Concealed Silences and Inaudible Voices
in Political Thinking

Concealed Silences and Inaudible Voices in Political Thinking

Michael Freeden

OXFORD
UNIVERSITY PRESS

OXFORD
UNIVERSITY PRESS

Great Clarendon Street, Oxford, OX2 6DP,
United Kingdom

Oxford University Press is a department of the University of Oxford.
It furthers the University's objective of excellence in research, scholarship,
and education by publishing worldwide. Oxford is a registered trade mark of
Oxford University Press in the UK and in certain other countries

© Michael Freeden 2022

The moral rights of the author have been asserted

Impression: 1

All rights reserved. No part of this publication may be reproduced, stored in
a retrieval system, or transmitted, in any form or by any means, without the
prior permission in writing of Oxford University Press, or as expressly permitted
by law, by licence or under terms agreed with the appropriate reprographics
rights organization. Enquiries concerning reproduction outside the scope of the
above should be sent to the Rights Department, Oxford University Press, at the
address above

You must not circulate this work in any other form
and you must impose this same condition on any acquirer

Published in the United States of America by Oxford University Press
198 Madison Avenue, New York, NY 10016, United States of America

British Library Cataloguing in Publication Data
Data available

Library of Congress Control Number: 2022943056

ISBN 978–0–19–883351–2

DOI: 10.1093/oso/9780198833512.001.0001

Printed and bound by
CPI Group (UK) Ltd, Croydon, CR0 4YY

Links to third party websites are provided by Oxford in good faith and
for information only. Oxford disclaims any responsibility for the materials
contained in any third party website referenced in this work.

For my family

Acknowledgements

I would like to express my gratitude to the Leverhulme Trust for awarding me a Leverhulme Emeritus Fellowship, enabling me to carry out research for this book.

My warm appreciation is due to the scholars and colleagues who rendered assistance, offered guidance, and responded graciously to my queries during the gestation of this book, in particular to Sergei Akopov, Sophia Dingli, Misa Djurkovic, Stefano Gandolfo, Theo Jung, Sudipta Kaviraj, John Keane, Michael Kenny, Adrian Little, Kate McLoughlin, Lois McNay, Ron Nettler, Eskandar Sadeghi-Boroujerdi, Aron Shai, Avital Simhoni, Quentin Skinner, Willibald Steinmetz, Rieke Trimçev, and Laurence Whitehead. Many others have played a silent yet significant role. It is the nature of scholarship that both they and I may not always be aware of such sources of inspiration.

I am also greatly indebted to the many participants in talks I gave in the UK and abroad, in person and online, whose stimulating comments and conversations helped to clarify and refine my thoughts on silence and its intriguing relationship with the political.

I consider myself exceptionally fortunate to have benefited from the constant backing of Dominic Byatt—the lead publisher of social and behavioural sciences at Oxford University Press. His encouragement, now and over many years, has been both invaluable and greatly heartening.

Michael Freeden

Mansfield College
University of Oxford

Contents

A Non-musical Prelude   1

Intermezzo: A Taster   9

I. INTERPRETING AND MAPPING: CONCEPTUALIZATIONS OF SILENCE

1. **Layers of Silence**   15
   1. Detectable and Hidden Silences   16
   2. Agentic and Non-agentic Silences   19

2. **The Political Elements of Silence**   25
   1. The Thought-Practices of Thinking Politically   25
   2. The Ubiquity of the Political   27

3. **Analysing Silence: Initial Considerations**   35
   1. Charting the Paths of Silence: Alternative Contours and Configurations   35
   2. Naming: Acoustic Purism and Semantic Latitude   41
   3. The Reach of Silence   46
   4. Alternative Non-silences: Sound and Noise   51

4. **Silence, Stillness, and Solitude**   57
   1. Silence and Logos   58
   2. Stillness   63
   3. Solitude   66

5. **Absence, Lack, and Removal**   73
   1. The Indeterminacy of Absence   73
   2. Radical Lack   77
   3. Removal   81

6. **The Dog that Did Not Bark: Listening for Silence**   91
   1. In Pursuit of Elusiveness   92
   2. Academic Predispositions   99

7. **Seven Modalities of Silence**   103
   1. The Unthinkable   104
   2. The Unspeakable and/or the Unsayable   104

viii   Contents

3 The Ineffable	112
4 The Inarticulable	116
5 The Unnoticeable	124
6 The Unknowable	126
7 The Unconceptualizable	127
8 Two Afterthoughts	131
8. Silence in Language and Communication	**137**
1 The Discursive Distribution of Silence	137
2 The Micro-structures of Silence	141
3 Uncommunicative Silences?	146

II. DECODING AND INVESTIGATING: SILENCES IN THE LIVED WORLD

9. The Temporalities of Silence: Theology, History, Anthropology	**153**
1 Theological and Philosophical Silences	153
2 The Silences of History	157
3 Tangled Linearities	161
4 Disciplinary Circumspection and Erasure	165
10. Superimposed and Invented Voice	**171**
1 Crowding Out	171
2 Dead and Unborn Silences	174
11. Tacit Consent and Attributed Consent	**181**
1 Locke's Tacit Consent: Unwritten Implications	181
2 The 'Silent Majority'	194
12. The Socio-cultural Filters of Silences	**201**
1 Buddhist Ineffability	202
2 Thresholds and Transitions	207
3 The Modalities of Silence and Their Social Roots	210
4 Dramatic Silences	215
13. State and Government Silences	**223**
1 The Quietism of States, Governments, and Constitutions	223
2 Neutrality and Abstention	228
3 Commemoration	233
4 Univocality	236
14. Ideological Assimilations of Silence	**241**
1 Ideological Networks and Ideological Spaces	241
2 The Proliferation of Ideological Silences	251
2.1 Liberal Silences	253
2.2 Feminist Silences	256

2.3 Anarchist Silences 258
2.4 Conservative Silences 258
2.5 Reformist and Radical Silences 259
2.6 Populist Silences 262
2.7 Nationalist Silences 263
2.8 Illiberal Silences 265

Coda **269**

Bibliography 273
Index 285

A Non-musical Prelude

A remarkable series of happenings took place in the world of art in 2018. Three parallel exhibitions were held in London of the work of Tacita Dean—the renowned British artist domiciled in Rome. I want to focus on one of them, comprising a series of videos that strikingly interweave silence and stillness, in which the dancer and choreographer Merce Cunningham sits silently and almost motionlessly in a chair, while John Cage's famed soundless 'composition' *4'33"*, conceived in 1952, is counted down by a metronome—a silence contained in a limited time-capsule, its ephemerality clocked in seconds.[1] Dean's interweaving and juxtaposing of those two different performances stimulates an enriched and layered interpretation. As is well known, *4'33"* involves a concert performance in which an individual sits down in front of a grand piano and does nothing for that segment of time except to close the lid at the beginning of each of three movements—'movements' in which nothing moves. The 'pianist' maintains silence against social and cultural anticipation, surrounded by an identifiable and visible audience placed in an unusual context, from which casual sounds of coughing and shuffling emerge, sounds that would normally be overridden by music emanating from the stage, and distinct from other sounds that are intentionally closed off by the acoustics and impenetrability of the concert hall structure.

It has almost become de rigueur to draft Cage into investigations of silence. But for the purposes of this book the point of the performance he contrived to stage is not the one he emphasized. It delivers more intricate and layered insights than merely serving Cage's intention to demonstrate the ubiquity of the 'entire field of sound' and the consequent impossibility of silence. Cage thought of his experimentalism as 'opening the doors of music to the sounds that happen to be in the environment'.[2] But, in addition and tellingly, *4'33"* contains significant socio-political and cultural implications. The resultant imperfect wall of silence is not an insulating physical edifice, but is intangibly located within the concert chamber, constituting a boundary separating the 'musician' and their audience. The silence impacts on that audience, now redefined primarily as spectators, and secondarily not as listeners to an artistic work but as hearers of sporadic noises that they themselves produce, as if they now were the surrogate 'artists'. Those noises punctuate a performance that is disruptive of a conventional cultural order—a surrealist situation of no music in a concert hall when the performer appears to be primed to play.

Concealed Silences and Inaudible Voices in Political Thinking. Michael Freeden, Oxford University Press.
© Michael Freeden (2022). DOI: 10.1093/oso/9780198833512.003.0001

2 Concealed Silences and Inaudible Voices in Political Thinking

The overriding feeling is one of absence: a soloist abstaining from their craft; and an audience tantalized by the unused piano and thus 'cheated' out of its expectations.

Silence, as will be seen throughout this book, can be as much a presence as an absence. But as an ostensible absence, it needs to be contextualized for the kind of absence it might be: resonating, obscured, or bemusing in its pattern-breaking unexpectedness. The intermittent rupturing of the silence by the unwitting participants in the performance—who 'create' an unscripted and unforeseen counter-performance of their own—lets through the uninvited disorder of the uncontrollable and the unintended. It also fragments the vital sound-producing capacity of human beings by switching off, regulating, and redistributing its production and reception. The surprise triggered by an unanticipated, contingent breach of expectations through introducing silence is matched by the arhythmic response of an audience inadvertently shattering its own context-specific codes of courteous, silent conduct.

In the second performance, it is not a group but an isolated individual who remains silent (plus the invisible camera operator and the person who marks time). By positioning Cunningham in a timed and mirroring homage to Cage—his by-then deceased life-partner—the appositely named Tacita Dean focuses however not on absence, but on stillness. Dean comments: 'Merce Cunningham sitting on a chair and holding his pose in silence is quite literally still life.'[3] In an interpretation of Dean's work, Marjorie E. Wieseman elaborates: 'Several works . . . represent birds or hares, live, dead, caged, or fettered, but nearly all are still, nearly all are silent. They remind us that stillness—intentionally or imposed—is part of life but also mimics death; that still life by another name is "nature morte".'[4] Nonetheless, the combined Cage–Dean creations produce a juxtaposition of the absence of sound and the absence of movement that entails both keeping quiet and being still. Note, by comparison, the observation of a classicist literary scholar, that 'to speak of one's silence means to perform an act of silence: to "do" silence.'[5] Indeed, even an unintentional silence can be an act, as it is still a state in which human beings discharge any number of practices unbeknownst to themselves.[6]

Cunningham was of course not perfectly still—unlike an inanimate object plucked from, or superseding, a live organism—but a being that had to breathe and blink. Nor did he mimic death: his stillness was an intentional tribute to Cage, enhancing the latter's originality and honouring his memory. The conjoined stillness and silence accompany Cunningham's deliberate performative presence, like a living statue—an established art/entertainment form, as distinct from Cage's previous withholding of a musical performance. But Cunningham's stillness is socially precarious, intimating an imbalance of power. Its fragility and ephemerality are resisted by him only temporarily, for he obviously possesses just a limited capacity to hold out motionless against the world, unlike the infinite capacity of a conventional artistic still life encapsulating the eternity of death or the separation of a fruit from its nourishing branches. That limit is amplified by the metronome literally and metaphorically counting down the finite and diminishing capitulation of stillness to the live body and—once we take our eyes and ears off the seated figure—the capitulation of silence to the enduring and penetrating sounds of the metropolis.

Cunningham's willing and perhaps wilful stillness is the counterpart of Cage's absent music—both events focus on a silent soloist under observing eyes as well as attentive ears. Significantly, though, even Dean's emphasis as a visual artist on a modicum of observable stillness intermittently succumbs to sound. We are in the presence of a silence that isn't quite silent and a stillness that isn't quite still. The legend informs us that there is 'ambient sound from Cunningham's other dance studio and the New York streets below'. These noises are less stochastic than those in the concert hall: the dance practice involves rhythmic noise patterns emanating from soft footfall, while the hectic street traffic has a familiar hum and growl of continuity. Both practices illustrate that even stillness is not, as some linguists argue, merely the absence of sound.[7] Instead, they are both patently intertwined with vigorous movement in an environment of spatial activity—the converse of stillness—endowed with penetrating momentum. Cage regarded the awareness of one's surroundings—human and humanly produced—as an artistic and philosophical insight.[8] Here, rather, the sounds emanate from an invisible and anonymous space, not from Cage's visible concert hall; and their normality intrudes on the artificially silent individual who is *caged in* by external crowds, while maintaining an aura of quiet dignity. The spatial and structural properties of an enclosed space are spelled out by an architectural theorist and practitioner:

> [T]he most essential auditory experience created by architecture is tranquility. Architecture presents the drama of construction silenced into matter and space; architecture is the art of petrified silence. . . . An architectural experience silences all external noise; it focuses attention on one's very existence. Architecture, as all art, makes us aware of our fundamental solitude. . . . Adjacent sounds, far or near, pose questions of proximity, safety, and threat.[9]

Silence, tranquillity, stillness, and seclusion—those overlapping yet nuancedly distinct concepts—constitute one of the many clusters through which human beings interact with their surroundings.

Interpreters of Cage, as well as Cage himself, regard *4'33"* as the composer's intentional fashioning of an alternative performance in its own right, a statement about sound rather than silence. But Cage is also acclaimed as celebrating the irregular naturalness of noise and sound. The audience can then be regarded as an agent that, without being directed, collectively and unsystematically produces incidental noise.[10] At its world premiere, Cage requested the windows of the hall to be opened to let sound in, defying the acoustic rationale of the auditorium.[11] Cage later observed that 'there is no such thing as an empty space or an empty time. There is always something to see, something to hear. In fact, try as we may to make a silence, we cannot.'[12] The effect of this contrived, musically unannotated, silence/non-silence is specifically to lift a barrier so as to accentuate the seamlessness between silence and sound and, importantly, the centrality of the act of listening. In this case the ersatz listening is to oneself and those immediately around one, as part of a group united by a preconceived but frustrated purpose—enjoying a concert—that does not materialize. Yet those present engage all the while in low-scale noise and motion that infiltrates the silence and exposes its tenuousness and porousness. While the 'pianist' intentionally attempts to produce silence, the audience unintentionally subverts what Cage sees as a 'mission impossible' to begin with. Silence is revealed as an intrinsically important conceptual category that does not necessarily entail the eradication of noise. In that, it differs from the profound quietude typically, though never completely, evoked by stillness.

Cage is now valued as a seminal figure in countless writings on silence that preponderantly underscore his insight that pure silence does not exist. Edgar has pointed out that the relation between silence and sound in Cage's experimental music is indeterminate and arbitrary, deliberately challenging the order, formality, and harmonies of the dominant classical European tradition in which silences are dictated by a musical logic.[13] But from the perspective of this book such interpretations, valuable as they are, should not underplay another, under-elaborated dimension entirely: the unintended, broader, and directly political features of the *4'33"* experiment and the lessons that political theorists can derive from it. Indeed, under the gaze of political theory Cage's experiment offers an instructive complexity both ingrained in *4'33"* and augmented in Dean's videos of Cunningham. Those artistic events interrogate silence by means of a rich constellation of politically fertile and significant elements that saturate the performance throughout.

Cage in particular was focused on breaking down the walls held to distinguish sound from silence by ushering sound *into* silence, just as he admired the architectural schools that by means of glass and light brought transparency and nature into the physical walls of buildings—a major proponent of that genre being Mies van der Rohe. Of Marcel Duchamp's painting *The Large Glass*, Cage wrote: 'It helps me to blur the distinction between art and life and produces a kind of silence in the work itself. There is nothing in it that requires me to look in one place or another or, in fact, requires me to look at all. I can look through it to the world beyond.'[14] The flooding in of silence melds with the spontaneous sounds of nature. That view of architecture as an integrating dynamic is itself political as well as psychological, standing as it does in stark contrast to architecture's alternative insulating role. Silence as tranquillity is achieved through a contrasting introversion/extroversion of perceptions and moods vis-à-vis diverse environments, in which barriers—those political constructs par excellence—can be dismantled as well as erected.

Looking more closely, *4'33"* is replete with some of the most ubiquitous characteristics of the political. They include the multiple asymmetric confrontations of individual versus group; the fragility, unpredictability, and reversibility of power relations; the manipulation of conduct and reaction; the confounded and blocked anticipation of action and event; the disruption of order, instantly replaced with alternative socio-cultural patterns of variable durability; the depiction of social activity as disaggregated rather than holistic; the drawing of performative boundaries that fluctuate between fixity and permeability, whether physical or cultural; and the dictating of strict instructions to the managers of the concert hall, to the simulating pianist, and to the inactive choreographer. *4'33"* is also a construction of highly organized and controlled precision; a far more meticulously disciplined form of delivery than even the most rigorously performed musical recital. Silence is arranged in seconds: each of its three 'movements' is sequentially timed at 30", 2'23", and 1'40". The closure of the piano lid prior to each movement adds to the sense of the boxing-in of silence by means of a solid partition, the cutting-off of access to musical sound making—a boundary formation Cage is nonetheless eager to refute. In all the above, silence occupies the ambiguous and indeterminate area between absence and presence, a thread that informs all its political manifestations. None of this is central to Cage's own understanding of silence which is shorn of inherent semantic, communicative, and philosophical import. Instead, he presents it as an acoustic condition positioned at the confluence of inevitable adulterating components. As a literary critic comments, Cage's approach 'involves a break with the concepts of content, control, interpretation and continuity. Ideas become unnecessary.'[15] The elaborate construal of silence—a vital dimension of its various analyses, including the one offered in this book—is irreverently brushed aside, despite the intensely political, aesthetic, and rhetorical scenarios Cage himself conjures up.

In the case of the Cunningham videos, their political dimension encompasses several elements. Here too both silence and stillness are revealed as subject to social direction through artistic expression. Cunningham is being managed through a conflation of two intertwined silences-cum-stillnesses constructed by Dean. He is persuaded to constrain himself in space by engaging in the kind of motionless symbolic activity that is the very antithesis of his professional persona as a master of movement, but that nonetheless complements the verbal silence normally present in dance. He is also persuaded to constrain himself in time through the dictatorial, relentless tempo of the metronome closing in on a conclusive end and release. Cunningham's statuesque silence is of a particular kind: it is seemingly uncommunicative and emotionless, in contrast to what is usually conveyed through the performing arts. Nonetheless, the result is to imbue an individual with gravitas, to emphasize his stature as a figure commanding respect: in short, to draw out the political dimension of this particular scenario.

This subtext is not immediately evident as a set of political occurrences and interpretations when viewed as a series of artistic and performative events, but it is nonetheless very much apparent at the moment in which appropriate disciplinary frames and filters are brought into play. I now proceed from this evocative artistic creation to a staccato sampling of several representative ways in which silence is found in discourse and aphorism. Following that brief intermezzo, the first two chapters of Part I tender some general thoughts on silence and outline the specific, yet expansive, view of the political to which I subscribe. That interpretation of the political is intricately intermeshed with myriad forms of human endeavour and activity, and it also provides the foundation on which a complex and multi-layered treatment of concealed, semi-hidden, or coded silences can build. The core of the book is occupied with spelling out, illustrating, and analysing a diverse array of topics pertaining to these master-themes. They involve interrogating literatures, conceptualizations, and events of silence, and in turn registering their own epistemological and cultural muting—all of which have a bearing on the place of silence as a shaper and conduit of political life and thought.

Notes

1 Tacita Dean, *Merce Cunningham performs STILLNESS*, 6 x 16 mm colour films (2008). Exhibited at the National Portrait Gallery, London, 2018.

2 J. Cage, *A Silence* (Middletown, CT: Wesleyan University Press, 1961), pp. 5, 8.
3 T. Dean, 'Cumulus Head', in A. Harris, A. Hollinghurst, and A. Smith (eds.), *Tacita Dean* (London: Royal Academy of Arts, National Portrait Gallery, The National Gallery, 2018), pp. 8–9.
4 M. E. Wiseman, 'Still', in Harris, Hollinghurst and Smith, *Tacita Dean*, p. 191.
5 S. Montiglio, *Silence in the Land of Logos* (Princeton, NJ: Princeton University Press, 2010), p. 289.
6 D. Kurzon, *Discourse of Silence* (Amsterdam/Philadelphia, PA: John Benjamins, 1998), p. 25.
7 M. Ephratt, 'The Functions of Silence', *Journal of Pragmatics* 40 (2008), p. 1911.
8 K. Ferguson, 'Silence: A Politics', *Contemporary Political Theory* 2 (2003), p. 62.
9 E. A. Danze, 'An Architect's View of Introspective Space: The Analytic Vessel', *Annual of Psychoanalysis* 33 (2005), pp. 109–124 at p. 106, referring to J. Pallasmaa, 'An Architecture of the Seven Senses', in S. Holl, J. Pallasmaa, and A. Perez-Gomez, *Questions of Perception, Phenomenology of Architecture* (Tokyo: A+U Publishing, 1994), p. 31.
10 A. T. Kingsmith, 'A Deliberate Silence: The Politics of Aural Materialism', in S. Dingli and T. N. Cooke (eds.), *Political Silence: Meanings, Functions, and Ambiguity* (London and New York: Routledge, 2019), p. 119.
11 F. Ramel, 'Silence as Relation in Music', in Dingli and Cooke, *Political Silence*, p. 147.
12 Cage, *Silence*, p. 8.
13 A. Edgar, 'Music and Silence', in A. Jaworski (ed.), *Silence: Interdisciplinary Perspectives* (Berlin and New York: Mouton de Gruyter, 1997), pp. 311–328.
14 As edifyingly discussed in Branden W. Joseph, 'John Cage and the Architecture of Silence', *October* 81 (1997), pp. 80–104; quotation on p. 92.
15 J. Pérez, 'Functions of the Rhetoric of Silence in Contemporary Spanish Literature', *South Central Review* 1/1–2 (1984), pp. 108–130 at pp. 113–114.

Intermezzo: A Taster

The everyday language addressing silence, and its accompanying understandings and usages, is inventive and extraordinarily diverse, pointing the way to a huge reservoir of variations. It might be instructive to sample as a taster, in no particular order, some of the ways in which silence may possess political significance. Here is a preliminary, and by no means comprehensive, selection of features offered for those who would still insist on locating silence at the margins of the political and underplaying its political prominence—an attitude still common among many logocentric students of political philosophy, thought, and science. Most of these features will be explored in greater detail throughout these pages. In line with the perspective adopted in this book, the chosen examples pay more attention to unplanned than to intentional silences and sidestep deliberate and forceful silencing. However widespread that latter category is, and however emblematic of the invasive aspects of the political, it is not the topic of the enigmatic silences with which this study engages.

- One can either purposely choose to be silent or be incapable of expressing that choice for reasons that may be physical, psychological, conceptual, or cultural.
- One may be embarrassed or shocked into silence.
- One may not care to give voice as a sign of apathy, or be reticent about, or not conscious of, one's silence.
- One's silence may be understood by others as voice, as is the case with so-called tacit consent, or one's voice may be understood as silence, or rendered incomprehensible, even when sounds or words emerge, if an unfamiliar linguistic or vocal register is employed.
- Others may uninvitedly impose their voice on a person's silence by substituting themselves for those in whose names they claim to speak.
- In some instances, the term 'silence' can misdescribe or obfuscate the facts of the matter: the 'silent majority' may neither be mute nor constitute the greater number.
- Self-imposed silence is an act of control over self as well as—deliberately or unintentionally—over others, but it may reflect fear, discomfiture, incomprehension, or impotence.

- Verbal incapacitation due to ignorance may be a function of adverse social circumstances or personal ineffectiveness.
- Silence may reflect a shying away from, or blindness to, ideological dissonances that could potentially undermine core belief systems. (The phrase 'turning a blind eye' is far more prevalent than the more appropriate 'turning a deaf ear', suggesting the superior appeal of the visual over the aural in metaphorical usage. That occasionally necessitates treating them as mutually exchangeable in this book.)
- Silence may reflect confusion, alienation, or anomie. Those silences may indicate a partial failure to (re)conceptualize and align one's relationship to a social environment, and 'the absence or suspension of established role expectations',[1] but they do, however, comprise a conscious awareness of perplexity and unease.
- Taciturnity may signal the unawareness that an issue exists, or that the speaker has (unintentionally) nothing to say, in addition to its signalling compliance, complicity, acquiescence, or self-defence.
- Those who speak may be regarded in some contexts as acquiring a superior political ranking over those who are silent; that is often the case with office holders occupying different positions on social and political hierarchies. Yet the saying 'silence is golden' establishes, conversely, its high ranking order.[2]
- Alternatively, the traditional injunction 'children should be seen and not heard'—apparently originally directed at women or maids—could be interpreted as a sign of modesty, inferiority, marginalization, or hostile tolerance. Movement and action—more difficult to suppress—are in such cases, oddly perhaps, less intrusive than speech, the stifling of which confines the potential voice to a socially deferential position. That kind of silence is often unconscious and self-controlled, while in fact imposed by external social norms as well as threats.
- Silence accorded by others *to*, or directed *at*, an event or person—the silence of passing over something—may indicate (if intentional) or be interpreted (if unintentional) that they are insignificant, negligible, sidelined, treacherous, or not worth the mention. Ostracism is one such instance.
- Silence may be pursued as a boon or a socially advantageous desideratum within the frame of human interaction, extolling it as virtuous, as in some religious orders, or it may be excoriated as a political and moral betrayal, as with the claimed silence-cum-neutrality of Pope Pius XII with respect to Nazi Germany.

- Silence may be perceived as a sign of resilience or dignity. It may also imply assurance and poise, particularly in the context of certain fantasies of confident masculinity epitomized by the phrase 'the strong, silent type'.
- Silence may be burdensome and dispiriting. As shops were closing during the galloping onset of the 2020 coronavirus pandemic, resulting in the demise of bustling social and economic interaction, a BBC correspondent commented on the 'heavy, oppressive weight of silence' at the Oxford Westgate shopping centre.[3]
- The contextual occurrence of a silence may be politically decisive or dramatic.
- Silences may be random or accidental, or they may be paced and patterned.
- Silence is occasionally seen as a resource, or even an exchangeable commodity prone to marketization: 'You will receive protection in exchange for your silence.'
- Silence may be a metaphorical as well as an actual denoter of death, as in the command: 'silence that person!'.
- Emotional or performative acts may take place in verbal silence resulting from inarticulable feelings.
- Socially practised, culturally conventional silences may legitimate events or histories (commemorative silences) or they may delegitimate them (the proposal was met with a stony silence).

All those instances, though far from exhaustive, are indicative of the complex and inextricable interweaving of silence with the political.

Notes

1 K. H. Basso, '"To Give up on Words": Silence in Western Apache Culture', *Southwestern Journal of Anthropology*, 26/3 (1970), pp. 213–230 at p. 227.
2 W. Sobkowiak, 'Silence and Markedness Theory', in Jaworski, *Silence*, p. 49.
3 BBC News at 6 p.m., 23 March 2020.

PART I
INTERPRETING AND MAPPING
Conceptualizations of Silence

In studying the intertwinement of silence with political thinking, we need to back away from any assumption that there is a sharp divide between 'theory' and 'practice',[1] a distinction that has proved impossible to maintain. Theorizing about politics should not be parachuted ready-made from above into the world we inhabit and experience. It emerges straight out of that world: extracted from it, pieced together from it, and continuously retested against it. Because the theory of silence is locked into its practices, the investigative strategy of this study follows two paths. Part I focuses on analysing and classifying approaches to silence, interspersed with illustrative and clarificatory examples. Part II reverses that emphasis: it focuses on a series of more detailed case studies, linking them with the variegated and general characteristics of silence explored in Part I. The investigator's task is to step back gently and momentarily from the lived world so as to fashion the perspectival distance from which to identify silence's patterns and problematizations, while remaining anchored in that world, always with its political overtones and undertones in mind.

Both parts of this book refrain from any tendency to essentialize silence as a unitary, undifferentiated phenomenon. Part I enquires into the relationship between categories of silence and specific features of thinking politically, emphasizing the macro-hypotheses and conclusions that sifting through an abundance of silences can produce and map. Part II probes into the particulars of silences, paying greater attention to specific types of social custom and to several distinct intellectual and artistic stratagems. In disparate ways they account for, convey, and illuminate the multiplicity of silences we experience—and, crucially, fail to experience or recognize.

1
Layers of Silence

Exploring silence involves examining a variety of ways in which something is made seemingly out of nothing. The acoustic nothingness of silence is transformed by the human spirit, mind, imagination—call it what you will—into an intricate force that shadows the vistas and recesses of our existence, always endowed with a transformative capacity even when effected surreptitiously and concealed to ourselves. The concept of silence, and the designation of certain kinds of natural phenomena and social conduct as silent, are plainly a human invention. The universe knows no silence, not because silence is inaudible and seemingly imperceptible, but because it is meaningless to attribute silence to the cosmos.[2] We will have cause to question that imperceptibility below but, in any event, what is certainly not meaningless—in our being-in-the-world—is to identify, and allot weight to, the idea of silence, the shapes into which our creativity moulds it, and its impact on our practices. Our thought-processes and our linguistic caesuras forge a goodly part of the reality we experience and by which we live.

Silences in general, and politically meaningful silences in particular, are normal, ubiquitous, and everyday elements of human expression and signification, irrespective of whether they appear or are encountered as absences, lacks, blockages, obfuscations, disruptions, oases of calm, reflective pauses, or indications of virtue and respect. Silence is an inseparable part, and counterpart, of human language and emotions; and engaging in silences is—*inter alia*—what human beings do as a matter of course. Silence is ineliminably woven into the expanses of human thought and experience, and accrues crucial importance when approached in its dual capacity, as practice and as phenomenon: first, as an integral element of the ways people communicate and discourse with one another—discourse here being understood as performative as well as verbal—and second, as the frequent subject of analysis, discussion and comment in both vernacular and professional languages, as an object of curiosity, desire, veneration, or fear.

Of course, the mere state of silence does not formulate theories, because they would have to be expressed and conveyed through human agency and optimally through logos: through word, symbol, and voice. Thinking and theorizing can take place *in* silence, but silence is not thinking. It is up to us as students of silence, first, to supplement silence with an articulate scholarly intervention in its meaning and production and, second, to recognize and identify the many political roles and functions that silences discharge; indeed, to break down silences into distinct and separate forms that invariably arise from silence's conceptual, linguistic, creative, and acoustic contexts. For silences become salient only though the networks and interrelationships that shape them. We need to discover how silence provides or accompanies patterns of human conduct that are amenable to analysis and deciphering. These patterns constitute a means of interaction that runs parallel to, and often intersects with, language and speech. The ways in which people practise silence or simply fall silent, its interpretation and decoding, cover a huge spectrum. All that is to contend that silence is a permanent systemic feature of human experience and discourse, not just an occasional interlude or a disruptive shaking-up of thought and language. It partners speech, voice, word, and deed sometimes as a tremor, a substratum, a whispering, or, contrariwise, as a conspicuous complement, serving as a semantic and performative container of messages. Whether stochastic and asymmetric or rhythmic and regular, it is a dynamic ingredient of the human mind, a functioning component of communication, be it above or below the adjustable line of detectability.

1 Detectable and Hidden Silences

Grasping that range of silences is made more demanding because the obvious modes in which silences are intimated, known, understood, and consciously adopted—the act of repressive and imposed silencing is the salient one, but far from typical—all too often eclipse their equally consequential unintentional, unpremeditated, and often imperceptible forms that occur in innumerable instances. Principally, we need to draw at this early stage a crucial distinction between (a) silence as an active participant or undercurrent that leaves discernible marks and traces in a discourse and is constitutive of it, and (b) silence as an undetected or unacknowledged feature that is buried under action and voice, its successful discovery albeit increasing the future chances of similar quests. The first category has to do with the kind of absences and lacks that leave a residual impact on the world we experience, a theme that will be addressed in Chapter 5. Alternatively, it also encompasses silences such as meaningful pauses, taboos, or a deferential reticence to speak that inject a particular value into different aspects of the political. The manner in which such practices intervene in discourse—or more accurately are assimilated into it—can be significant in affecting order and disorder, generating intensity, exercising control and limits on space, or opening options up. This category pinpoints ways in which we employ or react to silence in confronting, handling, or managing thought and discourse and will be discussed in Chapter 7.

The second category, however, concerns a multitude of hidden or unacknowledged political occurrences that are sealed off from us. Submerging or brushing aside experience is its most prominent facet, cementing social information and knowledge under layers of subsequent events or narratives and rendering them missing in a very specific way: unnoticeable and unacknowledged. But this category also displays a further fundamental subdivision, between silences that hide something—*silenced voices*—and silences that are *themselves* hidden—*silenced, concealed silences*. Silenced voices—including unmindful acts of self-silencing—may need to be deciphered or accepted for what they are: practices of non-disclosure triggered by external or internal inhibitors, such as unquestioned rules and customs. As a rule, these silences are socially normalized. When noticed, they are frequently a cause for concern, regret, protest, and frustration—a phenomenon familiar to us in many walks of life and much explored, and berated, in modern genres of scholarship that prize transparency. Notable among those are silences of women, of ethnic groups, or of newcomers to a society. They may dwell amongst us reflecting current social (im)balances, yet be anchored in past historical circumstances. We may even surmise their presence without clear evidence that they are occurring. The usual response to their subsequent retrieval is: 'It's high time those voices were heard and acknowledged', 'justice has been restored', 'Oh, I never thought of it in this way!' or even—when particularly unsavoury by current ethical standards—'these voices should best be left unheard'.

By contrast, concealed silences require spotting and excavating and their removal is far more complicated than simply granting, encouraging, or retrieving voice. These are silences buried at a deeper level. They may be lost, abandoned, or unintelligible voices from the past, products of agency that has now ceased to function or to be relevant. More emphatically, they may be silences whose very existence has been erased both evidentially and epistemologically, to the point that they cannot be identified as silences to begin with. For, like Russian dolls, the silences of which we are conscious may deflect our attention away from deeper silences trapped inside them. Here the formidable challenge is twofold. The first is to identify and decode those numerous, unconscious, and non-agentic, or indirectly agentic, silences that are undetectable and impenetrable to the mental apparatus as the disposal of members of a given society: the participants-cum-listeners. Nonetheless, those silences intersect with people's daily social lives and practices and ultimately, if and when breached, uncover more than they conceal. They illuminate, channel, pace, and unsettle patterns of political thinking and are inseparably part and parcel of that thinking. An example could be the former—and, in countless cases, present—rigidity of gender roles that disabled any critique or resentment from being directed at their generic and unhampered existence. It is not only that concrete individuals were socialized into silence on such matters, or that social convention disabled their potential to be voiced, but that there frequently was no inkling of the topic being enmeshed in silence, no conceptual framework within which it could be placed—so profound was its inaccessibility to those who were subject to that muting. Although gender inequalities were plainly experienced by those at the sharp end, the very option of challenging silences about gender was switched off and hence unavailable, and the circumstances in which they happened had become incomprehensible. Conceptually and etymologically the silence didn't exist for them because the condition in question commanded neither public nor private recognition.

The second—and no less pertinent—reason for concealed silences possesses its own challenges. Their likelihood is less commonly explored because they are initially (and often durably) undetectable also to the observer and the scholar, yet they too play a major role in shaping a political landscape. Their impact may well be immediate, but identifying that impact—feasible only with a different, possibly more recent, conceptual toolkit—may take generations and even centuries. Among others, as will be illustrated in later chapters, they will be found in certain historical and anthropological knowledge-frameworks. Those specific, double-bind, silenced silences—as a lived social practice and as a researchable object of analysis—that appear in several guises throughout this study are the most pervasive, the most subtle, the most curious and intriguing, and also those that carry particular political import in human conduct and encounters. If—and that is a big if—and when they are nonetheless retrieved, a predictable response might be 'I never knew that had happened or was even possible', or from a persistent scholar simply 'eureka!'.

In sum, with regard both to silenced voices and to concealed silences, we should be concerned with the endemic non-materialization of voice that is ignored, unnoticed, untheorized, covered up, or reinterpreted by political theorists, all because they do not, or do not yet, possess epistemic expectations—and consequently methodological tools—that could incorporate and recognize some silences for what they are: absences, lacks, or removals. The reason that we have not been trained as political theorists to cope with silence lies largely in the ongoing predilection of most mainstream political philosophers to regard people as rational, autonomous, and purposive agents, from which they infer that agents' capacity to articulate their thoughts and express their wills is a distinctive and fundamental human characteristic that is permanently in play. That belief may be held by broader swathes of people—'the idea of the public as normatively locutionary', as Ferguson observes. He elaborates reprovingly: 'If silence is that which means the lack of articulation, and such an articulation is the primary—even sole—means of creating and continuing community, then silence is incompatible with community and society.'[3] One may recall in this connection the double colloquial meaning of dumb as mute as well as stupid. And one can note that people are more likely to be intermittently locutionary alongside significant stretches of voicelessness for numerous reasons to be elaborated in the course of this volume.

2 Agentic and Non-agentic Silences

Silence is a phenomenon that invites a reaction, mild or emphatic. Some deem silence in general, as well as specific silences, to constitute a disconcerting vacuum. Consequently, sporadic and uncoordinated efforts to fill it are imported through thought and speech, alongside more planned and structured responses. Silence is made to serve other masters that mould it into shape—whether as an asset or a defect, an integral feature of human experience, a disruptive break, or simply a colourless slate on which matters of consequence may be inscribed. We live in intellectual and artistic times when we are frequently exhorted to 'take silence seriously'.[4] That entails not only reverting to silence as an established mark of respect but respecting the very presence of silence, social as well as supposedly natural. In certain circumstances silence 'possesses' greater gravity than voice, as if those associated with it carry particular weight, have a compelling reason to hold their peace, are honoured with special prestige, or are making a commendable effort. After all, on an elementary level it has been common among political theorists to regard power as the successful ability 'to get *a* to do something he would not otherwise do',[5] or as changing 'the probable pattern of specified future events'[6]—including preventing something from happening that would otherwise have happened. Silence is endowed with the same qualities, in that it can spur on or generate a shift in human and social conduct just as it can stem a flow of occurrences that was in the process of coming to pass. In either case it effects a staple and central political role, more often than not secreted at least in part beyond human awareness. But silence is not an agent or a doer. It has no will or purpose other than that metaphorically imposed on it by human interpreters and story tellers.

For philosophers and theorists who subscribe to the idea of purposive agency as defining humanity, silence is perplexing. And because, consequently, they have not developed an analytical apparatus to deal with the absence of articulation, they either overlay silence with agentic significance as ersatz articulation—as we will see in conjunction with Locke's tacit consent—or they exclude it from the sphere of scholarly interest. A related viewpoint is expressed as follows: 'If speech is action, then silence is failure to act';[7] an Austin-inspired statement that is trebly unsatisfactory: first, by committing a logocentric error, as silence may involve non-verbal acts; second, by overlooking the act involved in suppressing, or withdrawing from, the option of speech, which we might call a 'silence-act'; and third, by excluding unconscious or unintentional practices from the category of acts. From another critical perspective, the centrality of deliberative agency has been questioned by observing that 'the absence of deliberation is viewed as a tragic failure to meet a threshold of citizen agency marked out by speech'.[8] The linkage of silence with the failure of a given public is telling, and it is exacerbated by a seeming unawareness of 'silent thoughts' as well as a puzzling disregard of the obvious possibility that the human body can act without voice. Nonetheless, associating the problem with the normative—rather than scientific—quest to give some kind of voice to the inarticulate circumvents a more fundamental epistemological issue. What is missing in those approaches is an awareness of the possibility that silence may indicate a problematic, whose strange, voiced non-existence is baffling. Silence consequently demands a scholarly response to those views designed, more often than not, to annihilate rather than explore it.

Although concealed silences do not have exclusive billing in the pages of this book, they occupy centre-stage. The minutiae of their hiddenness display several nuances and gradations that require further elaboration. Here are six of them. First, silences can be overlooked when they *are not the product of conscious agentic choice*. Unquestioned acquiescence to 'received truths' about the absolute authority of religious injunctions, or the assumed superiority of certain classes of human beings and their associated life chances, will be found in this category. Scholars who contend that the only socially significant silences are those that are willed, wilful, and purposeful neglect unconscious silences as foci of analysis and strip them of noteworthiness and intellectual significance.

Second, silences that are *not recognized as silences* by a specified public who could have potentially discerned and borne witness to them, and therefore fall by the wayside unperceived. Such silences may, for example, present themselves as unheeded gaps or hiatuses, or fail to register as meaningful themes prominently absent from a discourse, or be the product of bypassing a conversation by means of non sequiturs or switching the subject, whether deliberately or inadvertently.

Third—underlining the political focus of this book—there are silences that possess salient political features but in the main are *not identified as political*, either by social actors or by scholars. The implicit power that weaves its way unnoticed through the silent parts of some marriage ceremonies, whether between the about-to-be-wedded partners or between officiator and congregation, discussed in Chapter 11, is a telling example. Silence may in this case be detectable in one sense, but its main political expression goes largely unheeded and unconceptualized.

Fourth is the category of *obscured and eclipsed silences* caused by discourses that concurrently dominate the airwaves and drown them out. Arrogating the right to speak in the name of unsuspecting, not just unwilling, others—silent majorities are a salient case in point—quashes not only their voices but also the potential impact of whatever silences they may have wished to register. That muting through the displacement of agency is another variant of the political processes implanted in silence, constraining and redirecting thought and language.

Fifth is a grouping specific to human verbal discourse, the emitting of *ostensibly meaningless sound or noise* that, although obviously not acoustically silent, substitutes functionally as an ersatz for certain social silences as it cannot be intelligibly listened to, as distinct from heard. Linguistic barriers as well as indecipherable forms of expressiveness or performativity render the hearer unreceptive to those effectively 'inaudible' stimuli and impervious to their meaning. We shall return to this theme in Chapter 3, and when discussing the 'inarticulable' in Chapter 7.

Sixth—and these constitute the deepest forms of concealment—are the already-mentioned silences *blocked by epistemological constraints* on what can be known in a given culture at a stated time-span. The task of the scholar is further complicated because concealed silences can themselves move in and out of undetectability: known silences are later buried and unknown silences emerge as secret or disregarded evidence. Those kinds of silence are broken, restored, or rearranged when epistemologies undergo transformation. Added to that is the theoretical problem that gnaws away at any scholar of silence—namely, that not all unknown silences will become knowable. That realization is of course common to another detecting practice—archaeology—whose mindset partly strikes a chord with silence scholars.

At this juncture, it is worth advancing a subtle distinction between unconscious and unintentional silences. A person can be unaware of or oblivious to the silence surrounding a potentially significant matter when—from an external viewpoint—voice and speech could have been a viable alternative. That silence is clearly concealed. But a linguist such as Kurzon contends that silence may be unintentional but not unconscious, accompanying that with the observation that 'people are sometimes silent without meaning anything specific by their silence'.[9] Linguistics, after all, often focuses on known silences such as pauses, ellipses, and hesitations. Their frequent unintentionality does not rule out an awareness of their existence or of the availability of voice to bridge it. A break in one's thoughts, or the petering out of a discussion, could happen without being deliberate, and it can take place in public view or hearing. Because the existence of that silence is not inaccessible to those who practise it, it is not *concealed*.

That said, both unconscious and unintentional silences are significant in this study because of its emphasis on the meanings that *we*—as political and cultural observers and theorists—can attribute *to* people's silences, irrespective of whether they are equipped to do so themselves. All this bears out the finding that investigating silence cannot be limited to agency and particularly not to the politically harmful suppression of agency.[10] Agency is of course often central to the production of silence, and agency can of course frequently suppress voice. Those political phenomena are not in doubt. The point, however, is different. As often as not, human beings are silenced by non-agentic social devices and practices that are not aimed at repressing individual freedom of expression and action but that nonetheless impede speech and intelligibility, bringing about silence in a non-conspiratorial manner.

All the same, implicit in Kurzon's contention is the possibility that people's silences exhibit a weak form of their own agency inasmuch as the subject knowingly desists from speech or sound, but for reasons they are unable fully to control or account for. If there is a will to be silent under such circumstances, it will not be resolutely autonomous or reflective. The production of human silences can therefore occur in hybrid shape, under circumstances that blur any stark distinction between autonomous agency, heteronomy, and cultural or psychological constrictions, such as when personal religious beliefs or sexual orientation are concerned. All these should be as important to political theorists—indeed, of paramount value to them—as are practices of wilful, domineering, hostile, and manipulative silencing, in which we are well inured as members of our societies. As a feature interlocked with the practice of thinking politically, concealed silences may be disruptive and perilous (though not necessarily transgressive) but they may equally *disrupt ruptures* by suppressing obstructions or smoothing them over, thus contributing to social equilibrium and order.

Finally, although the preceding sections have emphasized unintentional and unacknowledged silences and that will continue to be the case, this study will accord suitable space and significance to the central and prevalent instance of intentional silence. It recognizes and analyses those deliberate and socially organized silences that are not perceived as pernicious, unwelcome, or enforced. The willing compliance with many categories of silence—say, commemorative silences—clearly does not conceal them, but at the same time may not reveal a full awareness of their political implications, many of which will be submerged and observed routinely. Intentional silences, too, contain unintended consequences of concealment. In order to appreciate the peculiar features of concealed silences, they need to be placed alongside the practices of the open silences in which societies regularly, or sporadically, engage. Silences are always subject to degrees of hiddenness and a broader panoply can help in teasing them out.

Notes

1. I. Kant, 'On the Common Saying: "This May Be True in Theory, but It Does Not Apply in Practice"', in *Kant: Political Writings*, ed. H. Reiss (Cambridge: Cambridge University Press, 1991), pp. 61, 63.
2. See also M.-L. Achino-Loeb (ed.), *Silence: The Currency of Power* (New York and Oxford: Berghahn, 2006), p. 1.
3. Ferguson, 'Silence: A Politics', pp. 53–54.
4. J. G. Zumbrunnen, *Silence and Democracy: Athenian Politics in Thucydides' History* (University Park, PA: Pennsylvania State University Press, 2008), p. 50.
5. R. A. Dahl, 'The Concept of Power', *Behavioral Science* 2 (1957), p. 204.
6. N. W. Polsby, *Community Power and Political Theory* (New Haven, CT: Yale University Press, 1963), p. 3.
7. R. Langton, 'Speech Acts and Unspeakable Acts', *Philosophy and Public Affairs* 22 (1993), pp. 293–330 at p. 314.
8. T. Rollo, 'Everyday Deeds: Enactive Protest, Exit, and Silence in Deliberative Systems', *Political Theory* 45 (2017), pp. 587–609 at p. 600.
9. Kurzon, *Discourse of Silence*, p. 18.
10. Here I take a different path from that pursued, among others, by Dingli and Cooke, who focus specifically on 'aggressors seeking to silence' and the ways in which political silences are purposefully and even strategically engaged to respond to them ('Political Silence, An Introduction', in Dingli and Cooke, *Political Silence*, pp. 2, 7).

2
The Political Elements of Silence

1 The Thought-Practices of Thinking Politically

A key aim of this study is to marry the pursuit of known and silenced silences with the attributes of political thinking. Those attributes both account for the many different ways in which silences are veiled and reveal the multiple features of the political that can be unlocked by interrogating a sizeable array of silences. In all such cases, the practices circling around and through silences significantly include the recurring patterns of thinking in which human beings engage—in other words, our thought-practices. Among them, *political* thought-practices[1]—whether acknowledged, concealed, or misrecognized by the individual, group, or society in question—will differ from culture to culture, and will further vary internally within any cultural, geographical, or social entity. But they all nonetheless share several universal features of political thinking. For 'universal' read not uniform or identical, as held by some abstract normative theories, but ubiquitous and omnipresent in disparate contextual dimensions, whether temporal or spatial, and often at different degrees of intensity.

Political thought-practices invariably revolve around six defining axes: arrogating finality—having the last say—in decision making for collectivities, which includes the capacity for boundary drawing; distributing social, ideological, and ethical significance through prioritizing specified social arrangements and events above others; mobilizing, withholding, or withdrawing public support for communal and group discourses and activities; articulating and implementing cooperative or conflictual measures in managing social interaction; constructing and projecting collective future-oriented plans and visions; and exercising power and influence by employing persuasion, rhetoric, emotion, and menace as well as through utilizing suppression and cover-ups.[2]

Undeniably, silence plays a central role in each of the six axes, not as a side-constraint but as an indispensable catalyst and constituent. First, it underlies the wielding of, as well as the yielding to, conclusivity, facilitating the inclusion of groups into, or their exclusion from, political arenas

Concealed Silences and Inaudible Voices in Political Thinking. Michael Freeden, Oxford University Press.
© Michael Freeden (2022). DOI: 10.1093/oso/9780198833512.003.0004

through stratagems such as naturalizing their membership and compliance or, conversely, obfuscating their conformity to governance. The making and breaking of boundaries is a quintessentially political practice, and it *ipso facto* pertains to the boundaries of silence. Second, it aids in ranking and assigning weight to the standing of diverse political actors, enhancing and endorsing their existing position through eliminating potential challenges to their assigned prominence or, conversely, diminishing their roles by drawing a veil over their merits. Third, silence assists in securing, channelling, or nullifying social resources and stimulants, respectively filtering the consent, acquiescence, or dissent on which political agents, institutions, and ideologies depend. Fourth, it smoothens or dislocates the socio-political order by affecting stability or conflict through supplying uncontested continuity or introducing rupture, and by regulating the spatial relationships within those orders—distancing groups and communities from one another or connecting them. Fifth, it manages the political construction of time—past, present, and future—necessary to aid or resist political identities and futures, including the sidelining or reconstruction of collective memory, the resequencing of measured discontinuities, hiatuses, and stoppages, and the provision of a tabula rasa for prospective social potential. And sixth, silence intensifies or quashes the impact of ideas, arguments, and events that bear collective import, modulating their circulation, reception, and transformation, adding timbre and edge to the verbal and performative contexts in which it is inserted. In doing all that, silence attaches further telling nuances to the discernible and the shaded areas of the political and to the complexity and range of political expression. Put starkly, the political is inoperative and unimaginable without its accompanying and intersecting silences, shaping, blending, and blocking at every twist and turn.

Although it is a commonplace to politicize silence by associating it with power, the almost inseparable conventional association, let alone equation, of power and politics is far too blunt. That association singles out power as the central, monolithic, and undifferentiated feature of politics, stretching it beyond its usefulness as a decisive but not sole feature of the political. Rather, power needs to be approached as a subtle and flexible amalgam of variants that include influencing, reasoning, withholding, pleading, acquiescing, and so on, held loosely together by 'power' as a generalized conceptual umbrella term. Consequently, many political facets of silence cannot be reduced to brute, crude conceptions of power revolving around constraint or domination, even though the latter host numerous commonplace instances of force or violence. Instead, addressing silence in its manifold political modes refines its investigation as a resourceful and enhancing ingredient of the political in its larger sense, a sense that is played out throughout this volume. Those who rest content with overemphasizing the negative consequences of the silence–power conjunction themselves indulge in a silence about power's socially beneficial, or functionally necessary, aspects.

The distinctive understanding of politics that guides this study needs therefore to be clear from the outset. Importantly, it accounts for the multiple, and sometimes seemingly unconventional, ways in which the instances and categories of silence that pervade societies may be regarded. In so doing, it contrasts with other strategies for exploring silence in political thought. One such strategy might be to draw up a list of what political philosophers and theorists have said on the subject and whether silence has an important role to play in their *oeuvre*. John Locke may well top that list for his exceptional contribution by means of his notion of tacit consent and he will indeed be given his due in following sections, as will several other distinguished individual thinkers. Alternatively, many treatments and analyses of politics refer by that term to the conduct of public affairs in which competition, even struggle, over policy making determines the fortunes and fates of people—and peoples—in and across nation-states and, to a lesser degree, in regional and municipal settings. That understanding is at the back of the mind of any person who claims, whether apologetically, proudly, or dismissively, to be apolitical or anti-political in possessing no interest in the political realm.[3] Here silence may relate either to the puzzlingly inexplicable invisibility of the political to certain observers, or to a perception that includes only strife and antagonism within its purview and bypasses the rest—in both instances a regrettable and strange disconnect from substantial areas of politics' dominion that may well evaporate under closer scrutiny.[4]

2 The Ubiquity of the Political

An underlying confusion consequently cuts across analyses of the political. On the one hand, it is a particular specialization—policy-oriented and organizational—in which general social decision-making institutions and leaders are identified that vie over legal, or at least legitimate and authoritative, status, occupying the upper echelons of hierarchical power relations and located in traditional or commonly recognized institutional settings. Politics in that sense is something that happens 'out there' in circles disconnected from what 'ordinary people' do. In the UK those circles have in recent times been referred to as the 'Westminster bubble'. On the other hand, politics is understood as a ubiquitous feature of human thinking, conduct, and transactions that pervades human life in varying degrees of permeation. I have supported that latter approach to political thinking as a broader, collective set of practices not confined to outstanding individuals, nor one occurring merely and predominantly at state or governmental level, or exclusively attached to rulers, legislators, administrators, parties, electioneering, and the like, but discernible at all levels of human articulation and social interaction. Formal, institutional politics is rarely silent; it is a steamroller of action, noise, and directives funnelled into spheres of control and opposition—though it will frequently pursue objectives on the sly. The story of the political in its extensive silenced mode, on which this book principally focuses, is found in wider and far more diverse areas of social life and thought. And when it comes to silence, at all those colloquial, demotic levels, as Huspek and Kendall assert, 'alternative political words and meanings may be imported into or emerge out of and express speakers' everyday experiences and needs, in ways that provide speakers with specific rationales for either actively contributing or withholding voice from the political arena'.[5] What applies to this overarching view of the political applies *ipso facto* to the manner in which the everyday political dimensions of silence are investigated here. Those dimensions notably also include unknowingly withholding voice, being incapable of articulating it, or having it culturally precluded.

Performativity, it needs saying, is intertwined with the political as the sphere in which doing, changing, reshaping, and desisting from action (clearly an action in itself) takes place. Literary theorists have for a while been aware of the significance of the replacement of mimesis with performativity, but their insights are equally germane to students of political discourse: 'Since the advent of the modern world', writes Wolfgang Iser, 'there is a clearly discernible tendency toward privileging the performative aspect of the author-text-reader relationship, whereby the pregiven is no longer viewed as an object of representation but rather as material from which something new is fashioned'.[6] Two corollaries of this statement should be borne in mind as we delve into the interplay of silence with the political. The one acknowledges that politics, and its attendant silences, are universal happenings centrally focusing on the social dynamics of human transactions. The other recognizes that the political is also the domain of constantly mutating interpretative viewpoints located in the eyes of the researcher as well as the participant. It inverts Marx's celebrated 11th thesis on Feuerbach,[7] by contending that the practice of interpreting the world always entails changing it. Interpretation in a social context is a directly political act, no less than material activity can be. Politics involves both benign and damaging interventions—whether physical or by giving as well as withholding voice. Interpretations of social life are *ipso facto* interventions in the ways we engage in that life.

An obvious consequence of the approach to the political expounded here relates to the sources that feed into it. This volume not only makes use of professional political arguments of academics alongside utterances emanating from 'political' groups and individuals, as customarily understood. It also includes what, for want of a better phrase, is labelled 'popular culture', as well as literary works or personal narratives. The criteria for inclusion relate primarily to the insights and knowledge that can be gleaned from an abundance of cultural constructions. They do not invariably summon up the 'quality' of an argument as seen through the more typical specialized eye of a political theorist, but opt for the quality it portrays in illuminating the human processing of silence, including its concealed impact. Broadening and deepening the remit of political theory requires a searching purview of that kind that may challenge disciplinary constraints. It expands the logic I attempted to lay out in *The Political Theory of Political Thinking*[8] but does so with reference to this one, understudied theme of silence.

This is not to claim that *every* human discourse, activity, and inactivity—including the production or adoption of silences—is saturated with overwhelming political significance, merely that they all have a political dimension, whether sizeable or slight, just as they all have an economic dimension relating, say, to their exchange value. We are not addressing here the conscious, personal disavowal of the political, but the common scholarly insistence on its intermittent absence. Yet a human relationship or social happening devoid of any political features is inconceivable, just as one without psychological features would be. Hence the much-vaunted notion of depoliticization that has been making the rounds in recent years makes little sense. Depoliticization is itself a revealing term, since the prefix 'de' indicates a deviation from the default social setting of 'politicization'. In effect, however, the word 'depoliticization' merely obscures other political evidence by skipping over it. That unreliable and deflective unnaming or misnaming of large swathes of human transactions silences them, omitting their fundamental role in shaping political understandings and communication.

Nor is that to contend that the *full* range of political features will be found in every practice and thought-practice; those features will occur in variable and fluid concentrations and mixes, bestowing a diverse and fluctuating weight and complexion on any human relationship. In any given social occurrence there will be a political element, but it may be thick or thin, overpowering or diluted, recurring or casual. The onus on the scholar is to identify which features of silence shed light on, are conjoined with, and amplify, the diverse incarnations of 'the political' and, equally, which dimensions of political thinking may be embedded and revealed in the multi-layered potential of silence.

To give an example, catching a bus to town does not appear at first glance to be a pronounced political act, and in most cases it isn't interpreted as one. Yet it is a highly typical example of the ordinariness and routine of political processes, acts and thinking. Indicatively for our purposes, it contains a collection of practices that are not only fundamentally political, but silently so, taking place without the participant's acknowledgement or awareness of their political character, thus serving to illustrate the third type of silenced silence identified in Chapter 1, section 2. Those practices include choosing a destination (identifying a future aim, planning the means to attain it and deciding on the timing); standing in a queue (accepting and participating in an orderly ranking of access rights to a public good); purchasing a ticket (obeying a law that demands payment for services and the evidence to prove that compliance); instructing a person to act, by ringing a bell to make the driver stop (intervening in and controlling a course of action); and accepting the temporary authority of the driver—delegated by the bus company—in navigating through a pre-arranged route. None of these practices may be knowingly observed or materialize, and any one may be infringed and flouted, but even such resistance, challenging, or disobeying counts as a palpable political occurrence; indeed, a particularly obvious one.

Of course, the purposes of the journey may be saliently and deliberately political—attending a demonstration, travelling to a polling station, or defying a racially imposed ban—but their centrality is all the more likely to obscure the equally consequential but cloaked political acquiescences we perform daily and habitually. Nor does identifying the political aspect of catching a bus cancel out other—often more compelling—readings. Using a public conveyance is a practice heavily imbued with cultural, economic, and environmental dimensions, as long as we grant that those intertwining fields, too, are saturated with the political, just as they in turn saturate it with *their* disciplinary properties. Concurrently, the silences that may be interwoven in, or located under, political practices across the spectrum of human endeavour and creativity accrue political meaning of their own by design or default. They will be fully integrated into the diverse attributes of the political, and they will do so in the multiple ways that any particular context serves to influence the relative weight or 'audibility' of the silences it hosts. That is what this study attempts to investigate—an investigation held together not only by the evidence of diverse silences, known and unknown to those who live them, but by the idea of silence and its impact on human self-comprehension, conjuring up alternative worlds of anxiety, mystery, hope, serenity, or mundanity. The political silences one encounters may be trivial or momentous, disturbing, disorienting, disconcerting, and embarrassing, or reassuring, facilitating, and unifying. They may be crucial to decoding speech and thought, or not worth the paper on which they are unwritten, but they all impart information with which students of politics should be familiar.

Added to the above is another fundamental observation about the nature of this book. It brings us back to the enforced and knowingly restrictive silencing of individuals and groups—the most conspicuous and upsetting silence, because the easiest to observe and witness. There already is a considerable and well-developed body of scholarship on those politically prominent forms of deliberate, calculated silencing that ascribe to it often maliciously stifling exercises of social constraint and repression, as well as parallel attention to the determined and resistant counter-power that repression evokes. That body concerns topics such as the frequent, purposive muzzling of individual people as an oppressive act; the suppressive muting or erasing of cultural and religious beliefs and rituals; the subduing and eradication of gendered, racial, ethnic, and national viewpoints and demands; the concealing and defensive silences that individuals may adopt separately and knowingly for the purposes of deception or protection; the conspiratorial silences in which they may collude; and even the defiant, angry, or sullen silences to which they may be reduced, often classed among the 'weapons of the weak'. Both the dispossession of voice and the dispossession of the right to silence are products of the exploitation of unequal power structures and relationships.

It is indisputable that the power to inhibit and subjugate voice is of central concern to social life and most readers might expect it to appear in a book linking the political with silence. It will occasionally appear in the margins of this study, but not as a central theme of the broader story of power in political thinking and performance. The justification for such refocusing is not only that those themes have already been thoroughly and perceptively mined in professional analyses and in non academic fora, but that there is so much more to say about further extensive confluences between silence and the political. As one anthropologist has commented, in an observation pertinent to many other disciplines:

> In much anthropological literature, a silence is most often treated as secrecy, political subjugation, avoidance or repression—all active forms of agentive, if not expressly violent, *silencing*. This may explain the lack of attention in anthropology to silence as a form of communication or expression in its own right, one that does not rely on the normative logic of speech for its own objectification.[9]

There is a related challenge to be negotiated. Consequent on their dual attention to consciously suppressive silences and to normative standards for ethical politics, many political theorists strongly prefer to approach issues of silence from the perspective of democratic principles and arrangements, suspiciously eyeing silence as a bad—undesirable and in need of expunging. That perspective is applied chiefly to the enabling of substantive participatory citizenship in contemporary states, when silence is thought of as a disadvantageous and commonly damaging deviation from the vocally expressive and publicly committed standards democracy requires, and from the premium assigned to multiple conscious and agentic motives.[10] While that viewpoint is frequently referred to here—how can it not?—the concerns of democratic participation and citizenship empowerment do not encompass the full range of political thinking and expression germane to appreciating the politics–silence nexus. In this book, ideal-democratic modes of argumentation merit analysis primarily as evidence of discursive patterns that are grist to its particular investigation, but they are wholly distinct from the lodestar of its undertaking.

In sum, the ethical value or disvalue of deliberate silencing—central as it is to other contexts—is not the guiding principle of this book. Its objective does not include formulating a programmatic agenda of remedial solutions to the wilful suppression of voice. Rather, its sights are aimed chiefly at the incidence and intricacy of non-volitional and non-agentic silences in societies, for they are paramount in illuminating and comprehending the underexplored political seams in human affairs. Those rightly concerned about insidious political oppression and muzzling would do well to acquaint themselves also with the huge volume of concealed silences running across societies, irrespective of whether they possess harmful or beneficial effects on human flourishing.

Ultimately, there is a strong underlying link between silence and the political. Silence both *is*—in its multiple appearances in social life—and is *conceptualized*—as a modifier and catalyst of thought and language—as generating changes of tempo and mood, speeding them up or slowing them down. Modifying, generating, changing—making a difference in collective human life and conduct—are all core political phenomena. Silence is a non-musical counterpoint of discourse, either accompanying it simultaneously or held in abeyance and coiled to spring out. And it tracks—interdependently and independently—the patterns and regularities of speech and word, of grammar and signage, whether as mirror or as contrast.

Notes

1. On political thought-practices see M. Freeden, *The Political Theory of Political Thinking: The Anatomy of a Practice* (Oxford: Oxford University Press, 2013).
2. Ibid., pp. 34–35 and *passim*.
3. See, for example, M. Huspek and K. E. Kendall, 'On Withholding Political Voice: An Analysis of the Political Vocabulary of a "Nonpolitical" Speech Community', *Quarterly Journal of Speech* 77/1 (1991), pp. 1–19.
4. See M. Freeden, *Ideology Studies: New Advances and Interpretations* (Abingdon and New York: Routledge, 2022), pp. 95, 187–188.
5. Huspek and Kendall, 'On Withholding Political Voice', p. 6.
6. W. Iser, 'The Play of the Text', in S. Budick and W. Iser, *Languages of the Unsayable: The Play of Negativity in Literature and Literary Theory* (Stanford, CA: Stanford University Press, 1987), p. 325.
7. 'The philosophers have only interpreted the world, in various ways; the point is to change it' (K. Marx, 'Theses on Feuerbach', in *Early Writings* (Harmondsworth: Penguin, 1975), p. 423.
8. Freeden, *The Political Theory of Political Thinking*.
9. R. Norum, 'Trading Silence for a Voice: Ethnography of Lack for the Contemporary Classroom', *Teaching Anthropology* 9 (2020), pp. 93–97.
10. For an example see the special issue edited by Mónica Brito Vieira, 'Silence in Political Theory and Practice', *Critical Review of International Social and Political Philosophy* 24 (2021); and S. W. D. Gray, 'Mapping Silent Citizenship: How Democratic Theory Hears Citizens' Silence and Why It Matters', *Citizenship Studies* 19/5 (2015), pp. 474–491.

3
Analysing Silence: Initial Considerations

1 Charting the Paths of Silence: Alternative Contours and Configurations

'For it is all very fine to keep silence, but one has also to consider the kind of silence one keeps', counsels Samuel Beckett through the voice of his anonymous protagonist.[1] There are several rich literatures and source materials on which to build an account of the variegated and vital parts silence plays in human societies, their cultures, language, and political imaginations. I shall draw from them both systematically and intermittently, commencing by identifying some of the more prominent and promising macro-clusters that deserve investigation. They supply alternative conceptual codes and formative patterns through which to fashion understandings of silence. The ensuing theoretical frameworks exist in both competitive and complementary proximity, inspired as they are by plural disciplinary persuasions, temperamental nuances and preferences, and diverse methodological toolkits. The result is an exciting cabinet of treasures from which the scholar can pick.

The options for mapping silence are complex, presenting several plausible axes of classification that stand in a complementary relation one to another. They cut through the oscillations and undulations that permeate our mental and experiential interactions with silence, each offering its own dimensions and strata of understanding, and all abounding in rich takings for the connoisseur of socio-political silence. This section submits four such tentative mapping schemes, not as a pick-and-choose exercise but as alternative, parallel, or intersecting vistas, each with its own allure. The third and fourth schemes, as will be seen, play a particularly significant role in the arguments of the book. The idea is to show the potential versatility of silence scholarship and to explain where this book is located on that broad compass.

Scheme A emphasizes the *psychological or sociological roles* of silence in individual and social conduct and their impact on motivation and action. Five types of these silences stand out: aspirational silences, existential silences, solidaric silences, positioning silences, and fear-inducing silences. They all display salient kinds of overt and conscious conduct with clear political characteristics, while rarely possessing an awareness of their broader concealing powers.

Aspirational silences are those craved as objectives to be attained on the route to personal purity, self-understanding, or spiritual transcendence. They generate the kind of purposive goal-oriented activity that is one of the defining attributes of the political, and they can pertain either to particular individuals or to communities, and are common—but far from unique—to many monastic or reclusive practices.[2]

Existential silences are those regarded as natural, non-judgemental features of the human condition; consequently, their existence is rarely problematized by those who practise them. They anchor silences in acceptance of the world and its conservation, appealing to the order and durability that underpin human projections of the political, often with pronounced emotional undertones, and frequently aligning with environmental concerns.[3]

Solidaric silences are those that evoke feelings and memories of social togetherness and interdependence. They serve to strengthen the group dynamics that are produced by political interaction. Although most commonly found in ceremonies, they may also signal an understood but non-verbal affective intimacy and rapport among individuals who feel comfortable among themselves, consolidating an awareness of community and reinforcing networks of cooperation.[4]

Positioning silences arrange or confirm the relationships between members of a society, creating spaces—distant or proximate—appropriate to the organization and distribution of status, prestige, and authority. They tend to reinforce allocations and sequences of social roles found chiefly in formal or quasi-formal political and social networks, signalling deference, respect, or orientation towards the unfamiliar.[5]

Fear-inducing silences foster a sense of apprehension, vulnerability, and fragmentation. They may be displayed as a backing-off from a perceived antagonist or enemy, precede a potential subjection to hostile forces, reflect anxiety in response to state authority, or disable open social intercourse.[6]

All these conceptualizations of silence, and their contextualized manifestations, are fractured and varied. For example, blockages to speech and expression can involve magnitudes of volume or loudness, or sets of cultural, psychological, and epistemological inhibitions that conspire to impede speech even before it is voiced, or the privacy of the silence-practising individual. They require careful judgement in the attempt both to hone distinctions and to identify the unavoidable looseness of classificatory boundaries. Scheme A and its categories help in understanding the ways in which silences affect how people behave and the attitudes they adopt, but they do not address the central problematics raised in this book. They will flit in and out of other classifications, adding to them texture and nuance.

Scheme B addresses some of the *alternative epistemologies* in which the study of silence figures saliently. It is broadly comparative, distilling the interpretation of silence through different approaches to knowledge, and calling for an intellectual flexibility incurred by switching across epistemologies. That involves detaching the study of silence from the restrictive logics that diverse disciplines impose on them, and reaggregating them in the form of major perspectival constellations that interlink only tangentially, and that utilize their own languages of presentation. Four such constellations commonly take shape by means of the human imagination and temperament as well as through scientific elucidation.

The first constellation approaches both silence and stillness as artistic and poetic phenomena, often revealing themselves as possessing an emotional intensity or a mystical aura through which to appreciate, and identify with, the human condition. It is one of the most universal means of representing and communicating silence, in view of its direct appeal to sensibilities that cannot be recreated by discursive arguments and treatises.

The second constellation is a more technical and scientific exploration of silence as itemized silences. It sees them as constitutive of the grammatical and linguistic forms of speech that are integral to human communication, expressed in rhythms and sequences. It is alert to the mechanics of metrics, intervals, pauses, pacing—the mathematics and geometry of silence. It figures prominently in Chapter 8, which adds a missing piece to the conceptual and epistemological leanings of Part I.

The third constellation regards silence as an active participant in forging the organics, rather than the mechanics, of our immersion in life. It fashions the ways in which we perceive ourselves in the world and in relation to one another: a crucial mode of counterpoint that draws together shades, binaries, ambiguities, liminality, and the temporality at the core of social existence. It gives vent to the concrete ways of living of which silence is an essential part.

The fourth constellation calls for the detecting and unpacking of complex sets of codes through which instances of silence—whether concrete and empirical or conceptual and analytical—make sense. Its aim is to interpret the patterns and distinctions through which silence intervenes in, partners, and shapes human reflection and practice. It is oriented towards teasing out the discernible manifestations of silence as an introduction to its opaque facets that, in their own right, constitute a pervasive and valuable branch of learning.

Scheme C now takes us to an elaboration of the fourth constellation of Scheme B. The other three constellations of Scheme B remain important dramatis personae throughout this book but are not accorded centre-stage in its pages. Scheme C, however, underpins many of the analytical claims of this study, spelling out six major clusters, in no order or priority, that dominate the interpretative landscape of silence.

The first cluster—mainly the subject of Chapter 5—gathers around absence, lack, nothingness, emptiness, void, or acoustic silence. It recruits dualisms and dichotomies in addressing silence in terms of presence and non-presence, a thing and its opposite.

The second cluster steps away from abstract conceptual analysis. Instead, it approaches silence in terms of its linguistic and rhetorical usage. Here silence is a phenomenon or experience that takes place in the 'real world' and it triggers thoughts, ideas, and reactions that alter anticipated mindsets. In so doing, silences fashion patterns of knowledge and understanding that abound with cultural and political significance. That includes allowing for the mental and emotional rhetorical force of the word 'silence' itself. We find it extant, for example, in the literary *oeuvre* of Virginia Woolf or Harold Pinter, who employ silences to indicate states of mind or undercurrents in everyday behaviour. But they also play a significant role in the specialist field of discourse analysis, addressing meaningful silences in speech.

The third cluster investigates the silences that set up barriers and hiatuses. They parcel out and punctuate domains of experience and activity, and delimit, as well as structure, the possibilities of language. This cluster addresses silence as a constraining intervention in the organization of information and communication and in the regulation of social relationships. Conversational breaks and sequences, emotional reactions, or religious injunctions concerning the unsayable populate this cluster and are addressed utilizing insights from diverse disciplines.

The fourth cluster denies the separateness and exclusionary nature of silence as a phenomenon opposed to speech and signification, preferring to regard it as a complex and indispensable facet of human language and being. By blending voice and muteness into inseparable and complementary forms of human thought and discourse, it integrates silence into normal patterns of human expression. The teachings of Buddhist philosophy concerning non-dualism and ineffability are such an instance, explored mainly in Chapter 12.

The fifth cluster, to which Chapter 4 is devoted, examines the intersection between silence, stillness, and solitude, introducing ideas and experiences of immobility, serenity, spatiality, and spirituality into the field. It extends silence beyond a human practice to embrace natural, physical, and transcendental properties that human beings ascribe to the non-materiality of forces around them, or to their mimicking of such forces. That ascription of silence undoubtedly masks its origination in a human practice, though the quest for solitude reimmerses human beings into the natural world.

The sixth cluster is a practically oriented grouping focusing on concrete and specific examples of silences embedded in numerous cultural contexts, secular or religious, as instances of everyday living. It regards silence as encompassing a plurality of discrete occurrences, each of which should be considered separately as an anthropological or ethnographical exemplar of social practices. Silence among Finns, ritual silences, and historical forgetfulness count in this category.

The six clusters do not of course lend themselves to be treated singly in complete isolation from the others. While some are accorded their own chapter, they all spill over into other sections and chapters. Yet each one needs to be borne in mind as a distinct analytical stratum through which our subject-matter can be mined and sieved.

All three schemes outlined so far are different ways of cutting the cake thematically, and taken separately they make no claim to comprehensiveness or inclusiveness. Instead, each contributes to laying out diverse reference points through which to extract accumulative and often overlapping insights into silence. They are epistemological macro-vistas on silence and they cover several of the most instructive areas in which light may be cast on the nexus of silence and the political. The remainder of the book will not be devoted to running systematically through each of those mapping schemes in the sequence just outlined. Rather, they serve as storage silos from whose abundance topics, insights, and viewpoints will be chosen as and when appropriate.

Scheme D, however, homes in specifically on *concealed* silences—the primary focus of the book—selecting seven substantive micro-modalities: the unthinkable, the unspeakable/unsayable, the ineffable, the inarticulable, the unnoticeable, the unknowable, and the unconceptualizable. They constitute the heart around which the findings of this study circulate. This scheme is reserved for Chapter 7, which awaits a journey through the indispensable clarificatory stations on that path addressed respectively in Chapters 4, 5, and 6. All the macro *points d'appui* adumbrated in the previous pages will be referenced and utilized in different measures and order in the course of the book, as and when they can be best put to use. My hope is that these themes and categories may be seen as the nucleus and adumbration of larger and more ambitious programmes of exploring political silences that future scholarship might wish to consider.

By way of elucidating the standpoint of this study, there is of course another literature emanating from religious and ethical compasses that explores and extols silence as a substantive good. Rooted notably, though not solely, in interpretations of Christianity and Buddhism, silence is celebrated as virtuous, sacred, spiritually cleansing, or wholesome, both for the individual and for society. These understandings too have their place in this volume, but primarily as windows opening on to the political patterns that typify them. I allude to them only when relevant to the more direct scholarly concerns of a student of political thought focusing on evidence and experience.

This study refrains as far as is possible from adopting prescriptive or normative stances, nor does it probe in depth the creative and poetic aesthetics of silence or—for that matter—the scientific facts of its physics and acoustics. To the extent that it engages in advocacy, it is only to advocate the merits of investigating the role of silence in conceptualizing political thinking, without recommending or disapproving. That also involves detecting the political features of silence alluded to and present in other classes of human thought—from cultural studies to drama to psychoanalysis. Its overarching commitment is to the endeavour to extend and deepen a professional appreciation of the political and to expand the remit of what political theory can bring to the table of scholarship. Nor does this volume lay claim to the certainty of indisputable knowledge on silence, or any other matter. Rather, it follows the Weberian precept of understanding, of *Verstehen*, with its corollary of the openness and tentativeness of interpretation.[7]

A final note by way of concluding this methodological and classificatory set of vade mecums: every one of these groupings possesses a keen and unmistakable political edge that confirms the ubiquity and sophistication of political thinking and practice in silent domains not commonly held to exhibit political clues in profusion, if at all. They hold out novel possibilities for transforming the world of silences into a promising and fertile domain of political theory. As students of politics, when silences are silenced—usually for the actors as well as their fellow human beings—we need to know why. Specifically, which class of constraint or blockage comes into play, are those impediments of consequence or the product of the routines of social life, and what do they add to the interpretative tools we can wield in our pursuit of the political wherever it is placed? As agents and actors, however, those lived silences are concrete and localized. There are no silences other than those we conceive and sense, albeit often retrospectively or with the help of others. They are not open-ended and unstructured, nor ought they to attract any manner of interpretation to fill an apparently empty space. Emphatically, silences are not the 'spaces in between'. Rather, they happen while conjoined *with* speech, conduct, and expression. They are not simply caesuras or pauses—the kinds of silence prominently in the sights of grammarians and linguists. They come into their own as making room for both emotion and reflection—always already present in speech and performance—enabling those qualities to breathe and collect themselves. The task of the analyst is to run any single instance of silence past several epistemological and ontological frameworks, applying a reasoned and imaginative construal of the contexts—ideational, cultural, historical, and conceptual—in which silences may be elucidated, all along acquiring knowledge of the most significant political forms and patterns that silences evince through anchoring them in, and alongside, our particular disciplinary allegiances. As a sign in the Horniman Museum, London, reads: 'It depends on those who pass by whether I be tomb or treasure, whether I speak or am silent depends entirely upon you friend, do not enter without desire' ([Theodor]Von Holst, 1810–1844).

2 Naming: Acoustic Purism and Semantic Latitude

The Swiss thinker, Max Picard, was moved to write: 'Silence is an autonomous phenomenon. It is therefore not identical with the suspension of language ... it is creative, as language is creative; and it is formative of human beings as language is formative, but not in the same degree.'[8] Paradoxically or ambiguously, in approaches such as these silence is imaginatively allotted a named presence called 'silence'—even when merely signifying the presence of an absence. As Margaret Atwood comments, 'What isn't there has a presence, like the absence of light.'[9] Naming, be it of silence or of anything else, is an exercise in classifying a phenomenon, occurrence, or event, in assigning identity and singularity. It does not deny the variety that silence contains, but addresses its distinctiveness. Naming is therefore already a political act of enclosure and limitation, an imposition of human will and imagination on the world. The human capacity to label, mould, and create reality through words and concepts is well known. In the case of naming silence, it is a peculiar shaping of something that in its strong version seems not to *be there* as an auditory manifestation—ostensibly, but nonetheless disputably, a type of deep unreality. Yet whereas it designates a condition that may have no designatum in a material or even empirical sense, it nonetheless denotes an idea—itself consisting of many different variants—that people may entertain in their minds.

Naming, of course, has its own limits. The very naming of God as ineffable—a topic to which we shall return—has been called into question by the Gnostic Basilides: 'That which is named [ineffable] is not absolutely ineffable, since we call one thing ineffable and another not even ineffable. For that which is not even ineffable is not named ineffable, but is above every name that is named.'[10] The strong version of silence thus tantalizingly oscillates between a general state of elusiveness and numerous particular firmings-up of its meanings. As Sells neatly explains: 'That mode of discourse begins with the aporia—the unresolvable dilemma—of transcendence. The transcendent must be beyond names, ineffable. In order to claim that the transcendent is beyond names, however, I must give it a name, "the transcendent".'[11] We will encounter many instances of the political relevance of that version. As an aside, one might add that *naming* a person as 'silent' or 'unexpressed' can bring with it a peculiar associative twist. In introducing one of her 2018 exhibitions, Tacita Dean wrote: 'Even my own name has forever tied me to ideas of silence.'[12]

In their weaker but nonetheless equally important versions indicated in Chapter 1, section 2, the objects or events covered by silence may be heard but cannot be *verbalized* or *understood*—that is to say, cannot be meaningfully thought of, listened to, or experienced—due to a rupture between origination and reception at any point in the potential spread of conceptualization and its subsequent transmission in language. This requires elaboration, as it deviates from familiar colloquial understandings of silence. One of the fundamental modes of classifying silence is to divide its analysis into an acoustical phenomenon in the domain of physics—including non-sound and its linguistic sub-type, non-speech—and a socio-cultural one relating to human practices. In distinguishing between acoustic and communicative silence, Sobkowiak berates scholars who view silence as an undifferentiated phenomenon, although he chooses to do so solely on strictly linguistic criteria.[13] The consequent proposition running through this book is that only at a minimum does silence concern the scientific, physics-anchored state of non-sound. Whether that is its purest form is arguable.

The weaker sense of silence, then—communicative and sensitive to symbol formation—includes non-meaningful sound and its semantic sub-type, non-meaningful speech. This second grouping is acutely pertinent to a study of political thought-practices, first, because of the interactive nature of the political as a social activity involving communicating with more than one actor and, second, because this book is chiefly preoccupied with the subcutaneous socio-political manifestations of silence. Sound may be merely unintelligible when conveyed in a foreign tongue, as famously expressed by Shakespeare, penning Casca's reaction to a comment by Cicero: 'for mine own part, it was Greek to me'.[14] But it may be a more fundamentally incomprehensible set of sounds that has no direct, substantive epistemological value. At most, the production of human sounds could itself occasionally be decoded as a practice rather than a random eruption, but unless a person is gagged there is insufficient evidence to suggest that those sounds stand in for a specific silenced message. We provisionally reserve judgement on whether human vocal noise might silence a *voice* that is buried under an inability, or failure, to speak or to articulate, or whether it indicates a buried *silence* unrecognized by the noise emitter as well—a casualty, perhaps, of states of unknowability and unawareness that will be further discussed in Chapter 7.

In contradistinction to Sobkowiak, I do not interpret communicative silence solely as 'that which is deliberately produced for communicative purposes'.[15] That only covers part of the field. First, communicative silences are frequently filtered through pronounced cultural and political construals without any awareness of their being intended for communication—that is, they are not an *invariably deliberate* form of imparting information to others. Whatever communicative value they may have can equally be a by-product of factors beyond individual control or agency—a shocked silence, for example, has considerable communicative power. Second, given that the production of human sounds and speech possessed of meaning to their producers may not be convertible to meaning decodable by their recipients, that has the effect of extending the notion of silence to the *reception* pole of the relationship. For, to reiterate, if speech is a practice that transmits meaning, incomprehensible speech is reduced to sounds that serve *effectively* to silence their enunciators, who are thwarted in their semantic transmission exercise, consequently excluding their recipients from the communicative loop. Furthermore, incomprehensible speech may possibly deny its hearers from obtaining socially valuable information (untranslatability is the most obvious case, but far from unique)—even if, as will be emphasized, that is not always the case with certain sounds, such as keening.[16]

As a rule, though, the social impact and effects of unintelligible speech are indistinguishable from those of silence, and qua silence possess political significance, predominantly that of disorientation, alienation, withdrawal, or even resentment. In a context where human speech does not register as a decipherable practice by its prospective recipients, or where the function of words is altered to convey emptiness, as signalled in the avant-garde literature of the twentieth century with its 'retreat from the word',[17] a justifiable methodological case can be made for stretching the idea of silence conceptually, not just metaphorically. A parallel instance is the silence of incomprehension or irritation with which some contemporary music is met by audiences. While laden with meaning for its composer and those trained to listen to it, for others tuned in to classical arrangements of harmony, consonance, or melody, it is mere cacophony. In such cases, sound and meaning apparently part company—though not as rhythm, emphasis, timbre, or volume—and silence adopts a cultural guise (sifted through aesthetic criteria), rather than a physical and acoustical one, epitomized in the phrase 'this music does not speak to me'. To that extent, silence is reinforced as a human artefact, hewn out of language but capable not just of defying and negating but of complementing it in unexpected ways.

Ultimately, it transpires that even the strong version of silence—acoustical absence—may endow a phenomenon that plainly eludes and transcends the senses with the signs and properties of reality, so that we nonetheless 'perceive', 'encounter', and 'listen to' such complete absences in our everyday experience. When that happens acoustical silence, too, can be loaded with political meaning. Noticing it, talking about it, thinking and theorizing it, all bestow palpable ideational body on silence. Silence is made to live among us; it is reified. As Vainiomäki contends, 'it would be possible to think of silence as a *signified* somewhere out there in the "real" world, beyond the reach of our perceptions and sensations'[18]—though not of our sensibilities. It is not only a feature of an existing yet soundless thing; it becomes a weighty entity in its own right, a powerful concept and idea in our comprehension of the world: think for instance of epiphanies born out of solitude. And powerful players, by dint of that power, are *ipso facto* prominent inhabiters of the political world. Conversely, the weak version of silence—when apparently meaningless sound is involved—throws up a heuristic and conceptual challenge, that of exploring the nature of the manifold impediments to the discursive transmission and interpretation of meaning itself. Clearly not all noise is meaningless—as will be seen below in Carlyle's raptures about industrial machinery—but gibberish in the ears of the hearer is as close as one can get to an acoustic proxy to silence, the result of semantic barriers that mimic absence.

Following from the above, a parallel simplistic claim requires rebuttal: the claim that, if acoustics are the criteria, silence appears to be undifferentiated and subject to a straightforward binary—there either is silence or there isn't. On that view, although sounds may be several, and voices be overlapping and competing, there is a uniform oneness about silence: there are no multiple silences (as distinct from multiple sources or circumstances that elicit silence, or—notably—substantive analytical categories of silence). Indeed, when considered on its own, silence does not seem to indicate plurality or diversity. But several significant counterarguments can be drafted. First, as already contended, on a semantic level incomprehensible sounds and words constitute a cultural if not literal silence. A cultural silence is capable of harbouring many layers possessing considerable political significance relating, say, to social isolation, a dearth of educational opportunities, or an inadequate capacity to express thoughts and desires. In a very different cultural frame, by contrast, some articulations of voice are considered to belong to the category of silence. Ancient Greek literature registers different degrees of silence that can include 'in a low voice' or 'hushed'. There too one finds rudiments of a political distinction, as when 'in a low voice' means privately, not to be overheard.[19]

Second, silences do not have to come in the guise of one big thing—an argument forcefully made by Michel Foucault:

> There is no binary division to be made between what one says and what one does not say; we must try to determine the different ways of not saying such things, how those who can and those who cannot speak of them are distributed, which type of discourse is authorized, or which form of discretion is required in either case. There is not one but many silences, and they are an integral part of the strategies that underlie and permeate discourses.[20]

Finally, we should not only query the monolithic *oneness* of silence as a macro-phenomenon but unpack the *unity* of any specific instance of silence. That is to say, silences may be bundled in multiple, parallel but discrete, variants of emotional force and intellectual provenance within what appears to be, on the surface, an ostensibly single episode of silence. A particular commemorative silence can evoke memory, or pain, or conformity; a shocked silence can radiate surprise, or horror, or revulsion; a deferential silence can connote respect for tradition, flattering obsequiousness, or a sense of stratified worthlessness. Even when pertaining to an apparently unique case, a socially practised silence can be internally fragmented and diverse, while experienced as temporally and spatially specific. Sider has put this well: 'Specific silences are crucial ... to making culture shared, inclusive and simultaneously exclusionary ... but never through simple and neat separations ... Of special importance here ... is the breathtaking clarity of certain politically central silences—their absolutely unmistakable meanings—along with an indefiniteness so profound it makes the silences evasive, nearly irresistible.'[21] The components and strata of all those species of silence can stack up in micro-form for quite different reasons and yet produce the impression of an integrated macro-silence. And another thing: in any given community several silences can circulate separately. This refers not to their diverse meanings and roles, or the many emotions and responses collapsed into a single 'event' of silence. Rather, different groups within a society can 'own' alternative and even opposed silences, to the extent that—in a twinned mirror-image juxtaposition—one group's voice is another group's silence, each occupying competing zones of unawareness, forgetfulness, or epistemological opacity that define its identity.[22] In liberal societies, while one group can follow legal conventions of privacy and non-disclosure, another group will insist on openness and transparency. But the latter group may shy away from using language deemed by it to be 'politically incorrect', while the former may object to 'private' religious practices they consider to be abusive or discriminatory.

3 The Reach of Silence

The findings of this book affirm silence as a hotly contested concept that discharges vital social and political roles, occupying different positions in lore, culture, and science. Our imaginations not only are attuned to specific silences but conjure up silence as a defining ingredient of experiences across the span of human existence. That is borne out by the many other disciplines attracted by silence as to a magnet. Linguists and grammarians measure and catalogue the frequency of silences interspersed in speech—many of which indicate social or psychologically induced rhythms—and unlock their intent and meaning. Anthropologists clock obligatory and internalized social silences incorporated into ritualized encounters, such as when strangers initially meet, or in communal gatherings for purposes of worship or commemoration, or they attempt to decode the manner in which cultures are written out of national histories. Sociologists and social psychologists note mental frames that focus on certain features of human conduct while shrouding and ensnaring others in the unhearability and invisibility of irrelevance. Those insights reveal the key political element of allocating significance to actions and events by ranking them in order of importance, an allocation that does not usually take place on an intellectual, premeditated level. Psychoanalysts explore deep silences that are blocked, repressed, or transformed into psychosomatic behaviour. We find accounts and explorations of silence in philosophy, history, music (as illustrated in the Prelude), theology, law, and everyday language—again, often with a political edge and subtext. Literature and poetry abound with countless evocations of silence as awe inspiring, enchanting, menacing, moving, purifying, pacifying, despairing, segregating, or mystifying—always exercising a powerful hold on the human imagination and spirit. Silence is ascribed an energy that stirs and stimulates thought and feeling, or closes in on them. It is endowed with the dynamic capacity to induce change, or the retarding capacity to curb it.

We also find silence directly scattered through the history of political thought, albeit mostly recognized or acknowledged rather than debated, though we will come across notable exceptions in later chapters. Yet silence still is a manifestly underdiscussed theme in political theory, and only slightly less so in political philosophy. A decade ago, John Keane complained about political silence that 'its study is reckoned properly to belong elsewhere ... semiotics, anthropology and socio-linguistics'.[23] Although students of politics have begun to engage with the concept of silence and with the practices it adumbrates and stimulates, it has yet to be accorded the prominence that its multifarious forms merit as a weighty element of the political. Several green shoots of inquiry are surfacing but as yet there is no substantial corpus that could be assembled into a political theory of silence, let alone taught as such. There are several reasons for the persisting tendency of silence to fly under the radar of most scholars of politics and political thought: in part because they are chiefly schooled in complex debate and verbalization, in part because the occurrences of silence tend to be attributed to human agency as inhibitors of expression, in part because those who do explore silence, among them some critical discourse analysts, are suspicious of it as a pernicious outcome of abusive power and all too often wish to expose and eliminate it, and in part because there still is an emergent need to develop new and flexible linguistic and conceptual tools to get to grips with silence's diverse political meanings.

The topic of silence displays no constants, no timeless components. Like any other question occupying the human mind, it has undergone continuous mutation over time that alters its salience and significance across academic disciplines and the creative arts, in an elaborate mixture of upheavals and adjustments to fashion, prejudice, and epistemology. Importantly, those changes occur at different speeds in which parallel developments form sustaining connections alongside increasing misalignments. Religiously induced silences may dissipate with secularization but are unequally distributed across societies and faith communities, surfacing or receding at different historical moments. Silences affecting zones of personal privacy and family life may be long-standing but nibbled at the edges when challenged by ethical demands for transparency and scrutiny. Silences may be enshrined in confidentiality agreements that are invisible to third parties but begin to erode under the pressure of public accountability. The persistence of silences applied to the histories of certain ethnicities will depend on the salience of the specific ethnicity in the public spotlight. Silences pertaining to the identity of minors may slowly gain acceptance as protective shields. Silences sustained by taboos will be recalibrated rather than eliminated as the nature of social taboos shifts across customs and conventions. As a rule, though, silences have become more volatile and violable, buckling under curiosity, prurience, openness, or the power of the media.

Advances as well as discarded tendencies in anthropology, literature, psychoanalysis, linguistics, and theology play their various parts in this never-ending trajectory of human experience and the production of knowledge, as the balance of their cultural interventions and interlinkages ebbs and flows. Joined by other fields of human endeavour, they all contribute to determining what counts as political, in the process resetting its shifting boundaries. Those unceasing practices of disciplinary redesign and popular readjustment also make their mark on the many ways in which the political amplifies, diminishes, and alters understandings of silence. At any point in time such understandings both tighten and scatter. What seems to solidify does so ephemerally, and what spreads out in unanticipated directions needs occasionally to be reined in by discursive patterns, however tentative.

These paths of inquiry demand closer consideration in two directions. The one, 'siloed', perspective looks at mutating representations of silence in the intertwined disciplines of political theory and political philosophy. It examines the extent to which changes in the purposes, styles, and subject matter of political theory generate shifts in the meanings and social roles of silence. Does the quest for order, or the focus on leadership, or the pursuit of justice, or a belief in social evolution, or a subscription to dialectics and binaries, or the assumption of universalism, account for the profusion, variability, and dispersed effects of the silences that inhabit those themes? Are silences, not least concealed silences, more typical in some of those foci than in the others? As will be seen in subsequent chapters, order and leadership can be silently cemented by tradition and social conservatism. The rigidity of most justice protocols may exclude voices of mercy and charity, or disable languages that do not conform to legitimized legal procedures. Evolutionary theory may be tone-deaf to the normality of disruption and chaos; binaries skip over crucial nuances; universalism affords a low level of magnification that cannot spot the vital small print of divergent cases.

A further raft of questions arises that merits sustained historical and sociological investigation, and which can only be adumbrated here. Are the more fertile or intense repositories of silence likely to relate to class or social standing, to past generations rather than recent ones, to traditional rather than modern cultures, to reinforcing the overlooked concerns of women or gender-fluid people rather than men, and to the underage rather than the legally adult; or is it more apposite to talk of varying and cross-cutting combinations of any of those? Are the preoccupations of political theorists and their arguments supported or undermined by the silences, often uninvited, they encounter or unknowingly host? Does any of this matter more to one field of political theory—normative, interpretative, empirical, critical—than to another?

The other, 'diffused', perspective tracks the inputs of neighbouring disciplines into thinking politically about silence. It reinforces Keane's observation that one may glean quite different understandings of silence through other academic fields. But there is a major additional layer of potential knowledge. Those understandings also reflect different conceptions of the political embedded *within* each of those disciplines, often covertly, inextricable from their own assumptions and findings. The result is a remarkable two-way traffic across often elusive disciplinary boundaries.

In one direction, accordingly, from a viewpoint emanating in the field of political studies, it soon transpires that the political features and thought-practices central to the expansive view presented in this study are not only the properties of the domain that, in ordinary and constricted parlance, is termed 'politics'. They take in multiple fields of human inventiveness and interaction, permeating and cutting across other areas of knowledge, albeit in different measures, while applying some of the divergent emphases we have already explored and will continue to explore in the chapters to come. Understandably, the theorists and practitioners in any given discipline cannot be expected to devote the kind of analytical sharpness, intellectual energy, and painstaking detail to neighbouring disciplines—including the field of politics—that they invest in their own. Specifically, not all the actors and scholars in those other fields are alert to the remarkably divergent *political* implications for silence entertained by their own disciplines.

In the other direction, the discrete manifestations and treatments of silences detected in other disciplines—where such silences may well have a commanding control of the disciplinary terrain, or at least a prominent presence in it—will interact with and reflect their own diverse, possibly idiosyncratic, political understandings that thread through those fields of learning. Those intimations of the political from the other side of the nominal fence are fortunately available for export. Political theorists who enter the loosely demarcated territory of those scholarly domains may emerge with invigorated insights into their own vocation, notwithstanding that those trespassed on may raise the cry of misappropriated goods. Anthropologists will focus on a variety of social groups, communities, and tribes in a shift of emphasis away from state organizations, and highlight myth and ritual as shoring up political practices. Students of religion bring with them powerful understandings of authority and its extra-social inviolability. Authors of fiction will experiment with, and add intricacy to, the observation of individuals in nuanced, fragile, and unsettled chains of influence and hostility, or depict the heavy hand of the law in its clashes with free will and rebelliousness. Philosophers may invoke ideal-types as categories of analysis, abjuring the messiness and inconclusiveness of institutions tasked with meting out justice. That vital experience of intellectuals foraging-cum-borrowing presents a second-order decoding challenge that a political theorist of silence must undertake, and it is one that considerably enhances the available analytical panorama. The conclusion—heretical for some, perhaps—is that we need to be more *undisciplined*, that is to say, less committed to standard matrices of presuppositions, axiomatic ground-principles, and orthodox methods when disaggregating and querying the disciplinary rules that obscure silences—and their profusion of meanings—in each conventional area of scholarship.

In a change of tack, an intriguing ingredient adds spice into the mix so far. The historical silences, gaps, absences, and removals discussed above are humanly produced, knowingly or not. They are epistemic and contextual, and they are contingent on cultural and social practices, conventions, and traditions. But there also exists a permanent and largely solid physical basis that accounts for gaps in human understanding and limitations on its expression. The significance of what is missing and silent in our thought patterns gains credence through a very different disciplinary apparatus: neuroscience, whose findings are largely absent from the discourses of political theorists. In his analysis of the two spheres of the brain, the psychiatrist Iain McGilchrist has drawn attention to their disparate functions. The left hemisphere identifies parts, particulars, and components of knowledge and has to do with skills, accuracy, abstraction, routine, precision, planning, instrumentalism, and the concrete manipulation of our surroundings: 'this grasping, this taking control, this piecemeal apprehension of the world, this distinguishing of types, rather than of individual things—takes place for most of us with the right hand (controlled by the left hemisphere)'.[24] It is also repetitive and hence conventional. The right hemisphere is more holistic and organic; it has to be experienced, learned, understood, and intuited. McGilchrist references the neurologist Oliver Sacks in contending that music possesses that quality of 'an actual binding of nervous systems': 'It has a vital way of binding people together, helping them to be aware of shared humanity, shared feelings and experiences, and actively drawing them together.'[25] The capabilities of that hemisphere include empathy, humour, and irony, some of the qualities that 'permit the understanding of language at the highest level, once the bits have been put together', and enabling 'the making sense of an utterance in its context'.[26] However, although it is reflective and encompassing, its eschewal of accuracy and the fine points of detail causes silences to appear between the cracks.

Comparing the two furnishes important lessons about what we know and what is obscured or unavailable. The main 'silencer' is the left hemisphere, for 'isolating things artificially from their context brings the advantage of enabling us to focus intently on a particular aspect of reality. ... But its losses are in the picture as a whole ... whatever can't be brought into focus and fixed ceases to exist as far as the speaking hemisphere is concerned.'[27] And by being that which cannot be spoken, being ungraspable—in the domain, no less, where speech is naturally produced—a deep and irremovable silence descends on it, which can produce a sense of fragmentation that may bring on mental illness. Yet in the past that muteness had been compounded by a parallel silence afflicting some scholarly perceptions of the right hemisphere. McGilchrist writes: 'Until recently everything about the right hemisphere has been shrouded in darkness.' It too, after all, 'was considered to be silent, and to the verbal left-hemisphere way of thinking, that means dumb.'[28] The twin silences of the unfixed (discounted by the left) and the purposeful (discounted by the right) require a merger of their opposites in order for human brains—and minds—to perform optimally. Without interlinking the parts with an awareness of 'betweenness', the constricting and misleading dualism between spirit and matter persists.[29] That interlinkage does not produce the indeterminate non-dualism of Zen-Buddhism we shall presently encounter, but a coherence that enriches knowledge. And it opens another door to appreciating the political as implanted in the corporeal mental functions of directing, organizing, planning, and controlling as well as integrating, improvising, offering critical perspective, and fellow-feeling. The silences of the human mind are in part the result of the imperfect coordination and contrapuntal positioning of the two sets of skills, exacerbated by mutual misrecognition—misrecognition, as will become clear in the chapters to come, being one central cause and attribute of silence.

4 Alternative Non-silences: Sound and Noise

Silence is partnered with two conventional opposites, sound and noise. Sound can be generated by voice, in the form of speech or of song. It can be transmitted as music; and it can be naturally rhythmic, as are the crashing of waves or the murmuring of trees in the wind. We have already noted previously that, when voice and speech are indecipherable to the listener—a foreign tongue, or a stream of nonsense words—they may become mere noise to the recipient. Human sounds such as those may be transformed into social silences, though not—as in keening or wailing, for instance—when the noise follows a recognized cultural pattern. Noise, of course, is itself sound, but usually denotes a distinct sound unpleasant to the human ear. It can often be grating, shrill, animalistic, alarming, or disorienting, though not necessarily devoid of meaning, nor invariably unpatterned. In any case, we may become accustomed to some noises, either human or non-human, and take them in our stride—the clackety-clack of wheels on a railway track, the patter of raindrops on a window, the boisterous commotion in a school playground: in those cases noise may meld into decipherable and familiar, even comforting, sounds. But it is the sudden, unpredictable, or very loud noises that are particularly disagreeable or rattling, even when recognizable—such as the shelling of a town, an air raid siren, the slamming shut of a door or a loud clap of thunder. Langton remarks that 'one way of being silent is to make no noise. Another way of being silent—literally silent—is to perform no speech act.'[30] But that narrows the options. First, it should be clarified that making no noise includes being still as well as being acoustically and vocally silent, as in refraining from rustling and shifting when a person is hiding. Second, Langton's observation relates only to what agents do as sound emitters rather than their broader responses to noise—those responses being a vital component of thinking politically as well as reacting emotionally.

The intriguing question is: if silence is considered to be the paired opposite of both sound and noise, can those two latter categories consist of identical or similar kinds of silence, or is the type of silence that contrasts with noise fundamentally different from the silence that contrasts with mellifluous or intelligible sound, let alone the human voice—and thus more likely to incur deprivations of valuable stimuli? And is there political mileage in those putative differences? The *Oxford English Dictionary* (*OED*) draws a distinction between freedom from noise and abstinence from speech, a characterization that implies discrete domains of silence. The one entails a sanctuary from external disturbance; the other, desisting from activating a normal human aptitude. By contrast, freedom from speech and abstinence from noise would be odd pairings indeed. Silence as freedom from noise indicates that subjection to the latter is an imposition on our ability to function properly, and one that demands individual relief and then release, a liberation. Put more emphatically, the absence of noise is a resource,[31] and resources are enabling and empowering. Abstaining from speech, however, suggests an entirely different scenario: a person-centred retreat (unintentional or voluntary) from meaningful verbal social contact. Saunders has plausibly contended that silence 'is more complicated' than noise. By contrast, silence more than finds its match in the profound and unlimited subtleties of speech.[32] The exclusion of either leads to very different consequences. Yet both the silence of noise elimination and that of human muteness involve manifestly political circumstances—in the one case, the casting off, or blocking, of sensory intrusion in order to shield the undisturbed exercise of human capacities; in the other, the withdrawal from certain areas of human communication and cooperation for any number of reasons—social, physical, or psychological—that are not always immediately obvious.

Noise, at worst, is jarring and chaotic, and the silence that signals its termination clears a mental and physical space in which orderly, reasoned, or creative activity can commence or resume. Unlike abstinence from speech, its elimination or reduction underwrite the conditions for purposive behaviour. 'Stop this noise' (the frustrated demand of a teacher confronting unruliness) and 'I can't stand this noise' (the anguish of someone enduring a numbing cacophony) are equally requests for respite on a conjoined physical and psychological level, and for order and equilibrium on a political one. The removal of hindrances, whether human or extra-social, has always been regarded as a political capacitator—an occurrence revolving around the management and suppression of constraints, even when there are select instances of noise that carry their own clear political messages. As for abstinence from speech, it may be restrictive, but that does not in any way imply that verbal quietude is dehumanizing. Thus, extending the merit of silence to all art forms, Susan Sontag contends:

> Behind the appeals for silence lies the wish for a perceptual and cultural clean slate. And, in its most hortatory and ambitious version, the advocacy of silence expresses a mythic project of total liberation. What's envisaged is nothing less than the liberation of the artist from himself, of art from the particular art work, of art from history, of spirit from matter, of the mind from its perceptual and intellectual limitations.[33]

In its most general sense, the sound–silence pairing raises a fundamental ontological issue concerning what precedes what. It plays out an intricate juxtaposing of force and inertia, in which the force of sound is introduced into a state of silence. The French philosopher Maurice Merleau-Ponty harked back to that initial state, though specifically in relation to language and speech: 'Our view of man will remain superficial so long as we fail to go back to that origin, so long as we fail to find, beneath the chatter of words, the primordial silence, and as long as we do not describe the action which breaks this silence.'[34] As Toadvine elaborates, the movement from silence to expression and reflection begins as pre-reflective experience: a mute dialogue of the body with nature that also 'divines the world's presence' through non-linguistic significations in the perceived world—an incipient reflexivity that seeks expression.[35]

Of course, it is quite plausible to maintain the reverse, that silence is the absence of primordial sound.[36] Rather than annulling or shutting out sound to obtain or uncover originary silence, the issue can be reconfigured as brushing aside silence to reveal initial sound. Scientists assert that 'the real universe is not silent, but is actually alive with vibrating energy. Space and time carry a cacophony of vibrations with textures and timbres.'[37] In a move mirroring Cage's exercise on the piano, sound then becomes the alternative default position. The postulated rivalry between the initial starting points of sound and silence pits one scenario against the other, complicated further by supporting arguments for either standpoint that can be gleaned from theology, philosophy, or anthropology. In two crucial senses, however, neither symmetry nor polarity applies here. First, whereas total silence is a conceivable pole, it cannot be matched with total sound. Second, human sensibility to sound, and especially to voice, is richer and more multivalent than to silence in its simple acoustic, sensory receptibility—as distinct from the multiple interpretations of tonality through which we unpack, filter, and probe our comprehension of silence and our emotional reactions to it. This issue will be pursued further in the following chapter.

Notes

1. S. Beckett, *The Unnamable* (London: Faber & Faber, 2010), p. 19.
2. See, e.g., J. F. Teahan, 'The Place of Silence in Thomas Merton's Life and Thought', *Journal of Religion* 61 (1981), pp. 364–383, on the goal of calming interior consciousness and of union with God.
3. See, e.g., E. Kagge, *Silence in the Age of Noise* (London: Viking, 2017).
4. D. Tannen, 'Silence: Anything But', in D. Tannen and M. Saville-Troike (eds.), *Perspectives on Silence* (Norwood, NJ: Ablex, 1985), pp. 93–111 at p. 95.
5. R. L. Johannesen, 'The Functions of Silence: A Plea for Communication Research', *Western Journal of Communication* 38 (1974), pp. 25–35.
6. See, e.g., K. Neuwirth, E. Frederick, and C. Mayo, 'The Spiral of Silence and Fear of Isolation', *Journal of Communication* 57 (2007), pp. 450–468, who identify, among others, patterns of conformity based on ignorance that lead to the self-suppression of opinion.
7. M. Freeden, 'The Professional Responsibilities of the Political Theorist', in B. Jackson and M. Stears (eds.), *Liberalism as Ideology: Essays in Honour of Michael Freeden* (Oxford: Oxford University Press, 2012), pp. 259–277.

8 Max Picard, *The World of Silence* (Chicago, IL: Henry Regnery, 1964 [1948]), p. xix.
9 M. Atwood, *The Blind Assassin* (London: Bloomsbury, 2000), p. 395.
10 Quoted in D. C. Matt, 'Ayin: The Concept of Nothingness in Jewish Mysticism', in Robert K. C. Forman (ed.), *The Problem of Pure Consciousness: Mysticism and Philosophy* (New York/Oxford: Oxford University Press, 1990), p. 123. See also D. MacCulloch, *Silence: A Christian History* (London: Penguin, 2014), pp. 58, 62.
11 M. A. Sells, *Mystical Languages of Unsaying* (Chicago, IL: University of Chicago Press, 1994), p. 2.
12 T. Dean, 'Artist's Book', in Harris, Hollinghurst, and Smith, *Tacita Dean*, p. 106.
13 Sobkowiak, 'Silence and Markedness Theory', pp. 43–44.
14 William Shakespeare, *Julius Caesar*, Act I, Scene 2.
15 Sobkowiak, 'Silence and Markedness Theory', p. 44.
16 See the discussion of keening in Chapter 7 below.
17 I. Hassan, 'The Literature of Silence', *Encounter* (January 1967), pp. 74–80 at pp. 76, 81 (quoting George Steiner).
18 T. Vainiomäki, 'Silence as a Cultural Sign', *Semiotica* 150/1–4 (2004), pp. 347–361 at p. 353.
19 Montiglio, *Silence in the Land of Logos*, pp. 12–13. Compare this with the observation on a theatrical 'sotto voce' in Chapter 4.
20 M. Foucault, *A History of Sexuality*, vol. 1 (New York: Pantheon, 1978), p. 27.
21 G. Sider, 'Between Silences and Culture: A Partisan Anthropology', in Achino-Loeb, *Silence: The Currency of Power*, p. 151.
22 See Chapter 5.
23 J. Keane, 'Silence and Catastrophe: New Reasons Why Politics Matters in the Early Years of the Twenty-first Century', *Political Quarterly* 83 (2012), p. 662.
24 I. McGilchrist, *The Master and his Emissary: The Divided Brain and the Making of the Western World* (New Haven, CT: Yale University Press, 2009), pp. 96, 112.
25 Ibid., pp. 97, 104.
26 Ibid., pp. 125, 127.
27 Ibid., p. 115.
28 Ibid., pp. 127, 129.
29 Ibid., pp. 399, 401.
30 Langton, 'Speech Acts and Unspeakable Acts', p. 327.
31 M. Crawford, *The World Beyond Your Head* (Penguin, 2016), p. 11.
32 G. R. Saunders, 'Silence and Noise as Emotion Management Styles: An Italian Case', in Tannen and Saville-Troike, *Perspectives on Silence*, pp. 165–183 at p. 175.
33 S. Sontag, 'The Aesthetics of Silence', p. 14. http://www.ubu.com/aspen/aspen5and6/index.html
34 M. Merleau-Ponty, *Phenomenology of Perception* (London and New York: Routledge, 2002), p. 214.
35 Ibid., pp. 469–470; T. Toadvine, 'The Reconversion of Silence and Speech', *Tijdschrift voor Filosofie* 70/3 (2008), pp. 457–477 at pp. 466–468, 471, offers a cogent critique of Merleau-Ponty's account of the transition from silence to reflective expression.
36 But see the complications resultant from the term *tohu va bohu* in Chapter 9.
37 Craig Hogan, 'The Sounds of Spacetime', *American Scientist* 94/6 (2006), p. 532.

4
Silence, Stillness, and Solitude

A guiding argument of this book is that, in all its individual or social discursive manifestations, the salient and powerful political dimension exhibited by silence is not a side-effect or marginal phenomenon but a core constituent of the conscious or unconscious thought-practices in which we engage, and of the ideologies we espouse. It is present throughout our political discourses; it sunders them, amplifies them, and cloaks them in enigma. It can signify both something and nothing. We marvel at the silence of human solitude; we register the silent though noticed absence of others; we respect the silence of honouring the dead; and—to switch to very concrete practices—some railway companies have introduced carriages in which silence is required as a social virtue and respecter of others' space, while airport lounges market 'silence' to the wealthy.[1] Counter-intuitively, silences can be detected; they can interrupt, eclipse, disorient, delight, pain, tease, or be played with.

Every one of those silences, and more, also adopts claims to its ubiquity, exhorting us as political theorists to consider silence as integrated into our patterns of political thinking and discourse: in our conceptualizations of our place in the world and the forces that impact on us; in our observations about what a person does to another; in the ethical and institutional conclusions drawn from that interchange; in the opportunities and temptations silence affords to rush in and take possession of the ostensibly vacant space; in impeding, regulating, or propelling individual and collective will; in the human nullification, or relief, or helplessness, or puzzlement, accompanied by absence and frustrated by an intimation of something wanting. In all those, the concept of silence and its multifarious patterns should take pride of place alongside the practices, ideas, and happenings that demand the attention of political theorists.

We now move from the macro to the meso. In beginning to unpack some of the conceptual undergirdings of silence amongst its multitude of incarnations in familiar and typical vernacular discourse, as well as those expounded in scholarly renderings, two salient terminological groupings positioned at their centre will be addressed in turn. The first, already encountered in Tacita Dean's artistry, is the subject of this chapter, the intersection between silence and stillness; the second, in Chapter 5, is the subdivision of silence into absence and lack, also previously and briefly introduced. Neither set of terms is in a dichotomous or binary relationship with its partner—as will be seen, each pair both diverges and overlaps, sometimes adopting sharp outlines, at other times displaying fuzzy contours. In addition, there is a third, somewhat subsidiary, wheel in each pairing, respectively solitude and removal, which may allow the expansion of the pairings into two tripartite groupings.

Stillness can occupy a conceptual space unconnected to silence: when located on a conceptual map of proximities, it is to no small extent found outside the boundaries of silence, encompassing notions of calm as well as quietude, which offer a qualitative gloss on stillness way beyond its mechanical state of immobility. By contrast, the pairing of absence and lack is a central and more clearly bipartite subdivision of silence itself, denoting two categories internal to the concept that imply loss rather than value. Notwithstanding their widespread usage, both pairings fall far short of encapsulating the field entirely; intertwined and alongside them are other important concerns. But both serve to draw us into an intricate web of cross-cutting and interlocked issues, reminding us that the concept of silence is replete with interwoven distinctions, rendering unworkable neat taxonomies in which each classification can stand on its own perfectly insulated from the others. The point, though, is not to chase after that illusive wholeness but to explore what each categorization, despite its boundary problems, can bring in its wake.

1 Silence and Logos

Powerful as the Cage–Dean artistic representation of silence and stillness is, and evocative as is its political decoding, the scene needs to be extended. Keeping quiet has now to be appended to silence alongside stillness. For the time being, the notion of solitude will be kept in reserve as a socially significant state that is bereft of the defining acoustical silence the other conditions possess. Silence, keeping quiet, and stillness all involve broad brushstrokes that display a degree of vagueness and polysemy and, as already stressed, their nuances will frequently overlap. Indeed, in common language all three distinctions are often elided under the aegis of the overarching concept of 'silence'. I will often abide by that conceptual abbreviation but not when the distinction is germane to a specific issue or when it runs the danger of eroding crucially important types of silence unrelated to the mere abstention from speech. Stillness—*selenium* in Latin, *Stille* or *Ruhe* in German, and *le calme* in French—refers more broadly to tranquillity and quietude, not only to the acoustic silence which it incorporates. It can also be associated with human inaction and motionlessness (*Unbeweglichkeit, immobilité*), as well as with inanimate objects and voids. Keeping quiet—*taciturnitas, Schweigen, se taire*—identifies the willed capacity of a potentially animate agent to abstain from their natural ability for meaningful vocalization or sound and to hold their tongue, and I will refer only to *human* agency in that context. By contrast, Kurzon has noted that 'being silent' is a stative that has no active equivalent.[2] Keeping quiet, however, appears to suggest purposiveness or at least knowingness—a conscious refraining from speaking.[3] But a caveat must be attached. Central reasons for keeping quiet may also reflect a prior incapacity to articulate, or to comprehend the rules of communication prevalent in a given social setting, as well as a disorienting deficiency in pertinent information.

Notwithstanding the weight that has to be accorded to the conceptual stretching of silence, the epigrammatic sentence 'in the beginning was the word'[4] remains a potent articulation of the primacy of voice and verbalization in religious, cultural, and philosophical epistemologies. The beginning of logos must therefore be a credible starting point for any exploration of human silence. Consequently, the binary 'speech–silence'—whether affirmed or disputed—demands prominent attention and will constitute a key concern throughout this study. As Maitland notes in her probing study of silence, if the word was in the beginning and if what preceded it in the Judaeo-Christian tradition was 'without form and void', as the Book of Genesis has it, then even silence was absent prior to creation. Silence only became conceptualizable when words, language, and speech came into being.[5]

Indeed, the rationale of exploring silence in the humanities and the social sciences largely shifts to voice rather than sound as the *point d'appui*. As Petschke observes of voice: 'There is no sound to which human ears and brains are better attuned nor whose absence is more keenly felt.'[6] One might thus well assume that when a defining feature of human existence is frequently identified as the capacity for speech and language, human taciturnity seems an oddity. There are of course staging posts in between. *Sotto voce*—literally, under the voice—is a deliberate lowering of pitch, usually as an aside to oneself or to the knowing involvement of a theatrical audience. In a switch of allegiance that is always a political (re)association, it uncouples an actor from the community treading the theatre boards and engages an alternative group with which to commune temporarily. The primacy of speech rules the roost in everyday perception, even when speech is delivered as an aspect of performativity. In ancient Greek literature, *aglôssos* (being tongueless) refers to an inadequate speaker. Ineffective speech is absent speech, a non-language.[7] Notably, even reading to oneself—subvocalization, when the mind and minuscule larynx movements mimic the sound of words—is sometimes described as 'silent speech'.[8]

There is, however, a completely different evocation of silence in literature that sits at a double crossroads: between voice and silence, and between conscious handling and inadvertent presence. That is the phenomenon of the inner voice, including a voice unspoken even by the storyteller. Drawing attention to Jacques Derrida's discussion of thought in the Western philosophical tradition as a soliloquy or inner voice, Petschke remarks that 'even those subjects who remain silent must submit to the hegemonic dictates of the voice'.[9] The inner voice may be intimated, it may only be there for the discerning reader to detect, or it may slip out of the grasp of reader and author alike. An illuminating example is offered in Laurence's study of Virginia Woolf, exploring how Woolf's characters are represented in her fiction by transposing their presence from the external world of action to the inner life of mind, feeling and sensation, and imagery. Woolf creates a 'lexicon of silence of gaps, gulfs, pauses, fissures, cracks, and interludes', employing 'metaphors, punctuation and rhythms of silence'. The silence is there, if at all, to be experienced in its richness and its indeterminacy: 'silence points out language's mask: the uncertainties and limitations of interpretation in literature and life'.[10] The control of the text by the author is imprecise and unsteady, not quite able—or willing—to encapsulate or pinpoint the reveries of her protagonists, giving in instead to the irregular flow of their moods.

Woolf is balanced on the cusp between the deliberate evoking of silence as a laden and capacious presence and the recognition of its hiddenness for author as well as character. One heeds Merleau-Ponty's contention: 'If the author is a writer, that is, if he is capable of finding the elisions and caesuras which indicate the [character's] behaviour, the reader responds to his appeal and joins him at the virtual center of the writing, *even if neither one of them is aware of it*.'[11] Nonetheless, as Laurence contends, Woolf wields 'a planned "alternation" of rhythm that is carefully structured into her text'.[12] Order and design are some of the integral political features at the disposal of an author, in this case accompanied by a double silence: of the personae and of the quasi-concealment of the literary devices that are not immediately clear to the casual reader.

But the binary 'speech–silence' is far too general. Non-speech can fall into a variety of distinct categories, some of which are culturally internalized across societies in ways quite distinct one from another—and to that extent not the product of deliberate willing. First, silence may be the absence of language and that may include the cultural abstinence from speech, or the state of something becoming unsayable. Second, because—as already observed—silence may be interpreted as the absence of *conveyed* meaning when language itself is transformed into noise under certain conditions of incomprehension, that acquires marked political significance. Targeted words that make sense to the utterer and that may be heard but not understood as speech are a failed exercise of influence. Hence, when an anthropological study notes a common pattern among listeners to interpret 'the universal acceptance of silence as a form of withholding'[13]—while linking withholding to power—the universality of that reaction warrants a double counter-contention. It is not only that the repeated attribution of silence solely to agentic intentionality belies the fact that withheld power is equally the by-product of assimilated and obscured cultural and institutional conventions. Even more to the point, silence cannot be wholly and universally associated with withholding in the first place, given its numerous codes of expressivity that indicate active and interventionist semantic signalling. That argument is central to this and subsequent chapters.

A third option challenging the speech–silence binary—illustrating the central political feature of impacting on the practices of the world—may be found in some Catholic writings, when silence is charged with the gift of eliciting movement: 'in every silence there is something of the spoken word, as an abiding token of the power of silence to create speech'[14]—as if a potent force were left hanging, irrepressibly propelling a verbal response. That idea is reformulated by the French philosopher Roland Barthes, writing that 'silence has in fact a "speakerly" or "speechly" substance'. 'Notice the paradox,' he continues, 'silence only becomes sign if one makes it speak.'[15] Granted, but it would be preferable to desist from the metaphor of silence speaking, when that idea would be better expressed by presenting silence as a conveyor of messages to, and stimulator of imaginations in, those who experience it. Nonetheless, the emotive and quasi-mystical role that silence plays in some discourses is well illustrated by the explorer Erling Kagge, who casts it in the role of a transformative political actor, imbued with qualities that *speak* to people. In his words, 'To speak is precisely what the silence should do. It *should* speak, and you should talk with it, in order to harness the potential that is present. ... Nature spoke to me in the guise of silence.'[16] It is far from clear whether Kagge's nature is an independent bearer of attributes or whether human beings project nature's properties onto it. An any rate, the co-relationship between a silent and a stillness-inducing nature is palpable in explorers' accounts; when the 'voice' of nature is nonetheless compatible with its majestic stillness.[17] Barthes, more subtly and perceptively, if less lyrically, portrays silence as an interactive relationship between two human beings:

the one transmits silence to another, who does not necessarily receive it as silence—a possible failure of communication or of interpretation.[18]

In a very different poetic mode, silence is conjured up as actively malevolent and transgressive in Paul Simon's lyrics to his famous 1964 song with Art Garfunkel, 'The Sound of Silence'. There it becomes a deadening force that absorbs and disturbs human speech and contact: 'People talking without speaking/People hearing without listening/People writing songs that voices never share/No one dare/Disturb the sound of silence'.[19] The 'sound' produced by silence is a counter-sound of echoes and whispers in a cityscape emptied of human warmth and touch, itself the antithesis of nature. Social atomization and alienation characterize what effectively is a political dystopia.

The silence–speech relationship attains special significance in certain strands of Buddhist philosophy, in which speech and silence may be one and the same, dismissing their dichotomous existence. Whereas the relationship between silence, speech, and meaning may seem to be complex and intertwined in 'Western' eyes, in much Buddhist thought that complexity is normalized, anticipated, or eliminated. Thus, in his *Wanling Lu*, Huangbo Xiyun—the influential practitioner and teacher of Zen-Buddhism—states: 'Speaking is silence (*yu ji mo*); silence is speaking (*mo ji yu*); speaking and silence are non-dualistic (*yumo bu er*).'[20] The Buddhist insistence on non-dualism has launched a new branch of study, liminology, that explores the limits and boundaries of language, especially those between speaking and non-speaking. As Youru Wang elaborates, liminology refers to what prevails on a supposed border or threshold, transcending, blurring, or even negating it, and generating endless possibilities of transformation. Limits clearly do apply in the world, but 'the notion of an absolute, immovable limit, along with the notion of a separated realm of transcendence, is apparently abandoned. Limitlessness or what is beyond the limit is considered inherent in the limit or limitedness.' Tellingly, 'the limit simultaneously affirms and subverts itself through the limitlessness it invariably carries within'.[21]

Insisting on the non-existence of fixed boundaries between speech and silence is crucial to those worldviews and philosophical conceptualizations. Silence is then no longer an absence any more than speech is, nor is it a lack because that would imply the potential towards a clear presence, as suggested in Chapter 5. Some of these issues within Buddhist philosophy, with its own understandings of thinking politically, await further consideration in Chapter 7. For now, it is instructive to contrast Buddhist non-dualism with a completely distinct disciplinary and linear framework typical of theories of linguistic communication. Those theories reject two extreme misconceptions, that silence is either the 'foreign opposite' of speech, or that speech and silence are identical. Instead, they hold that 'the entire system of spoken language would fail without man's ability to both tolerate and create sign sequences of silence-sound-silence units'.[22] Such disciplinary divergences amply demonstrate that the identification, let alone the meaning, of silence becomes indisputably contingent on the knowledge apparatus through which it is filtered.

2 Stillness

If raw, unadulterated acoustic silence is the complete absence of sound, stillness predominantly combines the absence of sound with the absence of movement, as Dean so brilliantly captured. And even though nature is hardly ever completely still and motionless, it is often the case that conceptualizing silence as stillness endows it with the specific advantage of appearing to be the initial, 'natural', state, preceding life itself, astrophysical evidence to the contrary. In that version, noise and speech subsequently punctuate stillness or constitute forms of active energy and power that appear to rise out of stillness, only eventually destined to surrender to it. In discussing stillness, Barthes observed that it was an attribute either of nature or of divinity, conjuring up the notion of a 'timeless virginity of things, before they are born or after they have disappeared'.[23] Significantly, the ontological pairing sound–silence raised in the previous chapter is replaced by the more 'dignified' or eloquent pairing of silence with stillness. Stillness does not appear to be coterminous with void but a form of quiescence—evoking gentleness rather than nothingness. It usually prefigures something about to be or draws a curtain over something that has been, marking a transition in a chain of being. That attribution notably attaches a temporal, even circular, form to a calm nonexistence that frames existence. In employing the verb 'born', Barthes signals the dialectical interdependence between stillness and life, ultimately held in a synthesis. Barthes' spiritual account can only be granted in a metaphorical or imaginary sense, but it also has strong implications for the human element between those two poles. By contrast, in Zen-Buddhism a profound state of silence-cum-*stillness* is not unsettled by speech but compatible with it. The Japanese term *moku* 'implies silence *per se*. The idea is silently to enter the absolute realm of infinite stillness which is not disturbed by speaking and cannot be broken, but rather endows speaking with a depth of meaning.'[24]

One may well query the ubiquity of certain types of environmental and religious thinking that postulate the notion of the natural and the divine versus forms of energetic intervention or of inscribing—namely, the 'artificial' or the 'manufactured'—that are then reduced to harmful influences. Does it complicate matters that the divine creation of the world, of both sound and quietude, can itself be understood in several religions as a Godly act of supreme power, an archetypal political and sovereign act of willing and implementation, both final and unchallengeable?[25] As culturally induced dualisms draw them apart, patterns of political thinking thrust them together.

For that matter, stillness can also have strong negative and unpleasant undertones indicating death—as with a stillborn child—or the incapacitating cessation of vital activity. Discussing the ills of mass production, Picard surmises that 'the stillness that exists when machines stop working is no silence but ... an emptiness in the [factory] worker's life'. The 'great power of the labour process' is that 'it has established itself outside the sphere of discussion'.[26] A restorative silence is spliced and replaced with an oppressive, draining stillness—a blankness removed from human control. It covertly anaesthetizes the political support for the industrial system, threatening to dislocate it.

In his scathing critique of industrialism Thomas Carlyle offered a veritable paean of praise to the disjuncture between silence and stillness, and the precedence of the former over the latter, while according noise an unusually positive presence. Silence had value mainly as a means to preferring certain kinds of noise over human talk. In contrast with 'eternity's stillness',[27] Carlyle extolled the earthiness of work as noise that circumvents the logical sterility both of much speech and of idle chatter. Referring to silence stretching through time and space, associated respectively with infinity and eternity, Carlyle mused: 'Stars silent rest o'er us, Graves under us silent! Between which two great Silences, do not, as we said, all human Noises, in the naturalest times, most preternaturally march and roll?' The silent mysticism of meditation evident in some of Carlyle's writings was now located in practical physicality.[28] Human energy was channelled into 'the hum of all our spinning cylinders, Trades-Unions, Anti-Corn-Law Leagues and Carlton Clubs ... through all thy Ledgers, Supply-and-demand Philosophies, and daily most modern melancholy Business and Cant, there does shine the presence of a Primeval Unspeakable'.[29]

In 'these loud-babbling days' Carlyle honoured the fundamental 'talent of Silence', combined with the materiality and performativity of the English.

> The cloudy-browed, thick-soled, opaque Practicality, with no logic-utterance, in silence mainly, with here and there a low grunt or growl, has in him what transcends all logic-utterance: a Congruity with the Unuttered! The Speakable,

which lies atop, as a superficial film, or outer skin, is his or is not his: but the Doable, which reaches down to the World's centre, you find him there!

That capacity, 'unsung in words, is written in huge characters on the face of this Planet—sea-moles, cotton-trades, railways, fleets and cities, Indian Empires, Americas, New-Hollands; legible throughout the Solar System'. All these were testimony to 'the much-honoured, illustrious, extremely inarticulate Mr. Bull!' Ultimately, wedged between the central silences and stillness, 'Deeds are greater than Words. Deeds have such a life, mute but undeniable, and grow as living trees and fruit-trees do.'[30]

Carlyle refused to deem ambitious social and political projects as constructs of ideas and disputation. They were the hard graft of unquestioning labour conducted silently and wholeheartedly: their language was not the sound of speech but the noise of industry, and that specific noise was reassuring and wholesome. Deeds, then, have the luxury of accommodating an unfathomable depth of silences, carrying an amplitude that speech can only cut short. Importantly, the grand political projects—empire, international trade—testified to the matter-of-fact concreteness of politics as the sphere of material activity rather than verbalized intellect and schemata. In that concrete sphere things were achieved, changed, and made to happen, often by captains of industry capitalizing on the robust nature of the English worker, expressing the physical and transformative power invested in the collective can-do attitude of English workers and entrepreneurs. To the question 'which silences matter?' Carlyle's response is that human silence matters. Non-human, mechanical noise does not count as breaking a silence, particularly when it is in the service of human enterprise. To the question 'What counts as silence?' Carlyle's response is that silence does not require stillness or inactivity—unlike certain religious practices, or the allure of wildernesses for those who experience them as uplifting. The human capacity to work and expend energy is a performative language more powerful than speech and rhetoric—the latter lacking the vitality to change the world—and in no need of articulation. The dual contrast with, and similarity to, Nietzsche's pronouncement is intriguing: 'The greatest events', he wrote in *Thus Spake Zarathustra*, 'are not our noisiest but our stillest hours. Not around the inventors of new noises, but around the inventors of new values, doth the world revolve; inaudibly it revolveth.'[31]

To conclude, the very idea of phases of existence parcelled out by the presence or absence of stillness has profound social and aesthetic consequences, as if human sound, movement, or restlessness not only possesses—in cosmic perspective—an ephemeral transience, but has a contaminating quality that defiles a once and future tranquillity. If it is the case that the vocal world inhabited by human beings tarnishes the purity that precedes it, and even the materiality that consolidates it, one might extract an order of aesthetic and social ranking from that sequence—and all exercises in ranking are also allocations of political significance.[32] Equally deserving of consideration is that when stillness is understood as absence of movement, it is not merely timeless, as Barthes notes, but negates spatiality as well.

3 Solitude

Barthes' deliberate blurring of the distinction between nature and divinity strikes a chord among celebrants of the primordial and of the pristine appeal of the wilderness. For the Psalmist in the Old Testament, the divine may itself be expressed through a powerful silence in nature: 'The heavens declare the glory of God. . . . There is no speech nor are there words; their voice is not heard.'[33] That silent nature can mainly be experienced on one's own; in the company of others, after all, speech is likely to break the spell sooner rather than later. The American explorer Admiral Byrd wrote of his solitary sojourn in the Antarctic in more secular tones:

> I paused to listen to the silence. . . . Here were the imponderable processes and forces of the cosmos, harmonious and soundless. Harmony, that was it! That was what came out of the silence—a gentle rhythm . . . it was enough to catch that rhythm, momentarily to be myself a part of it. In that instant I could feel no doubt of man's oneness with the universe.[34]

The existential silence of the wilderness may also delimit by containing as well as encircling. The celebrated early twentieth-century English explorer and adventurer, Gertrude Bell, wrote of her experience in the desert as 'silence and solitude fall round you like an impenetrable veil'.[35] Shielding, concealing, and cocooning, that veil is both a highly private and isolating phenomenon and the elevating, protective, select, and nigh-mystical garb of affinity. The atomism of acute individualism is interlaced with a consciousness of privilege and uniqueness, producing a distinct political footprint.

Even more telling is Kagge's identification of nature as an agent in a very personal, even intimate, relationship. As if both man and nature were now two extra-social entities, divesting themselves from the rest of planetary existence, the author is simultaneously alone and in a dialogue with another encircling presence, all the more precious for not being interrupted. 'I began a conversation with nature. My thoughts were broadcast out over the plains towards the mountains, and other ideas were sent back.'[36] While the notion of natural objects speaking and requiring careful listening to is widespread in different cultures, it has also come under criticism from some ethicists. Vogel maintains that dialogues and conversations must be reciprocal and that makes them indispensable to moulding the ethical sensitivity and mutual obligation that puts whatever we hear spoken to the tests of truth and reliability.[37] His argument may be a valid ethical objection to attributing speech to nature, but it overlooks another objection concerning the practice of hearing that is more pertinent to the discussion in these pages. For even in the unlikely event that nature were capable of speech, its purported voice would be transmitted not directly but through the 'intervention' or regulation of personal practices and cultural filters. These place the complexities of reception, interpretation, and decoding at the heart of listening, irrespective of their ethical purpose or truth value.

Kagge inevitably brings with him the conceptual vocabulary of the political as an activating vision: 'Antarctica has a mission as an unknown land.'[38] That was felt by him when a large group at a South Pole base shared the sensation of holding a stone, each 'without uttering a word'[39]—one of many instances of collectively observed silences. If, in his words, experiences of silence are both an end and a tool,[40] silence serves a purpose as well as being an enabling condition—its empowering impact, as well as its role in making a difference, are some of its political capacities. For power is always about making something happen that would otherwise not occur, or pre-empting something that would otherwise ensue. Kagge's silence also appears to generate a sense of spontaneous emotional togetherness that mitigates solitude, tellingly replacing and mirroring the commonality more usually ascribed to shared speech, to logos.

On a separate but interrelated route as an artist and specialist in sound studies, Salomé Voegelin evokes the silence of solitude as a sensorial experience through which she can hear herself amidst soft sounds, in an incomplete and contingent process of self-knowledge: 'The silent landscape at dawn affords me the space of anticipation: to find the language of its sounds without a preconceived vocabulary; to meet them momentarily in my perception and produce a sense about myself within their silent density rather than about them.'[41] Here silence is a transformative unlocking agent that in turn prompts human agency, articulation, and creativity—a political dynamic propelling solitude into sociality.

Solitude has long been held to be the romantic supplement to both silence and stillness. One may call to mind Edmund Burke's passionate outburst:

'All general privations are great, because they are all terrible; Vacuity, Darkness, Solitude and Silence.'[42] Yet the latter two states are far more commonly detached from the former two. Wordsworth, the pre-eminent poet of solitude, of loneliness as being alone, offered a different, and more familiar, pattern of four conjoined states of mind: 'Thus did I steal along that *silent* road, My body from the *stillness* drinking in, . . . Above, before, behind, Around me, all was *peace* and *solitude*.'[43] In his *Ode on Solitude* the precocious twelve-year-old Alexander Pope lauded solitude—not in a wilderness but in the seclusion of family-owned property—for offering the prospect of 'health of body, peace of mind, quiet by day, sound sleep by night', in a setting where a man could 'breathe his own air, in his native ground'. For him, solitude and silence did not require the vast stretches of unpopulated nature, but were enmeshed with a sense of concrete, localized belonging, rootedness, and security in a rural domain. Particularly evocative, if melodramatic, was the plea 'thus let me live, unseen, unknown; thus unlamented let me die'— through which solitude was transformed into a concealment in which even the grieving for a departed life was effaced, silencing its memory.[44] An active and fulfilling existence beyond the gaze of others was only enabled, of course, by drawing up protective boundaries in both space and time around those who would desire that insulation—but, clearly, such boundaries could only be erected and respected by those against whom Pope sought a private haven. Hence, paradoxically, solitude was a function of political will, cooperation, and the laws of property.

By contrast, a master of the modern theatre such as Beckett overlays conventional distinctions one on the other when his narrator recalls: 'Yes, in my life, since we must call it so, there were three things, the inability to speak, the inability to be silent, and solitude.'[45] Blurring and intertwining, rather than separating, was increasingly taking over as the prevailing prism through which to correlate speech and silence in discrete ontological and conceptual combinations, all of which displayed an indeterminate fluidity that reflected the erosion of political and social solidities.

The frequent incorporation of solitude into the nexus of silence-related conditions evidently raises additional issues. Curiously, the merits or demerits of solitude as quietude were rarely broached in seventeenth- and eighteenth-century treatises (the involuntary solitude of Defoe's *Robinson Crusoe* being more concerned with economic self-sufficiency, religious observation, and the physical and emotional perils and challenges of an isolated existence). Initially, solitude was discussed with an express emphasis on its being the converse of (often urban) sociability, or a step on the quest for mental well-being, neither of which placed silence at centre-stage.[46] That latter construal remained half-hidden, a largely unintentional instance of the concealing gaps of scholarship, more likely to be noted by twentieth-century experts cautioning against 'risking sanity in a high-risk encounter with [the] prolonged silence and self-examination' induced by monastic life and retreats. As Vincent observes of a central underlying theme, repeatedly to be confirmed in other historical contexts in subsequent chapters, 'There is a need for what might be termed a quiet history of British society. Too little attention has been paid to the intermittently organized, often silent, re-creative practices that have been and remain a vital presence in the lives of most men and women in the modern world.'[47]

Politically, solitude could be an embodiment of the yearning for freedom and for individual, stand-alone, independence, denying the priority of supportive networks and the role of a sustaining social order, eschewing the quotidian experiences of social conflict, and opting for the utopian vision of an alternative lifestyle. But it is far more complicated than that. Solitude hovers between a strong affirmation of one's private emotional persona and the immersion of self into an extra-human world promising communion and connectedness, exceeding the everyday exchanges of interpersonal communication. It is one of many manifestations that capture the balance at the core of the political: its simultaneous disaggregative and holistic bind, a balance almost too fragile to put into words. It can also be found to apply to a national trait. As one study asserts: 'Nordic silence means retirement to solitude and non-communication',[48] a partial product of geopolitical environments. Perhaps in the case of Finns, that closedness and suspicion of strangers could contribute towards hampering their intercultural contacts. But it may simultaneously strengthen the social characteristics that bestow on them a unique, unspoken identity.

Notes

1   On silence as a commodity see J. Biguenet, *Silence* (New York and London: Bloomsbury Academic, 2015), pp. 9–12.
2   On the possible semiotic relationships between silence and stillness see Kurzon, *Discourse of Silence*, pp. 15–17.
3   Ibid., pp. 1–2.
4   John 1:1.
5   S. Maitland, *A Book of Silence* (London: Granta, 2009), p. 118.
6   K. Petschke, 'Agency without Voice? A Political Ecology of Vegetal Silence', in Dingli and Cooke, *Political Silence*, p. 131.
7   Montiglio, *Silence in the Land of Logos*, pp. 84–85.

8. J. D. Smith, M. Wilson, and D. Reisberg, 'The Role of Subvocalization in Auditory Imagery', *Neuropsychologia* 33 (1995), pp. 1433–1454.
9. Petschke, 'Agency without Voice?', p. 131.
10. Patricia O. Laurence, *The Reading of Silence: Virginia Woolf in the English Tradition* (Stanford, CA: Stanford University Press, 1991), pp. 12, 33.
11. M. Merleau-Ponty, 'Indirect Voices and the Language of Silence', in G. A. Johnson (ed.), *The Merleau-Ponty Aesthetics Reader: Philosophy and Painting* (Evanston, IL: Northwestern University Press, 1993), pp. 76–120 at p. 113 (italics in original).
12. Laurence, *The Reading of Silence*, p. 34.
13. Achino-Loeb, *Silence: The Currency of Power*, p. 2.
14. Picard, *The World of Silence*, p. 9.
15. R. Barthes, *The Neutral* (New York: Columbia University Press, 2005), pp. 24, 26.
16. Kagge, *Silence in the Age of Noise*, pp. 11, 14.
17. See this chapter, section 3, on Gertrude Bell.
18. Barthes, *The Neutral*, p. 24.
19. Paul Simon, 'The Sound of Silence', https://www.paulsimon.com/track/the-sound-of-silence/ (accessed 17 September 2021).
20. Quoted in Youru Wang, *Linguistic Strategies in Daoist Zhuangzi and Chan Buddhism: The Other Way of Speaking* (London: Routledge Curzon, 2003), pp. 116–117.
21. Ibid., pp. 6, 83–85.
22. T. J. Bruneau, 'Communicative Silences: Forms and Functions', *Journal of Communication* 23 (1973), pp. 17–46 at p. 18.
23. Barthes, *The Neutral*, p. 22.
24. Shizuteru Ueda, 'Silence and Words in Zen Buddhism', *Diogenes* 43/170 (1995), p. 11.
25. Freeden, *The Political Theory of Political Thinking*, pp. 93–101.
26. Picard, *The World of Silence*, pp. 186–188.
27. Thomas Carlyle, *Past and Present*, Collected Works, vol. 13, book II, ch. 17 [1843]. https://www.gutenberg.org/ebooks/26159
28. See, *inter alia*, C. Persak, 'Rhetoric in Praise of Silence: The Ideology of Carlyle's Paradox', *Rhetoric Society Quarterly* 21 (1991), pp. 38–52.
29. Carlyle, *Past and Present*, book III, ch. 15.
30. Ibid., book III, ch. 5.
31. F. Nietzsche, *Thus Spake Zarathustra* (New York: Boni & Liveright, 1917), p. 142.
32. See Freeden, *The Political Theory of Political Thinking*, pp. 132–165.
33. Psalms 2:2–4. See P. Torresan, 'Silence in the Bible', *Jewish Bible Quarterly* vol. 31/3 (2003), pp. 153–60.
34. R. E. Byrd, *Alone* (Washington, DC, Covelo, CA, and London: Island Press/Shearwater Books, 1938), p. 85.
35. Gertrude Bell Archive, Newcastle University, Letters, 19 December 1913 (http://gertrudebell.ncl.ac.uk/letter_details.php?letter_id=24).
36. Kagge, *Silence in the Age of Noise*, p. 14.
37. S. Vogel, 'The Silence of Nature', *Environmental Values* 15 (2006), pp. 145–171.
38. Kagge, *Silence in the Age of Noise*, p. 15.
39. Ibid., p. 17.
40. Ibid., p. 86.

41 S. Voegelin, *Listening to Noise and Silence: Towards a Philosophy of Sound Art* (London: Continuum, 2010), pp. 108–109, 112–113.
42 Edmund Burke, 'Privation', in *A Philosophical Enquiry into the Origin of our Ideas of the Sublime and Beautiful* (Cambridge: Cambridge University Press). doi:10.1017/CBO9781107360495.028
43 William Wordsworth, *The Prelude*, Book Fourth, Summer Vacation, ed. Jonathan Wordsworth (London: Penguin, 1995), lines 385–389. Italics added.
44 Alexander Pope, 'Ode on Solitude' (1700), poetryfoundation.org/poems/46561/ode-on-solitude. I have benefited from David Vincent's fine book, *A History of Solitude* (Cambridge: Polity Press, 2020), which expounded upon Wordsworth's and Pope's meditations.
45 Beckett, *The Unnamable*, p. 114.
46 Vincent, *A History of Solitude*, pp. 27–29.
47 Ibid., pp. 35–36.
48 K. Sajavaara and J. Lehtonen, 'The Silent Finn Revisited', in Jaworski, *Silence: Interdisciplinary Perspectives*, p. 271.

5
Absence, Lack, and Removal

Comprehending silence as something that is not—a non-presence—is always going to be an abiding and ineliminable practice. Unsurprisingly, the idea of 'absence' appears to be its strongest and most definite form. In that guise, most easily accessed through philosophical ontologies and theological doctrine, it is indistinguishable from nothingness. It stretches far beyond something that merely isn't contingently there (e.g., Louis was the only person absent from the meeting), or something that has been annihilated (e.g., sucked into a black hole), or removed (e.g., by a palimpsest that overlays or erases traces of a past). Rather, the fullness of absence—if one be permitted to put it in such a paradoxical form—is what absolutely cannot and does not exist *ab initio*, except that it has no *initium* either.

1 The Indeterminacy of Absence

In ordinary language, however, the absoluteness and primacy of absence is mitigated. It is intertwined with partner notions that cut into its ideational space while concurrently retaining their own distinctiveness. Conventionally, silence is largely thought of not solely as an absence (whether desirable or deplorable) but as a lack (indicating a deficiency). In discourse it is understood as something 'not there' or, conversely, missing, in either case dialectically opposed to the presence of sound or speech. However, absence appears to indicate a 'primitive' binary, while lack suggests a more complex notion of movement in time. Answers to the question, 'what goes on when there is silence?' are split into 'nothing goes on' and 'something goes on'. That is a very simplistic response to an immensely intricate issue, ranging across different disciplinary approaches and separate ontological systems. Commentators then endeavour to attach varying grades of significance to what may lie behind those two separate but interwoven terms. In everyday language the meaning of both terms seems to lean in the direction of 'nothing goes on'—certainly in contrast, say, to psychological, anthropological, literary, or religious accounts—yet here too nuances, as well as hairline fractures, abound.

Concealed Silences and Inaudible Voices in Political Thinking. Michael Freeden, Oxford University Press.
© Michael Freeden (2022). DOI: 10.1093/oso/9780198833512.003.0007

That needs further amplification. In common parlance, absence and lack are defined by two different characterizations of what they are, more readily grasped through dialectically pointing to their opposites: a presence in the first case, and a sufficiency or an abundance in the second. So while at its starkest absence is one branch of a zero-sum dichotomy, lack indicates a shortfall, implying a scalable comparative. Unavoidably, some definitions and colloquial usages of absence and lack overlap, but it is also possible to detect a nuanced variance: absence can suggest an emptiness that may not be the result of removing a presence but may precede it or follow it ontologically (the human lifecycle is prone to be understood in that way by many secularists and atheists); while lack may signal a defect or a failing—the non-appearance of something expected or at least available—but also denote an undeveloped, and even unrealizable, potential. As Merleau-Ponty put it, a lack is 'asking to be made good'.[1] To illustrate, the process of acquiring verbal skills—though not the ability to vocalize—exemplifies such a temporary shortage,[2] indicating an insufficient capacity, rather than absolute incapacity, to communicate. The tying in of lack to 'potential' diverges from some approaches for which it is no more than 'an absence with negative connotations'.[3] It also positions it in touching distance of 'vacant', which refers to something unfilled or unoccupied—though that implies the availability of a holding framework already reserved for occupancy, not necessarily suggested by 'lack'. The potentiality of lack also places it in close proximity to the term 'latent', defined by the OED as 'hidden, concealed ... present or existing, but not manifest, exhibited, or developed'.[4]

Nonetheless, an important difference between lack and latency can obtain, as in the renowned sociologist Robert Merton's seminal distinction between latent and manifest functions. He defined a latent function as referring to objective consequences for a person, group, or social and cultural system that 'contribute to its adjustment or adaptation' but are 'unintended and unrecognized'.[5] Leaving aside Merton's typical methodological preference—for that time—in favour of adaptation rather than, say, disruption, the key word in this context is 'unrecognized'. It steers our understanding of silence-cum-latency beyond those intimations of lack that are suspected, inferred, or may emerge, invoking instead a process already in train but unnoticed.

Maitland contends that reducing silence to either a lack or an absence renders it powerless for a culture that sees power in speaking.[6] But that underplays the hidden energy that may be stored in lack and, contrariwise, the unsettling vacuum that may hang over absence. In ordinary, non-professional, language it is arguably easier to identify a specific lack than a specific absence. When a lack is noticeable, it is for the obvious reason that it points to an unfulfilled anticipation—we are *aware* of something missing or unprovided. To judge something as lacking is to call attention to a particular incompleteness, even if we cannot always put our finger on it. The 'cheating' of an audience of its expectations has already been discussed in the Prelude.[7] But to refine matters further, an absence—unlike a lack—may not only be invisible and inaudible; it may well be general as well as unknowable, so that we have no clues where to look or even whether there is anything to look for. True, when reading out a roll call, the response may be 'present' by the addressee or 'absent'—after a short silence—by the roll reader, but that simply identifies and personalizes a known absentee in a given set of individuals, offering a very concrete and circumscribed use of a philosophically abstract and intangible notion.

One contention about the relationship between absence and silence, emerging chiefly from the field of discourse analysis, is that 'we will only perceive absences when there is a potential for them to be significant and, therefore, meaningful'. On that understanding, as Schröter and Taylor contend, 'epistemologically salient cases of absence' only surface 'when we can hold something that gets not said against the possibility of saying it'.[8] Absences are then restricted to those that seem to acquire a state of specificity, to which there must be a 'thinkable alternative', something imaginable. That thought has also been succinctly expressed by Glenn: 'Like the zero in mathematics, silence is an absence with a function, and a rhetorical one at that.'[9] The writer Kazuo Ishiguro, often referred to as a master of the unspoken, has reacted reflectively to the fashioning of his art by saying: 'It's not good enough just to say, you know, look at what's not said because, you know, millions of things are not said . . . you're going actually to try and structure the unsaid things as finely and narrowly as you structure the said things.'[10] In such instances, each possible path—out of several options—that human silences take may well have its own particular patterns that rigorously mirror the logics of the spoken.

This speaks to the power of the writer, able to choose and even to control absences that can only be intuited by the reader. But for the scholar it constitutes a precarious activity, postulating possibilities that may never materialize. The poetic and imaginative licence of the literary artist exceeds and cuts through the disciplinary constraints of plausibility that are professionally imposed on the political theorist, who has to proceed with greater caution. Ultimately, the unavoidable problem with these 'epistemologically salient cases of absence' is the unremitting transformations that epistemological templates undergo, as new epistemologies edge out older ones and saliences rise and fall. It concerns the tricky issue of listening *for* silences, to which we shall return in Chapter 6. Put slightly differently, we are alerted to the operation of a meta-silencing of a higher order: the ontological is stifled by what is currently available epistemologically. What is or may exist is overlaid and rendered opaque by what we think we know or can be known, not by as yet inaccessible or inapplicable epistemologies. For example, in critical discourse analysis the political component is uncovered through exposing a conflict, or juxtaposition, between the expressive capacity of individual agency and its socially constructed rationing and management. In such cases the socially hegemonic features of such constraint—understood by most discourse analysts as deep-seated oppression and inequality—require filtering out and expulsion in order to eliminate the deceptive silences they produce. That demands a sharp appreciation of such hegemonic features—an appreciation always already mediated by frames, predilections, and dispositional preferences at the heart of critical discourse theory, and thus liable to be clouded over by its own ideological biases.

There are of course absences that undeniably lie beyond the remit of discourse analysis, nor do they have a parallel in logos. Absences may be felt, sensed, or intuited without potentially putting them into words. A feeling that God is absent in the life of a believer is difficult to pin down verbally and may absorb other intangible absences. Not every absence will have an alternative, twin, explicitly utterable presence—as distinct from merely having the presence of the concept of 'absence' itself. For that is to rely excessively on paired dichotomies and to undervalue the possible ambiguity of absence, so central to forms of Buddhist thought, as well as the unknowability and unconceptualizability of some absences, to be aired in Chapter 7. Alongside perceptible absences there exist equally important imperceptible ones—imperceptible either to speaker and hearer alike, or to the hearer alone—that are consequently non-specific.

Yet another facet of absence needs to be recorded here, pertaining to issues of negativity. In its literary incarnations, touched on in Chapter 6, absence may leave muffled traces or stimulate an intuition sensed through a gravitation towards other meanings or figurative allusions. In its theological incarnations, explored in Chapter 7, it relates to the unsayable and the ineffable.

Last but certainly not least, there is another matter that should be borne in mind. In much silence scholarship, the authors of silence—its producers—are the subjects of attention, rather than its consumers or interpreters. Speech acts, too, have suffered from an asymmetry of treatment. Far more has been written on intentions, perlocution, and distortion than on the nuanced shades of their reception or consumption. That applies no less to absences of speech and textual omissions: the intended or unintended *reactions* to, or *interpretations* of, silence in a given population are a significant part of human thinking and communication, yet their investigation is underdeveloped, not least because relevant scholarship has a tendency to opt for socially common absences that are not particularly challenging. Sifianou rightly observes of recipients and consumers of a social interaction that 'it is usually the absence of what is conventionally anticipated which loads both speech and silence with negative meaning and impolite implications'.[11] Such disappointed discursive expectations—for example, applying to modes of address, courtesies, timing, or information—can have a deflationary effect on those affected but nonetheless do not touch the deepest layers of absence.

The marking and unravelling of distinctions in the nexus explored in this chapter can only be achieved in part. Nor is the required conceptual mapping resolved by examining some of their philosophically technical usages, though there appear to be some attempted clearings in that thicket. For instance, theories associated with Jacques Lacan handle lack in a decidedly distinctive manner, to which we now turn. Ultimately, a word of circumspection needs to be sounded: as with other major mapping schemes, neither absence, lack nor—as we shall presently see—removal tells the full story of silence. Defining silence by what it is not, what it no longer is, or even by what it might be—holding that it signifies some kind of blankness or inadequacy— cannot meet its prolific implications within the political sphere. And yet, all the above distinctions gradually build up an arsenal of meanings, and their subtle divergences remain conceptually valuable.

2 Radical Lack

The concept of lack still has some way to go as an organizing idea in exploring political thinking. But in one sphere—the application of Lacanian theory—it has made considerable headway, leading to a surge of research and analysis. In one instance it has even been accorded the heading 'a new paradigm: the concept of lack in political theory'.[12] For the followers of Jacques Lacan, including Slavoj Žižek, lack revolves around the inescapable harm inflicted by conflict, antagonism, and exclusion, papered over by a quasi-Marxist— but very partial—characterization of ideology as a purveyor of illusory and distorted social relations. They entertain the notion of an underlying Real that cannot be articulated or communicated, and for which the inferior and incomplete terms of language must be substituted. Although the possibility of the Real can be contemplated, imagined, or fantasized, it cannot be expressed or reified. As Wardle puts it, 'The Real also describes that which is impossible to signify and therefore impossible to describe through language. This includes phenomena without a signifier and everything that exists outside of human knowledge, but also includes certain objects and experiences that cause excessive amounts of trauma.'[13] Consequently, the inadequacy of language is no other than a manifestation of a radical lack.

The theory of radical lack holds that the reality we live is always a limited representation—or misrepresentation—of the Real in its unattainable fullness; hence the symbolic always fails to characterize the Real, leaving an unaccountable excess of meaning that constitutes an ineluctable lack. For Lacan, it is a lack of *jouissance*, the drive to enjoyment that animates human beings yet whose totality is doomed to elude them. Instead, they have to make do with a constricted *jouissance* that is managed through the symbolism of discourse. Imagination and flights of fancy create the illusion that the Real is attainable,[14] and this promise of wholeness—while always subject to different ideological incarnations—is a recurring political fantasy in societies; most recently, for instance, in populist fantasies about the 'people' as a socially all-embracing, undifferentiated, nation. Ernesto Laclau and Chantal Mouffe have expressed this well, identifying the process as one that retains the hegemonic function of articulating meaning by constructing the unity of society out of its very lack, out of antagonisms and dislocation.[15] In all this, lack is constitutively endemic, while the 'voice' of representation cannot convey the foundations from which it draws not merely imperfectly, but fantasmatically. Indeed, one finds here a hint of the superimposition of voice on the unsaid—a topic more akin to removal and the subject of Chapter 10—although the representing voice is heavily curbed when juxtaposed with the unfathomable depth of meaning that the Real encompasses. As a rule, consequently, when superimposition occurs, one voice replaces—or more typically, usurps—another voice, or other voices, equally capable of utterance. By contrast, the defective representation of the Real stands in for a perpetually inexpressible voice.

Under the spell of Lacanian lack, we are in the grasp of a truly thick silence. The expressive part of any Reality surrogate merely stifles—unknowingly and with total inadequacy—the inevitable silent whole, not by screening it, but by deflecting an ungraspable sphere from any possible view and hearing. There is no point in getting wise to the gap between the Real and its misleading representations; there is nothing even the sophisticated scholar can do to remedy this. Whatever is concealed is beyond human understanding: that kind of lack cannot be overcome, substituted, or disguised—not because it is Godly or mystical but because its silence is ontological, and permanently so. The challenge is hence not that of replacing a pinpointed muteness with language but one of an inexorable and fruitless confrontation with the enormity of silence itself. Unlike vernacular usages of lack that may imply an agent's awareness of it, this notion of lack is a scholarly philosophical tool that thrives not only on its very invisibility and inaudibility in ordinary discourse, but on its insulation from any knowledge of the Real itself. Obviously, it can only be surmised if one shares that modus operandi of deducing—or is it intuiting?—reality.

Outside Lacanian usage, lack far more typically harbours the possibility of a movement from silence to voice in a journey leading from shortfall to abundance, in the course of which a stultified silence is gradually shed. Jacques Rancière's philosophical scheme offers one route to correcting that lack of voice but it is more tortuous than simply unfolding human potential. He envisages the oppressed and hitherto silenced people (those who do not count) as disrupting the complacent saturation of those in power (whom he calls the police) through creating a dissensus, by means of either a lack or a supplement to the illusion of fullness fostered by those in control. The political can offer the glimpse of a lack in what can be sensed and perceived. Concurrently the power of the demos lies in its being 'an excessive part—the whole of those who are nothing'[16]—and in that manner more potent than current power arrangements allow. In that process of revealing gaps, fissures, and misalignments, consensualism—always for Rancière a form of silencing heterogeneous voices—can be questioned.

But Lacanian lack is of different order. It departs from the possibility of the unfolding or unfettering process sought by critical theory, as the route is not convoluted but wholly imaginary. It adopts a feature that could be associated with absence: it is *not* specific. But it is also not capable of being revealed. It is hidden in a way that cannot be presumed or discerned. In effect, it is a silence suspended between lack and absence—it is both there and not there, casting a shadow over the drive to *jouissance* and fulfilment, attesting to an ineluctable unavailability: another manifestation of the ambiguity typical of many interpretations of silence within and outside the orbit of 'Western' culture. Like all notions of lack in a social context, Lacanian lack is potentially dynamic: it has a propelling drive that impacts on subjects and their environments. That accords it nascent political, action-oriented force, bursting to be labelled. It is thus a special case of the general contention expressed in Chapter 3, that naming silence—and for that matter, nothingness—assigns them a linguistic and conceptual presence. It is a special case because the affective drive of Lacanian lack is merely one of weak *jouissance* that can never come to fruition. Consequently, it cannot generate proper understanding, because its dynamic is loosely invested in shifting and impermanent linguistic signifiers.[17] Hence naming Lacanian lack can only be tentative and liminal. And yet the general features of lack also apply in the distinct register of Lacanian analysis, precisely because naming can also confer a modicum of durability on its object. As Fink observes of the relationship between Lacanian drive and naming,

> There is no lack if something is not named. Lack only comes into being by being named. Otherwise it is simply the way an animal experiences hunger: It may be intense and lead to ferocity, but as soon as it is satiated, it is forgotten. But if it is named, it can be re-presented at any time, long after the hunger has been satiated; it can live on, persist.[18]

So, paradoxically, the naming capacities of voice and speech endow the constitutionally silent Lacanian lack with the facility to radiate intellectual and emotional energy.

In the grand scheme of thinking politically—the search for finality in human affairs—absence and lack line up on opposite sides. Silence as perceived lack carries with it the unfolding of a process in the making, though sometimes barely that. While that unfolding possesses a teleological undertow, it is subject to bumps in the road and occasional derailments, and it may render finality unattainable as complete closure. But silence as absence is a silence of a different order of inaudibility. By not allowing the anticipation of controversy and dissatisfaction, it purges those clearly political elements in an act of elimination that is itself blatantly—and quite normally—political. It is an 'end of the story before it began' finality, not a 'converging on an end-state' finality.

Symbols and signifiers adumbrate what can be said, however inadequately—a standpoint less radical than adopted by the advocates of the totally inexpressible Real, but nonetheless papering over fundamental insufficiencies in the human capacity to fashion and then convey meaning. Crucially, they provide the language through which individuals and groups can construct always fragile and fluid identities; but they also mark the limits of the sayable and the conveyable, so that silence is assigned to a realm where signifiers as referents cannot tread assuredly. Because the realm of signifiers and symbols is subject to constant modification by human imagination, fantasy, and misstep, silence swirls around those boundaries. It is continuously moulded and rechannelled into new areas while ejected from others, both gaining and losing territory in the process of the tenuous and provisional meaning making assigned to language. When a signifier is drafted to fill up, or colonize, as much available semantic space as possible—a frequent characteristic of ideological morphology[19]—it appears to crowd silence out, but in effect it merely indicates its looming omnipresence immediately outside the signifier's dominion. Hence language is not only a means of ending silence; it potentially reveals, and alerts to, silent absences; in particular, experiences that cannot be put into words and communicated.

That said, there is a clear distinction between Lacanian lack and two other salient methods of analysing language in a social context. First, critical discourse analysis, as already noted, deems signifiers to exercise the clear role of obfuscating and blurring the traces of exploitation, subjugation, and distortion, exhibiting a scholarly confidence in decoding language that Lacanian theory does not share.[20] Second, the morphological analysis of ideology— through its key process of decontestation—focuses on the ordinary language selection of particular conceptions of a concept from among the multiple meanings a concept carries. It interprets that process as an attempt to silence and delegitimate all other meanings that concept can conjure up by excluding them from consideration, often with only a vague awareness on the part of the disseminators of ideology that they are employing that practice.[21] Bypassing Lacanian argumentation, the analyst of ideologies regards such banished voices as unexpressed, not inexpressible.

The distinctions discussed so far may launch us into very different conceptual fields with their own normalities, normativities, irregularities, temporalities, and evaluations. Indeed, it is common to regard silence in general as 'teeming with potentiality'.[22] That vitality is *ipso facto* political, activating, and holding the key to social change. By contrast, the true nothingness of the absence of existence, a blackness eclipsing even Lacan's Real—the deep nothingness had the universe not been formed—transcends unnamed desire. Its total absence, beyond even the humanly coined words 'vacuum' and 'void', disabling time and space themselves, is profoundly unimaginable, let alone unnameable. Its political dimension lies not in what can counter it, for that is fundamentally impossible, unmanageable, even nonsensical. It lies in the ephemerality and precariousness it confers on the allegedly constant properties of the physical, social, and intellectual worlds we experience. Inescapable temporality and fragility are the political underbelly of the ultimately fruitless and elusive quest for finality in which political language is wrapped.

3 Removal

As indicated above, the pairing absence–lack has been recently extended to a triad. The increasing sophistication of historical research, anthropological evidence, and psychological insight have been joined by an equally robust component, removal. The term does not refer to something non-existent or incomplete but to something erased. The additional subtlety it brings implies the loss, or entombment, of what had previously existed and was perceptible. Whether or not the residue it may have left still carries an impact remains an open question. In line with the focus of this study, I leave aside intentional and wilful deletion, highlighting instead exclusions that have come to pass through unfolding social practices, changing historical circumstances, rising epistemologies, or accidents of fortune. The silence of removal is striking only for those who have prior relevant knowledge about events, arrangements, or discourses that used to be noticeable—and noticed—but have since become obscured or expunged.

Inspired by Marxist critiques of capitalism, Tie has noted that 'the phenomenon of absence . . . comes to be at risk of being absented from thought'. Consequently, different schemes attempt to reify that absence in an endeavour to dismiss it.[23] That version of absenting does not proclaim ontological absence as nothingness; instead, it wipes a slate clean because issues and problems are mounted in frames that make them either discardable or inaccessible. That constitutes removal rather than absence pure and simple. And that is the ultimate triumph of the political. Given that the quest for finality is a chief attribute of political thinking—even if it is ultimately fated to fail, only to be replaced by a new 'finality'[24]—the elimination of controversy and contestation is one powerful mode of maintaining control over human thought-practices. It does not involve the deliberate quashing of an issue but enlists a double move: first, brushing something under the carpet, and second—in an epistemological sleight of hand—conclusively removing the covering carpet from view while it still is actually there, and doing so simply by deactivating our ability to discern both it and what it conceals. That effect was famously discussed—albeit on a more restricted conceptual level—by Peter Bachrach and Morton S. Baratz sixty years ago in their renowned analysis of power as non-decision making, as part of their critique of the methodological bias of positivists and pluralists who pursue power's measurability.[25] While that imperative is no longer an issue for most political theorists, students of political silences have broadened their preoccupation from the more standard removal of the knowledge of an act, event, or process through hiding it, to moving up a gear by obscuring the concealing device itself. It is quite conceivable that, in both cases, when a person is made aware of that absence they will deny that it is an absence in the first place, just as a person who *feels* free (e.g., the happy slave) may protest at being informed that on any objective criterion she is unfree. But there still is a third level of removal—not only total unawareness of the specific existence of a concealing carpet and its subsequent effacement but a general denial of the very practice of concealment itself. That entails moving from epistemology to an ontology that banishes concealment from its purview. There is no better silencing than that, and it does not involve subscribing to a complex philosophy such as Lacan's theory of lack. A parallel to that dimension of concealment may be found in Derrida's observation: 'There is a secret of denial and a denial of the secret.'[26] It is the corresponding secret of silencing, surpassing the silencing of a secret, that we have in mind here; given always that the secret itself becomes inaudible and invisible.

The most common forms of removal are found in changing historical narratives, in the projection or repression of different segments of individual personality, in the competition among groups to establish their identity and interests in a crowded field, or in the modification and ditching of academic and investigative frameworks—this latter theme to be reserved for the following chapter. Forms of removal do not possess the immediacy that can be assigned to perceptions of absence and lack, which is why they are reliant on the hindsight supplied through unfolding temporalities and innovations in scholarship. Silence can of course remove memory directly. In these cases, however, voice is not replaced by silence, but by newer voices crowding out the old. Older happenings and discourses are ousted by functionally equivalent happenings and discourses that drown their predecessors in their wake. Silence here is simply—and momentously!—the buried transformations to which, due to their drawn-out nature, few can testify. Removal in the sense applied here is not mere obliteration but substitution. A well-known example is the rewriting of Russian school textbooks after the fall of communism. Airbrushing the narrative of the previously hegemonic Marxism-Leninism, history textbooks switched to a far greater emphasis on the cultural and national identity of Russia deriving from pre-Soviet Russian history.[27] Those kinds of deliberate substitution will attract closer consideration in Chapter 10.

In his reflections on Haitian history, *Silencing the Past*, the historian and anthropologist Michel-Rolph Trouillot breathed life into that social practice that has become increasingly commented on, yet still remains undertheorized.[28] Removal becomes pivotal to his perceptive comments on the accumulation and usages of historical evidence: 'The presences and absences embodied in sources . . . or archives . . . are neither neutral or natural. They are created. As such, they are not mere presences and absences, but mentions or silences of various kinds and degrees. By silence, I mean an active and transitive process. . . . One engages in the practice of silencing.'[29] And he continued emphatically, extolling 'archival power at its strongest, the power to define what is and what is not a serious object of research and, therefore, of mention'.[30] Very true, undoubtedly, as long as we realize that such activity is not necessarily or even typically intentional, nor does it embody the manifest agentic desire to superimpose one voice over another voice, or introduce a voice where it was previously absent. The random and unplanned preservation, or careless and indifferent mislaying, of information, and the silences they elicit, occur just as much as the deliberate concealment and tampering with facts. Those practices are political because they are humanly induced and culturally flavoured as well as favoured. They make a difference and change the course of events, of forgetting, and of collective memories. Unthought history is there to be retrieved from its oblivion, in the process ousting some of its usurpers.

It is of course also plausible to assume that different traces of past discourses and evidence endlessly intermingle with parallel and overlayered silences, some easier to detect than others, some deeper than others—if you wish, a palette of silences. Nonetheless, according recognition to a hitherto silenced group is as likely as not to mute or diminish voices previously accorded salience—such balances often tend to be zero-sum ones. The lesson to be derived from such empirical evidence, rather than from mystifying evocations, is to cultivate an awareness of a multiple field of contending, clashing, overlapping, or stochastic silences. That entails their unpacking as a spectrum of separate silences created under unique conditions—a microscopy of silences as distinct from a singular, embracing one. Parallel silences about social roots, contending cultures, resisting or deferring to leadership, and communal visions may coalesce, but possess their own origins and rationales.

One of the main arguments bearing out the endemic silences of history parallels the morphological approach to ideology, except that it is based on the inevitable incompleteness of historical evidence. The guiding tenet of ideology studies, by comparison, holds that no ideology can contain the totality of conceptual parts available to it, because some parts are logically incompatible with others. In a remarkably acute analysis, linking those silences with the political distribution of significance and with the exercise of influence and future control, Trouillot writes:

> Silences are inherent in history because any single event enters history with some of its constituent parts missing. Something is always left out while something else is recorded. There is no perfect closure of any event, however one chooses to define the boundaries of that event. Thus whatever becomes fact does so with its own inborn absences, specific to its production. In other words, the very mechanisms that make any historical recording possible also ensure that historical facts

are not created equal. They reflect differential control of the means of historical production at the very first engraving that transforms an event into a fact. … As sources fill the historical landscape with their facts, they reduce the room available to other facts.[31]

As we shall see below with regard to ideologies and ideological conceptualization, 'sources occupy competing positions in the historical landscape. These positions are themselves inherently imbued with meaning since facts cannot be created meaningless. Even as an ideal recorder, the chronicler necessarily produces meaning and, therefore, silences.'[32] We will revisit Trouillot's analysis of Haitian history in Chapter 9, but note that comparable features can be seen in literature, where the silences produced by the narrator, whether intended or not, vanish into obscurity. 'Silence in the literary context is ubiquitous and indispensable, even if not perceived as silence. Literature and art are replete with silences—those things not presented, not explained, not told—some germane and others irrelevant. The presentation of "reality" is necessarily selective, implying omission or silencing.'[33]

More recently, Little has argued in similar vein that

> the past in political temporality is not just concerned with multiple narratives of historical trajectories to the present, but also, vitally, it is focused on *the competing nature of these narratives* … relationships between policies and specific outcomes can not only be explained in different ways, but the act of explaining things in different ways denies, undermines, invalidates or delegitimises alternative accounts of the same phenomena.

And he adds tellingly: 'This competition is often highly political in itself as it calls into question truths that are fundamental to the self-identity of proponents of alternative narratives.'[34] Denial ('it never happened'), undermining (subverting by sowing doubt), invalidation (disproof or nullification), delegitimization (withholding recognized status), displacement (inserting a narrative at the expense of another), and blocking (anticipatory barring of something before it becomes established) are all forms of silencing voice and argument in varying degrees of intensity that account for, or reinforce, removal.

Billig arrives at similar conclusions about removal from a discourse studies and psychoanalytical perspective: 'As one matter is spoken (or written) about, so others are kept from immediate dialogic attention. Where topics of conversation become ritual, what is habitually spoken about may be dialogically functioning to prevent, as a matter of routine, other matters from coming to conscious, conversational attention . . . such dialogues . . . might also create their own silences.'[35] Parallel silences effected by removal may be found in the identification of repression as a defence mechanism. Freud employed the term to indicate circumstances in which 'the subject attempts to repel, or to confine to the unconscious, representations (thoughts, images, memories) which are bound to an instinct . . . [the satisfaction of which] would incur the risk of provoking unpleasure because of other requirements'.[36] Melanie Klein later elaborated on that in her discussion of the splitting of the ego: 'In repression the more highly organized ego divides itself off against the unconscious thoughts, impulses, and terrifying figures more effectively.'[37] In an echo of the layered silencing procedure that removes the concealing practice itself from view, Wilfred Bion wrote: 'Where the non-psychotic part of the personality resorts to repression as a means of cutting off certain trends in the mind both from consciousness and from other forms of manifestation and activity, the psychotic part of the personality has attempted to rid itself of the apparatus on which the psyche depends to carry out the repressions.'[38] Any awareness of the technique of covering has been removed and blocked. All traces of the silencing mechanism are recoded in dream form or expressed through parapraxes that ultimately require professional deciphering.

More recent sociological analyses of identitarian politics approach forms of social exclusion through separate, but reinforcing, sets of arguments. Theories of identity based on perceptions and images of the body in a social context play an instructive role in helping to detect the ubiquity of instances of silenced personal and group experiences. McNay has expanded on the observation by the cultural sociologist Pierre Bourdieu that 'the visible, that which is immediately given, conceals the invisible which determines it'.[39] She contends that barriers to political participation and mobilization are addressed by some political theorists in what Bourdieu terms a 'socially weightless' manner that overlooks their internalization as corporeal dispositions. The inability of some people to express their marginalization 'is the effect of the incorporation of structural violence into the body which is then lived in the euphemised form of a habitus of acceptance or resignation'.[40] Accordingly, a term such as 'complicit' cannot encapsulate the totality of forces operating on, and in, the individual. The silence induced by that condition is not the result of specific and deliberate agentic oppression and the knowing collaboration of a 'victim', but of 'a persistent, lived background condition of stigmatisation and purposelessness'.[41] Its consequence is an enduring social and legal misrecognition and bypassing of the claims of underrepresented and unappreciated sections of society. That misrecognition is undoubtedly a matter for ethical concern, but it concurrently comprises a dual empirical finding: first, that silences become ingrained in the concreteness of physical and psychological existence; and second, that the inability to express important group interests—interests that are vital to social equilibrium more generally—is not an intrinsic human condition but located in particular historical settings.

For Bourdieu, that appropriation of discursive space is entrenched in a structural political domination. While Foucault tends to consider disciplines as ultimately knowable systems of organizing knowledge, Bourdieu significantly leans not towards intentionally or systemically imposed subjugation but towards a non-volitional 'censorship' as a sociological given, one that stems from hemming in the occupants of certain social positions through culturally legitimated forms of discourse and articulateness, whose internalization may lead to silence. He writes: 'Among the most effective and best concealed censorships are all those which consist in excluding certain agents from communication by excluding them from the groups which speak or the places which allow one to speak with authority.'[42] That exclusion can be unconscious as well as conscious—which renders even the term 'censorship' controversial. Intentionality is never the be-all and end-all that can account for political thought-practices, just as rationality is never the sole key to their content.

More broadly and perhaps more commonly, currently existing groups are written out of ongoing discourse. One of the most common examples is the use of the term 'Man', which includes only silently—and sometimes not even that—'Woman' (and more recently in emerging discursive custom, also gender-fluid individuals), yet for long periods of time knowingly excluded classes of non-whites. As Mirabeau admonished the French National Assembly in 1789, 'Are the colonies placing their Negroes and their *gens de couleur* in the class of men or in that of the beasts of burden? If the colonists want the Negroes and *gens de couleur* to count as men, let them enfranchise them first.'[43] Foucault's celebrated treatment of discourse repeatedly drove home the argument that disciplines constituted a system of control in the production of discourse. 'Not all areas of discourse are equally open and penetrable,' he wrote, 'some are forbidden territory (differentiated and differentiating) while others are virtually open to the winds and stand, without any prior restrictions, open to all.'[44] Keller observes of Foucault's analysis: 'Discourses are structured by mechanisms of exclusion and empowerment that produce "scarcity" in the fields of serious speech acts' due, among others, to their origins and the standing of their utterers.[45] And it is that scarcity that can reduce potential voice to silence; it is either quantitively drowned out in a flood of other voices, or qualitatively devalued and struck off as lacking sufficient respectability.

Notes

1. Merleau-Ponty, *Phenomenology of Perception*, p. 213.
2. *OED* online (accessed 29 June 2017).
3. A viewpoint rightly criticized as inadequate by X. Guillaume, 'How to Do Things with Silence: Rethinking the Centrality of Speech to the Securitization Framework', *Security Dialogue* 49/6 (2018), pp. 476–492 at p. 480.
4. *OED* online (accessed 26 April 2020).
5. R. K. Merton, *Social Theory and Social Structures* (Glencoe, IL: The Free Press, 1957), p. 63.
6. Maitland, *A Book of Silence*, pp. 120–121, 130.
7. On the role of unexpected silences as challenges to power see T. Jung, 'Mind the Gaps: Silences, Political Communication, and the Role of Expectations', *Critical Review of International Social and Political Philosophy* 24/3 (2021), pp. 296–315.
8. M. Schröter and C. Taylor (eds.), *Exploring Silence and Absence in Discourse: Empirical Approaches* (Cham, Switzerland: Palgrave Macmillan, 2018), pp. 5–7.
9. C. Glenn, *Unspoken: A Rhetoric of Silence* (Carbondale, IL: Southern Illinois University Press, 2004), p. 4.
10. Kazuo Ishiguro, interviewed by Alan Yentob, *Imagine*, BBC 1 TV, 29 March 2021.
11. M. Sifianou, 'Silence and Politeness', in Jaworski, *Silence: Interdisciplinary Perspectives*, p. 79.
12. A. Robinson, 'The Political Theory of Constitutive Lack: A Critique', *Theory and Event* 8/1 (2005).
13. B. Wardle, 'You Complete Me: The Lacanian Subject and Three Forms of Ideological Fantasy', *Journal of Political Ideologies* 21 (2016), p. 305.
14. Y. Stavrakakis, 'Jacques Lacan: Negotiating the Psychosocial in and beyond Language', in R. Wodak and B. Forchtner (eds.), *The Routledge Handbook of Language and Politics* (Abingdon: Routledge, 2018), pp. 82–86.
15. E. Laclau and C. Mouffe, *Hegemony and Socialist Strategy* (London: Verso, 1985); E. Laclau, 'The Death and Resurrection of the Theory of Ideology', *Journal of Political Ideologies* 1 (1996), pp. 201–220.
16. D. Panagia and J. Rancière, 'Dissenting Words: A Conversation with Jacques Ranciere', *Diacritics* 30/2 (2000), pp. 113–126 at p. 124.
17. C. Kølvraa, 'The Discourse Theory of Ernesto Laclau', in Wodak and Forchtner, *The Routledge Handbook of Language and Politics*, p. 106.
18. B. Fink, *The Lacanian Subject* (Princeton, NJ: Princeton University Press, 1995), p. 126.
19. See M. Freeden, 'The Morphological Analysis of Ideology', in M. Freeden, L. T. Sargent, and M. Stears (eds.), *The Oxford Handbook of Political Ideologies* (Oxford: Oxford University Press, 2013), pp. 115–137.
20. See for instance R. Wodak, *The Politics of Fear* (London: Sage, 2015).
21. See Chapter 14.

22 N. Billias and S. Vemuri, *The Ethics of Silence* (Cham, Switzerland: Palgrave Macmillan/Springer, 2017), p. 143.
23 W. Tie, 'Radical Politics, Utopia, and Political Policing', *Journal of Political Ideologies* 14 (2009), p. 255.
24 Freeden, *The Political Theory of Political Thinking*, pp. 22–25.
25 P. Bachrach and M. S. Baratz, 'Two Faces of Power', *American Political Science Review* 56 (1962), pp. 947–952.
26 J. Derrida, 'How to Avoid Speaking: Denials', in H. Coward and T. Foshay (eds.), *Derrida and Negative Theology* (Albany, NY: SUNY Press, 1992), p. 95.
27 J. Zajda and R. Zajda, 'The Politics of Rewriting History: New History Textbooks and Curriculum Materials in Russia', *International Review of Education* 49 (2003), pp. 363–384.
28 Michel-Rolph Trouillot, *Silencing the Past: Power and the Production of History* (Boston, MA: Beacon Press, 2015 [1995]).
29 Ibid., p. 48.
30 Ibid., p. 99.
31 Ibid., p. 49.
32 Ibid., pp. 49–50.
33 Pérez, 'Rhetoric of Silence', p. 117.
34 A. Little, *Temporal Politics: Contested Pasts, Uncertain Futures* (Edinburgh: Edinburgh University Press, 2022), p. 13.
35 M. Billig, *Freudian Repression: Conversation Creating the Unconscious* (Cambridge: Cambridge University Press, 2004), p. 223.
36 'Repression', in J. Laplanche and J.-B. Pontalis, *The Language of Psycho-Analysis* (London: Hogarth Press, 1985), p. 390.
37 M. Klein, 'On the Development of Mental Functioning (1958)', in M. Klein, *Envy and Gratitude and Other Works 1946–1963* (London: Hogarth Press, 1984), p. 244.
38 W. R. Bion, *Second Thoughts: Selected Papers on Psycho-Analysis* (London: Maresfield Reprints, 1984), p. 52.
39 P. Bourdieu, *In Other Words: Essays Towards Reflexive Sociology* (Stanford, CA: Stanford University Press, 1990), p. 127.
40 L. McNay, 'Suffering, Silence and Social Weightlessness: Honneth and Bourdieu on Embodiment and Power', in S. Gonzalez-Arnal, G. Jagger, and K. Leon (eds.), *Embodied Selves* (London: Palgrave Macmillan, 2012), p. 236.
41 Ibid.
42 P. Bourdieu, *Language and Symbolic Power* (Cambridge: Polity Press, 1991), p. 138, also p. 97.
43 Trouillot, *Silencing the Past*, p. 79.
44 M. Foucault, *The Archaeology of Knowledge and the Discourse on Language* (New York: Pantheon, 1972), pp. 224–225.
45 R. Keller, 'Michel Foucault: Discourse, Power/Knowledge and the Modern Subject', in Wodak and Forchtner, *The Routledge Handbook of Language and Politics*, p. 74.

6
The Dog that Did Not Bark: Listening for Silence

This chapter switches the focus away from the components and characteristics of silence to one of the most demanding challenges facing those who study it: how can concealed silences be accessed, if at all? Although the varieties of meaning contained in the notions of absence, lack, and removal possess hidden, nameless, or unimaginable 'properties', many of them denote what some observers or analysts might reasonably assume to be present from another vantage point, yet puzzlingly isn't. 'Something is missing here' is an intuition that points to an unexplained blank or gap. For that reason, we are talking here not about a void, but about a qualified absence: a cultural and epistemological absence internal to a discourse that—as external observers of silences—we may well identify and decode as a conspicuous omission. Even then, omission can be nigh-invisible, yet the silence it evokes might not be a total darkness but a concealing faintness, and intimations of what is muted can be discerned through what is assumed to exist beyond that diaphanous veil. Why are these women silent in the face of social practices that condemn them to subordinate status? Why is deistic creationism accepted unquestioningly in so many cultures? Why is hereditary leadership so often taken for granted? Just as an eruption on a distant star can emit signals that careful, meticulous, and often serendipitous scanning may pick up, so the absence associated with some forms of silence may occasionally be sensed by imaginative deduction and exogenous social epistemologies through which we can resort to cultural detective work, or to ideological decoding.[1] Either way, silence is in the mind not of the unaware participant but of the beholder, or—more aptly—it weighs on the mind of the unhearing yet perplexed and curious scholar or observer. As can be surmised from the above thoughts, we are now considering how to address the other response to the question posed in the previous chapter, 'what goes on when there is silence?'—namely, 'something goes on'. Those 'goings on' occupy the preponderant interpretations of silence in ways that impact powerfully on the practice of thinking politically.

1 In Pursuit of Elusiveness

'There is no way', writes Blommaert in his critical study of discourse, 'in which we can linguistically investigate discourses that are absent, even if such analyses would tell us an enormous amount about the conditions under which discourses are being produced.' The problem, he adds, is that of looking 'inside language *as well as outside it*'.[2] That is an apt comment, but the question of *how* to look outside is the one demanding particularly careful attention. Like Conan Doyle's 'curious incident' of the dog that did not bark in the night-time, silence may be bemusing or troubling when noise, or voice, is anticipated. Those are the kinds of silence that may pass unnoticed by the general public. But there is a need to deal with the confounded expectations of that astute private detective Sherlock Holmes or, more to the point, the non-fictional scholar or observer inured in analysing language yet harbouring a suspicion that something isn't quite right. They may prompt questions such as: Do I detect silence on a particular issue? Why is there silence on this matter? And what is the silence about?

These are serious and evocative issues for political theory. The problem in this instance is not that of interpreting a particular silence as if it were a practice of political actors who bite their lips. The war slogan 'Keep mum—loose talk costs lives' was targeted at specific social contexts. The Omertà observed among the Mafia is part of a code of internal loyalty to protect and promote the (criminal) interests of a group, a practice sometimes referred to more generally as an impermeable 'wall of silence' that blocks out hearers and listeners, a selective silence that erects an obstacle between one field of discourse and another. In those more concrete cases of keeping silent, although silence cannot be heard, it can be listened to; its keepers may exhibit other forms of behaviour that provide us with clues to their quiescence; and its immediate causes might be identified. The dog was silent because there was no need for it to bark in the first place. It recognized the intruder in the act of a stealing a horse from the stables as a trainer, and consequently did not raise the alarm.[3] In the dearth of sufficient clues that incident would occasion a contested silence that in theory could be ended when explanatory speech is resumed. Here Holmes or, rather, Conan Doyle simulates the role of the scholar equipped with the external skills that can identify situations where silence appears to indicate a lack rather than an absence, but in this narrative turns out to be a non-event.

The *OED* defines 'to hear' as 'to have the sensation of sound', 'to possess or exercise the faculty of audition'; but to listen is 'to give attention with the ear to some sound or utterance; to make an effort to hear something', and even more specifically, to 'make an effort to catch the sound of'.[4] Jean-Luc Nancy has offered a different distinction between hearing and listening. To hear is to understand the sense, but to listen is to strain towards a possible and not immediately accessible meaning: 'To be listening is always to be on the edge of meaning.' That meaning is mediated via tuning-in to a sonorous, vibrating, musical, and quasi-physical presence: '"Silence" in fact must here be understood [heard] ... not as a privation but as an arrangement of resonance ... as when in a perfect condition of silence you hear your own body resonate.' And it is matched by listening that, tellingly, is 'an intensification and a concern, a curiosity or an anxiety'.[5] Nancy's view that hearing implies understanding is incomplete as it disregards the problem of deciphering speech and sound or a failure to decipher them. His interpretation of listening is more apposite. It entails absorbing an exuding, radiating pulsation of meanings that is experienced through silence. Listening conjures up a penetration into a deeper layer of silence that requires subtler and more persistent decrypting. In psychoanalytical practice, however, listening is both internal and external, involving mutual and interleaved sequences of speech and silence: 'The analyst listens to the patient who in turn listens to the analyst's interpretations and/or silence. Then the analyst listens to the fate of his reinterpretations or silence.' In those sessions the analyst detects something 'over and beyond what is continually surprising in the discovery of the unconscious world ... what my patients had to say or could not say were clinical answers to theoretical questions that I had yet to formulate'.[6] Exchanged silences as well as spoken words deliver insights barely conceived, let alone heard. Here contextualized silence under sharp scrutiny opens up the possibility of generating new knowledge.

But there is a further challenge, relating to a silence that does not even constitute a recognized arrangement of behaviour—such as the patterns surrounding the analyst's couch—because it does not exhibit the minimal features that a practice requires: namely, a recurring regularity that is either conducted through participant awareness, or possesses the potential to make sense to practitioners within their epistemological universes. Such a silence is not only physically soundless but conceptually 'inaudible' and undetectable to those who are its subjects. It is not possible simply to listen *to* that silence because we do not know from the context which particular silence, if any, is obvious. Those elusive, tucked-away silences can be anywhere and nowhere; they may come and go, re-emerging emphatically, or vanishing without trace like black holes swallowing up their own evidence. Here only the questioning observer might be able to provide the requisite distance. Crucially, that requires scholars to execute a decisive switch from solely listening *to* silence to also listening *for* silence: listening for the many silences that not only cannot be heard but cannot be meaningfully identified by the unwitting owners of such taciturnity, and that consequently cannot be broken by them. It is at least less daunting a task to listen for isolated and individuated concealed silences than to contemplate the possibility of a continuous, vast mass of inaccessible silence.

'Listening to' involves the auditory senses; but 'listening for' involves the mind and the imagination. The caesura between the two is implied in Foucault's observation: 'Things murmur meanings our language has merely to extract; from its most primitive beginnings, this language was already whispering to us of a being of which it forms the skeleton.'[7] Intimations of voice may need particularly careful aural sensitivity, but it still is listening *to* an acoustic stimulus. Searching and listening *for* concealed voices, to the contrary, may detect profoundly non-agentic, or extra-agentic, silences and they can only be overcome when replaced with a missing piece of hitherto obscured understanding or decipherable evidence—a task requiring mental and intellectual agility and inventiveness.

As Jean-François Lyotard tellingly observed in one context, the historian must 'break with the monopoly over history granted to the cognitive regimen of phrases, and he or she must venture forth by lending his or her ear to what is not presentable under the rules of knowledge'.[8] And he set down the following challenge: 'What is at stake in a literature, in a philosophy, in a politics perhaps, is to bear witness to differends by finding idioms for them.'[9] That identifies two roles for the interpreter: locating a socially and psychologically meaningful silence—part of the sleuthing work that a student of silence must pursue—and advocating an intervention in that silence, as a witness, an analyst, an external observer, by suggesting the words, or phrases, that capture what silenced and inarticulate individuals cannot enunciate by themselves.

If a path cannot be found to put the appropriate phrases in the mouths of those condemned to silence—and it cannot because, in Lyotard's view, the depth of their silence lies precisely in their inability to voice their grievances—then another voice must be imaginatively propelled into the void. That voice—of the student investigating silence and states of inarticulateness—must appeal to a set of perspectives capable of connecting with sufficient language to translate muted experience and feelings into phrases. To continue the quasi-legal analogy utilized by Lyotard, adjudicators may arise capable of weighing up the possibilities and of suggesting that they are able to impress their conceptualizations on the situation. Offering such a decoding is not tantamount to arguing that it is correct or even necessary, merely that it may be one way of either making sense of the situation, or showing that the specific silence begs sufficient questions to bring it to the attention of all the parties involved.

Nonetheless, silence scholarship needs to discern between the eventual savviness of analysts as they broaden and hone their professional sphere of understanding, and the attitudes of general publics. Although those publics do not aspire to, nor are they concerned with, producing a body of complex perspectives on the nuances of silence, that is of no matter. They are a vital object of interest to students of political thinking. If we are concerned about silence as a social phenomenon—not merely as the academic pursuit of a small group of people who share specialized intellectual curiosity—we must also incorporate the thought-practices typical of the societies that we study and explore their more restricted receptiveness to concealed silences.

In literary theory, the study of negativity—as distinct from negations or denials—exemplifies another practice of 'listening for', although even listening is too active a description of what occurs in this case. Negativity relates to the blanks that cannot be deduced from a text or the empirical world. It does so by 'play[ing] against something and thus bear[ing] the inscription of that something'.[10] It does not therefore scan *for* something but provides an intimation of its own self-effacing and inaccessible operation, as with the imprint on a pillow that may indicate the multiple occasions that preceded it.

Even so, all those potentially detectable silences involve what one study terms 'slipperiness'.[11] In the absence of conclusive evidence for what a presumed silence signifies, we need to exercise interpretative judgement. That may not satisfy 'precisionists' who are unhappy with the indeterminacy of hermeneutic practices, but we are dealing here with opening up the boundaries of understanding, not with forensically tying up the evidence that comes into view. Plausible conjecture is a reflective way forward, always awaiting and, indeed, welcoming contrary interpretation when it arrives on the scene.

There is another variant of 'listening for' that is quite common among scholars, but too restrictive for the purposes of this study: namely, being alert to discriminatory language or to insensitive depictions of people and their practices. A representative example may be gleaned from the otherwise very useful insights proffered by Achino-Loeb and her collaborators. In many ways they are illuminating and edifying, but they are diluted by subscribing to largely pejorative conceptions of ideology and of power, referring to false and true consciousness in a Marxist or post-Marxist mode. Those phenomena are seen to manipulate agents through heavily overemphasizing the inhibiting and dominating role of social structures at the expense of agency—such as consigning women to a nurturing role or promoting the virtues of markets, rather than protecting individuals from their harmful effects. All these are indisputably ethical and social concerns that no political theorist should ignore or underestimate, but they do not encompass the full field that should stimulate the interest of a student of political thinking and its practices.

Achino-Loeb rightly observes that 'the very activity of identity formation is an analytic practice, whether undertaken by outsiders or insiders—one that involves delineating boundaries of relevance and salience ... in order to understand the degree of authenticity of identity we need to unpack the contexts that produced it, veiled as they are by multiples of the unsaid or of the purposely muted'.[12] Yet this passage, while illuminating in some ways, raises major theoretical questions. The issue of authenticity is troubling, implying as it does a true or pristine human and social identity—even within the bounds of particular cultural settings.[13] Nor is the unsaid automatically the predominant outcome of a distorted social framework. As by now should have been made abundantly clear, it can reflect the inevitable epistemological codes and screens that human knowledge and psychological mindsets construct— beyond the grasp of participant and, often, of observer alike. Some unspoken thoughts may be cognitively recognized and understood, no doubt, but there are alternative reasons for not being able to bring something to the point of expression. To that extent, not all silences can be said to be 'glossed differently' as cloaking pernicious power structures.[14] Otherwise we are led on a path that may regard all and every kind of silence as a *failure* of social arrangements as well as a product of ideological engineering—a stance that reinforces the frequently held assumption that silence reflects malicious or incompetent forces at work.

Listening *for* silences is of course followed by attempting to listen *to* them. However, listening to soundlessness while bereft of other clues, rather than solely investigating the implied or muffled voices buried underneath strange and unaccountable absences, raises the demands on scholarship to another level. Some silences come to be interpreted as perplexing or curious beyond the identification of a blockage or impediment that arises from the give and take of conscious human action, or even unconscious human bias. They call up the effort to *catch the silence* of an absence. That demands deeper exploring and decoding. Scholars need to employ their analytical powers and accumulated understandings in order to probe profound absences, and that requires a resourceful listening to, and reflection on, what should or might have been heard had the epistemological obstacles that disable certain kinds of conceptualization and expression been removed. In disciplines that are fundamentally logocentric and language-based, such as political theory, listening—and its equivalent, reading—need to be complemented by searching for those obstructions, if indeed that is what they are. For—lest we be carried away by the excitement of detective work—not every silence necessarily masks a potential code of interest. Yet, analogously to the vocation of archaeologists, we need to start digging in order to satisfy ourselves one way or another.

Listening for silences can help to identify two variants of thwarted expectations. The one involves a context in which a participating group of individuals is gradually made aware of what is missing. It concerns the eschewing of certain implicit conventions. Quentin Skinner has observed of the ghost scene in *Hamlet* that the expectations of the audience are initially frustrated by the unexpected omission of what the time-honoured content of the scene would have traditionally demanded: namely, some praise from the ghostly father for his son. Yet in the course of the play the more discerning audience is made to realize that such a surprising silence is a rhetorical device designed to spell out the opposite message: paternal misgivings about Hamlet's capacity to act.[15] Silence involves a code shared by some, but overlooked by others.

The other variant, to which we shall return in Chapter 7, relates silence to the deeply unconceptualizable. The absolute acceptance of God in a multitude of cultures, confounding the questioning practised in secular societies, renders atheistic beliefs incomprehensible by means of *any* conventions that the participants could have shared, except one: sacrilegious transgression. The absence of discourse concerning a Godless society normally goes unnoticed by a profoundly religious and traditional people, and could only be picked up and listened for by an external ear, epistemologically pre-trained in such matters. The listening and reading skills of linguists, too, may lead them to similar conclusions: those unschooled in listening to specific socio-linguistic codes possess no algorithm with which to interpret a linguistic silence based on ignorance or incomprehension.[16] Alternatively, as with many discoveries, a silence may simply be innocently susceptible to serendipitous insight, like Hans Christian Andersen's little boy literally and metaphorically seeing through the emperor's new clothes. In that sense, any expectation is retrospective and not of the moment and—like spotting a new celestial object—it may well be a hit or miss exercise.

Achino-Loeb asserts that 'the semantic space of silence is marked by the experience of presence disguised as absence', indicating attempts to repress and hide awareness of the pursuit of self-interest, predominantly that of class. She argues that silence, as an act of withholding, exists only in the ear of those listeners who 'willingly or willfully ignore or veil the pregnant presence' lurking behind different silences.[17] But the profound silences for which one must listen are an important exception to that rule. Although it is by now uncontroversial to claim that structure and epistemology are endowed with the potential to shape human lives, their typical forms cannot merely be encapsulated by the concrete will to manipulate, coerce, dominate, control, and—above all—to dissimulate. The notion of disguising, however, has an agentic ring to it, an act of intentionality or complicity, as in the *OED*'s definition: 'To conceal or cloak the real state or character of (anything) by a counterfeit show or appearance'.[18] The conundrums of silence may be 'part and parcel of the veiling process that accompanies the wielding of power',[19] but certainly cannot be reduced to that. Silence in the context of human communication isn't just wielded; it may be passive or introverted without a puppet-master lurking in the shadows. Nor, for that matter, are all self-chosen silences imposed by an external force, either directly or culturally: the silence incurred by grief may have very different and nuanced causes.

Importantly, meaning transcends agency, and not only when it is incomprehensible to every one of the parties to a human transaction. This summons up Paul Ricoeur's famous phrase, 'the surplus of meaning',[20] when agents communicate or let on more than they intend to or are aware of. That happens to be a fairly normal occurrence in language, due to the impossibility of individual control over the manner in which, subsequent to its initiation, an utterance or text wends its way once it is let loose on the world and undergoes multiple 'translations'. This shifts our gaze once again onto reception, reflecting the ways in which sets of messages, simple or complex, are imparted to, or are understood to be imparted by, an audience, both targeted and general. Whether deliberate or not, silences too carry their own surpluses of meaning.

Alternatively, voices may obscure, override, or appropriate silence, aggressively, arrogantly, or unknowingly, in a manner apparently not dissimilar to painting over a portrait that can only be identified through scientific imagery techniques. The analogy is not accurate, however, because a painting occupies a defined space, the area of probing is circumscribed, and the painter is often known; whereas identifying obscured voices is confronted with a multiplicity of unforeseeable possibilities from any direction. Of considerable interest here is not talking *over* another *present* voice and thus suppressing it—i.e., not removing it—but talking *instead of* another imagined *absent* voice whose identity, whether individual or collective, is impersonated and arrogated in its inevitable absence by the speaker. One instance of that practice pertains to ancestral or envisaged future generations, whose present voices are patently unavailable, yet who are invoked—at times usurped, to use blunter language—to deliver messages of great social and cultural significance. The superimposition of voice will be discussed at greater length in Chapter 10.

2 Academic Predispositions

A significant category of silence found mainly in professional academic circles refers to research frameworks, when the requirements of a scholarly methodology debar the consideration of specific types of evidence or curb interpretative leeway. Among academic communities those methodological choices often are the subject of intellectual dissent and disputation, wedded as they are to diverse ontologies. Those who subscribe to them can be impervious to alternative readings, having invested rationally and emotionally in their theories—and often built a career on their understandings. A central instance is the commitment to dichotomies—a key tool in the history of philosophical analysis and political argumentation—of which Chantal Mouffe is a prominent contemporary example. Drawing on Carl Schmitt's overworked friend–enemy dichotomy, she has infused the analysis of the political with the practice of antagonism and its less confrontational cognate, agonism. Politics, on that increasingly common view, is tantamount to the domain of conflict and is sharply contrasted with a liberal consensualism that, by default, is relegated to epitomizing the anti-political.[21] No space is set aside for the many attributes and nuances of the political that either lie between the two poles or, more saliently, conjure up other political features—coexisting alongside contention and dissensus—that are just as constitutive of the political, such as mobilizing support, ranking collective priorities, or anticipating social futures. Acknowledging a research procedure that recognizes that the political can occur abundantly 'in between', or 'alongside', or 'together with', ensures that those other elements are free to bark in the night-time.

Another dimension of the distortion that dichotomies can inflict on understanding the political is the obfuscating effect of the liberal–conservative binary in attitudinal research common in US political science and political psychology. It is a method of organizing findings that greatly oversimplifies the empirical complexity, nuance, and diversity apparent in the field and ill serves its many streams and tributaries. It may well be that a false binary, all too often saturating the field of US ideology studies, is convenient for statistical or psychological analysis but it is detrimental to the knowledge and comprehension of what the ideological terrain actually includes.[22] The result, yet again, is a coating of undetected silence about vital gradations and irregularities.

A further element inhibiting some forms of scholarship relates to the suspicion directed at vernacular forms of expression and speech that are harboured by several political philosophers because they deem those forms to be incapable of carrying intellectual weight worthy of serious analysis. Ostensibly 'inferior' political thinking in everyday, demotic, or ideological modes—the argument goes—cannot be subject to appropriate 'superior' ethical and ontological scholarship. It is therefore ignored and silenced as a category that could elicit significant knowledge. Under the belittling gaze of philosophical purists, that is occasionally even the fate of the entire field of ideology studies.[23] Another silencing factor, to which Émile Durkheim drew attention over a century ago, was the internal obstructions that beset scholars themselves—like any other human beings—against the grain of conventional expectations, alongside the intuitions that propelled them. There was a 'concrete and living' aspect of science 'which is in part ignorant of itself . . . there are habits, instincts, needs, presentiments, so obscure that they cannot be expressed in words, yet so powerful that they sometimes dominate the whole life of the scholar'.[24]

Dichotomies are often found in the company of a neighbouring concept: rupture. While a dichotomy is a theoretical device borrowed from the field of formal logic, rupture is a physical and sociological example of a dislocation that splits an anticipated continuity, located in real time–space axes. Ruptures signify breaks and fissures that lack the implied artificial symmetry or predictability of a binary. They can occur at any point, as well as at many points, in the path of an event, an idea, or a process. A recent study comments that late-twentieth-century theories of ruptures 'connote a moment of temporal evacuation—the void that the hiatus of their break opens up'—but they also rehearse 'the definitive ontological structure of what is perhaps the grandest narrative of all, namely the Judaeo-Christian conception of creation ex nihilo'.[25] In other words, small and large silences combine: micro-gaps of disconnectedness are accompanied by the construction of macro-narratives out of nothing. Homing in predominantly on the dramatic effect of ruptures—say, a revolution, a transformative technological invention such as printing, or the rise of a new belief system such as Christianity—is of course illuminating; but it covers up the partial and layered discontinuities and flare-ups that are far more common than caesuras and sea changes. Accordingly, exploring some of the more subtle instances of silence's presence in the political world requires a shift of perspective. Here the notion of shading can help. Shading is an essential constituent of portraits or landscapes, using gradations of tone and contour lines to create a stronger or weaker representation of an individual image or conveying the features and atmosphere of a broader view. It is just as applicable to voice and its muting, affording glimpses of communicative activity, whether fleeting or more durable, and ensuring that certain segments of discourse, thinking, and expression are not simply obscured or polarized.

Theories of dichotomies or of rupture do not factor those subtleties into their resolute and adamant schemata. The theoretical neatness that immutable binaries afford sidesteps the more ubiquitous casual opposites—or simply variances—that might comfortably tolerate readjustment and compromise. Dichotomies are designed to construct a world in which gaps are sealed by ontological fiat, eliminating possible conceptual spaces between the components of an intellectual order. The silences that overwhelm them are squeezed between tectonic plates that carve out boundaries and eliminate scalar distinctions and subtleties, stifling the recourse to tools that could encourage the shading emanating from multiple perspectives and micro-evidence. Ruptures, to the contrary, open up gaps so yawning that a whole range of intermediate, empirically determinable, steps is obscured. In both instances, vital elements of social life are muted, their undeniable presence subsumed or eradicated in a theoretical scheme that eschews complex characterization of socio-political interaction. As a method of generating an overconfident, even brutalist, sense of the world, that starkness stands in marked contrast to the ethereal erasure of certainty through the ambiguities ushered in and welcomed by Zen-Buddhist silences—a philosophical structure whose treatment of silences permits the embrace of imaginative ambiguity. In that worldview, anything and nothing can be detected. Nor do the principled hesitancy and doubt evinced by reflective liberals tolerate a world of polarities as a matter of course. The acts of concealment, built into the fundamental ideational conviction or commitment of schemata of dichotomization and rupture, need to be listened for and detected to do justice to a field in which silence can obscure promise, suggestiveness, and variability.

Notes

1 Melani Schröter, in *Silence and Concealment in Political Discourse* (https://www.academia.edu/2379290/Silence_and_concealment_in_political_discourse, pdf, section 3, 2013) has observed with respect to deliberate and evasive silences that 'the work of . . . establishing evidence of what a person could have known at the moment where such a claim [i.e. a refusal to comment] is made, seems to be more of a detective's task than a linguist's research question'. That is all the more the case when the silent person is oblivious to the issue on which they are silent.
2 J. Blommaert, *Discourse: A Critical Introduction* (Cambridge: Cambridge University Press, 2005), p. 35. Italics in original.
3 A. Conan Doyle, 'The Adventure of Silver Blaze', in *The Memoirs of Sherlock Holmes* (London: George Newnes, 1894).
4 *OED* online.

5   J.-L. Nancy, *Listening* (New York: Fordham University Press, 2007), pp. 5–7, 21.
6   H. Faimberg, *The Telescoping of Generations* (London and New York: Routledge, 2005), p. 2.
7   Foucault, *The Archaeology of Knowledge and the Discourse on Language*, p. 228.
8   J.-F. Lyotard, *The Differend* (Minneapolis, MN: University of Minnesota Press, 1988), p. 57.
9   Ibid., p. 13.
10 Budick and Iser, 'Introduction', in *Languages of the Unsayable*, pp. xi–xxi.
11 A. J. Murray and K. Durrheim, *Qualitative Studies of Silence: The Unsaid as Social Action* (Cambridge: Cambridge University Press, 2019), pp. 9–10.
12 Achino-Loeb, *Silence: The Currency of Power*, pp. 10–11.
13 For a cultural analysis of authenticity see M. Umbach and M. Humphrey, *Authenticity: The Cultural History of a Political Concept* (Cham, Switzerland: Springer, 2017).
14 Achino-Loeb, *Silence: The Currency of Power*, p. 11.
15 Q. Skinner, *Forensic Shakespeare* (Oxford: Oxford University Press, 2014), pp. 2, 85.
16 Ephratt, 'The Functions of Silence', p. 1926.
17 Achino-Loeb, *Silence: The Currency of Power*, p. 2.
18 OED, https://www.oed.com/view/Entry/54411?rskey=ZeHBRo&result=2#eid (accessed 4 February 2020).
19 Achino-Loeb, *Silence: The Currency of Power*, p. 3.
20 P. Ricoeur, *Interpretation Theory: Discourse and the Surplus of Meaning* (Fort Worth, TX: Texas Christian University Press, 1976), p. 55.
21 C. Mouffe, *On the Political* (London: Routledge, 2005).
22 See, typically, T. B. Edsall, 'Conservatives Are from Mars, Liberals Are from Venus', *The Atlantic*, 7 February 2012; J. Sterling, J. T. Jost, and C. D. Hardin, 'Liberal and Conservative Representations of the Good Society: A (Social) Structural Topic Modeling Approach', *Sage Open*, April–June 2019, pp. 1–13.
23 See Freeden, *Ideology Studies*, pp. 11–13.
24 É. Durkheim, *The Division of Labor in Society* (New York: The Free Press, 1964), p. 362.
25 M. Holbraad, B. Kapferer, and J. F. Sauma (eds.), *Ruptures: Anthropologies of Discontinuity in Times of Turmoil* (London: UCL Press, 2019), p. 5.

7
Seven Modalities of Silence

In Chapter 3 it was suggested that silences may be found under several rubrics, each of which gathers the explanandum in separate constellations. One mapping scheme explored silences as emotionally or motivationally linked to human conduct. Another scheme included artistic, technical, contrapuntal, or conceptual arrangements of silence recognized in professional thinking or in everyday life. And a third identified six macro-clusters that carry the interpretative weight of elucidating silences. Last but not least came a fourth scheme, dedicated to the modalities of concealed silences that now demand detailed attention. Those modalities—all saturated with salient political import—are the unthinkable, the unspeakable/unsayable, the ineffable, the inarticulable, the unnoticeable, the unknowable, and the unconceptualizable. Some revolve around the axes of how silence is encountered as a subjective lived event or non-event, whether prompting taciturnity or forming obstructions in the path of communicability. Others act as a pre-emptive undercurrent beyond subjective cognition, disabling the capacity to formulate certain thoughts or feel certain emotional states, let alone give them voice or act out their existence. Despite the inevitable slippages between the modalities that will be examined in this chapter—in particular, the overlaps between some of the words used to identify them—the distinctions to which they refer possess a robust nucleus and are both analytically and heuristically valid and widespread.

The first four modalities concern the major ways in which silence intervenes in, shapes, and manages human expressiveness. The sixth and seventh relate to silences beyond human awareness—indeed, at the very limits of epistemological or ontological reach that consequently occur extraneous to discourse. Even their absence is ungaugable; hence they cannot participate in crafting the complexities of discourse; and in some accounts the unconceptualizable may not be relatable to silence at all. The fifth modality, however—the unnoticeable—is an outlier both to the first four and to the last two. It shares with the former group the presence of epistemological constraints on conveying knowledge. It shares with the latter group the presence of circumstances that sever the very accessibility of human agents and agency to evidence or knowledge. As a result, it may indicate the inability or failure of

Concealed Silences and Inaudible Voices in Political Thinking. Michael Freeden, Oxford University Press.
© Michael Freeden (2022). DOI: 10.1093/oso/9780198833512.003.0009

an entire given population—not just external observers or future scholars—to recognize some, or any, of the features of a discourse as it takes place—not because it is hidden, distorted, or unarticulated but merely because it lies outside the sphere of interest, knowledge, or perception of those who pass it by.

1 The Unthinkable

The unthinkable, as the *OED* puts it, has come to refer to something that exists as a possibility but is 'highly unlikely or undesirable',[1] as well as ethically unacceptable. For instance, 'it is unthinkable that in our society people accused of witchcraft should be burnt at the stake': that social practice has been eliminated or cannot be tolerated. True, we can continue to imagine it happening, but we cannot envisage it actually taking place in the here and now. The unthinkable can also indicate a possible future catastrophe: 'A no-deal Brexit may be unthinkable but that doesn't mean it can't happen.'[2] Most instances of the unthinkable concern the elimination, deflection, or switching off of a mode of thinking through external constraints, partially internalized. It may signal a rigid adherence to a rationality that rules out certain happenings as absurd or perilous. More commonly, it suggests an emotional taboo on, or psychological abhorrence at, a line of argumentation at various levels of consciousness and self-awareness. Its political import is found in the exclusion of specific misleading or harmful occurrences from the realm of the socially and intellectually permissible, thus channelling the discursive options at the disposal of policy makers at all levels, and often securing that exclusion through the appeal to a powerful set of values. However, because words are never sufficiently determinate in the meanings to which they refer, they often involve more than one modality. In different vocabularies the unthinkable may stretch to include the unknowable and the unconceptualizable. Such conceptual overlaps will be revisited in the course of this chapter.

2 The Unspeakable and/or the Unsayable

Among all the modes discussed in this chapter, the relationship between the unspeakable and the unsayable best illustrates the intricacy and pliability of linguistic indeterminism and the looseness to which it points. For any endeavour to establish clear-cut boundaries between words or between concepts is akin to drawing lines in the sand. The two terms may indeed converge strongly, but the semantic force-field they inhabit may equally pull them asunder, assigning some of their connotations to the inarticulable or the ineffable. Nonetheless, many scholars use them interchangeably and for that reason they are grouped together in this section, notwithstanding reservations already mentioned or about to unfold. The sub-heading indicates that simultaneous identity and non-identity.

References to the unspeakable cannot evade Wittgenstein's much overquoted injunction that has become an aphorism of popular culture: 'Whereof one cannot speak, thereof one must be silent.'[3] That may be interpreted, first, as a comment on the limits philosophy encounters with regard to understanding and to offering an explanatory and representational account of some questions, such as morality, the sacred, or the ur-sources of scientific knowledge. Second, also explicitly construed by Wittgenstein, there are things that cannot be put into words, although they may be intuited, assumed, or evoked. They may reside at—or just outside—the cusp of awareness and expressibility, but we can know, or feel, their existence.[4] A third, somewhat different, philosophical rendering is summoned up by Picard, for whom that form of silence emanates from 'a literally unspeakable fund of reality', an 'original state of things' not accounted for by the later advent of language. Fourth, on a more general and colloquial level, it can work as an observation on the meaningless or superficial nature of the sayable due to miscomprehension, the impossibility of articulation, or the casual use of language: in other words, if you can't get something right, for heaven's sake keep quiet.[5]

None of these usages matches the specific implications of the 'unspeakable' in everyday language. In commonplace usage it refers to a notion or event that elicits deepest revulsion and repugnance, not to a happening of which philosophy cannot make sense. It relates to the morally horrific, the physically disgusting, the psychologically abhorrent, to something that is known but cannot, or ought not to, or is too awful to, be described or brought up. That silence is adopted out of respect for the cultural and ethical sensibilities of the potential audience as well as the potential speaker—say, forms of systematic murder, mutilation, or torture, or blatantly racist monikers—often on the grounds of shielding the self and others. Here, proscriptions of expression obtain, both imposed and internalized, although in recent times they have attached to, and detached from, a fast-changing rota of topics. Emotionally, it may also be incredibly painful and damaging for a person to speak of certain events: the silence of many Holocaust survivors about what befell them is an example, as is that of those who have gone through other harrowing war and torture experiences. The personal and social prohibitions surrounding rape, sexual abuse, and incest that involve trauma or humiliation cover 'unspeakable' experiences that for many are difficult to overcome or make public.

Both the unthinkable and the unspeakable serve as conversation stoppers or, more accurately, conversation preventers—a protective silence that may help in averting considerable upheaval. Whereas the unthinkable can be internal and private, the unspeakable is best seen as an extra-legal 'restraining order'—culturally and ethically clued up—on actual speech and conversation. In that role, silence can play a significant part as one of several order-preserving mechanisms, a main feature of the political. In what is currently the most arresting instance, the explicit utterance of the 'N' word in contemporary (mainly but not solely North American) discourse, unless employed within certain genres of African American interpellation, carries with it severe socio-cultural penalties of anger, outrage, and ostracism that have curbed its usage, even in scholarly contexts of analysis, interpretation, or historical reconstruction that do not employ it in a defamatory sense. Its unspeakability ensues mainly when used as a form of direct address, or a concrete referral to a known group. For others, who are not addressed and who merely hear it spoken or have read it, it may nonetheless arouse psychological and emotional distress or embarrassment, whether direct or vicarious. Paradoxically, its erasure from permitted vocabularies (though not from dictionaries) serves to silence and expunge a particularly egregious chapter in black history that can only be fully evoked by the acknowledgement of the actual historical (and contemporary) debasing force that such phrasing inflicts, both acoustically and semantically, rather than by screening it behind a neutered and abstracted initial carrying considerably reduced impact. Foucault's acute comments on the proscriptions associated with sexuality apply by now far more emphatically to race: 'what is inexistent has no right to show itself, even in the order of speech where its inexistence is declared; and that which one must keep silent about is banished from reality as the thing that is tabooed above all else'.[6] But in a remarkable shift away from those in positions of formal authority, or from those who have controlled cultural practices historically by burying them in silence, people who have justifiably rebelled against past discriminatory and confining verbal practices—practices that have targeted groups with whom they empathize and whose fates they share—now agitate, together with their supporters, for a group-protecting, silencing censorship—or from another perspective, ethical monitoring—in which one mode of containment is replaced by another.

The political import of the unspeakable is threefold. First, it concerns the establishing of cultural and potentially solidaric norms and symbols of conduct that direct the trajectory of public discourse and that cannot be gainsaid. Second, it shields against the unsettling of social balance by supressing the kinds of destabilizing and fissiparous nonconformity and harm that might challenge a particularly brittle equilibrium. Third, it assigns cultural and social ownership over words, phrases, metaphors, even entire arguments, whose uninvited 'purloining' is considered to be a breach of group intellectual property rights, powerfully entrenched in emotion. The associated concept of cultural appropriation as applied to language—'don't tread on my culture zone'—condemns prospective borrowers and users, under intense political pressure, to resign themselves to the status of fenced-off non-owners, a status that demands their silence. This striking extension of property and privacy claims guards against the theft of identity and heritage, and the raiding of cultural capital, particularly when a culture is perceived by its supporters and would-be preservers as vulnerable, fragile, and representative of a valuable minority (locally, nationally, or globally).

Crucially, though, each of the three features also possesses alternative consequences. The unifying and solidaric role will always be subject to a countervailing set of prescriptions that curb freedom of expression. Suppressing destabilization involves cementing rival equilibria that may well turn out to be just as difficult to justify and enforce. Determining the sayable invariably sports a repressive dimension, hard to be pinned down as that may occur in both apparently open and apparently closed societies. And blocking the fertile intermingling of language impedes the assimilation and development of vocabularies over time, not least in wiping out instructive traces of past points of implosion. As so often in similar instances, resistance to cultural appropriation can be interpreted either as a manifestation of inter-cultural hostility or as liberation from contamination, even from annihilation.[7]

The existence of silences within silences is especially resistant to expression. Typically, they occur as cultural or religious effacements of areas of discourse that disable or disincentivize the legitimacy of certain voices that may arise from within their midst. In a renowned essay entitled 'Can the Subaltern Speak?' G. C. Spivak considered the cultural and political capability of colonized peoples at 'the margins (one can just as well say the silent, silenced center)', marked by the epistemic control and violence of the educated colonizers: 'men and women among the illiterate peasantry, the tribals, the lowest strata of the urban subproletariat'—all of whom constitute the 'unacknowledged subjects'.[8] This masks a second silence obscured by those— often class-focused Marxists—bent on calling out the first one: namely, that the silenced social groups are not an undifferentiated social collectivity of the oppressed, the disempowered, or the alienated. Instead, such silenced categories contain a multitude of diverse and heterogeneous individual and group voices, each of which may undergo and experience different manifestations, areas, and intensities of silence. Those voices are subsumed under a tendency to generalize and homogenize. Silences within silences raise several intertwined issues: the question of their dispersed and layered densities, the consequent scalar difficulties of unearthing them, and their centrality as operational determiners of social existence fractured into its multiple (mis)perceptions.

That is yet another example of methodologies and analytical frameworks acting, undetected, as silencing instruments no less than rulers and institutions do, and often buried within ideological worldviews that are rarely identified as such. The uneven and fluctuating distribution of silence is a prominent factor in its social grip and its effects on political discourse; a distribution possessing a malleable and often transient impact on the inability to speak or even to gather thoughts. That distribution may reflect different cultural mores, patterns of socialization, changing psychological sensitivities, or epistemological vocabularies, all of which contain manifestations of the political. In Spivak's critique a 'Western' intellectual epistemology appears to the colonized as alien. For, as Spivak maintains, 'there is no unrepresentable subaltern subject that can know and speak itself. . . . The problem is that the subject's itinerary has not been traced so as to offer an object of seduction to the representing intellectual.'[9] And she perceptively adds: 'If, in the context of colonial production, the subaltern has no history and cannot speak, the subaltern as female is even more deeply in shadow.'[10]

One of the reasons for that additional sub-stratum silencing, Spivak argues, lies in catachresis—the inaccurate or misused employment of words. Adapted from Derrida, it refers to a particular type of silencing:

> the violent and forced abusive inscription of a sign, the imposition of a sign upon a meaning which did not yet have its own proper sign in language. So much so that there is no substitution here, no transport of proper signs, but rather the irruptive extension of a sign proper to an idea, a meaning, deprived of their signifier. A 'secondary' origin.[11]

Such abuses or eradications, however, need not only be forced; they can equally be the consequence of intellectual or investigative sloppiness or disinterest. Those too are forms of silencing, perhaps lazy ones, but silencing nonetheless. Here again, the fissured diversity of the world's micro-silences is shown to resist aggregation into an all-encompassing macro-silence, both as to what and who are being silenced and as to the linguistic and discursive processes that bring about silence.

The social constraints on questioning and pondering, however, can unravel in many ways, not just through epistemic annihilation or deliberate muting. In Tennessee Williams' *Cat on a Hot Tin Roof*, centring on a family crisis in which a terminal illness has been concealed from the patriarch, his daughter-in-law Maggie reflects:

> When something is festering in your memory or your imagination, laws of silence don't work, it's just like shutting a door and locking it on a house on fire in hope of forgetting that the house is burning. But not facing a fire doesn't put it out. Silence about a thing just magnifies it. It grows and festers in silence, becomes malignant...[12]

However, that gnawing effect of the unspeakable with its connotation of taboo, morphing into harm—one of the consequences of the unsayable—may occur not only deliberately, but through forgetfulness, or because what is unconsciously concealed in thought and conceptualization tends to erupt in unexpected circumstances. Silence is indeed a magnifier, because its scent puts us on the trail of the enigmatically elusive or the factually painful. When what is missing suggests a blockage rather than an unfathomable absence, even in the realm of the psyche, we traverse into the domain of the political, first, to the extent that blockages are power interventions that have human origins; second, to the extent that they are capable of being removed, as indeed they cruelly and dramatically are at the climax of Williams' play; and third, to the extent that their removal can be thwarted. Kølvraa has put this nicely: 'whatever a discursive order excludes returns to haunt it'.[13]

The kind of 'unspeakable' referred to here is also distinct from the 'undiscussable' and the 'unmentionable' that Zerubavel has explored in his illuminating 'elephant in the room' study. The unspeakable is more than an 'open secret' or an 'uncomfortable truth' that involves a tacit agreement to brush something under the carpet in a collective 'conspiracy of silence'.[14] Indeed, that conspiratorial denial upends the well-known notion of tacit consent—the central theme of Chapter 11—by replacing it with its inversion: the consent to be tacit. But, to re-emphasize, I am only incidentally concerned with practices and habits of intentional denial—practices usually involving not so much a lone elephant as an entire flock of gaze-averting ostriches—although unquestionably denial too has a conspicuous political dimension. The psychological roots of the unspeakable—which makes *Cat on a Hot Tin Roof* far more than a study of willing collusion—are embedded in the emotional recoiling from imparting or reiterating certain types of information, which can then be reinforced through cultural codes demanding acute circumspection.

The unspeakable is not simply the turning of a blind eye—or the clamping shut of a jaw—caused by embarrassment, deference, knowing complicity, or protectiveness. It indicates the impeding of an individual's discursive potential when coping, coming to terms with, or suppressing very disruptive or distressing knowledge, or when confronting unpalatable words. If the sources of the unspeakable may be highly personal, the results of that practice have clear social and political aspects: the asymmetrical distribution of that modality of silence across a community both paves the way for other priorities and leaves open and chafing wounds that have ideological and cultural consequences in shaping mindsets and reactions to public policies and to events. The unspeakable has an element of hybridity about it, always hovering between the unpremeditated and a low level of intentionality, when conscious but sub-rational brakes are applied to stop an utterance, even a thought, in its tracks.

Foucault offers an instructive intervention in locating both the unthinkable and the unspeakable not as underlying or foundational characteristics of human experience but squarely in the sphere of concrete and local discursive practice. 'Whether talking in terms of speaking or thinking, we must not imagine some unsaid thing, or an unthought, floating about the world, interlacing with all its forms and events. Discourse must be treated as a discontinuous activity, its different manifestations sometimes coming together, but just as easily unaware of, or excluding each other.'[15]

Lastly, a couple of observations on the *unsayable*, which will reappear in slightly different guises in sections 3 and 7 of this chapter. The unsayable is literally something that cannot be said because there is no possibility of either saying or naming it, not because it is too repulsive or outrageous to voice, or because a particular individual cannot articulate it (the subject of section 4). One of its most striking instances is found in Samuel Beckett's theatre of the absurd *oeuvre*. Beckett was a remarkably eloquent and self-conscious inquirer into the unsayable, and the most troubled by the slippery interplay between silence and speech. In his *The Unnamable*, Beckett's unidentified person embarks on an elusive and doomed search for silence, a silence that is already within and around them: 'Where do these words come from that pour out of my mouth, and what do they mean, no, saying nothing, for the words don't carry any more.' And: 'the words are there, somewhere, without the least sound, I don't feel that either, words falling, you don't know where, you don't know whence, drops of silence through the silence'. Or again: 'If I could speak and yet say nothing, really nothing? . . . But it seems impossible to speak and yet say nothing, you think you have succeeded, but you always overlook something, a little yes, a little no, enough to exterminate a regiment of dragoons.'[16] A continual unnaming and naming signals the utter precariousness of the sayable about the self: 'First I'll say what I'm not, that's how they taught me to proceed, then what I am.'[17] Marais comments that in language, the narrator 'must seek, find, and so recognise, a self that precedes and exceeds language, and which is therefore in the silence'. But that search only produces 'failed and incomplete representations of an absent self'.[18] The semantic silence of words, amidst the deliberate torrent Beckett periodically pours from the mouths of his characters, runs through many of his writings. But if his words seem to be an unrestrained *mélange* incapable of papering over the elusiveness of human existence, they exhibit a pattern and repetitiveness that evoke their own range of submerged meanings, however ambiguous or indeterminate.

Wolosky observes: 'This longing for silence, for a self "impassive, still, mute" . . . as the ultimate expression of self, repeatedly marks Beckett's texts, inscribed in their very rhythm of utterance.' It is, she continues, 'a namelessness that truly evades representation, that represents nothing'.[19] The unsayable—in this as in other instances—is a case of the broader issue of negativity which, as Iser suggests, is 'far from negative in its effects, for it lures absence into presence, but by continually subverting that presence, turns it into a carrier for absence of which we would otherwise not know anything . . . making that which is inaccessible both present and absent'.[20] We are back in the circle, vicious or virtuous, in which absence inevitably signals both nothing and the something ingrained in the mental, imaginative, and linguistic effort in summoning absence up.

There are of course more concrete and empirically grounded notions of the unsayable. Historical research into the politics of the sayable has established inevitable limitations on the relationship between the sayable and the doable in governmental transactions and commitments. As Steinmetz has demonstrated in his study of speech-acts in nineteenth-century British high politics, political leaders are often unable 'to find the right words at the right time'; that is to say, they fail to control their own words, as well as the reception and impact of the language they employ. Older phrasings of a problem are unconsciously replaced by newer ones,[21] and something will be lost in their restating. Put differently, what is left unsaid and silenced may be the consequence of institutional and personal incompetences, or of the inability to keep abreast of efficient modes of expression and articulation and hence to bridge the gap between promises and their resonance. Discursively, future-oriented promises concerning collective action, irrespective of the chances of their realization, are a key feature of thinking politically. Culturally, they stand on the cusp between the unsaid and the unsayable—unsayable at the time, but not at *any* time.

3 The Ineffable

The unspeakable may mutate not only into the unsayable but into the ineffable or the unutterable. Unlike the first two modalities of silence, the ineffable is restricted to religious, mystical, magical, spiritual, and some philosophical sub-cultures, as well as genres of philosophical transcendentalism. Such cultures contain in their midst large or small pockets of devout conduct or entertain strong beliefs about the non-material world. In the main, the ineffable spans both a rigid injunction about what *must* not be uttered and a denoting of what *is* unutterable—features increasingly missing from fast-mutating, lax, or accommodating secular societies that experience the erosion of such boundaries.

A prominent instance may be found in negative theology or apophatic thought, prevalent in many religious currents, which regards God as unimaginable and incomprehensible, reducing any germane utterances to negative assertions on what God is not.[22] The tradition of 'de-activating' God, even of querying whether the move from nothing to something in the story of creation emanates from God, seemed to suggest a complete transcendence—as exemplified in Gnosticism—from the concrete, empirical world by insulating God, or the idea of God, from a social context. By contrast, adherents to other traditions of mysticism—for example, Jewish kabbalists—sensed that 'the philosophical unmoved mover was incompatible with the traditional Jewish view of God as a living, responsive being'.[23] Accordingly, they restored God's pivotal status as an originator, a doer, a creator, and not least a communicator and master of language, thus repoliticizing him as the decisive source of human (and non-human) shape, form, and action. This has occasionally been taken further in Hasidism, referring to the nothingness—the *ayin*—that underlies the world, the concealing and concealed silence of the totally unknowable. As Matt elaborates: 'The ego cannot abide *ayin*; you cannot wallow in nothingness. In *ayin*, for an eternal moment, boundaries disappear. *Ayin*'s "no" clears everything away, making room for a new "yes"'.[24] Here the reinstating of boundaries counterweighs the most profound and intangible of silences.

A different practice involves shedding the elements of disgust and horror surrounding the violation of ineffability and replacing them with awe, reticence, even superstition. As one seventeenth-century exegetical commentary observed of Jewish religious practice, 'wee grant the name Iehovah, not in respect of the letters [Yhvh], but of that which is thereby signified, the nature and essence of God, to be ineffable'.[25] Commenting on the views of the theologian Meister Eckhart, Sells observes of God's naming: 'The first name is the tetragrammaton, a name that is unpronounceable and thereby, through its silence, protects the one so named from linguistic reification.'[26] But the letters, too, follow a chain of escalating unutterability and unprintability. Invoking the taboos of sanctity and mystery, the name of God in orthodox Jewish practices travels from the vowelless tetragrammaton 'Yhvh' to 'Yehova' (adopting the vowelization of 'Adonai'—the, or my, Lord/s) and thence to 'Ha'shem' (the Name). Yet again, God's appellation cannot be pronounced by means of a proper noun and is effectively indicated as an ethereal presence, as the name that precedes all names. In highly orthodox circles the sequence is further contracted to the written spelled abbreviation 'Ha' ('the'), eradicating any vestige of the name, denoting its complete ineffability or, alternatively, constructing a protective wall around a core aspect of religious belief: namely, the non-materiality of God. That silence becomes unmediated and naturalized, as it evokes an internalized constraint heavily reinforced by reverence and the fear of consequences—a political hemming in and closure of belief.

For the Greeks, sacred mysteries were not to be spoken about, for fear of desecration. In Plato's *Sophist*, the Stranger says to Theaetetus, running some modalities of silence together: 'Do you see, then, that not-being in itself can neither be spoken, uttered, or thought, but that it is unthinkable, unutterable, unspeakable, indescribable?'[27] Montiglio notes in this context that 'at the heart of the Greek notion of the unspeakable in its religious sense we do not find the impotence of language, but its dreadful powers'.[28] And respecting divine authority, St Paul 'was caught up into paradise, and heard unspeakable words, which it is not lawful for a man to utter'.[29]

In all these instances, the injunction to desist from speech and its written representation controls both personal and group behaviour. Referring to creative writing, the author and critic Claude Mauriac observed: 'The writer who pits himself against the unsayable must use all his cunning so as not to say what the words make him say against his will, but to express instead what by their very nature they are designed to cover up: the uncertain, the contradictory, the unthinkable.'[30] On a very different dimension, the historical reluctance to discuss death among or in the presence of elderly or seriously ill people—including the social suppression or euphemizing of discourses on ageing—may be seen as a protective shield combining the fear of the old and ailing, the embarrassment of their interlocutors, and a general cultural recoiling from infirmity, reflected also in the glossing over by medics in conversation with their patients.[31] Such silences may be as awkward and painful as their converse. That is only partly counterbalanced by the relaxing in recent years of some of those silences under an ethos of greater openness and transparency, even one of blunt outspokenness.

Among many philosophers it is not uncommon to approach the distinction between the unspeakable and the ineffable with a different problematic in mind. As Chien-hsing Ho asks, 'can we *speak* meaningfully of something by saying that it is *unspeakable*?' That question is posed as a challenge to those 'ineffabilists' who assume that there is a transcendental reality that cannot be expressed by concepts and words—a question that thinly intersects with Lacan's theory of lack and the Real, but does so only through replacing fantasy with otherworldliness. Ironically, Ho notes that 'most ineffabilists have chosen to remain silent on this issue'. But, he asks, reproducing St Augustine's musings, if one can say of anything that it is unsayable, has it not just been said?[32] And in that case are not all attempts to describe ineffable experiences reduced to an equality of inappropriateness, as Yandell argues?[33] The conclusion points in the direction of a notion of the *profoundly* inexpressible that cannot be reduced to the unsayable but can only be indicated obliquely— for example, metaphorically according God specific attributes, even though we cannot access knowledge of him. In sum, the silence invoked here avers that 'mere linguistic knowledge is no substitute for the true experience of the ineffable'; hence whatever the intellect offers in that quest has to be negated.[34]

Finally, we enter markedly different territory through Derrida's extensive and complex theories. Derrida regards the shifting of allusions to the ineffable—notably in traditions of negative theology—as 'hyperessential' and distinct from his own deconstructionist challenges that break language down and prise it apart. He critically interprets negative theology as 'a silent intuition of God', intimating 'a being beyond being',[35] held to possess a loftier essence. In resorting to the idea of being beyond being—as one commentator elucidates—'such reference is not so much subverting a positive theology [the knowability of God] as replacing it. "Hyperessentiality" is still fundamentally an ontological statement.'[36] In Derrida's own words, 'God is refused the predicate of existence, only in order to acknowledge his superior, inconceivable and ineffable mode of being.'[37] Edifyingly, given also that in the scriptures God is the source of order emanating out of primordial disorder,[38] Derrida calls out hyperessentiality because it 'reestablishes and strengthens the order it puts into question'.[39] Put differently, Derrida's view of negative theology contains some of the originary components of the political, which are exercised through the divine self-assumption of sovereignty and the power vested in the act of creation.[40] It is not that the politics comes back in; it has never been removed. As Derrida notes in his discussion of Foucault's history of madness and psychiatry, the latter presents that history as an archaeology of silence, 'the misfortune of the mad, the interminable misfortune of their silence, is that ... when one attempts to convey their silence *itself*, one has already passed over to the side of the enemy, the side of order'. Foucault's identification of madness entails both the pairing of reason and madness and their separation. The appeal to rationality evokes the orderly metaphysics of the political realm, but silence too has its order and logic.[41]

Just as significantly, in introducing his notion of *différance* Derrida 'concedes' that, while not reduceable to negative theology, it remains an unanswered, or unanswerable, question—and that is precisely his point. *Différance* refers to 'something' before the concept, but that something 'would be nothing, that no longer arises from Being, from presence or from the presence of the present, not even from absence, and even less from some hyperessentiality'.[42] This signification of deep nothingness is not just beyond words but beyond conceptualization. Hence it cannot even be dead silence, just as silence could not be attributed to the non-existence of the universe, as what never existed cannot be defunct. Whereas apophatic theology aims at 'absolute rarefaction, toward silent union with the ineffable', that movement could only occur through systematically negating all the stages of positive theology in a discourse of its own, and in so doing becoming interminably coextensive and interwoven with it. That means, contends Derrida, that 'the apophatic moment cannot contain within itself the principle of its interruption. It can only indefinitely defer the encounter with its own limit.'[43] The problem enmeshes the scholar of speech, caught between its presence or absence. For the very question 'how to avoid speaking?' is already cast in language, even if only non-spoken language.

At a minimum, denial and effacement leave an unheard trace. Following Georges Bataille, Derrida observes that in attempting to silence meaning, silence inevitably silences itself and slides towards other words that can exercise control or sovereignty.[44] *Saying* that, pointing out the non-meaning of silence, the political reasserts itself. Sovereignty is the control of discourse by refusing meaning or making sense, let alone fixing it. The sovereignty of silence is exercised furtively by inserting rupture into a text or discourse; through introducing unknowledge and chance, thus interrupting articulated language. *Différance* is thus uneasily located between two modalities of silence, the ineffable and the unconceptualizable, satisfying the attributes of neither. In deference to Derrida's *différance*, I will defer further discussion of his intimations of the unconceptualizable to the last section of this chapter.

4 The Inarticulable

The inarticulable relates to something that exists at some level of experience but cannot be put into words, as distinct from something that cannot be uttered or that is beyond grasping. It may indicate a profound internalized inhibition or trauma—and every inhibition models, or mimics, the political practice of a constraining intervention in movement or expression. It may be beyond the emotional and imaginative abilities of a speaker to pinpoint and convey a state of mind, or an experience, to self and to others. And it may be due to a paucity of sufficient linguistic tools or the result of employing a wrong or inadequate linguistic code, referred to by Langton as 'perlocutionary frustration'. On this latter possibility she observes of a slave: 'Something has silenced his speech, not in the sense of rendering his spoken words inaudible or written marks illegible, but in the sense of depriving those sounds and marks of illocutionary force: of preventing those utterances from counting as the actions they were intended to be.'[45] And it may pertain, as in Merleau-Ponty's understanding, to the omnipresence of 'tacit language', a 'lateral or oblique meaning which runs between words' as a matter of course. For him, that could be discovered through painting or poetry. 'Why should the expression of the world', he pondered, 'be subjected to the prose of the *senses* or of the concept?' Poetry 'must completely awake and recall our sheer power of expressing beyond things already seen or known'.[46] But the inarticulable may also reflect a more fundamental incapacity on the part of the unaware or optionless agent. It runs deeper than indicating the hearer's incapacity to understand on grounds of language, culture, social rank, or lack of empathy. It also runs deeper than those cases of inhibitions arising out of embarrassment, shyness, or shame, over which a person has no control, as discussed by Kurzon.[47] While a distinct modality, it often overlaps the unsayable and the unconceptualizable. Though it cannot be verbalized as logos, it may be fathomed, divined, or afford an inkling of its existence on an emotional or intuitive level, though often only through the interpretative and releasing intervention by others.

A particularly trenchant analysis of the inarticulable is to be found in Lyotard's notion of the differend. While couched in moral terms of causing a wrong and suffering from it, it refers in semantic terms to an unbridgeable 'case of conflict ... that cannot be equitably resolved for lack of a rule of judgment applicable to both arguments'.[48] Using Auschwitz as a defining instance, and because the wrongs endured there cannot be conclusively addressed in legal language, Lyotard calls it a tort—a civil wrong that has harmful consequences, rather than a damage that can be redressed legally. Characteristically, the wronged party does not possess the language, the idioms, and the phrases to make a case that can be understood, or the validation apparatus to prove that it has been wronged. Lyotard has a clear moral agenda of ending, or at least diminishing, the inequality and injustice perpetrated on the wronged. He is outraged by their silence and, not least, by the disowning of their capacity to argue their case in a register that cannot be dismissed by truth- and fact-obfuscators. But his analysis points to a broader issue. Sometimes it is not the clash of epistemologies and ideologies that produces silence, but their placement in worlds that occupy not only separate but contactless spheres.

Silence for Lyotard is thus not only a negation but a deprivation. We may therefore see it not as a lack, which could be rectified, but as an absence that indicates a profound and immutable silence rather than a potentially transient one. That distinction is captured by his phrase: 'To be able not to speak is not the same as not to be able to speak.' 'Not to speak', he maintains, 'is part of the ability to speak.'[49] In other words, that ability entails a choice denied to a victimhood bereft of ability. Whereas Ricoeur's surplus of meaning was embedded in what one says, Lyotard identified a *deficit* of meaning: 'what remains to be phrased exceeds what they can presently phrase'.[50] He describes that, slightly oddly, as a feeling: 'one cannot find the words'—perhaps better characterized as an imprecisely articulated thought. Not finding the words is given a different meaning through Lacan's ultimately unattainable *jouissance*—the drive to enjoyment—discussed in Chapter 5. As Fink comments, 'experience in moments of rapture and ecstasy simply cannot be described. No words come at that moment ... it is inarticulable.'[51]

In socio-psychological terms, inarticulateness could intersect with Durkheim's notion of anomie. In that case, disorientation disables individuals from making sense of the epistemological and linguistic codes surrounding them, codes that permit both internal conceptualization and external communication. As a consequence of major social and economic crises, 'so long as the social forces thus freed have not regained equilibrium, their respective values are unknown and so all regulation is lacking for a time. The limits are unknown between the possible and the impossible.'[52] That articulative anomie will often hover on the verge of self-awareness but will produce an incapacitating and isolating silence, often with devastating consequence for the anomic individual. It should be distinguished from an unintentional silence dictated and internalized by an established social norm with which the agent has never achieved, or has lost, conscious familiarity.[53] Articulative anomie points to the absence of any such norm, not its unacknowledged authoritative standing.

A related yet distinct case may be provided by the specific silences found in Virginia Woolf's novels, applied to her binary gendered separation of women and men—in itself a common practice of political boundary setting. Laurence writes: 'Women are more often associated with the unspoken, the unsaid, and the unsayable, and men are more often associated with talk, in Woolf's novels.'[54] The unspoken is an ambiguous category amidst the classification offered in this chapter, indicating both an intentional suppression and an unconscious welcoming of silence, sometimes identified by a shift from verbalizing to other forms of physical expression. Here the concrete 'unspoken' does not constitute a barrier like the generalized and insurmountable 'unsayable'. It is a psychological and cultural state of mind that channels a gendered version of inarticulation into a quiet, substitute, quasi-communicative performativity such as a look or a smile. Those silences do not conform to views of ethicists of silence: namely, that silence is liberating and can generate creativity.[55] Although they could be, that is far from the given outcome.

A different situation arises when certain voices may be heard or encountered in a text, but the messages they aim to convey are incomprehensible or undecipherable to their targets and consumers, so that they are effectively smothered through their seeming incoherence. An instructive instance is provided by Corbin, relating how 'the silence maintained by peasant witnesses during judicial enquiries was often a sign of an incomprehension resulting from a mismatch between the law code and the many sets of norms operating throughout the country'.[56] Likewise, in connection with the legal right to silence, Ephratt cites an observation by Susan Easton that 'there is no evidence that the reasons for maintaining silence are always trivial. For weaker, ill-educated, inarticulate and poorer defendants, there may well be genuine fears of making themselves understood under cross-examination.'[57] Research conducted by the political scientists Huspek and Kendall notes that speakers are disadvantaged 'on account of a deficient mastery of a vocabulary of politics'. As they claim: 'Political words, learned early in one's life, may lose their original meaning; even if the words themselves are not forgotten, their meanings may either fade from memory or become confused.'[58] The silence in these cases is perhaps deliberate, but one mediated through the burden of ingrained cultural reticence. However, in contrast to the position adopted by Trevor Pateman, on whom the two scholars lean and who relies on Marxisant theories of the power of a dominant ideology,[59] they argue that 'a lack of mastery of a vocabulary preferred by the dominant culture may not necessarily entail a total absence of political awareness; however, it may entail a lack of a *specific* political awareness. Different vocabularies may express alternative forms of political awareness'[60]—and, we may add, consequently evince alternative corresponding (political) silences. In contrast, tellingly, a decision taken by a committee of the Israeli Knesset in 2004 limited the right to silence of public representatives on the grounds that the lack of linguistic competence does not apply to them, as they are 'expected to be well educated and fluent in [the] rhetorical use of the language code'.[61]

These instances offer an insight into the manner in which the overwhelming dominance of formal stabilizing and integrating political structures and languages holds the uninitiated in a vice way beyond their grasp, and brushes aside competing local thought-practices. In a neat turn of phrase, McNay calls this 'linguistic deauthorisation',[62] reinforcing Bourdieu's contention encountered above in a different formulation: 'The reality of linguistic legitimacy consists precisely in the fact that dominated individuals are always under the *potential jurisdiction* of formal law ... so that when placed in a formal situation they are doomed to silence or to ... broken discourse.'[63] Human speech may still be politically and socially muted if it remains overlooked, not because of its intended content but because it cannot surmount the barriers of interpretation and articulation. In extreme cases these become 'silences that convey the annihilation of the subject or the incommunicability between human beings'.[64] That is the politics of latent exclusion, or the politics of social and communicative fragmentation when the parts do not add up to an integrated whole. Formal law screens the informal politics behind it.

A study of silence in Russian cultural and mystical practices records that 'Pushkin vividly captured noises of the "multitude" with the abundance of words relating to inarticulate sounds', including to cry, wail, curse, groan, laugh, weep, scream, murmur, 'and yet, Pushkin says, "people remain mute"'. Mazour-Matusevich calls that 'silence of a noisy mass' social muting, 'characterized by the absence or incapacity of articulate, commonsensical, and transparent speech'. It ascribes 'the lack of public opinion ... [to] the general and socially shared distrust of logical discourse and reluctance to use words in a clear and straightforward fashion'.[65] The combination of a doctrine of mystical silence introduced from Byzantium and a culture of domestic speechlessness resulted in the emergence of Russian Orthodox elites who were 'wary and distrustful of public speaking. Throughout Russian history, the prestige of the coherent, practical and rational speech remained consistently low, and the prestige of silence consistently high.'[66] The significance of silence was embedded in the core political process of ranking that associated it with the respect and status initially accorded to mystical religious philosophers and then transferred to great literary *oeuvres*. As Mazour-Matusevich concludes: 'It is only logical that in a society where the elite chooses as its program the principle of silence, public opinion and [a] practical frame of mind are slow to materialize.'[67] A cultural paradigm thus endows silence with a power to limit the impact of rational discourse in the public domain, obstructing as a matter of course the critical questioning of patterns of thought and conduct.

The phenomenon of social muting differs fundamentally, say, from the legendary silence of the Finns, alluded to above in relation to solitude, which is regarded as a feature of individual temperament rather than of public comportment. But it also differs from targeted responses to the failure of linguistic and political communication. Thus, the more common instances of political protest that adopt the shape of organized and purposive group silences—such as the 'women in black' anti-war and violence vigils that have emerged since the late 1980s—intersect only partially with the type of social muting explored here and certainly do not imply articulatory impediment.

The inarticulate noises of Pushkin's multitude surface in a totally different context that bears witness to the political eloquence of some human non-verbal sounds, one such instance being keening. Famously in the 1980s, when words of persuasion directed at American soldiers failed the women protesters who surrounded the Greenham Common US nuclear missile base in the south of England, they embraced hands around the perimeter of the base as well as resorting to keening as a powerful language of emotion in a literal endeavour to pierce through the logocentric disconnect.[68] Although seemingly an arresting instance of Lyotard's differend, in which a dominant discourse blocks the recognition of the wrongs it produces, it came with a twist: here an alternative 'language' is nonetheless articulated by its users, while remaining unidentified as meaningful voice to its targeted audience. The actions of the women gave vent to frustration, sorrow, and a sense of bereavement, bewailing the impotence of dialogue and loss of humanity. It was an attempt to circumvent the inadequacy of rational conversation with the soldiers, who had heard their words but could not listen to their contents, let alone find a shared convergence point. The effective silence of failed verbalizing, and of having one's articulatory capacities culturally and socially stifled, gave way to physical performativity and to another kind of vocality, in which speech was replaced by a quasi-cacophonic practice. That practice was offered as a counterweight to articulateness, while doubling up as an act of collective mourning.[69] Another way of accounting for such protests is to 'realize that this sort of disruptive noise does not oppose silence, it *is* the collective silence of the oppressed'.[70] Silence may migrate across parallel sources and layers of political expression, and political theorists are tasked with the attempt to unravel those layers in their pursuit of comprehension and, when necessary, to achieve that by breaking through prevailing disciplinary constrictions.

Silences are common currency in the psychoanalytical process, both in psychoanalytical theory and in its clinical practice—as already noted with respect to patterns of listening. That becomes evident through a bunching reference to several modalities of silence discussed in this chapter. Bion wrote about the analyst–analysand context: 'But I did hear what he was not telling me, and that silence made quite a different noise; the pattern of what he didn't say showed that.' As Chris Mawson, the editor of Bion's *Collected Works*, commented: 'The unobserved, incomprehensible, inaudible, ineffable part of the session is the material from which will come the future interpretation that you give in so many weeks', or months', or years' time.' No less revealing is Bion's additional recounting of the session: 'I was listening to the silence; I was listening to the interference; I was listening to what came between him and me.'[71]

A different variation on the inarticulate quality of silence came from the pioneering psychoanalyst Sándor Ferenczi, interpreting a patient's sudden citing of the adage 'silence is golden'. The patient was 'in the habit of hoarding his words', and his choice of the aphorism suggested an unarticulated link with money as well as bowel evacuation in that 'taciturnity in and for itself means a saving (in use)'.[72] The decontextualized mention of silence became itself a means to cover up the inability to grasp what it substituted for.

The fundamental insight that silences display internal patterns is revealed in the psychoanalytical process, patterns distinct from the external rhythms to which linguists are attuned. And the insight that silence may be an interference not just in communication but in self-understanding is equally valuable to the political analysis of silence. Impositions, interruptions, manipulations, and systemic hindrances may all point to the unconscious control and blocking, rechannelling, or diverting of modes of thinking, feeling, or acting. While psychoanalysts focus on 'free-floating attention to what is going on in the session'—a form of unstructured receptivity and openness—logocentric political theorists, especially students of ideology, may be more literal in explaining their interpretations as decoding. Nonetheless, they both share a sense of having to be 'able to stand the pressure of watching that process',[73] whether intellectually or emotionally.

Of considerable bearing is the room in which analysis takes place—another structure that encases a human interaction. It provides a type of expected ordering with clear and private boundaries; whatever turbulence occurs within its walls is contained and secluded from the social world beyond the analysand–analyst relationship. Additionally, the silence is both directed against the external world and observed in the professional ethic of non-disclosure. On a third level, for the two individuals present, that room is itself 'a silent backdrop, sometimes mute, sometimes assertive, but always present. The room speaks and participates through materials, detail, form, light, air, space, and through silence.'[74] As an often overlooked and unacknowledged arena with direct political import, that space delimits, confines, penetrates, and determines the parameters of thought, perceptions, feeling, and imagination that both the parties experience and take away with them, serving as one possible channel for the inarticulate. What is more, as one analyst observed, there had long been a 'silent consensus' about using the couch in psychoanalysis. The couch constituted another supervening boundary that provided a 'protective shield', preventing the analyst's private space from being invaded by the patient's transference expectations.[75]

One prominent area encountered by psychoanalysts is that of trauma. As distinct from the unspeakable, which may involve a social and cultural *suppression* of speech and a reluctance to broach a subject when that is possible in principle, the incapacity to communicate trauma verbally—the inability to articulate a language through which to speak—is formed at a deeper level of *repression* rather than a conscious prohibition by the self or the surrounding society. Here 'non-spoken feelings and the pain of past traumata have been silenced'. Alternatively, 'the cessation of speech as dead-like is contrasted by disintegration into sounds such as screams and sighs'.[76] A study of the now adult children of Holocaust survivors talks of their 'mute scream[s]' as they are unconsciously 'deformed by the vestiges of a past which is not theirs, but which has been imposed upon them'. That second generation is 'trapped in a pitiless battle against the power of their parents' history and the history of our [twentieth] century'.[77] Such investigations testify to the silent and persistent control exercised by collectively lived-through events, as political violence percolates over time through the unconscious reactions of personal, and shared, psyches. Another manifestation of the inarticulable emerges through a psychoanalytical reading of two of Sophocles' plays: *Oedipus the King* and *Oedipus at Colonus*. John Steiner draws attention to the unconscious or half-conscious collusion among the chief characters in turning a blind eye to the obvious indications of Oedipus's parentage. 'Blind eye' has a special resonance in the case of Oedipus, but it is no less the directing of a deaf ear. By denying reality, silence guards against the enormity of articulating and then admitting to oneself the personal and normative perversion that has taken place.[78]

In another illuminating study of silences present among the next generation of Holocaust survivors that straddles the domain of anthropology and psychology, Carol Kidron raises several fundamental issues that merit closer scrutiny on a number of levels.[79] First, she takes on board the unconscious practice of tacit knowing that involves the extrapolation of indirect information, such as a child's observing tattooed numerals on the arms of their parents. That may occur at a level of partial awareness when the viewer is unable to interrogate that information or deduce from it the nature of the associated silences. 'These silent traces', Kidron comments, 'maintain an intimate and nonpathological presence of the Holocaust death-world in the everyday life-world.' Those traces are nonetheless chronological and detectable through other forms of behaviour engineered by past events or experiences, and differ categorically from Derrida's usage of trace, which is attuned to indeterminate representations of what is not present.

Second, because trauma entails the 'burial or repression of speech' and generates an ineffability beyond narrative, Kidron steps away from logocentrism and from therapeutic endeavours to give trauma voice. Instead, preferring ethnography to psychology, she is more concerned with silence 'as a medium of expression, communication, and transmission of knowledge in its own right or as an alternative form of personal knowing that is not dependent on speech for its own objectification' but is present as 'nonverbal, intersubjective, embodied, and material traces of the past in everyday life'. Kidron's methodological message resonates with the detection of silent emotive and physical presences, of which traumas are simply a part. As she expounds: 'By challenging reductionist readings of the survivor and descendant profiles as silent/silenced, emotionally wounded, and collectivized, anthropological research methods would allow the survivor and descendant subjects to articulate the experience of silence and the everyday practices of silent forms of interaction.' That could best be achieved through an ethnography that 'seek[s] phenomenological accounts of the silent presence of the past', given that the 'lived experience of embodying or interacting with traces of the past may not always be politically motivated or performed as acts of resistance or as capitulation to hegemonic indoctrination or appropriation'.

Although Kidron associates the political only with hegemony or personal empowerment, all her findings reinforce the manifestations of politics as a mêlée of normalizing, shaking up, deflecting, and manoeuvring conduct and thinking even as it is veiled in extra-linguistic silence—whether corporeal, performative, or emotional. It follows that when Kidron asserts that 'taken-for-granted mnemonic practices are constituted, sustained, and intergenerationally transmitted to create the silent yet no less living presence of the past', these too are political by nature. Exploring the political does not have to *be* motivated; it *may* motivate. Nor does its study have to convey empathy with individual burdens or offer restitution. The political simply happens, and scholars will want to know what it looks like.

5 The Unnoticeable

The unnoticeable involves a practice or event actually located in social time and space that does not spring to the attention of those who partake of it. As suggested at the outset of this chapter, that may simply ensue from the ignorance or indifference of the practitioners. Many features of the political have to be spelt out to become noticed, as illustrated in Chapter 2 through the practice of taking a bus ride to town. That type of silence is not a contributor to discourse, nor indicative of something missing. It is merely an understandable gap in information and its processing that can, in principle, easily be remedied. But the unnoticeable may have a deeper cause, when the happening is so taken for granted by given groups that it is beyond their recognition and comment. That has been famously captured by that master of social customs, Bourdieu. He contended that 'when the social world loses its character as a natural phenomenon ... the question of the natural or conventional character (*phusei* or *nomo*) of social facts can be raised'[80]—an observation no less pertinent to unqualified religious faith. Bourdieu made a seminal contribution to issues such as these through his central concept of the habitus, a system of unorchestrated regulating and underlying structures that generates fundamental social practices and that is limited 'by the historically and socially situated conditions of its production'. Consequently, 'the most improbable practices are therefore excluded, as unthinkable, by a kind of immediate submission to order' because 'the anticipations of the habitus ... give disproportionate weight to early experiences'.[81] For the sake of conceptual tidiness it is worth observing that Bourdieu's usage of 'unthinkable' differs from the category elaborated on at the beginning of this chapter, because it is socially obscured rather than subject to internalized taboos. Substituting 'unnoticeable' for Bourdieu's 'unthinkable' serves his purpose better. He expanded more clearly on the unnoticeable in another work:

> Because the subjective necessity and self-evidence of the commonsense world are validated by the objective consensus on the sense of the world, what is essential

goes without saying because it comes without saying: the tradition is silent, not least about itself as a tradition; customary law is content to enumerate specific applications of principles which remain implicit and unformulated, because unquestioned; the play of the mythico-ritual homologies constitutes a perfectly closed world, each aspect of which is, as it were, a reflection of all the others, a world which has no place for *opinion* as liberal ideology understands it, i.e. as one of the different and equally legitimate answers which can be given to an explicit question about the established political order.[82]

Bourdieu's reference to a silent, unnoticeable tradition suggests that it contains three salient elements. First, assumptions of self-evidence and 'consensus'—more accurately, conformity to deep-seated cultural parameters—work as cementers of ideational positions and foster a default screen of silence, in which an alternative agenda is intellectually imperceptible. Second, in many social settings the practice of questioning, the cultivating of curiosity, and the positing of experimental counterfactuals are too costly, bizarre, or out of reach, both socially and personally, and not at the forefront of closed, or reposing, cultural and epistemic orders. Third, the process of naturalizing a practice may involve replicating it to the point where it loses its salience and is performed mechanically or routinely—epitomized by the phrase 'second nature'. But Bourdieu refers to a level of awareness that not only sinks beneath recognition but resists rising to the level of recognition. Even the naturalness of that practice goes unobserved—a mark of the ultimate triumph of a social thought-practice. Modern ideologies may aspire to that triumph, but they will ultimately fall short of it.

Bourdieu, of course, is not alone in his insights. Rancière charges 'the ideal of consensus' with postulating 'objective equilibriums' that are 'precisely the negation of the political'.[83] Brubaker's cognitivist approach likewise regards constructs and categories such as ethnicity as frameworks and filters that 'shape what is noticed or unnoticed, relevant or irrelevant, remembered or forgotten'.[84] Zerubavel points out that 'personal information merely confirming default cultural assumptions is therefore rarely considered notifiable. . . . Whereas the abnormal is explicitly labeled, the normal needs no mentioning.' In such cases silence is applied to the 'culturally redundant and . . . semiotically superfluous'.[85] Bourdieu, however, takes the political implications further. Noting the social unanimity such doxa displays, he adds that 'The adherence expressed in the doxic relation to the social world is the absolute form of recognition of legitimacy through misrecognition of arbitrariness, since it is unaware of the very question of legitimacy.'[86] In such instances, the holy grail of legitimacy craved by political systems is delivered not by people, members, and citizens, but by obscuring whatever doubts those systems might have provoked in a silence nourished by ignorance, or reflecting a numbing lack of curiosity among some people. Unlike the notion of tacit consent borne out of a performative, indirectly political, awareness, here we are ushered into the sphere of widespread, even total, unawareness—a powerful and common indicator of socially significant silence.

There is a modification on the theme of the unnoticeable—*unrecognizability*—exemplifying the tenuousness of the boundary between silence on the one hand, and hearing, visibility, and awareness on the other. It concerns the failure of voices to register in the public domain, leaving them unrecognized to the point of blanking them out. The response to the murder of George Floyd in 2020, as part of extensive 'black lives matter' protests in major cities, was a political event on two quite separate levels. At immediate face-value it was a demand for a change in the treatment of black people in the USA, the UK, and around the world, especially at the hands of white social and cultural majorities and elites and by the police. While the high degree of explicit police violence in the UK was less prevalent than in the USA, slogans on the streets of London such as 'silence is violence' expressed a mood of considerable anger and frustration.[87] But at a deeper level, in terms of the practices of political thinking, it was an insistence on the re-ranking of the rights and standing of black citizens, residents, and visitors to a far higher position in the collective consciousness and the governmental agenda. The unrecognizable operates only on the nether range of a ranking scale of awareness, touching the lowest points such as 'barely noted' or 'irrelevant', and even when those small traces still exist, the claims they embody are effectively consigned to the realm of social silence. It is a silence not of deliberate exclusion but of ignorance that culminates in an apathetic relegation to the sidelines.

6 The Unknowable

The unknowable refers to instances when it is beyond human capacity to gather information about something or to understand it. In his discussion of truth and the indeterminate, Aristotle notes that a follower of Heraclitus—Cratylus—who held that 'nothing could truly be affirmed . . . finally did not think it right to say anything but only moved his finger'.[88] Here too slender boundaries permit the unknowable to mutate into the 'unsayable' in one variation on Wittgenstein's famous aphorism. A more banal example would be that we have no idea what human life on Earth will look like in a million years' time. The silence it induces, or *should* induce, suggests either resignation to the limitations of our current state of knowledge, or a deeper ontological impossibility of, or abstinence from, attaining understanding—an acknowledgement of human inadequacy or, perhaps, imperfection in the course of pursuing a finite, illusory quest.

The former United States Secretary of Defense Donald Rumsfeld was much derided at the time for speaking of 'known unknowns and unknown unknowns' but the phrases he chose aptly fit his two categories. In a news briefing in 2012 Rumsfeld said:

> Reports that say that something hasn't happened are always interesting to me, because as we know, there are known knowns; there are things we know we know. We also know there are known unknowns; that is to say we know there are some things we do not know. But there are also unknown unknowns—the ones we don't know we don't know. And if one looks throughout the history of our country and other free countries, it is the latter category that tend to be the difficult ones.[89]

That makes perfect sense, with the proviso that the unknown unknowns are intriguing not only in so-called free countries. Taking this one step further, those deep silences can be spliced into the unknown unknowns we will probably *never* know, and the unknown unknowns that we *might* have known under different contingent conditions of knowledge availability. Far from being conspiratorial, those latter silences are epistemologically concealed and hence 'inaudible' in a broad conceptual sense, though they might be revealed and retrospectively recognized as significant, if alternative cultural and conceptual readings that could unlock another way in become available.

Human impatience, imagination, mendacity, or delusion often ride roughshod over the warranted silences of the known unknowns, creating sound, speech, and performance that plugs and covers them. Such substitutions may not serve the world of verifiable facts, but they inject structure and order when inevitable silence is socially and politically unpalatable. By contrast, unknown unknowns are socially safe, but only until an encounter with a new source of information renders them politically combustible.

7 The Unconceptualizable

The unconceptualizable is the most elusive—and most intriguing—of the seven modalities. It signals a more fundamental ideational hiddenness that relates not to ignorance, inattention, opacity, or internal blockages but to the unavailability of an intellectual and cultural apparatus through which certain kinds of knowledge can be perceived and processed to begin with. It is a function of non-existing, or yet to change, knowledge paradigms unable to access impenetrable doctrines; of untutored groups; or of a dearth of radically revised findings about social life, which display various measures of incidence or impenetrability. While the unknowable may be imaginable but inaccessible, or wildly inaccurately imaginable as through the lens of science fiction, the unconceptualizable is invisible/inaudible to the population to which it applies and thus not an object of human reflection, articulation, or fantasy. In that it must be distinguished from the colloquial usage of 'inconceivable' which, as the *OED* notes, may be employed 'often with exaggerative force for "hardly credible", "incalculable", "extraordinary", of things which transcend common experience'.[90]

One pronounced example of the unconceptualizable was raised in Chapter 6. In profoundly religious cultures a literally Godless world cannot even be conceptualized. It addresses a question that cannot be posed, so intertwined is the notion of God in what it is to be human and to conduct a shared social life. The equivalent in the sphere of scientific theory is the impossibility of posing the question 'what happened before the Big Bang?' The question is invalid because physics denies both the theoretical and empirical possibility of a pre-Big Bang, and because to establish a beginning is only logical if *nothing* preceded it, thus avoiding an infinite regression to one beginning after another.[91] These are not legitimate concerns within the matrix of human thought. Maitland fittingly refers to the Big Bang alongside the religious myth of creation as 'an attempt to express the inexpressible' and associates the term literally with breaking the silence.[92] But the idea of the Big Bang is more than that. It is not the inexpressibility of the creation of the universe that the Big Bang dispels. Rather, it accomplishes two things. It confirms the intrinsic unconceptualizability of what did not occur prior to it; i.e., it draws a line over temporality. And it cements a basic understanding of the political as the drive to inject human order into extra-human chaos. To make this more relatable to the human mind, a narrative is woven that reintroduces temporality into a domain where time cannot, or does not, tread. An unconceivable silence or, more specifically, an absence beyond the reach even of silence can only end by conjuring up its very opposite, the almightiest of sounds.

Any discussion of the non-existence of beginnings returns us to Derrida's *différance*, dissociated from the ineffability arguments of negative theology. He offers an even more emphatic disavowal of conceptualizability and—for the purposes of this study—of silence as a definable proposition. For Derrida, the unconceptualizable concerns not just the unavailability of an intellectual or imaginative processing apparatus but a far more profound issue. Building on Freud, Derrida contends that the never-present unconscious sends out 'delegates or representatives' as a 'radical alterity', leaving only a trace that 'muffles itself in resonating'.[93] That muffling is the deferred silence of the unseen and unconceptualizable, elusive and ungraspable. *Différance* is an assemblage—in writing that becomes a grammatology—of indeterminate components, neither words nor concepts, that wait on other indeterminate differences, permanently deferring meaning. *Différance* lies not in any specific contents but in that woven structure.

Différance cannot be exposed and thus made to appear, because the logical consequence would be that it could also disappear. That logic cannot hold because *différance* is non-conceptual, not a present-being, and therefore does not exist as a substantive thing. If it did exist, we would 'be led to delineate also everything *that* it is *not*, that is, *everything*'.[94] In similar vein, something that not only isn't being heard, but cannot either begin or cease to be heard, eliminates silence both as concept and as an actual or potential property of the world. Derrida contends that consciousness in the form of the self-presence of a subject—'a silent and intuitive consciousness'—is wholly metaphysical.[95] That consciousness is not the central form of being, and not even the synthesized, incessantly reassembled 'effect' of embeddedness in a system of nuanced *différance*, because *différance* cannot tolerate the very possibility of opposites, sequences, or effects. The erasure effected by *différance* is also the ultimate—and arguably—only example of radical depoliticization, bereft of either time or space, because it obliterates a 'rightful beginning', an 'arche', and consequently the possibility of political foundation and government, whether through the Godly act of creation or its weaker secular counterparts.[96] In Derrida's rejection of a teleological ontology not only absence, but also the notion of lack-as-potential, has no place.

Like the unnoticeable, both the unknowable and the unconceptualizable do not relate to prohibitions or constraints that 'impose' or elicit silence. Unlike the unnoticeable, they occupy domains where meaningful speech and thought are completely beyond reach or unidentifiable to given groupings. But that is not quite the case with the ineffable and the inarticulable, for which practices of philosophy, religion, or emotional awareness may bridge the divide that inhibits interpretation. In a probing discussion of what he labels 'the unthought', Mohammed Arkoun has considered such silences as they manifest themselves in Islam, posing the question: 'To what extent are these [Muslim] protagonists aware of the ideological dimension of their discourse and historical actions?' Although Arkoun ties the unthought to the unthinkable, in terms of the categories discussed in this chapter his designation gravitates towards the unconceptualizable. On the other hand, it does not identify the unconceptualizable as an epistemic absence beyond grasp, as befits the full remit of the concept. Rather, it becomes a concrete conceptual process under which 'voices are silenced, creative talents are neglected, marginalized or obliged to reproduce orthodox frameworks of expression'. These acts of religious and cultural muting are eventually no longer perceived as such by the believers, being bundled into a sacralizing tradition, or what Arkoun calls a 'logosphere', a 'linguistic mental space'. This offers an instance of how the unconceptualizable is subject to paradigmatic shifts. A specific language will shape the articulation of thoughts and memory into a unifying *Weltanschauung*. It accounts for how Islamic values 'taught in Arabic to Indonesian, Bangladeshi or Tajik people, for example, share the same **unthinkable** about religion with the rest of the world's Muslims'.[97] What commences as practices of religious domination is excluded over time from social awareness, traversing the boundary towards unnoticeability in Bourdieu's sense of habitus and from there to epistemic inaccessibility.

Particularly edifying is Arkoun's exploration of the pincer movement of the silencing mechanism. Although, he contends, Islam has been subject to etatist control, 'the religious discourse developed by the opposing social forces shifted to a **populist** ideology which increased the extent of the **unthought**, especially in the religious, political and legal fields'.[98] The socio-political underpinning of unconceptualizability re-emerges as an internalized and unquestioning censorship practised also by those who have borne the brunt of that closure, incapable even of contemplating what has been silenced, let alone criticizing the consequences. Crucial, too, is Arkoun's awareness of the drawing in of scholarship and theorizing into this almost impenetrable ring of silence. 'That is why the historical summary I have just provided', he maintains, 'is strictly unthinkable in the historical and cognitive contexts in which Islamic thought has been imprisoned.' Its 'conceptual apparatus and horizons of meaning' disable the unlocking of the 'collective imaginaries' it employs.[99] This version of the unnoticeable emphatically brandishes the characteristics of the unconceptualizable. Such shadings and gradations inch silences across their modalities.

In contrast, the possibility of the unconceptualizable and consequently of profound silence recedes in Bourdieu's idea of liberal ideology that harbours a multiplicity of legitimate competing understandings of the political order—though it will be contended in Chapter 14 that liberalism contains its own, rather distinct, silences. To the discerning outside world the silence of the observed culture reveals what that external gaze considers to be a blinkered epistemic incapacity, whereas within that world silence is unnoticed, relentlessly shielded by routine, belief, safety, and taking experienced normality for granted. As Beckett's Vladimir muses: 'The air is full of our cries (*listens*). But habit is a great deadener.'[100]

8 Two Afterthoughts

Another variant of interest deserves brief mention: Michael Polanyi's category of tacit knowledge. Here silence concerns not the unconceptualizable but the *pre-conceptualizable*, a form of understanding that gradually unfolds in a manner grasped only retrospectively. Polanyi argued that tacit thought was a form of integrating the initially unintelligible particulars of experience, working back from a conceptualization of the whole. Through constructing a Gestalt, the active shaping of knowhow was made possible, but could not be specifically accounted for. Rather, people possess 'the intimation of something hidden, which we may yet discover ... we can have a tacit foreknowledge of yet undiscovered things'.[101] Some of the most fundamental processes of the human mind, relating to analysis and perception, occur prior to their being formulated and expressed. A temporal development moves from the unrecognizable to the recognizable and then turns back retrospectively to shed light on its own components. And the task of problem solving is thus future oriented: 'To trust that a thing we know is real is ... to feel that it has the independence and power of manifesting itself in yet unthought of ways in the future.'[102] A deeply ingrained and pre-social and non-transmittable silence initially cloaks two hallmarks of political life that subsequently emerge: the capacity for ordering and the drive to address the future. Polanyi's tacit knowledge is subtly different from Bourdieu's unnoticeable/unthinkable tradition insofar as it presents itself as a germ of incipient knowability that will grow into a fuller cognition, in contrast to the static and settled world Bourdieu describes.

Finally, section 1 of Chapter 3 mooted a number of paradigmatic constellations that characterize several traditions of thinking and creativity. Diverse genres of thought and questioning are particularly revealing in their juxtaposition. One question they raise in artistic and poetic garb is whether there are other paths to conceptualizing the unconceptualizable, and to what extent such paths are intuitive. An elucidating contradistinction in this context is found in T. S. Eliot's *Four Quartets*, which appears to stand in complete paradigmatic contrast to Derrida's analysis: 'And the end and the beginning were always there/Before the beginning and after the end. And all is always now.' Words, in Eliot's imaginative poetry, are not distinct analysable concepts. They stretch into the silence, or perpetual stillness, but 'decay with imprecision ... will not stay still'. Their pattern of movement is 'caught in the form of limitation between un-being and being'.[103] That ambiguity, found also in instances of Zen-Buddhism to which we shall turn in Chapter 12, offers an inkling—a trace, we may venture—of the structural separation-cum-overlap dominating Derrida's theorizing: in particular, Eliot's contention that the present—if its sense *could* be distilled—would have to embrace everything; 'all is always now'. Yet it departs in fundamental ways from the insistent unhitching of proximities generated by *différance* and from Derrida's principled unease at naming, defining, and temporality. Eliot's poetic and Derrida's philosophical imaginations address issues of liminality in discrete modes, sometimes in touching distance of one another, at other times producing their own silent gaps of misalignment.

Notes

1. *OED* online.
2. A. Rawnsley, *The Observer*, 26 August 2018.
3. L. Wittgenstein, *Tractatus Logico-Philosophicus*, Ogden and Ramsey translation (London: Routledge & Kegan Paul, 1922), Proposition 7, p. 56.
4. For a brief discussion see Budick and Iser, 'Introduction', in *Languages of the Unsayable*, pp. xii, xxi.
5. See *inter alia* A. Holiday, 'Wittgenstein's Silence: Philosophy, Ritual and the Limits of Language', *Language and Communication* 5/2 (1985), pp. 133–142.
6. Foucault, *A History of Sexuality*, p. 84.
7. For a general discussion see R. A. Rogers, 'From Cultural Exchange to Transculturation: A Review and Reconceptualization of Cultural Appropriation', *Communication Theory* 16 (2006), pp. 474–503.
8. G. C. Spivak, 'Can the Subaltern Speak?', in P. Williams and L. Chrisman (eds.), *Colonial Discourse and Post-colonial Theory: A Reader* (New York: Columbia University Press, 1994), pp. 78, 87.
9. Ibid., p. 80.
10. Ibid., pp. 82–83.
11. J. Derrida, *Margins of Philosophy*, trans. Alan Bass (Brighton: Harvester Press 1982), p. 255.
12. http://shsdavisapes.pbworks.com/w/file/fetch/76523768/ Cat%20on%20a%20Hot%20Tin%252 (accessed 23 July 2018).
13. Kølvraa, 'The Discourse Theory of Ernesto Laclau', in Wodak and Forchtner, *The Routledge Handbook of Language and Politics*, p. 96.
14. E. Zerubavel, *The Elephant in the Room: Silence and Denial in Everyday Life* (New York: Oxford University Press, 2006), pp. 2–3.
15. Foucault, *The Archaeology of Knowledge and the Discourse on Language*, p. 229.
16. Beckett, *The Unnamable*, pp. 86, 99–100, 13.

17 Ibid., p. 38.
18 M. Marais, '"A Step towards Silence": Samuel Beckett's *The Unnamable* and the Problem of Following the Stranger', *Journal of Literary Studies* 32/4 (2016), pp. 89–106 at pp. 96, 99.
19 S. Wolosky, 'Samuel Beckett's Figural Evasions', in Budick and Iser, *Languages of the Unsayable*, pp. 180, 183.
20 Iser, 'The Play of the Text' in ibid., pp. 336–338.
21 W. Steinmetz, *Das Sagbare und das Machbare* (Stuttgart: Klett-Cotta, 1993), pp. 13, 19.
22 For a brief summary see D. Braine, 'Negative Theology', in the *Routledge Encyclopedia of Philosophy*, https://www.rep.routledge.com/articles/thematic/negative-theology/v-1
23 Matt, '*Ayin*', p. 129.
24 Ibid., p. 145.
25 Andrew Willet, *Hexapla in Exodum: The Second Booke Of Moses Called Exodus* (London: Thomas Man, Paul Man, and Jonah Man, 1633), ch. VI, quest VI. https://quod.lib.umich.edu/e/eebo/A15408.0001.001/1:20?rgn=div1;submit=Go;subview=detail;type=simple;view=fulltext;q1=ineffable
26 Sells, *Mystical Languages of Unsaying*, p. 151.
27 Plato, *The Sophist*, http://www.gutenberg.org/files/1735/1735-h/1735-h.htm (accessed 15 June 2017).
28 Montiglio, *Silence in the Land of Logos*, p. 38.
29 2 Corinthians 12:4.
30 C. Mauriac, *The New Literature* (New York: G. Braziller, 1959), p. 81.
31 N. Coupland and J. Coupland, 'Discourses of the Unsayable: Death-Implicative Talk in Geriatric Medical Consultations' in Jaworski, *Silence: Interdisciplinary Perspectives*, pp. 117–152.
32 Chien-hsing Ho, 'Saying the Unsayable', *Philosophy East and West* 56 (2006), pp. 409–410.
33 K. E. Yandell, 'Some Varieties of Ineffability', *International Journal for Philosophy of Religion* 6/3 (1975), pp. 167–179 at p. 177.
34 Cf. Chien-hsing Ho, 'Saying the Unsayable', p. 421.
35 Derrida, 'How to Avoid Speaking: Denials', pp. 73–142 at pp. 74, 77.
36 Ivana Noble, 'Apophatic Elements in Derrida's Deconstruction', in P. Pokorný and J. Roskovec (eds.), *Philosophical Hermeneutics and Biblical Exegesis* (Tübingen: Mohr Siebeck, 2002), pp. 83–93 at p. 89.
37 Derrida, 'Différance', in *Margins of Philosophy*, p. 6.
38 See Chapter 9 on *tohu va bohu*.
39 Noble, 'Apophatic Elements in Derrida's Deconstruction', p. 92.
40 See Chapter 2.
41 J. Derrida, *Writing and Difference* (Chicago, IL: University of Chicago Press, 1978), pp. 34–36.
42 Derrida, 'How to Avoid Speaking: Denials', p. 79.
43 Ibid., pp. 80–81.
44 Derrida, *Writing and Difference*, p. 262.
45 Langton, 'Speech Acts and Unspeakable Acts', pp. 314, 316.
46 Merleau-Ponty, 'Indirect Voices and the Language of Silence', pp. 84, 89.
47 Kurzon, *Discourse of Silence*, p. 35.
48 Lyotard, *The Differend*, p. xi.

49 Ibid., p. 10.
50 Ibid., p. 13.
51 B. Fink, *Lacan to the Letter* (Minneapolis, MN: University of Minnesota Press, 2004), p. 40.
52 É. Durkheim, *Suicide: A Study in Sociology* (London: Routledge & Kegan Paul, 1952), p. 213.
53 That, by contrast, is the subject of Kurzon's unintentional internal silence. D. Kurzon, 'Towards a Typology of Silence', *Journal of Pragmatics* 39 (2007), pp. 1673–1688 at p. 1676.
54 Laurence, *The Reading of Silence*, pp. 35–36.
55 Billias and Vemuri, *The Ethics of Silence*, p. 17.
56 A. Corbin, *A History of Silence* (Cambridge: Polity Press, 2018), p. 94.
57 Quoted in Ephratt, *The Functions of Silence*, p. 1931.
58 Huspek and Kendal, 'On Withholding Political Voice', p. 3.
59 T. Pateman, *Language, Truth and Politics: Towards a Radical Theory for Communication* (Lewes, East Sussex: Stroud, 1975).
60 Huspek and Kendal, 'On Withholding Political Voice', p. 4.
61 Ephratt, *The Functions of Silence*, p. 1932.
62 McNay, 'Suffering, Silence and Social Weightlessness', p. 236.
63 Bourdieu, *Language and Symbolic Power*, p. 71.
64 Corbin, *A History of Silence*, p. 80.
65 Y. Mazour-Matusevich, 'Historical Roots of Russian Silence', *CrossCurrents* 64 (2014), pp. 295–311 at pp. 295–296.
66 Ibid., pp. 302, 305.
67 Ibid., p. 308.
68 L. Day, 'The Greenham Common Contest: A Participant Observer's Account', *Rain*, no. 62 (1984), pp. 3–4.
69 A. Cook and G. Kirk, *Greenham Women Everywhere: Dreams, Ideas and Actions from the Women's Peace Movement* (London: Pluto Press, 1983); Freeden, *The Political Theory of Political Thinking*, pp. 182–183, 195–196.
70 Sider, 'Between Silences and Culture', p. 154.
71 W. Bion, 'Brazilian Lectures: 1974, Rio de Janeiro', in *The Complete Works of W. R. Bion*, ed. Chris Mawson (London: Routledge, 2014), vol. VII, p. 121.
72 S. Ferenczi, 'Silence is Golden', in *Further Contributions to the Theory and Technique of Psychoanalysis* (London: Hogarth Press, 1926), pp. 250–251.
73 Mawson in *The Complete Works of W. R. Bion*, vol. VII, p. 121.
74 Danze, 'An Architect's View', pp. 122–123.
75 G. Moraitis, 'Prologue', *Pychoanalytic Inquiry* 15/3 (1995), pp. 275–279.
76 M. Ritter, 'Silence as the Voice of Trauma', *American Journal of Psychoanalysis* 74 (2014), pp. 176–194 at pp. 177, 180.
77 J. Chasseguet-Smirgel, 'Foreword', in I. Kogan, *The Cry of Mute Children* (London: Free Association, 1995), pp. xiii–xiv.
78 J. Steiner, *Psychic Retreats* (London and New York: Routledge, 1993), pp. 120–130.
79 C. Kidron, 'Toward an Ethnography of Silence: The Lived Presence of the Past in the Everyday Life of Holocaust Trauma Survivors and Their Descendants in Israel', *Current Anthropology* 50 (2009), pp. 5–27.

80 P. Bourdieu, *Outline of a Theory of Practice* (Cambridge: Cambridge University Press, 1977), p. 169.
81 P. Bourdieu, *The Logic of Practice* (Cambridge: Polity Press, 1990), pp. 54–55.
82 Bourdieu, *Outline of a Theory of Practice*, pp. 167–168.
83 Panagia and Rancière, 'Dissenting Words', pp. 123–124.
84 R. Brubaker, M. Loveman, and P. Stamatov, 'Ethnicity as Cognition', *Theory and Society* 33/1 (2004), pp. 31–64 at p. 47.
85 E. Zerubavel, 'Listening to the Sound of Silence: Methodological Reflections on Studying the Unsaid', in Murray and Durrheim, *Qualitative Studies of Silence*, p. 64.
86 Bourdieu, *Outline of a Theory of Practice*, p. 168.
87 See, e.g., J. Cobb, 'The Death of Floyd George in Context', *New Yorker*, 27 May 2020. https://www.newyorker.com/news/daily-comment/the-death-of-george-floyd-in-context (accessed 12 November 2021); J. Silverstein, 'The Global Impact of George Floyd: How Black Lives Matter Protests Shaped Movements around the World', *CBS News*, 4 June 2021. https://www.cbsnews.com/news/george-floyd-black-lives-matter-impact/ (accessed 12 November 2021).
88 Aristotle, *Metaphysics*, https://www.documentacatholicaomnia.eu/03d/-384_-322,_Aristoteles,_13_Metaphysics,_EN.pdf, p. 36.
89 Donald Rumsfeld's response to a question at a US Department of Defense news briefing on 12 February 2002 about the lack of evidence linking the government of Iraq with the supply of weapons of mass destruction to terrorist groups. http://archive.defense.gov/Transcripts/Transcript.aspx?TranscriptID=2636 (accessed 12 October 2017).
90 *OED* online (accessed 28 April 2020).
91 See M. Freeden, 'The "Beginning of Ideology" thesis', in *Ideology Studies*, pp. 99–105.
92 Maitland, *A Book of Silence*, p. 119.
93 Derrida, 'Différance', p. 21.
94 Ibid., p. 6.
95 Ibid., p. 16.
96 Ibid., p. 6. See also Freeden, *The Political Theory of Political Thinking*, pp. 93–100.
97 M. Arkoun, *The Unthought in Contemporary Islamic Thought* (London: Saqi, 2002), pp. 10–12 (bold type in original).
98 Ibid., p. 15 (bold type in original).
99 Ibid., pp. 17–18.
100 S. Beckett, *Waiting for Godot* (London: Faber & Faber, 1956), p. 91.
101 M. Polanyi, *The Tacit Dimension* (New York: Doubleday & Co., 1966), pp. 22–23.
102 Ibid., p. 32.
103 T. S. Eliot, *Four Quartets*, 'Burnt Norton' (London: Faber & Faber, 2001), p. 8.

8
Silence in Language and Communication

Many scholars regard silence as fully social and communicative, but communication does not entail controlled meaning. As Weller maintains, silence

> is not the opposite of speech but rather the far end of the continuum of uninterpretability that affects every kind of communication. It differs from other forms of sociality primarily in its opacity, in the way it resists the social controls that allow some speech to appear, in context, as unambiguous. All communication is subject to alternative interpretations, but silence more than any other keeps possibilities open and makes a final resolution impossible. . . . Silence will always pose irresolvable problems of interpretation, even as it demands interpretation.[1]

And yet, some silences display clearly discernible patterns and rhythms, and their consideration is the final step in the mapping process of Part I, now adding several insights gleaned from linguistics and communication with which to prepare for Part II.

1 The Discursive Distribution of Silence

Language, of course, contains its own order, but the manner in which its silences are organized can wield exceptional power over the listener or reader, and organization is always the domain of the political. Ferdinand de Saussure had already analysed the organization of language as a grammar of word networks in employing his distinction between *langue* and *parole*. Language contained syntagmatic relations in the form of specific sequences of units.[2] In focusing on the structural synchronicity of language, Saussure also drew attention to its temporal dimension: words—oral and written—are spoken one after another and listening or reading usually entails waiting for the meaning of a sentence to be revealed over time, however short its span may be. Consider especially the placing of the meaning-unlocking verb at the very end of German phrases, its initial grammatically induced silence hovering

Concealed Silences and Inaudible Voices in Political Thinking. Michael Freeden, Oxford University Press.
© Michael Freeden (2022). DOI: 10.1093/oso/9780198833512.003.0010

over the sentence and capable of enlisting any number of potential words to fill it. The speaker holds the recipient in expectant tension, or delayed gratification, up to the final moment when the meaning is retroactively fixed, and the previously silent verb is spoken. The social construct of grammar and to a lesser degree the rational rules of logic, not human will, manipulate the process of comprehension by ensuring that the act of listening will endure for the duration of the utterance.

Linguists have applied these emphases on order by marking silences in speech and even quantifying them, just as John Cage's concert work consisted of a silence counted down in exact time, contrasting a semblance of the precisely measurable and sequential with the haphazardness of audience uncontrollability. All those approaches involve the punctuation of silence with sound or noise, even if it is only the random coughing of the audience, or conversely punctuating sound and noise with silence, depending on one's starting point. They remain committed to a sequential chain. For Picard, adopting the grand view from silence, as it were, 'language is only of short duration, like a break in the continuity of silence'.[3] Linguists, to the contrary, examine the internalities of language, recording that although silence is crucially assimilated into discourse, smaller *silences* invariably intersperse speech and bisect it, extensively as well as minutely. Silence as a holistic imaginary is distinct from silence as a compound of siloed or stacked silences that appear to coalesce, although their origins, rationales, and significations consist of sets of discrete phenomena, united only in their soundlessness.

Whereas silence in and around language is to some extent conditioned by the structure of language itself, by its transmission from the brain to the vocal cords, and by the physiology of breathing, silence also reacts back on language and imbues it with crucial nuances of meaning. The *social* distribution of silence will be addressed in Part II, but the *discursive* distribution of silence is equally edifying as a political practice. Five political implications of discursive silence come to mind, of which only the first is definitely deliberate; the others hover between the intentional and the unplanned.

First, there is a silence of emphasis as a rhetorical strategy when tension is ratcheted up to heighten concentration or to induce anxiety—as in TV competitions where the host pauses dramatically before the winner is announced. Second, a reflective silence occurs when information is digested, alternatives are considered, or efforts to increase the cogency of an argument are put in place—as when a student directs a particularly challenging query at their professor. Such a silence is likely to be interpreted as internal silent speech in which the addressee mulls over a response. As Chafe indicates, 'the speaker is interested in the adequate verbalization of his thoughts. Pauses, false starts, afterthoughts, and repetitions do not hinder that goal, but are steps on the way to achieving it.'[4] Another interpretation of that kind of silence has found that pauses happen predominantly at boundaries between clauses, suggesting that a critical decision-making juncture occurs in which the future route of argument is chosen.[5]

Third, there are disjunctive silences, when a substantive break is introduced as a barrier severing one theme from the next—in the words of the acclaimed *Monty Python* comedy series: 'And now for something completely different'. That break may be either contrived or spontaneous and is chiefly a moment of adjustment to a switch of topic—the silence buried under the more obvious need to change gear, or a hiatus in a lecture indicating a new sub-section. Fourth, switching pauses occur among participants in a dyadic conversation. The political rhythm in that practice is unmistakable. Switching may involve two typical political elements: cooperation entails taking turns silently signalled by cues such as intonation, while competition over who controls the floor is typified by shorter pauses and more frequent interruptions. In the first case, pauses are a salient form of ordering and sequencing, possibly as a result of yielding—i.e., conceding power; in the second the break, sometimes through the very act of breathing, is an opportunity to be pounced on and curtailed more aggressively.[6] Fifth, and commonly, there are silences of uncertainty, when hesitation or indecision temporarily disempower the speaker and offer the opportunity for other interlocutors to 'muscle in' and take control of the direction of the discourse. Whether consciously or unconsciously, as the sociologist Erving Goffman observed: 'Undue lulls come to be potential signs of having nothing in common, or of being insufficiently self-possessed to create something to say, and hence must be avoided.'[7]

A sub-group of that category are silences that invite a response, when a gap is introduced as a voluntary interruption that enables another discussant to insert a new contribution to a discourse—think of the teacher peering silently but encouragingly round the room, hoping for someone to rise to the bait of the topic. When silence is met with silence, the purposeful silence of the teacher is a counter to the unwelcome silence of the students. Finally, an instructive case of hesitancy is to be found when lawyers ask questions of witnesses. Here the issue does not concern total silence—as in the example given in Chapter 7, section 2 when peasant witnesses were subjected to a culturally incomprehensible judicial inquiry—but relates to pauses that may lead the questioner to suspect whether something is being concealed, rather than recognizing the need for space for the witness to order their thoughts. Such silences, 'involving asymmetries of power in a confrontation between lawyer and witness,[8] pertain chiefly to perceived social status and expertise. They may be predictable, yet hardly deliberate or planned.

Linguistics highlights the rhetorical features of silence, and rhetoric has always had a political component, not only in its persuasive aims, but in its filtering impact on the salience of messages. But are there not other dimensions to studying linguistics that may well cause one to question what they have to do with the political? Several perspectives on silence relating to phonetic analysis—for example, the identification of ellipses or pauses—treat silences chiefly as mechanical or technical devices, measurable, and existing objectively in human utterances and their recording. Silence and sounds are then equally functional and requisite units of communication—units whose difference is obliterated through the coding assigned to them. Epistemologically, they share the empirical status of alternative, normal and unremarkable signs that make up segments of speech. Their investigation apparently cuts silence down to size, downgrading it as a source of mystique or power. Indirectly, it achieves the effect of neutralizing and routinizing the allure that other disciplines—indeed, other major branches of linguistics—tend to confer on silence. We must, however, take into account that neutralizing and routinizing always are a significant political element of control and ordering—a theme to be discussed below in Chapters 13 and 14.

In her study of shared silences dominating cultural narratives, Fivush notes—in a vein similar to Bourdieu's—that 'the canonical is the unmarked and therefore does not need to be voiced'. But she takes his analysis further. The normal, the expected, the unremarkable, confer a distinct politicization of their own: 'the freedom not to speak, to be silent, the freedom to assume shared knowledge that comes from a position of power', even if that freedom is only there for the observer to detect. Conformity to established and expected cultural narratives passes unnoticed. The need to speak, on the other hand, follows from the desire to justify a deviation from such norms.[9]

In spoken language the meaning of silences is more easily appreciated as interwoven with the verbal messages, even if punctuation conventions and the imagination of the reader assist in transporting some of those messages onto the printed page. Although most pauses in speech are minuscule interruptions, sometimes merely acting as 'a natural rest in the melody of speech',[10] a pause can distribute significance across an utterance and intensify its effect by eliciting changes in listeners' conduct and channelling their reactions in unpredictable as well as predictable ways. In texts the effect is slightly different. Brackets and new paragraphs intended to pace the narrative can double up by handing over the initiative to the readers, granting them the agency that enables the insertion of interpretative addendums, controlling the speed of absorption, or ignoring the proffered and directive gap at will. The stage is set for a silent and surreptitious power struggle between author and reader, opening a range of paths taken or not taken. In oral conversation, the hesitations and gaps in verbal exchanges—whether natural or planned—can assist in decoding a message,[11] for instance through weakening confidence in its contents. The ellipses commonly employed to denote an implicit omission in written texts—usually the creation of the recording writer, not the speaker—are a highly salient type of hiatus, indicating the ostensibly obvious, or clearing space for others to fill. Laurence remarks on nineteenth- and twentieth-century novels: 'Dashes and ellipses are a pattern in women's sentences that occurs again and again' in men's writing, obscuring women's silence by associating their speech with stammering and hesitancies.[12] But ellipses are a peculiarly ambiguous notation: they can be separators, interveners, absences, truncators, cultural demoters and political downgraders, or just random signs that signal nothingness. Or they can, like Hansel and Gretel's breadcrumbs, inexorably draw us into the next phrase in the sentence.

2 The Micro-structures of Silence

Communication theory has developed a corpus of analysis and theorizing with direct bearing on silence as a plentiful source of political thinking and carrier of political messages and instructions. To begin with, communication is an interactive social practice and both the sounds it transmits and the silences it contains should give political theorists much food for thought. Bruneau has notably, if implicitly, contributed to facilitating access to the politically communicative aspects of silence through the analysis of its patterns, rhythms, organization structure, and experience of time, and a detailed discussion of his arguments merits closer examination. One is the destruction of continuity through the alternation between speech and silence.[13] From the perspective of thinking politically, this amounts to the managed regulation of experienced reality. It encapsulates the normal expectation that social interaction is a disrupted flow of language, repeatedly requiring the listener to join the dots and impose an interpretative schema on the fragmented speech-acts of individuals. Expression then incorporates a navigation through hiatuses, and its reconfiguration is an exercise in piecing together and stabilizing information, engaging both reason and imagination. A variation on that theme is to converse with someone who occasionally swallows their words. Rather than asking frequently for a repetition of the unheard word—itself an interruption that elicits another kind of pause—the partner in conversation may bridge the gap silently though their imagination or guesswork, or simply settle for that disjointing absence.

Another of Bruneau's propositions is that both thought and speech reveal ways in which individuals control the time at their disposal.[14] By default, we may add, they also control the time of their interlocutors. Talking to a listener is always an intervention in their thoughts and deeds. Listening to, absorbing, and wading through silences has the same effect. To reiterate, those silences—their duration, their intensity, as well as their distribution across speech-acts—may have rhetorical intent but may also be unintentional and spontaneous, as interlocutors on both sides of the communicative relationship process information at different speeds. In certain speech situations, there is a correlation between the time span of a silence and the amplified intensity it conveys: silence then contains an inbuilt dynamism not as an internal attribute but as the product of human perception and feeling. Some of those silences will be mechanical—say, catching one's breath—but others, indicating miscomprehension, confusion, scruples, or embarrassment, as well as indications of deliberate displeasure, will contain considerable political significance. Both the listener and the scholar are pressed to decipher those fluctuating significances at relatively short notice within the diverse cultural contexts that trigger such pauses. For both, a rapid decontestation of contested silences poses the challenge of handling uncertainty. That interpretative decoding may be questionable, ranging as it will between plausibility and arbitrariness, but it is nonetheless at the very heart of the political quest for finality, for decisiveness and guidance in matters of common concern. Here silence offers notably fertile ground on which to address Ricoeur's 'surplus of meaning', and to tease out those silences harbouring particularly significant surpluses. They nestle in the rhythms and hesitations of mundane, everyday speech, touching on issues such as sincerity, complexity, articulateness, and assurance. Any surplus that silence engenders transfers the power of interpretation to the receiving interlocutor and offers a broad line-up of choice and opportunity.

A third thesis offered by Bruneau is the distinction between fast-time and slow-time silences. Fast-time silences occur in the immediate and automatic mental processing of speech. They are frequent but of low intensity. Slow-time silences invite semantic decoding and are primarily exercises in organizing stored information—say, by measuredly digesting it, or by laboriously trying to make sense of it. Tellingly, Bruneau sees slow-time silences as vertical and spatial movements through 'levels of experience and levels of memory',[15] although his description of those movements as willed needs to be qualified. It is not only that forgetting imposes unintentional silence on memory, but that our access to memory is far from measured, planned, or deliberate. The marshalling of time in the pacing of those pauses, or in the filtering and inadvertent (or uncontrollable) withholding of information, shapes the semantic field in which political identities are imagined and disputed. The art of communicating, or appearing not to communicate, impacts on the perception of dialogue, of human contact, and of the power exchanged between members of a community. Following on from Bruneau's analysis, it also imposes slow-time in such a way as to affect a listener's 'habitual level of tolerance for ambiguity'[16]—in other words, their patience, a vital component of thinking politically and of social coexistence.

Bruneau's fourth observation is his suggestive question: 'who will take the burden of speech?',[17] adapted from Susan Sontag's discussion of Bergman's film *Persona*. Sontag examines the relationship between two women—an actor who has stopped speaking and her nurse-companion—and observes how silence is transformed into a specific manifestation of control, in which saying nothing becomes 'a virtually inviolable position of strength' because the other person 'is charged with the burden of talking' and having to do the running in the relationship.[18] By singling out interactive silences that pile pressure on the interlocutors, it is possible to focus directly on the mute features of a power relationship that elicits discomfort, upset, or disdain, yet is compelling. That practice is located somewhere in the domain of who will blink first, except that (unlike in *Persona*) it is not necessarily a blatant exercise in manipulative control: Bruneau refers also to interactive silences 'used by many persons unintentionally or unconsciously'.[19] As so often is the case, silence can deliver a two-pronged product: first, the potentially permanent breakdown or stifling of a mutual set of social expectations and transactions, but—if not permanent—its subsequent precipitate ending through the psychologically or socially activated impulse to communicate. Silence is endowed with an active, loaded ingredient that may not only proceed through to its termination but is then carried on by its conversion into speech, as if in one continuous movement of time and affect.

The political features that percolate through the silences disclosed by linguistics and communication theory have their own distinct patterns and cadences that distinguish them from other disciplinary mindsets in which silence moulds and channels the political. Communicative silences may reveal boundaries of individual separation that are experienced as constraints on human interaction. Alternatively, they may emerge as statements of social interdependence (a linkage function[20]), hatched internally and surfacing in discourse—a testimony to recticular integration. In some instances, speech can morph into the shared silence of interlocuters. Thus, Baker recognizes the concealed finality drive of the political embedded in the prevailing power of a speaker when he observes that

> the underlying (i.e., unconscious and unpremeditated) aim of speech is not a continued flow of speech, but *silence*, for the state of complete equilibrium, marked by elimination of intrapersonal psychic tensions.... This silence is one in which arguments and contention, whether expressed or not, have vanished, to be replaced by understanding acceptance on the part of the hearer (or hearers) and satisfied contentment on the part of the speaker.[21]

Stilling the argumentative waters is a political achievement, even a victory.

Sontag adds pertinent reflections on the communicative constraints of silence in art: 'So far as he is serious, the artist is continually tempted to sever the dialogue he has with an audience. Silence is the furthest extension of that reluctance to communicate, that ambivalence about making contact with the audience which is a leading motif of modern art.' Whether this be a disinterest in anything but 'pure' art, or egocentric self-absorption, the implicit political act is bifold. First, it rejects the social preference to address individuals through the metier of 'artist', while concurrently craving the social recognition and ranking that most artists desire. Second, it exudes hostility to others: 'Most valuable art in our time has been experienced by audiences as a move into silence (or unintelligibility or invisibility or inaudibility); a dismantling of the artist's competence, his responsible sense of vocation—and therefore as an aggression against them.'[22]

Communication, then, takes us back to its inverse, solitude. Sontag's versions of solitude are different from the holistic solitudes of those who cherish communion with nature and the sense of feeling part of a non-human whole, as was the case with Kagge. They appear to have greater affinity with the renowned Trappist monk Thomas Merton, who wrote in his diary: 'In solitude, at last, I shall be just a person, no longer corrupted by being known.'[23] Denied solitude, people were subjected to a dehumanizing displacement in a metaphor suggesting political banishment: 'If man is constantly exiled from his own home, locked out of his own spiritual solitude, he ceases to be a true person.' The solitary life of monks, with its aspirational silence focused on 'transcendent and spiritual freedom', is integral, claims Merton, to any society that 'favours true liberty'.[24] And yet, silent communion is not always a monastic, or monadic, practice. It features in both religious and non-religious groups, and includes 'the action or fact of sharing or holding something in common with others; mutual participation'.[25] Merton expands on the communal union intertwined in a monastic silence: 'These two tendencies, the one solitary and the other social, always unite together in every form of organized monasticism'.[26] While Kagge and Merton appear to take part in a deeply political act of individual disengagement and atomization, of a retreat from the trappings of society, it is not bereft of a fellow-feeling with entities external to the self, carrying its own political implications.

The private mental happenings of silence prefigure and spill over into the publicness of speech, and that verbal creativity and contestation demands in turn refuge in the regenerative hiatuses that silence affords. The microstructure of linguistics and communication indicates how silence combines with speech to form a crude symmetry of tempo, a regulator of social contact. As noted in 'turn-taking' conversations, silences will signal the cessation of a segment that allows the interlocutor to pass the baton of speech onto another.[27] However, that often occurs not as relinquishing control but as a cooperative effort where the political features of integration, regulation, and sharing figure in what is a largely unplanned yet recognizable mix. The rules of etiquette—'do not interrupt'—superimpose themselves as an organizing mechanism. Notably, though, in a heated, angry, or emotional conservation—and when discursive courtesies are in short cultural supply—such finalizing silences are brushed aside, as one speaker cuts through another's speech and the silence needed for listening and for measured, paced, and reflective responses is curtailed, resulting in more chaotic exchanges.

Silence also offers access to resources stored in memory and retrieved unobserved, and at variable speeds, to be subsequently allocated to differentially ranked events and emotions, assigning them alterable weight and significance. Discussing historical narratives, Trouillot points to their 'unequal frequency of retrieval, unequal (factual) weight, indeed unequal degrees of factualness . . . some strings of fact are recalled with more empirical richness than others'.[28] Silent laboratories and testing grounds are fundamental to the regrouping of verbal messages and the redesigning of acts of attempted influence, whether successful or not, propelling and inducing shifts in conduct. In many cases, silence defuses and adjusts the tensions posed by spontaneity and indeterminacy and the instabilities they threaten, as well as the inventiveness they facilitate. The solidity and backbone supplied by the largely unspoken formal properties of linguistic intercourse can contribute to appreciating the thick political lode that runs through all human thought processes.

3 Uncommunicative Silences?

Many of these communicative markers have been highlighted in the dialogues Harold Pinter has given his characters. As Martin Esslin, who coined the term 'theatre of the absurd', observed in his now-classic study, Pinter 'transcribe[s] everyday conversation in all its repetitiveness, incoherence, and lack of logic or grammar . . . he registers the delayed-action effect resulting from differences in the speed of thinking between people . . . misunderstandings arising from inability to listen'.[29] Both acoustic and metaphorical silences tangle in fragmented exchanges. Indeed, they hardly are exchanges, as incomplete utterances pass each other like ships in the night, reinforcing individual isolation. Delayed action and reaction in conversation are a specific type of silence, of mismatched tempo and pace in which human coordination is disturbed—a political game of neutralizing or distorting mutual influence by calling purposive action into question.

Note, also, the political message in that literary genre: the communication—and its obliteration—engendered by semantic silence wields a haphazard, erratic, meaningless, unintentional, and uncontrollable force through words that can nevertheless have lethal effect. The power of randomness is paired with the powerlessness and futility of intention, will, and design; silence, once again, both is and is not. Ultimately speech is drained of significance and voice, as Beckett indicated in interview: 'The expression that there is nothing to express, nothing with which to express, nothing from which to express, no power to express, no desire to express, together with the obligation to express.'[30] Robinson put this nicely, observing that Beckett tended to regard 'our conversation quite empty of meaning, just words in fact, language on holiday'.[31] Even God, claims Lucky in his unexpectedly explosive tirade in *Waiting for Godot*, possesses 'divine aphasia'.[32] And Sontag observes of both Beckett and Kafka: 'The truth is that their language, when it is examined, discloses no more than what it literally means. The power of their language derives precisely from the fact that the meaning is so bare.'[33]

Beckett's silence-cum-nihilism is reinforced in *Waiting for Godot*, when silence is accompanied by an immobility found also in Tacita Dean's creative rendering, but with opposite effect. Through Dean's intrigued gaze and curiosity Cunningham's immobility exudes life and energy, while Beckett's protagonists have a strong whiff of death about them, of *nature morte*. Estragon's opening line, having failed to take off his boot, is 'nothing can be done'. The play ends with Vladimir: '"Well? Shall we go?" Estragon: "Yes, let's go." *They do not move.*'[34] And back to *The Unnamable*, to the unending turmoil of movement, stasis, silence, and the anarchic collapse of order, sequence, and categories:

> I'll wake, in the silence, and never sleep again, it will be I, or dream, dream again, dream of a silence, a dream silence, full of murmurs, I don't know, that's all words, never wake, all words, there's nothing else, you must go on, that's all I know ... it will be the silence, where I am, I don't know, I'll never know, in the silence you don't know, you must go on, I can't go on, I'll go on.[35]

Rather than inferring from this that the breakdown of communication is complete, there is no communication to begin with. It resembles the frantic running of a mouse around a maze, back to the point from whence it came—the silence of futility.

Understandably, silences have greater immediate force in a verbal exchange than on the written page. As an appendage to this section, Pinter's comments on his own work sarcastically offset the linguistic communicative theories that examine annotation techniques to denote silences. In a highly entertaining account, he offered this tongue-in-cheek riposte to over-exacting critics: 'In *The Birthday Party* I employed a certain amount of dashes in the text, between phrases. In *The Caretaker* I cut out the dashes and used dots instead. ... The fact that in neither case could you hear the dots and dashes in the performance is beside the point. You can't fool the critics for long. They can tell a dot from a dash a mile off, even if they can hear neither.'[36] Those dots and dashes, needless to say, are signs of separation. There is no joining of the dots here. Their aggregate, or even their linear sequence, points to no form or shape. They signify silence as disconnected, discontinuous, and non-organic.[37]

Uncommunicative silence does not add up to a whole: it is isolated from its own several component units, nor does it flow from the speech it mechanically interrupts. The holistic structure of silence as conveyed through literature, prayer, or the wilderness possesses powerful containing and immersing attributes. It is countered by the disjointed, staccato accumulation of grouped silences signifying moments in a disturbed and disturbing narrative, discarding the qualities of an integrated phenomenon. Its fracturing power lies in its efficacious undermining of tranquillity. In both cases, the impact on the engrossed listener or reader is to tailor contrasting reactions to the practices and rhythms they bear. Pinteresque silences can signal dramatic menace and design, and their relation to speech possesses a peculiar complexity. There is an arbitrary, seemingly nonchalant aspect of the way they are worked into the text—perhaps, on reflection, complementing the casualness of the violence they herald. Generally speaking, the engineering of readers' participation in the interpretation and coding of silence—a particular hallmark of Virginia Woolf's writings[38]—allocates reserved spaces for their powers of imagination and invention. That is doubly political: in its fostering of an alliance between author and reader, whether supportive or hostile, and in securing the readers' freedom to impress themselves on the text.

One method of distinguishing between silence and speech has been developed within the analytical formalities of markedness theory. Unlike Fivush's socio-cultural focus on silent, unremarkable conformity, its adherents label silence as the marked, unusual, 'functionally deficient' member of the pairing ('the prototypical non-communicator') and speech as the unmarked, 'obvious', 'normal' one. Silence then becomes 'the overall least formally complex communicative entity'.[39] True, in many ways silence is the more constrained term of the pair—it does not refer to a meaningful locutionary utterance, nor does it offer a metalingual route to query the structure of language. But the asymmetric distinction endorsed by that method, and the sterility of its notation, stand in stark juxtaposition to artistic, literary, and philosophical schemata. They are at least partially overshadowed by the remarkable semantic illocutionary force silence wields—the force that is exerted in and through an utterance or, in this case, a non-utterance—and one laden with its own sets of complexity. The theatre of the absurd emphatically puts silence, not speech, in the driving seat.

The political implications of the juxtaposition are clearly discernible. The linguistic perspective of markedness theory is primarily concerned with the forms and sequences of speech segments. It prioritizes speech over silence as the dominant pairing—silence being ranked lower, as exceptional or 'abnormal'; indeed, as formless. But when we move to the semantic properties of communication, as displayed in the theatre of the absurd literature, silence is given at least equal pegging with speech, being inextricably intermeshed with it. Pinter's plays, notably, apportion considerable illocutionary force to silence or, more specifically, to the frequent occurrence of silences that stochastically pepper his characters' speech, dialectically alongside the words that punctuate them. As Sontag notes more generally, 'Everyone has experienced how, when punctuated by long silences, words weigh more; they become almost palpable.'[40]

For Pérez, however, there is a difference between punctuation and printed spaces: 'the pauses indicated by punctuation constitute minimal intervals of "background" stillness; they are not perceived as silence per se. Greater duration is necessary for silence to be perceived.' By contrast, the conventions of the printed page are replete with silences that have a role quite different from those discharged by punctuation. As she observes, factoring in one of their most visible features: 'The space between printed words graphically recognizes those minimal silences which separate the spoken word, conferring and maintaining individuality.'[41]

And yet, to return to Tacita Dean filming Merce Cunningham, her use of a metronome confers measured precision and artificiality on silence, resonating with the technical, grammatical analysis of structure that can be associated with socio-linguistics. Pinter, to the contrary, abandons any show of formalism in his wonderfully pitched ear for replicating the ordinary speech patterns of everyday life and everyday people, even if in an oft-exaggerated manner. The faltering, fragile, and splintered conversations he brings to life disclose silence in a rough colloquial mode, far removed from the elevated silences that are regarded as pinnacles of spiritual endeavour, or the honed and stylized silences of cultured conversation. When sentences peter out, the space they were intended to occupy—and agonizingly or frustratingly do not—is overrun not by a lack or by a potential for more words but by a new finality of verbal detritus dissolving into existential inconclusiveness or the repetition of the banal. In this instance, as in countless others, politics has its mechanics and its organics, its aristocracies and demotics, its tight-lipped control and its shambolic disintegration, and silences are the trusted travel companions that adapt, terrain by terrain, to its paths, trails, and impasses, carrying with them the key to the diverse forms and deformations of thinking in a social setting.

Notes

1 R. P. Weller, 'Salvaging Silence: Exile, Death and the Anthropology of the Unknowable', *Anthropology of This Century*, issue 19 (2017), pp. 12–13.
2 F. de Saussure, *Course in General Linguistics* (London: Duckworth, 1983).
3 Picard, *The World of Silence*, p. 16.
4 W. Chafe, 'Some Reasons for Hesitating', in Tannen and Saville-Troika, *Perspectives on Silence*, pp. 77–89 at p. 78.
5 P. R. Hawkins, 'The Syntactic Location of Hesitation Pauses', *Language and Speech* 14 (1971), pp. 277–288.
6 See C. Trimboli and M. B. Walker, 'Switching Pauses in Cooperative and Competitive Conversations', *Journal of Experimental Social Psychology* 20 (1984), pp. 297–311; H. Mori, 'An Analysis of Switching Pause Duration as a Paralinguistic Feature in Expressive Dialogues', *Acoustical Science and Technology* 30/5 (2009), pp. 376–378.
7 E. Goffman, *Interaction Ritual* (New York: Pantheon, 1967), p. 36.
8 A. G. Walker, 'The Two Faces of Silence: The Effect of Witness Hesitancy on Lawyers' Impressions', in Tannen and Saville-Troika, *Perspectives on Silence*, pp. 55–75.

9 R. Fivush, 'Speaking Silence: The Social Construction of Silence in Autobiographical and Cultural Narratives', *Memory* 18/2 (2010), pp. 88–98 at p. 94. On markedness see later in this chapter.
10 Quoted in Ephratt, *The Functions of Silence*, p. 1927.
11 Bruneau, 'Communicative Silences', p. 20.
12 Laurence, *The Reading of Silence*, p. 85.
13 Bruneau, 'Communicative Silences', p. 18.
14 Ibid., pp. 19, 21.
15 Ibid., p. 26.
16 Ibid., p. 27.
17 Ibid., p. 28.
18 Sontag, 'The Aesthetics of Silence', p. 13.
19 Bruneau, 'Communicative Silences', p. 31.
20 J. Vernon Jensen, 'Communicative Functions of Silence', *ETC: A Review of General Semantics* 30 (1973), p. 249.
21 S. J. Baker, 'The Theory of Silences', *Journal of General Psychology* 53 (1955), pp. 145–167 at p. 161.
22 Sontag, 'The Aesthetics of Silence', pp. 3–4.
23 Quoted in J. Brox, *Silence: A Social History of One of the Least Understood Elements of Our Lives* (Boston, MA, and New York: Houghton Mifflin Harcourt, 2019), p. 212.
24 T. Merton, *The Silent Life* (Dublin: Clonmore & Reynolds, 1957), pp. 125, 132.
25 *OED* online (accessed 13 November 2017).
26 Merton, *The Silent Life*, p. 50.
27 Ephratt, *The Functions of Silence*, pp. 1919, 1926.
28 Trouillot, *Silencing the Past*, pp. 53–54.
29 M. Esslin, *The Theatre of the Absurd* (New York: Doubleday & Co., 1961), pp. 206–207.
30 S. Beckett, *Proust, and Three Dialogues with Georges Duthuit* (London: John Calder, 1965), p. 103.
31 C. J. Bradbury Robinson, 'A Way with Words: Paradox, Silence, and Samuel Beckett', *Cambridge Quarterly* 5/3 (1971), pp. 249–264 at p. 250.
32 Beckett, *Waiting for Godot*, p. 43.
33 Sontag, 'The Aesthetics of Silence', p. 25.
34 Beckett, *Waiting for Godot*, pp. 9, 94.
35 Beckett, *The Unnamable*, p. 134.
36 H. Pinter, 'Writing for the Theatre', in H. Pinter (ed.), *Various Voices: Prose, Poetry, Politics 1948–2005* (London: Faber & Faber, 2005), p. 20.
37 But for a suggestive distinction between dots as a form of suspension and dashes as a device for filling in by the reader with an intimation of haste, see Laurence, *The Reading of Silence*, pp. 107–110.
38 Ibid., p. 217.
39 Sobkowiak, 'Silence and Markedness Theory', pp. 46, 53, 55.
40 Sontag, 'The Aesthetics of Silence', p. 16.
41 Pérez, 'Rhetoric of Silence', pp. 108–109.

PART II
DECODING AND INVESTIGATING
Silences in the Lived World

While silences may unquestionably be absences, there is no absence of silences in the socio-political sphere. Silences may be central to a discourse or event—becoming their defining *raison d'être* or their modus operandi—or peripheral and incidental. Over time, their social distribution will wax and wane, vacating some territory while gaining new footholds, but they are always to be found in human conduct and thought-practices. Part II explores the particular ways in which issues that are experienced and lived through, such as tacit consent, silences of the state, arguments for non-duality, and narrative silences, alongside changing research proclivities, impact on the options available to societies and their ideologies. The lived world is interpreted here to comprise concrete behaviours and customs as well as intellectual and metaphysical paradigms held and commended by specific belief communities and philosophical schools.

In all those circumstances, theologies, philosophies, mysticisms, dramatizations, and temporalities have moulded and shaped the family of silences. Silence is endowed with prominent dynamic aspects, and although some silences prevent change, they are more likely to generate various kinds of momentum, disruptive or stabilizing. That activating or intervening capacity filters through diverse sets of cultural frameworks, through political constraints or establishing hindrances, as well as through opening up major spaces for ambiguities and routes that initiate political inventiveness and imagination. Consequently, silences are embedded not just in a plurality of political processes, but in all of them. They shake up and reconfigure thought, expression, and conduct in ways that are hugely significant. Operating at many social levels and spaces, their disruptive force may be direct, but they are also to be found in places where vagueness rules the roost or crises abound. Under those circumstances, silences become responding, even transformative, mechanisms to cope with political upheavals, failures, vacuums, breakdowns, or indeterminacies, serving as sifters, shock-absorbers, and regenerators. Considerations such as these assist in shifting the relocation of the entire subject of silence to a position more proximate to the principal concerns of scholars of political thought and discourse.

Cutting across disciplines and comparing cultural practices casts further light on the extraordinary versatility of silence in shaping the concrete social and political worlds we inhabit, and this book merely offers tentative forays into that extensive realm. A sub-specialization of 'comparative silences' may well lurk around the corner, awaiting a further raft of questions: Are there any detectable patterns about the clusters and correlations that silences form? To which kinds of silence are some societies more susceptible than others? Under which circumstances do certain silences become weighty yet remain unacknowledged? Which silences have an effect on various aspects of the democratic process?—a question not only of interest to political and ethical philosophers, but located within the domain of ideology studies. Those are questions to keep in view in the course of furthering our acquaintance with this book's concerns.

9
The Temporalities of Silence: Theology, History, Anthropology

This chapter selects some modes of processing silences evident in the imaginative and cultural traditions spread over the field of human creativity. It explores several prominent group practices and frameworks that draw out and consolidate aspects of the concept of silence and their political undercurrents analysed in Part I, demonstrating—through its sustained engagement with temporality—how silence is integrated into the fabric of human inventiveness and its tangible social practices, as well as its learned academic disciplines.

1 Theological and Philosophical Silences

The relationship of silence to temporality is especially prominent in two spheres: religious beliefs and historical narratives. Silence has a pivotal ontological role to play both in theology as a discipline and in many varieties of religious thought, as a defining bookending of human existence, with particular emphasis on beginnings associated with the drama of creation, and to a lesser extent incorporating a view on endings. Conceptualizations of history have seen a move from macro-temporalities to micro-temporalities. Former foci on grand theory, worldviews, ideas of monolinear progress, and constructs in which time is an undifferentiated phenomenon that opens and closes a cosmic or historical trajectory have been largely replaced by a detailed tracing of its disjointed and continual vagaries. Cutting silence down to size has been greatly abetted by the recent focus on handling time on smaller scales. It hardly needs stating that both the grand, seemingly cosmic silence and the silence that displaces or interrupts narratives and accounts of communal life are of human origin. The one is confidently broadcast by religions and philosophies that call forth silence's monumental centrality. The other is audible only through the combined perspectives of knowledgeable observers who frequently deplore—from their diverse standpoints—the

Concealed Silences and Inaudible Voices in Political Thinking. Michael Freeden, Oxford University Press.
© Michael Freeden (2022). DOI: 10.1093/oso/9780198833512.003.0011

historical silences they detect as distorting intrusions on social and cultural truths.

It was noted in Chapter 4 that, prior to creation, silence itself was thought to be absent—as might be inferred from the biblical expression 'without form and void'.[1] That is a translation, deriving in part from the Greek Septuagint and found in the King James Version, of the Hebrew *tohu va bohu*, signifying emptiness and barrenness. But the Hebrew phrase is also associated with another cluster of terms revolving around chaos and confusion—signifiers of disorder rather than absence. If one employs interpretative licence to integrate the two Hebrew senses, there is a movement from non-speech to speech and from non-silence to silence—in both cases a transition towards an orderly world. In that movement, silence too exhibits the quality of possessing its own rudimentary, underlying, order. That is not the same as claiming that silence is necessarily patterned—though, as we have seen, it may be in some of its forms. The claim, rather, is that the post-creation silence is *ex definitio* less impenetrable than the initial *tohu va bohu*. We know that, when deliberately designed and implemented, there is a very strong connection between order and silence in a range of social practices, past and present. But even when silence in the world might still seem random and disjointed, its disruptive quality always slots into intervals found in sequences of sound, speech, and noise. By dint of such insertions or interruptions silence acquires its own, second-order, patterning.

Christianity—particularly in the apocalyptic tradition—reinforces the idea of a silence that envelops the beginning and end of human time, tied to Godly creation. In the early Christian tradition, 'the unformed world before creation was silent' but the primeval silence of the beginning ultimately re-emerges as a transitional hiatus in the movement towards God's final judgement, at which point silences come to an end.[2] That judgement sheds further light on political finality: namely, its 'Godly' arrogation of closure and its conclusive determination of what cannot be denied. The secular political concept of sovereignty, with its defining feature of a decision-making process where 'the buck stops', mirrors the religious attribution of finality: the locking in of judgement through God's words and deeds.[3] Silence can thus not only be a vehicle of transformation, but precede it, heralding and heightening the enormity of the transformative judgement, for good or bad, with respect to the very essence of being human—literally the ultimate political decision. Because the political entails control over a beginning (as distinct from *the* beginning), and because sovereignty is control not only over space but over time, ethereal silence possesses both an apolitical and a political dimension. It is simultaneously the converse of the political—a non-happening—while signalling that the encircling of time between two eternities is a delimited, directed, and profoundly political phenomenon.

The stillness–silence conjunction discussed in Chapter 4 contains similarities to theological interpretations. In Barthes' hands, the pre- and post-frames of existence indicate its apolitical quality. He interprets stillness as extra-wordly, unplaceable, and atemporal, to be revered as ineffable and imponderably divine or mystical. Barthes read the ontology of the Greek poet and philosopher Parmenides to signify silence as encircling discourse, preceding and following it. It is 'the silent knowledge of the ineffable absolute'.[4] Thus, he too depicts silence as elemental and originary. Politics intervenes by breaking the silence, by overriding that absolute, and by shrinking the world to a new, finite, quasi-absolute directed at the affairs of men and women. That requires imposing a beginning on a non-beginning, enunciating the first as well as the final word, dictated through the fiat of the political as the monopolizer, instigator, and ultimate decider when conflicts and competitions over authority emerge from any corner of social life and thought. Through that process, the emergence of time immediately and *ipso facto* becomes political time: the sequential *shaping* and *ordering* of time is a quintessential political process.

Notwithstanding the idea of a quasi-theological fore-and-after silence being also central to several philosophical ontological positions, the latter can invest silence not only with order but with the power to mould and change—a more immediate political attribute. To illustrate, the philosopher Bernard Dauenhauer conceives of silence as an originary and fundamental driving force in relation to discourse—both launching and ending it—as well as pervading discourse at every juncture. He outlines a grand temporal ontological sweep with Hegelian undertones, in which even pre- and post-discursive silence are not bereft of meaning in the world but display an energetic dynamic. Dauenhauer writes:

> The multiple ways in which silence appears in conjunction with discourse allows the identification of three irreducible moments or parts in the temporal structure of silence. First, silence in all of its aspects originates or opens the way for something. It is a point of departure for the entire domain of discourse. But silence does not merely open the way for this domain as a whole. Silence, by its second moment, spreads out the domain by making possible the shifts from shape to shape and from level to level within the domain of discourse. Its second moment, in a variety of ways, preserves the movement within discourse which was inaugurated by virtue of silence's first moment. Finally, by virtue of its third moment, silence not merely closes off discourse but turns discourse in its complexity back

> upon its point of departure. That is, silence, precisely in its closing off of discourse, establishes the unity of the domain of discourse taken as a whole. . . . Discourse arises within the broad domain of experience by virtue of silence. . . . In its unfolding, in turn, discourse makes it possible for silence to appear as senseful.[5]

The notion 'In the beginning was the word' therefore refers not to the foundation of what was and can be, to a verbal Big Bang, but to a logocentric, political ordering of time. That is circumscribed by signalling a specific kind of order, inasmuch as that word is initially introduced through Godly will, not human verbalization, and it is confronted by its counterpart—an earthly silence. Earthly silence is central to most religious outlooks, but it highlights the inevitability of a ranking order in those religions that subscribe to a single, often all-powerful deity. It terminates consequent on God's utterances that launch and enable logos, and human beings capable of logos.

However, the deeply ingrained permanence that silence in the world appears to possess—be it in the shape of the stillness of wilderness, or of a solitude bereft of human and animal presence—begins to be replaced by a series of timebound and bracketed silences-cum-gaps. While the existential, macro-silences have profound philosophical and metaphysical significance that affect the entire category of the political, those time-bound micro-silences do much of their hard political work in the here and now. We already know that, when deliberately designed and implemented, there is a very strong connection between order and silence in a range of social practices, past and present. Prisons, monasteries, and the military rely on enforced periods of silence for disciplinary purposes or for carving out times for isolation or introspection as extreme forms of control.[6] Yet even without such regimenting intent, the silences built into human existence and into naturally occurring discourse are no less pivotal in the sporadic and piecemeal managing, separating, intimating, anticipating, and apportioning of thought and action, all distinct features that address in turn many core political properties.

The uneven distribution of silence in diverse cultural-religious conventions and rituals is telling as well. Individual silences or collective silences are matched with different occasions. In regular religious practices, silence is maintained, among others, when devotion materializes in religious ceremonies and edifices. Reverence and wonder are often translated into respectful silence—a voluntary subservience that, as with so many other human activities, is 'automatically' internalized and triggered by context and event: entering most houses of worship is accompanied by that expectation. Quiet contemplation in prayer is an instance of private religious silence, whereas monastic silence is, in addition, a mixture of self-imposed group discipline and hierarchical rule abiding. Indeed, for Thomas Merton such silences can contain, deflect, and stabilize, or perhaps neutralize, the irresolvable contradictions that constantly swell around thought and deed.[7] In Jewish and Christian group prayer in formal settings, speech and silence among the congregation and the officiators generally alternate in patterned sequences, necessitating cooperation as well as leadership, and the observance of unalterable procedures and performances. As with Buddhism, the purity of human spirituality is typically distilled in silences. Silence as awe, silence as turn taking, silence as communion, and silence as deference all contribute to demarcating social roles, assuring stability, continuity, and room for a partial retreat from everyday life, combining temporal and spatial categories. These are predominantly the positioning silences referred to in Chapter 3.

2 The Silences of History

Historical temporalities possess their own forms of complexity. They consciously or surreptitiously regulate the perceptions of social life, filtering and clustering particular amalgams of socio-political ideas and infusing them with meaning—the product of collective and contending human actions and traditions, not a reified element of the world. Historical narratives stitch together the hollows and breaks in their subject-matter, sometimes patching events and ideas onto each other in quasi-random fashion. Below that suturing operation, silences criss-cross each other, sometimes at different points of the same chains of events referred to, each laid out in parallel patterns: silences about origins, about allotting significance to various social groups, about victories and defeats. Those micro-temporalities are not players on the cosmic scene. But neither are they what the French philosopher Gilles Deleuze called 'little gaps of solitude and silence' in conversation, fashioned through the exclusion or muting of what the participant-narrator holds to be irrelevant or subversive.[8]

Rather, those gaps all have the same objective: enabling things worth saying to emerge, usually through the eyes of the astute and eccentric participant, or the discerning and detached onlooker. What transpires is a multiplicity of continuous, shifting, and interwoven temporalities of silence that accompany social life on ascending, descending, interrupting, and clashing tracks, abandoning the deep veneration and power assigned to the theological macro-silences as a primordial, dynamic, and largely linear force. The same—as we shall see in Chapter 14—applies to ideologies: they not only interpret silences; they are replete with silences that gloss over the contingencies of their narratives and mapping roles, sidestepping the interruptions inflicted on them by rival versions. In both cases, those assembled 'continuities' are often processed by those living through them as grand, macro-temporalities in their own right. By stapling disjoined and curtailed developments to one another through strategies of simulated continuity, often filled in with pieces of fabrication or legend, such discourses erase the unknown or the unspoken and facilitate the quasi-unintentional silencing of alternative stories, sacrificed to ensure the preserving of an imaginary line whose tracing is itself a major ideological practice.[9]

The question hanging in the air is this: is disguising the seams merely the blurring of specific transitional moments or, more radically, is it unfeasible to factor in the very possibility of disjuncture? The latter route would not be a case of silenced silences (silences about change or continuity) but an instance of silencing the very existence of silencing practices themselves—a process noted in Part I to which we now turn in concrete form.

Fictions, myths, and imaginaries are of course evidence of a way of cultural thinking, and when they are brushed aside in the cause of scientific empiricism and historical 'accuracy'—themselves forms of cultural thinking, of course—their loss enshrines another kind of silencing, that of the socially valuable as distinct from the scholarly correct. These silences may commence as individual manipulations and fantasies, but they are soon swallowed up in wider submerged beliefs held by groups. And let us be clear here: that is not just a question of eliminating, or skipping over, the histories of black people, or women, or the vanquished, or multiple sexualities. *Any* account of human histories is an act of silencing—through prioritizing and ranking, through forgetfulness or chance misplacement, through embarrassment or pride, whether intentional or unnoticed. Our confrontations with silence are never merely simple or direct, even if they are often experienced as such.

Chapter 5 alluded to sociological interpretations of silence emanating from structural maldistributions of power and voice, maldistributions that marginalize and even eliminate certain social groups and personal identities. But bringing in temporality as a constant process of rearranging voices—a process that renders some voices pronounced, others masked, and others vanished—produces a different terrain for silences. This terrain is revealed as acutely affecting language and action and as profoundly normal. That historicity extends beyond just focusing on the mutating power structures within the volatile balance of a society through the spectacles of sociology, important as they are. Nor does it rely on the continuous, closed, and solid hold of a tradition-pervaded habitus such as Bourdieu's. Instead, it examines the drawn-out, fluctuating, and disrupted fortunes of flowing and ebbing tides in the life of a nation, culture, or ethnic group, from which in the long run there is no escape, nor need there be.

Assume that we wish to track the lifespan of a particular manifestation of silence as it treads a path in the social world. If the phenomenon we call silence is a human construct, as suggested at the beginning of this book, on which defining milestones on that route ought we—as students of silence—to focus? Where and when does silence come into being as a socially remarkable or significant occurrence? We might do well to revisit Michel-Rolph Trouillot from whose pen came one of the most instructive and valuable analyses of the historical manifestations of silence. Trouillot argued that 'silences enter the process of historical production at four crucial moments: the moment of fact creation (the making of *sources*); the moment of fact assembly (the making of *archives*); the moment of fact retrieval (the making of *narratives*); and the moment of retrospective significance (the making of *history* in the final instance)'.[10]

Expanding the vista of Trouillot's historical trajectory, it reveals how human intervention generates silences by the very method of striving to eliminate them. This is not a case of causing or identifying an absence, of absconding with an idea or event and removing it from a larger totality—as so many theories of silence contend—but of producing a presence whose appearance on the stage replaces, and thus stifles, the existence of other, parallel or alternative, happenings, shrinking a totality into a series of particularities. Trouillot elaborated:

> theories of history rarely examine in detail the concrete production of specific narratives. Narratives are occasionally evoked as illustrations or, at best, deciphered as texts, but the process of their production rarely constitutes the object of study ... professional historians alone do not set the narrative framework into which their stories fit. Most often, someone else has already entered the scene and set the cycle of silences.

And most often, we may add, the process is that of removal, discussed in Chapter 5. In his study of Christopher Columbus and the Americas, Trouillot notes that divergent 'appropriations of Columbus's persona' cause silences to 'appear in the interstices of the conflicts between previous interpreters. The production of a historical narrative cannot be studied, therefore, through a mere chronology of its silences.' The danger is that 'chronology replaces process' and the assembling of linear continuity effaces context.[11] Furthermore, 'any historical narrative is a particular bundle of silences'.[12] Hence, as silences are weighted unequally, they cannot be addressed as if they were equivalent.

Trouillot's findings about Haiti underline how revisiting sources and evidence results in a ceaseless temporal redistribution of silences, as one selective arrangement of facts and construals queues up to replace another, and new gaps and concealments overrun porous narratives. The hidden shapes below the surface of the water, writes Winter, 'cannot simply be ignored because they are concealed at some moments and revealed at others'.[13] Trouillot notes of the Haitian revolution at the turn of the eighteenth and nineteenth centuries that it was 'unspoken among the slaves themselves ... the Revolution was not preceded or even accompanied by an explicit intellectual discourse', not only because most slaves were illiterate but because 'the claims of the revolution were indeed too radical to be formulated in advance of its deeds'[14]—they were at the time unconceptualizable. When silence jostles with silence under the gaze of changing horizons, the course of human history serves as a salient reminder that silence is no one thing. Important or trivial, durable or ephemeral, silences may be absences to be plugged and then reintroduced in a change of scholarly fortune, or they may be lacks awaiting completion, only to be chipped away at later. The unrealizable idea, say, of human equality that has motivated many reformers emerges periodically from the dark, only to be resubmerged by exposing it as a moth-eaten mantle through which emptiness gapes.

As is so often the case, later political systems are peppered with physical evidence of cultures swallowed up by their successors. Residual stories allowed to decay await the curiosity, sharpness, and epistemological conversions required to detect the many clues they leave behind. Like Edgar Allan Poe's purloined letter, they lie in full but frequently unrecognized sight, similarly to the archaeological ruins people walk by without noticing, and without registering the messages the stones divulge to those who can listen. There is now a rich literature on contested cultural heritage,[15] whether concerning the selective methods of historical display in museums or the reclaiming of lost or sidelined national-religious roots of major edifices, of which the cathedral-mosque Mezquito in Cordoba is a remarkable example. Its stratigraphy peels off layers of competing Christian and Muslim claims to the historical and religious ownership of the site, exemplified in the physical restructuring of the building from a Roman temple, later Visigoth church, then Muslim mosque, and finally Christian cathedral.[16] Each transformation wholly or partially silenced the voices and rituals of its predecessors; each had a narrative harking back to its 'original' status, eradicating the others.

Trouillot's concerns have resonance in many other circumstances. What he wrote of Haiti can apply anywhere: 'If some events cannot be accepted even as they occur, how can they be assessed later? ... can historical narratives convey plots that are unthinkable within the world in which these narratives take place? How does one write a history of the impossible?'[17] Archaeological finds, such as Arthur Evans' in Crete, can rescue an entire civilization from obscurity even when evidence has been tampered with or erroneously reconstructed, so that the stories nourished on a particular exercise of fantasy and imagination that suits the agenda of storytellers disguise the silences that still persevere. Evans' reinvention of Knossos through the modernism and ideological rifts of the early twentieth century superimposed a peaceful and feminist culture, with implicit lessons for contemporary Europe, on a period that was no stranger to warmongering. In Cathy Gere's interpretation, 'horror at the aftermath of the ignominious war that won Crete her independence caused Evans to turn his back on this evidence for Minoan belligerence and to reconstruct their world as a pacifist paradise'.[18] A silence that might be thought to be the deliberate, capricious licence of a historian wielding his scholarly authority becomes also the wishful thinking of an individual through which the collective hankerings of a later age are projected.

The renaming of several African and Asian states in recent decades is an attempt by their governments to extricate themselves from the dense fog of their colonial pasts and to unsilence their suppressed colonial 'pre-history'—itself a biased and distorting term. That 'pre-history' eliminates the crucial and multiple continuities of people and processes within those societies, while concurrently suggesting a past both undifferentiated and irrelevant, just marking time for the arrival of their externally imposed and redemptive Year One. Those new temporal frameworks magnify current perspectives out of proportion rather than exposing them in the main as brief (if often crushing) interventions in a society's timeline.

3 Tangled Linearities

Constructing narratives laces together sundry forms of human experience, whether recorded or imagined. Writing from the perspective of a literary critic, George Steiner's contemplation of the ineffable manner in which narrative structure wields its own adaptive force reinforces the departure from linearity. The truth, he contends, 'need not conform to the naïve logic and linear conception of time implicit in syntax. In ultimate truth, past, present, and future are comprised simultaneously. It is the temporal structure of language that keeps them artificially distinct.'[19] Linearity, of course, is not erased in personal experience. Maitland observes that her own subjection to silent solitude induced the loss of 'a sense of time passing' but valued that as a positive thing, as long as it is accompanied by the knowledge that the silence is bounded; i.e., that linearity will resume.[20]

Fivush adds a further element: biographical narratives, or what she terms life-scripts, of cultural groups become layered one over another. Alongside an overarching story about cultural and historical identity, minor divergent narratives pick holes in the master narrative and eliminate segments of it, or are themselves silenced. That occurs not because they are suppressed but because they flounder under the weight of the more established histories: 'in privileging certain aspects or evaluations of the narratives, other aspects or evaluations become more and more difficult to recall over time, and thus become more and more likely to remain silenced'.[21] An account of first-generation Mizrahi women who immigrated to Israel from Arab countries dwells on the reaction of a woman asking to tell her life story: 'My head is empty . . . because it is so full, it is empty.' The researchers comment on those 'subjects whose lives do not comply with centrist model[s] of the "proper" way of living': 'There is something that makes her many memories a burden and renders her voiceless, feeling empty in the head. Rivka lacks the language, the model that can make her life events communicable, meaningful to her listeners.'[22] Lack rather than absence is the operative term here.

It is not uncommon for the silences of 'migrants' versus natives to resonate deeply: first-generation immigrants are less likely to express their voices collectively and publicly as they gauge the measure of their new social positions and gain confidence in their switched country of residence. Equally, ethnic and racial groups may maintain silence through fear, alienation, unfamiliarity, or social introversion. Some of the most significant criteria of its distribution may be observed across divides of gender or of age. Women have frequently been socialized to be less assertive and vocal than men, and many have in addition been socialized to maintain low visibility outside the family or household. Their silences, especially as a group characteristic, are particularly revealing, implying status differences, educational practices affecting respect and manageability, and insufficient allocation of resources required for self-expression and development.[23]

Both in the spontaneous grass-roots telling of collective stories and in their professional recounting, gaps, overlaps, hues, and shadows weave a host of alternative patterns for the cloths that deck out the terrain. Importantly, none of this implies deliberate silencing. McNay notes, 'narrative is regarded not as determining but as generative of a form of self-identity which itself is neither freely willed nor externally imposed'.[24] As in the micro-analysis of ideologies discussed in Chapter 14, the small print holds circumvented data that is barely discernible in the supervening palimpsests that may originate from any quarter. A collection of narrative silences requires an array of disciplinary angles and scholarly apparatuses to do it justice, and its political ingredients call for an additional unravelling of the political. Narratives burying conflicts of authority, eliciting legitimacy, or implying benevolent futures surge in and out of view.

Those issues are also evident in anthropological studies. Substantively, anthropological knowledge provides an unlimited and fecund source of information about the distribution of silences in very diverse societies and their relation to social beliefs and practices. For the participants, as one scholarly work observes, silence may 'become so fragmented that either the meaning of the silence disappears altogether or it becomes deeply ingrained as a mode of thinking'.[25] Indigenous Aborigines are guided by cultural protocols in which communication with non-Aborigines as well as with some other Aborigines is characterized by silences. Those may signify ignorance of other mindsets, misunderstandings, or mistrust, including 'poison cousin' relationships, when people 'can't even look at or sit in the same car or room with one another'.[26] Culturally induced discomfort divides and segments people, and the stock-in-trade reaction is frequently a shrinking away from contact through silence. By acting as the outward manifestation of shutting up shop, silence becomes a political happening: a classifier, funnel, hindrance to, or neutralizer of, human relationships. Silence acts here not only as a segregator but as a built-in structural deflector of tensions and conflict applied to very specific situations and encounters. It is regulated not by reflective personal deliberation but by group conventions that secure a political order revolving around place, decorum, distance, and above all deep beliefs about nature and human life.

Silences within Aboriginal societies are accompanied at a more submerged level by silences engendered by the unequal meeting of settler and indigenous cultures. In his inquiry into the colonization of indigenous peoples in Australia, Paul Patton observes that even when colonization may occur in a 'noisy, Earth-shattering' manner, 'this does not exclude the possibility that it is also an ongoing, silent event. Even once it has been achieved, it continues to operate inaudibly, often in ways that pass unnoticed to those not directly affected.' But here too the linearity is fractured. In historical moments when legal decisions concerning the relations between indigenous and non-indigenous Australians are taken, they involve 'a return to earlier events of colonization, collapsing elements of the colonial past into the present and making these parts of the ongoing elaboration of the future'.[27] These fluid and countervailing flows of temporality are silent, little-recognized processes that simultaneously hold numerous perspectives and interpretations. Linearity operates as a form of silencing through contorting the complexity of lived reality, superimposing sequences on familiar time that are unrepresentative of human experience, memory, and grasp.

Nonetheless, linearity perseveres as the dominant historical frame. Despite the temporal complexity of lived experience in reshuffling and jumbling up different trajectories and perceptions of what is simultaneous and what is sequential, the idea of a 'past' and of a 'future' has momentous presence in human minds. That is epitomized in the memorable, if by now clichéd, opening line of L. P. Hartley's novel *The Go-Between*: 'The past is a foreign country: They do things differently there.'[28] The sense of distance sustains the past's unbridgeability; while the future may seem unattainable, at least in a form that offers hope or comfort. In a social setting, past and future generations occupy pride of place in communal histories, identities, and imaginations. And yet, both groups are silent—intrinsically and elementally absent—though the way that silence is filled varies. The past community will have actually existed (at least when there is convincing evidence to maintain that it did), so that it can be assigned imaginary views and beliefs based on the present restoration (rightly or wrongly) of their identities. This thought-exercise freezes time, development, and context in a frame of deliberate ahistoricity and is intended in the main to serve current ideological interests and goals. The future community, however, has to be conjured up as an act of imaginative projection, even if based on some calculation of probabilities, often aspiring to the best features of, and solutions to, current difficulties and problems. It is patently historical and reformative, seeking to correct and improve the present at some impending time of movable distance, although the plausibility of its utopian materializations may drift away considerably from actual experiences.

Yet on some accounts the very imagining of a utopia can project an impossibly distanced and timeless future, unlike prefigurative versions that lead from the present and that offer a blue-printed path inevitably fashioned out of current imaginations. The sociologist Ralf Dahrendorf characterized utopias as 'having a nebulous past and no future; they are suddenly there, and there to stay, suspended in mid-time or, rather, somewhere beyond the ordinary notions of time'. Moreover, they are 'suspended not only in time but also in space, shut off from the outside world'.[29] The gaps that distance them from the present with which we are acquainted are filled with an historical and sociological silence of absence, rather than with narratives that override and silence others.

Prior to devoting further attention to ideologies, we may note in this context the importance of their accounts of time. As decontestation devices that select certain conceptual meanings and arguments at the expense of others, ideologies conjure up and employ silences as part of the raw material at their disposal when they shape, and add lustre to, social events and practices or, conversely, when they excise and hide evidence, or when they facilitate the forgetting of social knowledge or—even more decisively—its irretrievable disappearance into oblivion. The questions of origins and natality exercise most ideologies as they seek to stake claims to exclusive territorial possession, to the source of their belief systems, and to the sovereign power of a people. Among the many tools at their disposal is the appeal to a 'state of nature', 'divine right', or to a 'first nation' status concealed in the mists of time by means of an informational silence.

4 Disciplinary Circumspection and Erasure

Anthropology does not only grapple with linearity. The manner in which academic disciplines themselves process or overlook silences occurs not just through competing narratives over time or in simultaneous coexistence. It is also coloured by methodological mismatches. As Aminzade and McAdam observe, 'in all fields of study, dominant theoretical perspectives tend to obscure as much as they reveal. By highlighting specific dimensions of complex empirical phenomena, leading paradigms render other aspects of these same phenomena more or less invisible to scholars.'[30] A revealing account of the historic arguments and tensions among Australian anthropologists who specialized in indigenous culture in the first half of the twentieth century sheds light on the interdependence between scholarly politics and disciplinary predilections on the one hand and the silences they instil among professional investigators on the other.[31] The disinterested application of the science of anthropology and the need for funding clashed with, and subdued, ethical concerns about the impact of government policies on the condition of Aborigines in the reserves they were allocated. Those 'cautious silences' were a mixture of academic socialization, ideological preferences, and the inevitable omissions—even when unintentional—generated by the intellectual paths they strode. Australian anthropologists also produced a further set of professional silences. Those of a traditional bent were focused on studying indigenous communities isolated as far as possible from colonial influence. They saw their mission as representing 'the virtually inarticulate Aborigines' and through public policy guiding them towards modernity. Their research consequently bypassed what they regarded as the increasing 'inauthentic' lived lives of indigenous peoples who partook culturally of urban life, and their silence on those interactions may have indicated a lack of interest. That 'fascination with the forms of traditional Aboriginal life ... was concerned with the pre-colonial social order to the point of blindness to the contemporary scene. It exhibited what might be considered a fetish for empiricism, a steady accretion of knowledge rather than dramatic disjunctions or radical reconceptualizations of the ethnographic material.' In the words of one scholar, the Australian anthropologist 'prefers a quiet existence, untouched by the latest foreign crazes'.[32]

Another investigation into ethnographical methods discusses instances of silence among Japanese day labourers and their impact on research findings. Given that silence in Japanese culture 'reflected social expectations in Japanese society, one of which is "the less said, the better"', and that 'it is often used unconsciously in communication', the interview techniques of American and British ethnologists were ill fit for purpose, focusing only on what participants say. Whereas often 'silence in interviews is viewed as resulting from the interviewees' lack of knowledge or interviewers' insufficient skills to elicit interviewees' responses', as well as an articulatory failure, it was preferable in this case to decode such silences both as a cultural norm and as a form of response, even as an attempt by the interviewee to control the conversation—a 'communication strategy'. Western research criteria themselves acted as silent silencers, blocking the non-verbal evidence that emanated from the face-to-face interaction and impeding the path to meaningful scholarship.[33]

These studies reinforce some of Trouillot's findings, but do so from the small-scale perspective of the working tensions and rivalries among anthropologists and their schools. Unlike history, which in cultural mode investigates events and knowledge trajectories over extended stretches of time, anthropology is distinguished chiefly by addressing and juxtaposing contemporaneous cultural and ethnographical evidence, as well as myths. The gaps of silence are therefore not contiguous or sequential but ongoing and concurrent. That propels researchers—anthropologists and ethnographers—into an active if not always totally mindful interaction with the societies they investigate, conferring a temporal immediacy on the intertwined silences that are found at the mutual points of contact.

Trouillot had himself submitted anthropology to scrutiny not, as previously, through his analysis of competing and truncated historical narratives, but through identifying a 'savage slot' conferred by the West on other cultures and that defined anthropology's 'geography of imagination' as the basis of that discipline. Its canon, he maintained, abdicated scholarly responsibility through its unquestioning silence rather than an eclipsing and eradicating one. The consequence was 'the erasure of the other's historical specificity', thus both hiding manifold alterities by collapsing them into an undifferentiated mass and treating non-Europeans as people without either history or historicity. In effect, 'anthropology needs to turn the apparatus elaborated in the observation of non-Western societies on itself, and more specifically, on the history from which it sprang'.[34] Its silence was nourished by a domineering metanarrative emanating from the prioritization of the 'savage' as a symbolic construct.

Delving deeper into the rationales of anthropology, Trouillot maintained that central anthropological concepts such as race were 'scientized' and deprived of political connotations. He saw them not as 'political silences as such—though there were enough of those also. They are silences *in theory* that shielded theory from politics or, better said, from the political.'[35] But that is not quite accurate: the ostensible removal of something from the political sphere is itself a process of organizing and redistributing political significance. Shielding is a pronounced political act by any account—in this case attempting to protect and ensure the 'benign' or 'neutral' status of anthropological research. Echoing a fundamental feature of ideologies as competitions over the control of political language, Trouillot went on to assert that 'definitional debates about culture are in fact battles over control of that conceptual core'.[36] The losers of such battles are silenced (at least temporarily) in the annals of learning. And they involve a silence concerning method: 'a recurring assumption behind the difficulties and silences ... about both culture and race is the illusion of a liberal space of enlightenment within which words-as-concepts can be evaluated without regard for their context of deployment'.[37] In an echo of the same problematic, an anthropologist studying the lives of Muslims in France claiming to be both Muslim *and* French noted that 'their claim to Frenchness involves a desire to be ordinary, what ... one of my interlocutors referred to as his "right to indifference", his right "to be forgotten"'. Those claims fell on the unsympathetic ears of French secular republicans, who insisted on their otherness. Her conclusion was that 'for as much as we try to represent what Trouillot called the "epistemological competence" of our interlocutors, their insights, and ours, are not always intelligible or thinkable'.[38]

The temporalities of silence are employed to perform very different political roles. The silences of the past can be challenged, interrogated, or refuted. The silences of the future, to the contrary, are beyond reach, untouchable, and fragile. But both categories of silence offer an ample platform within which to conduct contestations and struggles over policy. Phantom former populations are recruited to have their voices added and counted in the quest for legitimating current political choices, and links are forged with random and haphazard pasts. Prospective future populations may have their desires and interests named and identified in the ambition to direct historical change—an acute and current battle over constructing and controlling an unfolding and continuous teleology. That problematic can be explored, among others, not by fusing past, present, and future, and not by challenging linearity, but through a simple and typical form of handling past and future silences: recruiting new voices to fill them. The following chapter takes up that theme.

Notes

1. Genesis 1:2. See above, Maitland, *A Book of Silence*, p. 118.
2. MacCulloch, *Silence: A Christian History*, pp. 29, 49.
3. Freeden, *The Political Theory of Political Thinking*, pp. 92–109.
4. Barthes, *The Neutral*, p. 72.
5. Bernard P. Dauenhauer, *Silence: The Phenomenon and its Ontological Significance* (Bloomington, IN: Indiana University Press, 1980), p. 77.
6. Brox, *Silence*.
7. T. Merton, *Thoughts in Solitude* (New York: Farrar, Straus & Cudahy, 1958).
8. G. Deleuze, *Negotiations 1972–1990*, trans. M. Joughin (New York: Columbia University Press, 1995), p. 129.
9. For thoughts on that practice see Trouillot, *Silencing the Past*, pp. 5–8.
10. Ibid., p. 26.
11. Ibid., pp. 22, 26, 28.
12. Ibid., p. 27.
13. J. Winter, 'Thinking about Silence', in E. Ben-Ze'ev, R. Ginio, and J. Winter (eds.), *Shadows of War: A Social History of Silence in the Twentieth Century* (Cambridge: Cambridge University Press, 2010), p. 3.
14. Trouillot, *Silencing the Past*, p. 88.
15. See, e.g., H. Silverman (ed.), *Contested Cultural Heritage* (Urbana, IL: Springer, 2010).
16. D. Fairchild Ruggles, 'The Stratigraphy of Forgetting: The Great Mosque of Cordoba and its Contested Legacy', in ibid., pp. 51–68.
17. Trouillot, *Silencing the Past*, p. 73.
18. C. Gere, *Knossos and the Prophets of Modernism* (Chicago, IL: University of Chicago Press, 2009), p. 14.
19. G. Steiner, *Language and Silence* (Harmondsworth: Penguin, 1969), p. 31.
20. Maitland, *A Book of Silence*, p. 66.
21. Fivush, 'Speaking Silence', p. 95.
22. S. Nagar-Ron and P. Motzafi-Haller, '"My Life? There Is Not Much to Tell": On Voice, Silence and Agency in Interviews with First-Generation Mizrahi Jewish Women Immigrants to Israel', *Qualitative Inquiry* 17/7 (2011), pp. 653–663 at p. 655.
23. See, e.g., Malve von Hassell, '"Issei" Women: Silences and Fields of Power', *Feminist Studies* 19/3 (1993), pp. 549–569; Nagar-Ron and Motzafi-Haller, '"My Life? There Is Not Much to Tell"'.

24 L. McNay, *Gender and Agency* (Cambridge: Polity Press, 2000), p. 85.
25 Billias and Vemuri, *The Ethics of Silence*, p. 98.
26 Quoted in ibid., p. 102.
27 P. Patton, *Deleuzian Concepts: Philosophy, Colonization, Politics* (Stanford, CA: Stanford University Press, 2010), pp. 110–111.
28 L. P. Hartley, *The Go-Between* (London: Penguin, 1997), p. 5.
29 R. Dahrendorf, 'Out of Utopia: Toward a Reorientation of Sociological Analysis', *American Journal of Sociology* 64/2 (1958), pp. 115–127 at pp. 116, 117.
30 R. Aminzade and D. McAdam, 'Emotions and Contentious Politics', in R. R. Aminzade, J. A. Goldstone, D. McAdam, E. J. Perry, W. H. Sewell, S. Tarrow, and C. Tilley, *Silence and Voice in the Study of Contentious Politics* (Cambridge: Cambridge University Press, 2001), p. 14.
31 G. Gray, *A Cautious Silence: The Politics of Australian Anthropology* (Canberra: Aboriginal Studies Press, 2007), pp. 15–27.
32 P. Morton, *Fire across the Desert: Woomera and the Anglo-Australian Joint Project 1946–1980* (Canberra: Australian Government Publishing Service, 1989), p. 5.
33 M. Kawabata and D. Gastaldo, 'The Less Said, the Better: Interpreting Silence in Qualitative Research', *International Journal of Qualitative Methods* 14/4 (2015), pp. 1–9.
34 M.-R. Trouillot, *Global Transformations: Anthropology and the Modern World* (New York and Houndmills, Basingstoke: Palgrave Macmillan, 2003), pp. 13–14, 72.
35 Ibid., p. 105.
36 Ibid., p. 106.
37 Ibid., p. 107.
38 M. L. Fernando, 'Ethnography and the Politics of Silence', *Cultural Dynamics* 26 (2014), pp. 235–244 at pp. 240–241.

10
Superimposed and Invented Voice

1 Crowding Out

Controlling silence in concrete situations is a key political practice, involving the exercise of power. Its most conspicuous instances pertain to state or institutional suppression of speech and voice but, as has been the case throughout this study, those concerns—important as they are in other scholarly and ethical contexts—are not accorded undivided attention here. What does demand consideration within the investigative guidelines of this volume is another indicator of control, ubiquitous as well as effective. It manifests itself not through wittingly or unintentionally promoting or enabling specific social silences, but through a deliberate superimposition of voice whose effect is to crowd out other existing voices, who then become unheard. Complementing that practice is the invention of non-existing voices to fill the unpopulated spaces. Superimposition and invention encompass a range of interventions: muscling in, exploiting, or concocting, in an endeavour to dismiss rival discourses and narratives, drown them out, exercise sole control over public utterances, or more indirectly recalibrating them. This means taking advantage of an opportunity: the non-vocalization of an issue or an argument as a gap in public discourse, or—in quite a few cases—as the inability to articulate that was identified in Part I. Once again the issue is crisply adumbrated by Bourdieu:

> The political field is thus the site of a competition for power which is carried out by means of a competition . . . for the monopoly of the right to speak and act in the name of some or all of the non-professionals. The spokesperson appropriates . . . the words of the group of non-professionals, that is, most of the time, its silence . . .[1]

The term 'professionals' indicates not a formal position in a political structure but those who are adroit in influencing and pressing their views on others.

Illuminating in this context is the subtle distinction to which Spivak alerts us, that between *Vertretung* and *Darstellung*—most closely translated as 'standing in for' versus '(re)presenting'.[2] The relationship with silence is tricky. *Vertretung* is an 'instead of' concept: a person, group, or institution takes the place and discharges the work of another person, group, or institution. Representation may be conducted in good faith, but seen from the viewpoint either of numerical aggregates (e.g., those on the losing side of an election) or of certain sectoral communities who possess a common identity (e.g., a group of immigrants who worship in a particular religious framework), it is a practice highly susceptible to eliminating, forgetting, or ignoring any section of a particular population—politically, culturally, gender-related, and so on. It is, after all, a fallacy to maintain that any method of representation can reproduce the uniqueness of everyone, or the diversity of all; it invariably is a culling procedure. At the same time, however, silences are presentations, indications, or *Darstellungen* of thinking, feeling, and acting that possess the potential to impart an extraordinary amount of information about human and social conduct, selected from a broad and indeterminate pool.

Superimposition does neither: it does not stand in for other voices; rather it announces its own unilaterally. And it does not represent, illustrate, or convey the materiality or mood of the social entity in question. Instead, it reverses the flow, importing and injecting its own flavours into its selected population, though it may often resort to the false claim of being authorized to do so. Additionally, the act of superimposing introduces a further silenced differentiation: that between superimposing a voice on a silence while preserving some space for alternative voices, or—more expansively—colonizing all the space hitherto available for signalling and expressing existing voices so that no room remains for others. We may surmise that the former possibility oscillates between the authoritarian, the intolerant, and the highly prescriptive, while the latter goes the further mile and tends to be found on the totalitarian arc of the spectrum.

The typical methods of *superimposing* voice occur in three different trajectories, all retaining a connection to distinct moments of temporality: one sweeps aside other contemporaneous voices and asserts its own monopoly over public discourse (e.g., most right-wing populisms, a subject addressed in Chapter 14); another blocks out previous voices (e.g., the marginalization of the languages of first nations); and a third curtails prospective voices (e.g., employing sacred texts or customs to stifle religious or scientific innovation). A widespread method of *inventing* voice involves speaking in the name of two vast non-existing groups—the dead and the not-yet born, both obviously silent—while purporting to reflect their thoughts and wishes. Neither kind meets the test of 'standing in for' or giving expression to the features of such groups.

The monopolization of contemporaneous voices is in evidence when a phrase such as 'the will of the people' is exploited to indicate an undifferentiated totality, even when only a minority gave voice to whatever that will is assumed to entail. That rhetorical device—particularly powerful within the context of a democratic society—was extensively employed in the Brexit campaigns and debates in the UK during the referendum of 2016 and its aftermath, when the expressed views of 37 per cent of the electorate were magnified to include its entirety and crowd out—hence silence—any hint of a plurality of opinions.[3] The 'will of the people' is a highly effective silencer when democracy is interpreted as synonymous with crude majoritarianism. Under its spell, contrary voices lose their legitimacy, being at best heard disapprovingly but not listened to. Political silences of that magnitude are easier to manufacture and disguise when rallying cries about the national interest and threats to cultural integrity hog the stage, and dissenting voices are degraded into insignificance, even called out as a betrayal. Narratives promoting 'alternative facts'—a term employed by a senior counsellor to President Trump—erase the very existence of those they displace.[4]

On the blocking of past voices through superimposition, Fivush remarks: 'When silence is imposed, by self or by others, it can lead to a loss of memory and a loss of part of the self.'[5] As we have seen in the previous chapter, that loss led Trouillot to contend that 'the rhetoric of the Savage slot is what ensures that the voice of the native is completely dominated by the voice of the anthropologist',[6] spurred on by anthropologists who 'practised an advocacy by which non-Aboriginal people preferred to talk for Aboriginal people rather than enabling Aboriginal people to talk for themselves'.[7] That intervention in the expressive capacity of a person has obvious political repercussions. When voice is arrogated in that manner, it is immediately accompanied by the prominent political features of sovereignty and finality. It will also recalibrate, and probably diminish, the resources at that person's command, as well as impact on the quality of interaction with others in making a contribution towards a common pool of knowledge. Consequently, it establishes an unspoken hierarchy of significance.

As for the curtailing of future voices, certain interpretations of Islamic holy scriptures offer a particularly instructive instance of the manner in which a sacred text induces and superimposes silences affecting religious conduct. The distinction between the Qur'an as a recited and vocalized discourse and its textual canonization—the *mushaf*—marks a space in which silence prevails. As the scholar Nasr Abû Zayd contends, ' 'Ali, the cousin of Muhammad and his son-in-law ... described the *mushaf* as silent; it does not speak, but humans speak it out.'[8] Amir-Moezzi offers further detail. When ' 'Ali, the designated successor to Muhammad, was deprived of what his supporters considered to be his rightful role, the names of Muhammad's followers and of his family were deliberately excised from the Qur'an in an act of falsification. For those followers, the text was rendered unintelligible and became a silent book. Deliberate silencing can morph into future unknowability, a silenced silence without trace. This is where the hermeneutic mission was called upon: 'In order to recover its Word, the teaching of the genuine initiates—the imams, whose person and/or teaching are said to be "the speaking Qur'an" ... is henceforth necessary.'[9]

That reduction of the Qur'an to a silent text allowed for its 'political and ideological manipulation'. The authority of a written text establishes a fixity embedded in a very specific silence, in its distanciation from the everyday expressions of social and political life. That silence pits the power of a permanently unadaptable script—exploited by rulers and clerics for their purposes—against the power of a popular, though not quite democratic, moulding and shaping of a society by means of dialogue and debate, and threatens to make the latter inaudible.[10] Overall, an unavoidable tension obtains between the flowing and dynamic nature of verbal interaction and its freezing in sacralized writing, and that tension uncovers the social practices that govern fundamental ethical and legal injunctions. Although religious texts tend to inflexibility because they are understood as objects of devotion to divinely decreed and hence immovable will, the silence they consequentially impose on textual deviations may be countered by exegetical leeway, or by books such as the ones just cited. By contrast, other relatively rigid cultural artefacts, such as political constitutions, sanction textual amendments as a matter of course.

2 Dead and Unborn Silences

Inventing the voices of the dead requires less effort. It is tempting, often easy, and it harnesses a potent form of psycho-social force. Let me illustrate that through a personal experience. After a talk I gave some years ago to a department of environmental studies at a Japanese university, I was taken out for dinner by a senior faculty member. He assured me that the most important thing about the environment was to listen to the voices of the Japanese war dead. Back in my hotel, three thoughts went through my mind. The first obviously was that the dead cannot be listened to in any ordinary sense, inasmuch as listening entails an immediate and direct aural reception, and my host was not referring to recordings or written reflections. The second harboured a doubt as to whether concern for the environment was high on the wish list of Japanese soldiers prior to and during the Second World War, even though I did not query the sincerity of my host in believing that to be true. And third, that pronouncement elevated a particular group of citizens to the position of authoritative vehicles of the public good by dint of their 'heroic' status in having sacrificed their lives for the nation—a common convention in many societies. Their absolute silence afforded the opportunity to broadcast and validate messages of national import in their names, messages whose ethical and political significance would be prioritized over other voices (or silences). Pieters has observed that 'dead people do talk . . . if only because we imagine them talking'. He notes Petrarch's view that 'the conversation with the dead stands for a special insight in the course of things and for the transfer of a special form of knowledge that cannot be gained from everyday conversation or from the reading of "ordinary" texts'. And he quotes approvingly from Constantijn Huygens, the Dutch diplomat and poet: 'I prefer those who are mute to those who cannot be silent. They talk to me when I want them to.'[11]

But that is a completely different case from that of the Japanese soldiers. Pieters refers to an informed interpretation of what individual dead people have already expressed on relevant issues when they were alive. That contrasts with the veneration of the war dead as an undifferentiated and anonymous category, regardless of their (environmental) views. In his role as literary critic, Pieters sees specific dead people—writers, authors, and philosophers—as imparting highly meaningful messages, yet accepts that 'to read is to colonise and to force texts into saying what we as readers want them to say. The same could be said about our conversations with the dead.'[12] In those conversations, voice is projected onto past voices by refiltering them imaginatively, rather than merely treating them as a tabula rasa, a blanket absence of voice that is then utilized for a completely new set of fantasy-based narratives. The dead—especially the venerated dead, ancestors, martyrs, and those who died tragically young—provide a shielded space in which to anchor imported voice. Another variation of that practice entails (re)naming narrative voices. By assigning a new label to historical events, one narrative can displace a rival one. What on one account is Columbus' discovery of America can on another—as Trouillot astutely points out—be 'the Castilian invasion of the Bahamas', setting up 'a field of power' that was spatially controlled from Europe.[13]

There also is a curious variant of inventing non-existing voices, directed not at the dead but at the inanimate. Kagge's claims to be conscious of nature speaking, and conversing with it, were noted in Chapter 4. That variant raises the obvious question put by Vogel: 'in the evocations of nature's speech, who is it who is really speaking?' Can one indeed confer voice on an object intrinsically incapable of uttering, of conceptualizing and thinking, even of producing language and its dialogical dimensions, except in the imaginations of those who are amazed by it to the point of anthropomorphization? There is undoubtedly something appealing and reassuring in redescribing the world as a site of interaction and conversation, a place where sense and passion are accessible and transmissible at every turn and where the stark and unresponsive features of the environment may be tamed into benevolence. In that manifestation of silenced silences, nature's intimidating and supra-human silence is concealed and reduced to human scale. But as Vogel observes, that involves political danger: 'th[e] human speaker—like a sleight of hand magician, or more accurately like a ventriloquist—makes it seem that something else, the place, is doing the speaking ... the real speaker is being systematically hidden'.[14] Illicit and concealed power is, as we well know, profoundly unaccountable, not only on more obvious normative criteria, but as a free-floating force that evades communal regulation, ending up as simultaneously political and extra-political.

The other non-existent group—future generations—is less commonly referred to in terms of its silence, though the scientific extrapolation of current trends may increase the probability of predicting the content of those voices. Unavoidably, we participate in fashioning the options open to the non-existent, just as they may also be overlooked or forgotten, and just as the anticipation of their possible future, but currently mute, voices will shape ours. Barring unfathomable catastrophes, people will exist in the imaginable future, an assumption reflected in sundry discourses on our responsibilities towards them—'will exist' indicating a biological and statistical nigh-certainty. Thus, a document headed 'A Voice for Future Generations at the United Nations? Turning Words into Action'[15] comments on a UN report on establishing representation for what effectively are the silent unborn. Speaking in the name of past concrete individuals whom we could have known, may know, or about whom records may exist, is an entirely different prospect from representing hypothetical people and projecting our words into their unformed mouths. And yet, the moral and utilitarian cases for so doing are regularly acknowledged among ethicists as irrefutable, the aim being to minimize the harm we may now inflict on future people due to our present-centred activities. Current debates on the mitigation of the perilous effects of climate change are a stark example. They frequently employ language that projects urgency, intent, and agency on the unborn: 'future generations desperately need us to do something *now* in order to give them a *chance* when it's their turn'.[16]

There is an extensive literature on how to represent the interests of future generations in current social decision making, how to ensure that they benefit from a just allocation of resources, what rights they can claim from us, and what our duties towards them are. Most of the literature on the subject is understandably couched in normative terms and its ethical considerations are broadly agreed. Normative language assumes transparency and openness and only rarely postulates contention over competing normativities. Hence there is very little discussion of those who have not yet been born as unwilling, or unconsenting, objects of our will, visions, fantasies, and interests. One reason for that is an unquestioned universalism about the needs and desires of future human beings and about the requirement to 'represent' them according to the 'duties of environmental stewardship' that we already accord to the more vulnerable among the living.[17] Another argument resorts to an analogy with some of our obligations towards strangers,[18] of whom the unborn are an intriguing sub-group!

That universalism assumes the constancy of certain human voices and the interests they express over time and across space. Typically, and unsurprisingly, those interests—and the rights they are intended to protect—reflect a specific ethical view of the world today, even when embedded in scientific fact. In a recent book Peter Lawrence advocates 'giving voice to the interests of future generations by a proxy articulating their interests' and notes that 'presentist bias implies the negation of the "all affected principle" to the extent that future persons affected by decisions being made now are being denied a voice on the basis of bias or prejudice'.[19] The question whether the unavoidable silence of future human beings can be broken by producing their voices now is moot from discursive, historical, and comparative perspectives and requires shifting to a philosophical mode of universalism. That type of normative advocacy is, of course, legitimate and unexceptional within its own premises but it does not lend itself to the multiple messages towards which the interpretative analysis of discourse is attuned. Indeed, yet another way of conceiving of the transhistoricity of interests and rights derives not from an abstract universalism, nor from the scientific insistence on laws and regularities, but from the recognized case for regarding society as a continuous partnership through time; in Edmund Burke's famous words, 'a partnership not only between those who are living, but between those who are living, those who are dead, and those who are to be born'.[20]

To identify a section of any population as rights bearers carries unusually heavy import because rights are the supreme ranking device that trumps any other claims, needs, or desires. As a fundamental political practice, the bestowing of rights elevates the status even of the non-existent, let alone the living, and it enables the silent future to compete effectively with current members of a society and to secure a share of the valuable goods they distribute. In that competition, as with any special rights argument, other groups may lose out—for instance, those who have to bear the costs of such 'futureproofing'. In other words, the silent group of the unborn can wield considerable clout *in absentia* merely through bringing it into the unassailable circle of rights language. Of course, that is just another way of seizing an unusual opportunity for other interest groups to barge into the vacuum of absent voices in order to promote an agenda that speaks—so one is led to believe—for the non-existent, though probably more for the values and interests treasured by the self-appointed mouthpieces themselves. Silent futures, and the voiceless and hence resistance-free communities they may contain, offer similar opportunities for socialist ideologies to build their case—a characteristic that will be examined in Chapter 14, as will the distribution of protected rights to silence within liberal discourse. Conversely, silent futures are insulated from change by some schools of political philosophy that subscribe to universalizable and abstract theories of rights. In their view, the silence of future voices has no analytical or moral import because rights exist irrespective of whether their bearers want and claim them or not. Human intervention in the status of rights bearing is, therefore, pointless and the silence of the future, on that understanding, is irrelevant, being a 'voice-in-waiting' assumed absolutely by the theorist. Tellingly, the entry in the online *Stanford Encyclopedia of Philosophy* on intergenerational justice contains neither the word 'voice' nor the word 'silence'.[21]

Both superimposition and invention proceed by reverting to two common language stratagems that render the replacement of silence with voice unnecessary while achieving similar results. Those stratagems are embedded in the positivist and extra-human sanctuary of incontrovertible verification, rather than indisputable democratic values or ethical universalism. The one is represented through everyday expressions such as 'needless to say' and 'taken as read'—the misguided allure of self-evidence already elaborated on by Bourdieu. The other, the common phrase 'the facts speak for themselves', is designed to put an end to debate by appealing to a determinable truth. Facts, however, are voiceless and cannot utter any truths; they certainly do not engage in self-justification. What is at play, obviously, is that a human speaker ensures a particular interpretation of evidence through transferring it to the realm of an unrivalled and unassailable vantage-point, one where the unambiguous and singular 'voice' of inanimate facts is fabricated in a bid to nullify the need for possibly contentious human speech. Similarly, appeals by some policy makers from the social sciences community to 'evidence-based research'—largely construed as quantitative and statistical—indirectly silence claims of other genres of scholarship to promote the equal standing of qualitative or textual production and interpretation of knowledge. Such usages have been mirrored during the 2020–22 Covid-19 pandemic in the declarations of politicians that they 'follow the science', bestowing on science an incontrovertible aura of authority well beyond its reach, as well as a unity that masks scientific pluralism.[22] The result is a deflection of public doubting of governmental pronouncements through a culture-based—rather than scientific—silencing of human judgement, rendering the questioning of policy within a given framework of discourse impermissible and, indeed, absurd. If majoritarianism puts an end to opposing voices by a rhetorical fiat that transmutes it into an overwhelming singularity, an even more efficient way is to cut out the babel of human voices altogether. The power struggle is then waged between human imagination and agency on the one hand and their eclipsing and muting on the other, through paradoxically assigning voice to a non-human source, a 'speaking' scientific or commonly known fact that exists 'objectively'.

Notes

1. Bourdieu, *Language and Symbolic Power*, p. 190.
2. Spivak, 'Can the Subaltern Speak?', p. 72.
3. See, e.g., M. Freeden, 'Editorial: After the Brexit Referendum: Revisiting Populism as an Ideology', *Journal of Political Ideologies* 22 (2017), pp. 1–11.
4. http://edition.cnn.com/2017/01/22/politics/kellyanne-conway-alternative-facts/index.html
5. Fivush, 'Speaking Silence', p. 92.
6. Trouillot, *Global Transformations*, p. 132.
7. Morton, *Fire across the Desert*, p. 5.
8. Nasr Abû Zayd, *Rethinking the Qur'an: Towards a Humanistic Hermeneutics* (Amsterdam: Humanistics University Press, 2004), p. 12.
9. Muhammad Ali Amir-Moezzi, *The Silent Qur'an and the Speaking Qur'an* (New York: Columbia University Press, 2016), pp. 76–77.
10. Abû Zayd, *Rethinking the Qur'an*, p. 13.
11. J. Pieters, *Speaking with the Dead: Explorations in Literature and History* (Edinburgh: Edinburgh University Press, 2005), Epilogue. https://ezproxy-prd.bodleian.ox.ac.uk:2574/view/10.3366/edinburgh/9780748615889.001.0001/upso-9780748615889-chapter-7
12. Ibid.
13. Trouillot, *Global Transformations*, pp. 114–115.
14. Vogel, 'The Silence of Nature', pp. 149, 158–159.

15 http://www.youthpolicy.org/blog/youth-policy-young-people/a-voice-for-future-generations-at-the-un/ (accessed 23 October 2017).
16 S. Syropoulos and E. Markowitz, https://blogs.lse.ac.uk/businessreview/2021/08/23/taking-responsibility-for-future-generations-promotes-personal-action-on-climate-change/
17 P. Christoff, 'Ecological Citizens and Ecologically Guided Democracy', in B. Doherty and M. de Geus (eds.), *Democracy and Green Political Thought: Sustainability, Rights and Citizenship* (London: Routledge, 1996), p. 159.
18 W. Achterberg, 'Sustainability, Community and Democracy', in Doherty and Geus, *Democracy and Green Political Thought*, p. 179.
19 J. Linehan and P. Lawrence, *Giving Future Generations a Voice: Normative Frameworks, Institutions and Practice* (Cheltenham: Edward Elgar, 2021), p. 12.
20 E. Burke, *Reflections on the Revolution in France* (Harmondsworth: Penguin, 1968), pp. 194–195.
21 Stanford Encyclopedia of Philosophy online. https://plato.stanford.edu/entries/justice-intergenerational/
22 See, e.g., J. Basevic, 'There's No Such Thing as Just "Following the Science"—Coronavirus Advice is Political', *The Guardian*, 28 April 2020.

11
Tacit Consent and Attributed Consent

1 Locke's Tacit Consent: Unwritten Implications

What happens when silence is misinterpreted as a specific response to, or authorization of, another entity's actions? And what if that silence is indeed a token of agreement with a set of words or events? The epitome of that dilemma lies in the juxtaposition of the qualifier 'tacit' and the noun 'consent'. Its most prominent historical instance, reiterated in countless university courses on political thought, is Locke's notion of tacit consent in his *Second Treatise of Government*—although Hobbes, another stalwart of those academic surveys, preceded Locke in tentatively mentioning *en passant* that 'Silence is sometimes an argument of Consent.'[1] Yet most scholarly research has not been unduly perturbed by the compound concept. Indeed, it is often taken for granted, so closely is it assumed to correspond both to political and social practices and to a plausible variation on signalling democratic legitimation. Consequently, the remarkable thing about the scholarly analysis of Locke's tacit consent is its almost complete focus on what kind of consent it constitutes, or even on whether consent is necessary in the first place to legitimate a Lockean state, at the expense of the more fundamental challenge posed by silence, by the absence of voice, in comprehending and interpreting the political. Significantly, the drafting in of silence in this case occurs as a reaction (or non-reaction) not just to matters of indifferent or marginal concern, but to the weightiest of political commitments: an undertaking to be subject to, and obey, the laws of government. In that context, the word 'tacit', not the word 'consent', is by far the more intriguing of the pairing. Why Locke loads on silence something we might now call agreement, authorization, or, in a different vein, acquiescence, is one kind of question; but why the exegetical work on Locke is largely unconcerned with the significance of such a transmutation is no less curious.

The issue is not whether appealing to tacit consent is a reasonable or philosophically valid way of inferring consent.[2] It is, rather, what work does taciturnity do, or can it discharge, in a known population and what can it indicate to the political theorist focusing on political practices? Both Locke

Concealed Silences and Inaudible Voices in Political Thinking. Michael Freeden, Oxford University Press.
© Michael Freeden (2022). DOI: 10.1093/oso/9780198833512.003.0013

and his interpreters predicate a specific thought-practice concerning the extending (and appropriating) of political support on the absent speech-act, relying on alternative evidence that is at best circumstantial and at worst might be regarded as irrelevant to the ascribed task. As suggested above, it may be that some philosophical and political scholarship is not well geared to addressing the inarticulate, wedded as it is to identifying human beings as reflective, purposive agents. Conversely, the absence of voice is not identified by some scholars of political thought as silence in the first place—for instance, by those focusing on the body or the emotions as loci of interpersonal communication. It is, however, unlikely that Locke deliberately incorporated or implied such methodologies of exegesis in his text.

Famous and paradigmatic as Locke's exploration of tacit consent is, we are talking about a specific type of silent social practice that recurs in numerous contexts, both over time and across space. *Qui tacet consentire videtur* goes back to Roman times as a legal maxim, when it entailed that 'one who fails to deny or object to a claim, accusation, or statement of fact relevant to his interests must implicitly have done so because of its truth or validity, and it is therefore proper to construe the failure to deny or object as an admission'.[3] Alternatively, one may find tacit consent in different cultural settings, such as the traditional customs prevalent among the Igbo in Nigeria. *O gbalu nkiti Kwelu* ('he consents, who keeps silent') indicates an agreement to participate in the collective decisions of a community.[4] Locke's usage, however, is the most detailed, intriguing, and politically surprising of them all, and the thoroughness and inventiveness of his take on that form of silence merits special consideration. It is broader than the Roman case in not relating to a particular juridical occurrence addressed directly and personally that would normally require a response. But it is also more focused than the Igbo case, because when Locke refers to certain common practices engrained in civil life, he does so by homing in on explicit identifiable signals that emerge out of social silence.

Locke's indications of what constitutes tacit consent in the *Second Treatise* are few. They concern two features: possession and enjoyment. The first category consists of some measure of property or possession: owning inheritable land, and taking up lodgings, however temporarily. The second consists of unconstrained mobility when using what we might now term a specific public good: travelling freely on the highway. Having duly noted the difficulty of 'how far any one shall be looked on to have consented, and thereby submitted to any Government, where he has made no Expressions of it at all',[5] Locke goes for performative rather than vocal or verbal indicators of consent. But he does so unquestioningly and without anchoring his argument in an alternative exegetical frame. That, presumably, is why Locke never probes into the silence arising from the absence of voice and why he ultimately does not find it problematic, nor subject to more than one interpretation.

Put differently, Locke is himself silent about the analytical category of performativity—a concealed category implicitly comprehended but beyond the available mindset at his disposal. That contrasts with the recent readiness of many political theorists to depart from the predominantly logocentric conventions of their discipline: to recognize performativity as a major vessel of ideas and conceptual patterns, and to explore the political dimension of everyday non-verbal deeds.[6] Yet again, it befell a later age to detect what was once epistemologically inarticulable and unconceptualizable—though contingently, not essentially, so. Nonetheless, Locke's muted reference to doing, alongside promising, is ambiguous. Because performing an action can be decoded as a type of language—resonating, for example, in the current phrase 'body language' that relates to co-verbal communication[7]—it is possible that Locke understood that in a roundabout manner. Let's call this counter-contention A.

Counter-contention A implies that Locke's inability to conceptualize performativity nonetheless does not specifically detract from the significance of his focus on non-logocentric behaviour, *sans* any theoretical underpinning. The possibility of establishing political legitimacy no longer hinges on what liberal contractarians seem to insist on: mandatory rational deliberation and commitment. It is quite acceptable to argue—with Carlyle—against the subordination of deed to speech. People hindered from speaking are not consequently denied agency, nor need people whose voices are downplayed or disregarded for reasons of gender, age, or ethnicity be omitted from playing a political role. Non-speech is hence no disqualification for inclusion in the democratic, consent-valuing ambit. That method, associated by Rollo with a deliberative systems approach,[8] understands deeds as intentional bodily practices, and as such they can signal consent.

As it is, a scrutiny of Locke's recourse to intentional performativity runs up against two difficulties in accounting for his position: is it *intentionally* political, and is it intentionally *political*? Locke does not appear to emphasize the unintentionality of tacit consent to a government: he relates it to intentional practices from which he then infers high-level political significance. There appears to be a marked difference between Bourdieu's generalized, buried, and inadvertent legitimacy conferred on a society's practices as a whole, and Locke's specific understanding that tacit consent is to be interpreted as a targeted legitimating relationship in which the ruled empower a particular government—the rulers—to act and to demand their obedience. That difference derives not from different views on legitimacy but from different views on agency. Bourdieu contends that agentic consent to political ground rules is impossible if the grip of social conventions that guide conduct is unnoticeable.[9] Locke insists on the possibility of agentic consent extrapolated from what a people *does* in a territory under political rule. But he superimposes his own interpretation of agency and motivation on that people, even when it is unlikely to be a party to Locke's proffered insights, being unaware of them. So we slide back to a Bourdieuan terrain, in which a crucial aspect of modern political legitimacy could bypass Locke's 'people' entirely unnoticed.

To spell this out: from a Bourdieuan perspective, the domain of unintentionality and unawareness that may lurk behind taciturnity is the common condition of performing actions—namely, doing so without any grasp of the political connotations those performances might carry in the minds of others. If that is so, the implications of Locke's tacit consent are more subtle than it appears on the surface because the burden of interpretation decisively shifts from the agents to their unspecified contemporaneous observers and fellow-inhabitants, who constitute the bulk of a society. That move prioritizes the political judgement of the savvy observers over the actions of the unaware participants in tacit consent, whether the latter be naïve, undecipherable, or disengaged. Those imputed tacit consenters are consequently deprived of the opportunity to employ their agency, as due to their silence they cannot transfer that agency to a broader, uninvited social group. Correspondingly, the larger social group has not been empowered to conclude that the motives, sentiments, or allegiances of individuals going about their private business necessarily include the recognition of a government's authority. Tacit consent in Locke's version, then, is implicitly not merely held to be the consent to obey any number of laws and rules within a government's domain, but involves a preceding tacit consent to allow others to judge actions on behalf of any silent individual. It is not *intentionally* political; indeed, any political construal of silent personal and economic interactions is instilled externally.

There is also little purchase in transporting Locke's shadowy notion of performativity to contemporary perspectives on intentionality, as per Rollo's approach. Those perspectives are anchored in a political mindset alien to Locke. It is one in which consent, whether tacit or explicit, is locked into an ethos of participatory democracy. It is also one in which most contemporary political theorists of democracy—to the extent that they explore silence at all—are amenable to identifying signs of that ethos in assorted human silences. At best, Locke supports an embryonic association of performativity with proto-democratic inklings by means of the right to revolution, by which he understands negatively calling a halt to a legislature's breach of trust, rather than vocally and positively instructing it what to do. Indeed, Locke assumes that at the outset, and for a while—before the accumulation of abuses becomes intolerable—the mistakes and wrongs of rulers 'will be born by the People, without mutiny or murmur';[10] that is to say, significantly without deed *or* voice.

Conversely, Locke's examples do not pass an unequivocal test that they are intentionally *political*, as travelling on the highway may be sought for recreational purposes or in order to admire nature, visit a friend, or purchase dinner. To re-emphasize, the general focus on tacit consent in this chapter is on its role in voice appropriation; specifically, on cultural and conceptual supplanting or superimposition. It singles out a specific type of appropriation, or commandeering: namely, that of arrogating the voice of a particular public not only without their permission but often without that public being able to articulate its views under any circumstances. That would apply when a public is no longer, or not yet, in existence, as with past or future generations. Locke's public, however, is located squarely in the present and thus available for indicating express political views, so that his ascribing of non-verbal support when clearer and more visible signs of consent *could* be available is particularly problematic.

There is, however, a counter-contention B, available to those who query whether Locke's tacit consent is really politically silent. Some overt political consent may be involved in the practices of ownership and of renting. Taking up lodgings, as a rule, is preceded by an oral or written discourse concerning the legal, financial, and cultural arrangements and conventions it incurs. Perhaps the very act of intentionally entering into a contract—were that indeed to occur prior to taking up lodgings—may be interpreted as a political practice that mirrors and respects laws and agreements underpinned by states and governments. However, based on the textual evidence we cannot assume that Locke implied that possibility. He explicitly excluded commercial agreements such as 'Bargains for Truck, &c' from the political sphere. 'For 'tis not every compact that puts an end to the State of Nature between Men, but only this one of agreeing together mutually to enter into one Community, and make one body Politick; other Promises and Compacts, Men may make with one another, and yet still be in the State of Nature.'[11] As Kary notes of legal thinking in the late-seventeenth-century England of Hobbes and Locke, 'Contract was clearly a kind of agreement, in their time like our own, but back then it was commonly an agreement to enter into various kinds of formal relationships whose terms were defined by custom and the courts rather than by the will of the parties.'[12] And he adds: 'In the seventeenth century, one could agree to a sale, and be bound by all the rules that flow from the nature of a sale contract, whether one knew about them or not.'[13]

In short, renting property (and possessing property in general) is a practice into which individuals may well be socialized unwittingly, and that is achieved absent their consent for the macro-practice itself—the institution of property—which is embedded into the ideational habitus they occupy. Neither Locke, nor those in whose names he argues, are cognizant of the political nature of commercial contracts. Our current understanding of political theory includes within its orbit the small-scale, commercially practised, manifestations of the political that Locke did not recognize as constitutively political: negotiating, influencing, cooperating, deciding, rule heeding. But even had Locke included those micro-practices, it does not follow that what is political on a small scale has to involve, or be echoed in, the country's central government. Accordingly, localized and private transactions cannot in any case be deemed to signal blanket macro-approval for a government's overriding authority or for incurring political obligation. Nor is the problem of acting without the knowledge or consciousness of such macro-implications an indication of proper political consent. Quite plausibly, no such consent should be inferred from silences concerning property relationships in a society bound by traditional custom. Unawareness of the political nature of a performed practice is quite different from holding one's tongue, and one's nose, while clearly signalling a semblance of allegiance or loyalty. And the reach of silence does not end there. Identifying a *natural* right to estate only further obscures the lack of basal consent to that institution. For what is natural may require acknowledgement, but by definition cannot be generated by consent.

Dunn is thus right when he contends that 'Locke advocates government by consent as a means for realizing freedom and yet his concept of tacit consent removes all behavioural specification from the notion of consent.'[14] But if not behavioural specification, is there still performative generality? The activities Locke identifies apply to various walks of life and have no particular bearing on political agreement or legitimation. It is accordingly reasonable to suggest that, in the quest for a willing submission to government, Locke's arguments still conjure up an unhelpful and unsupportive silence. In so doing, he is culpable of enlisting an untransparent category—tacit consent—through which individuals are presumed to indicate a precise form of political thinking and action, even if they may have had no opportunity to incorporate it into their moral or conceptual universes.

But it is not just performativity that exercises Locke; it is the sheer concreteness of territorial location; it is not merely *what* people do that could, on its own, indicate consent, or *how* they do it, but *where* they perform it. On which ground do they place their feet; and in which social capacity do they do so as recognized members of a commonwealth, irrespective of whether they have submitted to government consciously and deliberately?[15] Tellingly, it transpires that politically silent people can move tacitly from ascribed consent to presumed non-consent simply by abandoning their territorial possessions and transferring their physical presence. It follows from Locke's exposition that a voluntary act of bodily movement and spatial relocation terminates political consent without a spoken word. Even assuming—for the sake of argument—the fallible assertion that economic transactions and mobility of person within the public space of the commonwealth do signal political consent, that very mobility can be exercised on a highway leading *out* of the country. Performativity of that kind can confer at best only transitory—thus weaker—political obligation on a person.

But here's the crux of the matter: in an extraordinary twist separating Locke's arguments from later practices of liberal democracy which he supposedly inspired, the silence attached to tacit 'consent' significantly allows for additional individual freedom. It permits a return to the state of nature, now as a stepping stone from which to exercise the option of joining or forming another commonwealth. In sharp contrast, speech in the form of an express agreement or declaration of consent within one's current commonwealth would irrevocably prohibit that move, being fixed to a politically delimited space and to irreversible time. As Locke explains:

> The obligation anyone is under, by Virtue of such Enjoyment, to submit to the Government, begins and ends with the Enjoyment, so that whenever the Owner, who has given nothing but such a tacit Consent to the Government, will, by Donation, Sale, or otherwise, quit the said Possession, he is at liberty to go and incorporate himself into any other Commonwealth, or to agree with others to begin a new one, *in vacuis locis*, in any part of the world, they can find free and unpossessed; whereas he that has once, by actual agreement and any express declaration, given his consent to be of any commonweal, is perpetually and indispensably obliged to be, and remains unalterably a subject to it, and can never be again in the liberty of the state of Nature, unless by any calamity the government he was under comes to be dissolved.[16]

For those *not* previously and expressly self-committed to join and be a subject of a polity, no political or legal utterance is required in order to be assumed to shed a personal and voluntary commitment to governance.

That requires only two kinds of action: an economic transaction divesting oneself of whatever possession that signalled—however debatably—the earlier so-called consent; and a physical move away from the location in which that 'enjoyment' initially occurred. Put differently, when silence is imported into the social and civic spheres, its institutional impact is variable and transient, reflecting specific institutional and ideological contexts. Silence accrues temporary political characteristics in circumstances heavily circumscribed by the materiality of ownership. It confers on the tacit section of the population what Hirschman famously described as the liberty to exit an organization, including a state.[17] With regard to Hirschman's triple matrix of exit, voice, and loyalty, there is no indication that Locke's silence is a protest, even an unvoiced one, nor is it the abdication of political loyalty, for that loyalty was never on the cards in the first place.

On that understanding, silence gives those who adopt it a unique and manifest political advantage over speech. The privilege—indeed the power—of silence enables the shuttling back and forth between the political and the non- or pre-political, unrecognized as that distinction itself may be for the taciturn individuals. Nor does it have to require re-entry into the same territory. It is unclear whether or not this means that those who were initially labelled as tacit consenters would ultimately come to recognize the overt practice of political consent and then proceed to reject it. At any rate, one may assume that the practice of consenting—once it is enunciated verbally by those content to vocalize it—becomes known to some and knowable in principle to all, because any number of individuals *will* have deliberately and overtly signalled their consent. That shuttling affords a flexibility—or alternatively, a political inconclusiveness—unburdened by the constraints of commitment induced by text or speech. Silence thus becomes, as Mikhail Bakhtin also contended,[18] the postponement of finality and of decision—those central attributes of the political—to be resumed or abandoned in a forthcoming territorial attachment. Silence is a condition in which indeterminacy can be either contained or masked, rendering it politically enabling and liberating.

Silence as empowering is likewise evident in the capacity 'to strike first'— an aggressive tactic of warfare straight from the political/military lexicon— that Hobbes cedes to those who do not 'love to consult': that is, who do not need to voice their self-doubts to others.[19] Their silence is not just a question of deceiving others.[20] It adds to the register of the conceptual attributes of silence an unexpected advantage in human interchange. As a literary critic elaborated in another context: 'Silence ... offers the possibility of choosing what to do first or next. ... Non-speaking gives man the power to enclose or disclose himself.'[21] Silence remains on the cusp of finality, the potential thoughts it harbours only decontested one way or the other when it is replaced by explicit language. As the unspoken facilitator of political choice, silence is a catalyst of freedom. Alternatively, however, it has been suggested that silence may afford a pause 'at the threshold of a decision';[22] effectively, one might contend, a gathering of energy in the guise of a launching pad from which a decision can emerge.

Nor is that all. What the analysis of Locke's text teases out is a conceptual attribute of silence—the opening up of space—that it shares with many other concepts when we encounter them in a social setting. The combination of stillness and silence as an abstract category may negate the spatiality of movement, but silence in its multiple concrete locations has a distinct spatial presence: it is here rather than there, or there rather than here. For those who love solitude and thrive in it, such as Kagge, silence indicates and enables a repositioning both physical and mental: 'Silence is a tool helping us to escape the surrounding world.'[23] In Kagge's case it is chiefly perceived as a shift from communion with the social to the non-social; but for Locke, the spatial move incurred by tacit consent is a shift from a *social* silence to what is—at least initially—a pre-social articulateness by dint of 'agree[ing] with others' to refound a commonwealth. Tellingly, that occurs in *vacuis locis*: an empty space that is currently socially and politically vacant, yet—if agreeing with others signals voice—vocal from the moment a new constituting accord is attained. Those entering a new political space are now pre-equipped with their previous knowledge of social life, and presumably with some of its political manifestations. Whether or not that was agreed in the past, one might assume that the second time around any show of silence by those individuals now residing in another commonwealth will lean towards consent: they—or those around them—will have become wise to the stakes involved. In fact, it is difficult to imagine that those previously tacit individuals, once having left a commonwealth and minded to establish a new one, will still be permitted merely to consent tacitly to their new polity, given that the chain of social fracturing through exit may persist.

The issue of tacit consent is hence not some marginalia in, or incidental to, Locke's writings. It accrues a significance larger than he may have intended, as it strikes at the heart of the ontology of politics and its standing as a nigh-equal counterweight to the primordial enormity of the silence it attempts to usurp. Inasmuch as Locke's silence is politicized through interpreting it as consent to laws and governmental authority, however dubiously or tentatively, the political becomes a major exploiter of silence as its vehicle. But it is simultaneously silence's major vanquisher. The strategy entwined in the rigid pairing of 'tacit' and 'consent' unwittingly endeavours to overcome the problematic of inserting the political into its antithetical absence. It does so both by replacing silence's ostensible emptiness with meaningful activity and by taming it through colonizing its continued presence. In the latter instance, silence is revealed to be in a state of political servitude. This may be approached on a complementary path, adopting Ricoeur's argumentation. Government, needy of the legitimization that its subjects' silence cannot provide, deploys an imaginative—and very possibly a spurious—ideological move. Harnessing the interpretation of tacitness as compliance assuages any doubts that may apply to the rulers' claim to legitimacy and consolidates the belief in the rightfulness of their authority.[24]

There is, however, an additional and quite distinct strand to Locke's discussion of tacit consent. We find that phrase intermittently in his *Essay Concerning Human Understanding*. But here it attaches to a different political dimension that does not quite possess the inventive originality of the *Second Treatise*'s undeclared role for silence. Locke's context now is not governmental legitimacy, but the emergence of social conventions. It is a silence located in horizontal socio-political relationships within a community rather than in vertical relations of authority, obedience, and political obligation that dart in and out of social life. Locke discusses the manner by which 'men commonly come by their principles' and his answer is through the socialization of doctrines into the 'unwary' young, 'confirmed to them, either by the open profession or tacit consent of all they have to do with'. The holders of such fundamental principles are silent about their validity and veracity. They 'never suffer those propositions to be otherwise mentioned but as the basis and foundation on which they build their religion and manners', and those doctrines 'come, by these means, to have the reputation of unquestionable, self-evident, and innate truths'.[25]

Famously, Locke disputes the innate, God-given, and natural recognition of virtue and vice, bemoaning the habit of men to 'stamp the characters of divinity upon absurdities and error'.[26] In a striking phrase, he identifies 'custom, a greater power than nature' as the reason that 'grown men, either perplexed in the necessary affairs of life, or hot in the pursuit of pleasures, should not seriously sit down to examine their own tenets; especially when one of their principles is, that principles ought not to be questioned'.[27] Notwithstanding Locke's singling out disparate *spatial* sites as conferring meaning on silence in his *Second Treatise*, the *Essay* reinforces the *temporal* claim to control origins and beginnings, grounding them in their inevitable liminal relationship with silence. It is another instance of creating finality by anchoring it to a historical process that buries and silences silence itself. In that role the political manages, or at least supersedes, all understandings of collective life. In that sense, too, politics and its representatives become Hobbes' 'Mortall God'.[28]

The silence induced by unquestionability is of course a form of unconceptualizability—not the ontological but the cultural impossibility of accepting that references to either God or nature may conceal humanly created, and hence malleable, thought-practices, and the consequent eradication of human curiosity when it comes to custom. In the *Second Treatise*, Locke had dismissed the effective universality of tacit consent, as in most instances neither tacitness nor consent need be evoked at all. Individuals are not debarred from voicing express consent and, conversely, they can knowingly opt out of signalling such consent. In the *Essay*, to the contrary, they cannot withdraw from consenting to custom-based principles of thought and conduct because of the eclipsing of the very silence from which those principles emerge. Socialization ensures that they know not that they are silent in their compliance with existing thought-practices. Hence, the *Essay* appears to reveal the prevalence of tacit consent, but dismisses as erroneous the possibility of all people universally subscribing to substantive values. As Locke observes, 'There is nothing more commonly taken for granted than that there are certain principles, both speculative and practical, (for they speak of both), universally agreed upon by all mankind.' However, he continues, 'But yet I take liberty to say, that these propositions are so far from having an universal assent, that there are a great part of mankind to whom they are not so much as known.'[29] It is that deeper practice of unquestioning acceptance, of *unknowingly* embracing a silence, that is nonetheless universal. As Locke notes: 'Thus the measure of what is everywhere called and esteemed virtue and vice is this approbation or dislike, praise or blame, which, by a secret and tacit consent, establishes itself in the several societies, tribes, and clubs of men in the world.'[30] By equating silence with unquestioning, it is in effect an *obscured*, silenced, silence. The 'tacit' employed in the *Essay* is beyond the ken of individual actors—being linked instead to internalized group routines— and is therefore decoupled from any inkling of voluntarism. Absent even an intimation of aware tacitness, any suggestion of pairing it with consent melts away. Consequently, the silence of custom is a category discovered only by the searching and discerning beholder, of whom Locke is one.

All this is an early precursor to Bourdieu's analysis of a tradition silent about itself, and of a perfectly closed regime of custom. It joins several other examples of such displacement. According to the Talmud, silent performativity stands in for vocal assent in the traditional Jewish marriage ceremony. The bride remains silent when hearing the groom's statement of betrothal and her taciturnity is converted into consent only by accepting the token given her by the groom.[31] In the Sahih Muslim book of marriage, a Hadith—recording the prophet Muhammad's words and actions—stipulates that 'a virgin's father must ask her consent from her, her consent being her silence. At times he said: Her silence is her affirmation.'[32] Reading silence as affirmation—that is, as near as possible to active agreement—associates it, too, with performativity. In both cases, given the relevant cultural and religious conventions, the woman is the mute object of those readings of silence. Hobbes' idea of performativity strikes a different note. His third law of nature states: 'That men performe their Covenants made: without which, Covenants are in vain, and but empty words.' Injustice is consequently defined as the non-performance of covenanting words, as the effective silencing, or emptying, of what those words signify. In the same chapter, those empty words are paired with silent speech, for 'The Foole hath sayd in his heart, there is no such thing as Justice'; in his heart, which does not rule out the occasional voicing of the thought.[33]

The convention of associating silence with political consent has continued to be well established in professional as well as in everyday experience. Jean-Jacques Rousseau's advocacy of popular sovereignty enabled him to claim that under conditions of freedom 'the silence of the people permits the assumption that the people consents'. He then explicitly avers that 'yesterday's law is not binding today, but for the fact that silence gives a presumption of tacit consent and the sovereign is taken to confirm perpetually the laws it does not abrogate while it has power to abrogate them'.[34] In the first citation, Rousseau employs his characterization of the general will as rational and universal, which permits silence to be comprehended as the product of free will, if in a passive register. In the second citation, however, silence significantly contains the active choice of doing or not doing, or speaking or not speaking. Power is inherent in the people, who are the sovereign qua lawmaker. Its silence is loaded with self-restraint in assessing the actions of government. The alternative power of the latter—when it oversteps the mark in invading freedom—arouses the 'sleeping sovereign'.[35] Silence thus obscures the juggling of power between the two primary political entities as well as the trumping force of the one—the sovereign people—over the other, the government.

The power ingrained in silence that facilitates doing or not doing is splendidly exemplified in the famous pronouncement of the marriage ceremony spelled out in the *Book of Common Prayer*: 'Therefore if any man can shew any just cause, why they may not lawfully be joined together, let him now speak, or else hereafter for ever hold his peace.'[36] On the linguistic and communicative surface, a continuous ceremonial silence constitutes a negative response at both the individual and collective levels.[37] But the issue is far more complex, and it concerns the fluidity, temporality, and dual directionality of power. In this instance, as in Rousseau's case, the silent power of those attending tapers out during a window of opportunity—for Rousseau's sovereign people a prolonged one, but in the marriage ceremony sharply curtailed—receding in the timespan between an initial promise of strength and the ultimate loss of resonance, and far more often than not ending in the finality of non-decision. For Rousseau, sovereignty—in this case the power to end that silence—still obtains even as its wielding normally diminishes in practice. In the marriage ceremony—with the congregation's tacit connivance—the officiating minister briefly transfers his or her power (which on one reading originates in divine will; on another, in social and anthropological convention), to any *individual* member of the entire congregation, rather than to the congregation as a whole. A calculated hiatus of silence 'interrupting' the proceedings is employed to invite its even more disruptive shattering. The common prayer procedure threatens to splinter the solidarity of the congregation joined in celebratory mode by implicitly inciting any person present to pit him or herself against the official. In breaking their silence, they undermine a sacrosanct ceremony and thus challenge the established social order. But when a silence of consent or indifference is preserved, it is quickly followed by the ebbing of power back to the minister, at which point the fleeting lack of protest is exchanged for its irreversible permanence.

Note that here reason may well be accompanied, or even replaced, by a forceful expression of emotion. Note also that—from the perspective of divine law—the congregation as a whole exercise no sovereignty at all, departing from Rousseau's understanding. Consequently, the potential individual challenge is not to the group but to the legitimacy of the ritual. The power of the officiating minister is over the ceremony, not over the laws of marriage themselves; hence, the silence is pregnant with power in a limited and concrete way. This practice shares some features with Sontag's *Persona* example,[38] in that silence shifts the burden of activity and responsibility from one individual to another, yet differs crucially in that its termination by the potential individual objector could cause serious social disruption, rather than the resumption of the 'normal service' of a dialogue.

These instances of silence point not merely to its unsettling nature, not even just to its interventionist and intrusive capacities, but to its potential subversiveness. When politicians are met by silence following a speech their authority is undermined, rather than affirmed by tacit consent. Silence may be commanding; it may have an unnerving side, as in Pinter's plays, but it also possesses an annihilating force, as if the lights were suddenly switched off. There are nonetheless other forms of silent unquestioning that, while inaudible, are not unknown to a group or society and that signify a very different mood. They conjure up an alternative configuration of political interactions, one conducive to social cohesion. In Locke's *Second Treatise*, and the mainstream political tradition building on it, being tacit relates to a bifurcated and problematic relationship between a governing sector and a governed civil group. But tacitness may be inwardly directed, identifying a particular feature of social coexistence. In such cases it singles out a positive feeling of mutual understanding or empathy shared by a group—perhaps intuitive, perhaps learned—indicating that 'we don't have to be told what this is all about; we recognize the circumstances'. As Zoe Williams has expressed it, in the context of overt distortions of national identity brought about by Brexit: 'a nationalism that goes unstated defines itself from within—its tacit understandings are its connective tissue'. It is a 'brand of social solidarity'.[39] Thus, what may seem to be a calculating usurpation of people's wills or a rhetorical spin on hesitancy and apathy has another, less sinister, aspect. It may indicate a genuine sense of communal camaraderie—a state of political unity that can be felt within a like-minded citizenry. In such circumstances the political occupies a subliminal dimension attached to individual psyches acting in concert in a manner so natural, and comforting, that it requires no overt expression. Alternatively, taciturnity may be a quasi-ritualistic affirmation of group rules. In Buddhist monastic practice, relating to the ordination of novices, transgressions, and internal disputes, a motion is put to the assembly and, in the absence of voiced opposition, the silence of the group is deemed to be agreement.[40]

2 The 'Silent Majority'

One conspicuous twentieth-century reincarnation of tacit consent has been the popularization of the phrase the 'silent majority', famously alluded to by President Richard Nixon in his 1969 address on the Vietnam War. In that speech he adumbrated a strategy supposed to bring about the end of that war without a defeat for US forces, and he pleaded for the support of 'the great silent majority of my fellow Americans'.[41] That phrase attained rhetorical longevity as well as electioneering force. Donald Trump used it in his campaign for presidential nomination in 2016. A political commentator had this to say:

In just about every stump speech he gives these days ... Trump can't stop using the phrase 'silent majority'. Sometimes he'll ask the audience members if they've heard it before and point out that it's been around for a while. And then he'll say that the silent majority feels abused, or forgotten, or mistreated. And usually, toward the end of his speech, Trump says that the silent majority is back.

The commentator singled out an explanation coming from an attendee of a Trump rally: 'The people that mind their own business, don't expect anything from anybody, and they're kind of quiet. They don't go around bragging. They're not activists.'[42] It is a silence of individualistic self-sufficiency combined with unstated faith in, or hubris towards, one's country. At the very least, it is not a source of political conflict or discontent. How different that looked in January 2021, when a violent mob burst into the Capitol, deluding themselves to be the vocal manifestation of the majority. That self-imagined majority was bent on expressing the voice of the people, a real-world majority of whom had just voted in a very different direction. Fantasies and falsehoods are great silencers of facts and truths, made all the more potent when genuinely believed. A more direct association with the populist rhetoric of confrontation was made by Richard Grenell, US ambassador to Germany, in 2018: 'we are experiencing an awakening from the silent majority—those who reject the elites and their bubble'.[43] It was a case of a member of the elite denouncing elitism, hiding his own colours.

The rhetorical construct of the 'silent majority' deploys very different layers of political meaning. It hovers, first, between a manipulative fantasy of control, namely attributing and superimposing putative voice on silent groups and, second, a crude—but exceedingly common—bestowal of collective life on an artificial block called 'majority' that fuses together an amorphous assortment of multiple voices *and* multiple silences, few of which are necessarily put at the 'disposal' of political leaders. As Brito Vieira has put it, 'the silent majority claim, especially where the reference group is large, disallows contestation in its own terms. It trades on the ambiguous and unverifiable nature of the evoked silence to resist falsification.'[44]

An entirely different gloss on political silence was put by the pioneering German political scientist Elizabeth Noelle-Neumann through her well-known phrase 'spiral of silence', which gave substance to the concrete existence of tacit dissent rather than tacit consent—an inverse silent minority. Although the decision to keep one's differing views to oneself may have been conscious, it was not identifiable as such in a social arena. As Noelle-Neumann explained:

individuals who notice that their own opinions are losing ground, will be inclined to adopt a more reserved attitude when expressing their opinions in public. ... The result is a spiral process which prompts other individuals to perceive the changes in opinion and to follow suit, until one opinion has become established as the prevailing attitude while the other opinion will be pushed back and rejected by everybody with the exception of the hard core that nevertheless sticks to that opinion ... the representatives of the first opinion talk quite a lot while the representatives of the second opinion remain silent.[45]

In this instance, silence covers the erosion of a political stance, reflecting the loss of confidence in its viability; hence the public perception persists that something undefined may be out there, but while it remains unarticulated its effect is assumed to wane or become less relevant.

The era of digitalization and the proliferation of social media have partially reversed the 'silent majority' phenomenon by bringing in their wake a novel type of political silencing. It is the product of a hyper-verbose electorate (or the trigger-happy and often heedless segments of it) rather them a quietly acquiescent one. Participation, in such instances, goes off the rails in a very personal and individualistic sense, streets apart from the ideals of an active communal and organic democracy, recalling instead theories of atomistic social structure that were applied to nineteenth-century politics. Indiscriminate over-information in the shape of a barrage of tweets and social media messages that rarely undergo self-censorship produces a cacophony that effectively desensitizes the capacity to separate the wheat from the chaff, like a haystack dropped over a needle. That quantitative eruption transforms the transmission and penetration of information. It acts as an ersatz, unintentional silencing of the substance of messages by blunting the capacity to absorb, listen to, understand, and discriminate among them. Some of the main ingredients of the democratic ethos—weight, articulateness, and group identity—are edited out and muted. And the maldistribution of voice is striking—a result not of malice but of successful and impersonal technologies at the disposal of the digitally and electronically capable. As one scholar of digitalization has maintained: 'No democratic theorist expects citizens' voices to be considered exactly equally, but all would agree that pluralism fails whenever vast swathes of the public are systematically unheard in civic debates.'[46]

The equivocality embedded in silence is a defining attribute of its political dimension. Political thinking approaches the ineluctable ambiguity of language in two ways. The first is by attempting to reduce ambiguity through decontestation: that is, through expressing a strong preference for one of the multiple meanings implied by a word or concept and ruling out the others. The second, to the contrary, is by promoting ambiguity so as to enable the addressing of disparate audiences simultaneously, thus maintaining the relevance of a particular discourse through maximizing its impact. The ostensible non-language of silence, however, serves ends that can support both options. When treated as a blank sheet on which human thought and text can be inscribed, silence provides a pliant base for those who wish to appropriate it. It can be decontested as either a positive or a negative utterance when referring to the specific issue to which it is associated. Positively, it may be ascribed to a broad—if frequently vague—contentment with the state of affairs in a society and the comportment of its government. Negatively, claiming the legal right to remain silent may often, but not always, be a wilful act of obfuscation, an act of moral fortitude, an insistence on privacy, or a form of clueless bewilderment. It may just as often alert us to the alienation of societies from the political frameworks that encase them. On the other hand, silence may be exploited as an absence, whether mysterious or opportune, that can fall into the hands of politicians and delay decision making—the latter case was exemplified in the initial silence of the Catalan government following the October 2017 referendum on whether to declare independence from Spain.[47] Politically, the nature of consent revolves around control and its elusivenes: the political finality of foisting voice on silence is matched by the ultimate metapolitical finality of silence itself.

Notes

1 T. Hobbes, *Leviathan* (Harmondsworth: Penguin, 1961), ch. 26, p. 313.
2 Such matters are considered critically by A. John Simmons, *On the Edge of Anarchy: Locke, Consent, and the Limits of Society* (Princeton, NJ: Princeton University Press, 1993), pp. 80–90; and J. Dunn, *The Political Thought of John Locke* (Cambridge: Cambridge University Press, 1969), pp. 131–136.
3 A. X. Fellmeth and M. Horwitz, *Guide to Latin in International Law* (Oxford: Oxford University Press, 2009).
4 G. O. Nwoye, 'Eloquent Silence among the Igbo of Nigeria', in Tannen and Saville-Troike, *Perspectives on Silence*, pp. 185–191, at p. 189.
5 John Locke, *Two Treatises of Government, Second Treatise* (New York: Mentor, 1965), section 119.
6 For a range of perspectives on political performativity see S. M. Rai, M. Gluhovic, S. Jestrovic, and M. Saward (eds.), *The Oxford Handbook of Politics and Performance* (Oxford: Oxford University Press, 2021).
7 Kurzon, *Discourse of Silence*, p. 13.

8. Rollo, 'Everyday Deeds', pp. 587–609; T. Rollo, 'Democratic Silence: Two Forms of Domination in the Social Contract Tradition', *Critical Review of International Social and Political Philosophy* 24 (2021), pp. 316–329.
9. See Chapter 7.
10. Locke, *Second Treatise*, sections 222–223, 225.
11. Ibid., section 14.
12. J. H. Kary, 'Contract Law and the Social Contract: What Legal History Can Teach Us about the Political Theory of Hobbes and Locke', *Ottawa Law Review* 31/1 (1999), p. 79.
13. Ibid., p. 91.
14. Dunn, *Political Thought of John Locke*, p. 142.
15. Locke, *Second Treatise*, sections 116–120.
16. Ibid., section 121.
17. A. O. Hirschman, *Exit, Voice, and Loyalty: Responses to Decline in Firms, Organizations, and States* (Cambridge, MA: Harvard University Press, 1970).
18. See T. Beasley-Murray, 'Reticence and the Fuzziness of Thresholds: A Bakhtinian Apology for Quietism', *Common Knowledge* 19 (2013), pp. 424–445.
19. Hobbes, *Leviathan*, ch. 11, p. 163.
20. On a different set of issues emanating from Hobbes' passage see P. Hayes, 'Hobbes's Silent Fool: A Response to Hoekstra', *Political Theory* 27 (1999), pp. 225–229.
21. E. Kahn, 'Functions of Silence in Life and Literature', *Contemporary Review* 194 (1958), pp. 204–205.
22. Billias and Vemuri, *The Ethics of Silence*, pp. 143, 161.
23. Kagge, *Silence in the Age of Noise*, p. 114.
24. P. Ricoeur, *Lectures on Ideology and Utopia* (New York: Columbia University Press, 1986), p. 13.
25. John Locke, *Essay Concerning Human Understanding* (Oxford: Oxford University Press, 1979), book I, ch. 2, section 22.
26. Ibid., section 26.
27. Ibid., section 25.
28. Hobbes, *Leviathan*, ch. 17, p. 227.
29. Locke, *Essay*, book I, ch. 2, sections 2, 4.
30. Ibid., book II, ch. 28, section 10.
31. Talmud, Kiddushin 3b. See https://momentmag.com/ask-the-rabbis-is-silence-consent/, 6 January 2020 (accessed 24 June 2020).
32. Imam Muslim, *The Book of Marriage (Kitab Al-Nikah) of Sahih Muslim*, Hadith 3308, https://www.searchtruth.com/book_display.php?book=008&translator=2&start=0&number=3308
33. Hobbes, *Leviathan*, ch. 15, pp. 201, 203.
34. J. J. Rousseau, *The Social Contract* (Harmondsworth: Penguin, 1968), pp. 70, 135.
35. R. Tuck, *The Sleeping Sovereign: The Invention of Modern Democracy* (Cambridge: Cambridge University Press, 2016); R. Douglass, 'Tuck, Rousseau and the Sovereignty of the People', *History of European Ideas* 42/8 (2016), pp. 1111–1114.
36. *Book of Common Prayer*, http://www.ccepiscopal.org/handouts/bcp-1662.pdf (accessed 19 October 2017).
37. Ephratt, *The Functions of Silence*, p. 1915.
38. See Chapter 8.

39 Zoe Williams, 'What Used to Define Us was Irony. Now It's Self-Importance', *The Guardian*, 30 October 2017.
40 R. E. Buswell Jr. and D. S. Lopez Jr., *The Princeton Dictionary of Buddhism* (Princeton, NJ: Princeton University Press, 2014).
41 Richard Nixon, *President Nixon's Address to the Nation on the War in Vietnam*, 3 November 1969, http://watergate.info/1969/11/03/nixons-silent-majority-speech.html (accessed 7 November 2017)
42 Sam Sanders, 'Trump Champions the "Silent Majority," But What Does That Mean in 2016?', NPR.org, 22 January 2016, https://text.npr.org/s.php?sId=463884201 (accessed 27 May 2020).
43 Quoted in E. Fawcett, *Conservatism: The Fight for a Tradition* (Princeton, NJ, and Oxford: Princeton University Press, 2020), p. 356.
44 Mónica Brito Vieira, 'Representing Silence in Politics', *American Political Science Review* 114 (2020), pp. 976–988 at p. 986.
45 E. Noelle-Neumann, 'Turbulences in the Climate of Opinion: Methodological Applications of the Spiral of Silence Theory', *Public Opinion Quarterly* 41/2 (1977), pp. 143–158 at pp. 143–144.
46 M. Hindman, *The Myth of Digital Democracy* (Princeton, NJ, and Oxford: Princeton University Press, 2009), p. 12.
47 'Spain Says Catalonia Leader Puigdemont "Unclear" on Independence', 16 October 2017, https://www.bbc.co.uk/news/world-europe-41632084 (accessed 10 December 2021).

12
The Socio-cultural Filters of Silences

The manner of the social distribution of silence is one of its most illuminating political aspects on every dimension. Where silence is prevalent, where it is profound and intense, where it shifts across time, to which changing issues it pertains, whether it affects some groups more than others, whether it is proximate to or remote from the principal concerns of political thinking and speech, and which culturally specific social practices encourage silence or, to the contrary, covertly override speech, are all strongly indicative of socio-political forces at play. Several examples have already been mentioned *en passant*, but it might be helpful to draw some themes together.

In everyday interaction, the firm grip of silence—as well as its lighter caresses—will herald, enable, or block a range of human capacities. Silence is either an integrator or an isolator, a unifier or an atomizer. Individuals may choose to encase themselves in it or assume that they are enveloped by it. In imagining that holistic relationship, they become part of a larger whole that takes them over and to which they are subjected, however beneficially they may conceive of it. Their autonomy is reduced by, and occasionally abandoned to, a guiding and immersive force, whether that be religion, music, or the solitude experienced in nature. Alternatively, individuals may be caught up in a deeply felt insulating silence that blunts or obstructs their capacity to act when such obstruction is physiological or psychological.[1] In both cases their critical awareness may be dulled, and their personal human agency curbed to the point where it cannot be wholly retrieved, extracted, and exercised, even when they feel liberated.

In focusing on silence as a regulator of quotidian social relations, it is important to reiterate two central guidelines established in this study. First is the appeal to an expansive understanding of the political, omnipresent at every level in the complex interplay of individuals and groups. Second, concealed and unheeded silences have enough weight, and merit sufficient analytical attention, to keep us busy and intellectually engrossed without recourse to the deliberate suppressing of the agency of others—an analytically distinct field.

Concealed Silences and Inaudible Voices in Political Thinking. Michael Freeden, Oxford University Press.
© Michael Freeden (2022). DOI: 10.1093/oso/9780198833512.003.0014

1 Buddhist Ineffability

We commence with revisiting the complex topic of silence in Buddhism, located at the finely meshed interstices of the religious, the mystical, and the philosophical, in a tradition where these distinctions are prone to dissolve. Buddhism straddles any putative divide between a lived life and theorizing about it, contributing to a mindset through which to conduct one's way in the world. In the early stages of the teachings of Buddha, silence does not endorse any view on questions concerning whether the world is eternal or finite or whether the soul is the same as the body. Those questions must remain undeclared, yet that silence on the Buddha's part may nonetheless be understood as affirming the futility of solving such metaphysical problems, hence insisting on their unknowability—although in this instance silence does not apply to beneficial knowledge about enlightenment and nirvana.[2] The *Vilmalakirti Sutra* effects a more emphatic link with the ineffable and with emptiness. It writes of Vilmalakirti's encounter with Manjushri: 'At that time Vilmalakirti remained silent and did not speak a word. Manjushri sighed and said, "Excellent, excellent! Not a word, not a syllable—this truly is to enter the gate of non-dualism!"' Burton Watson has commented that all things in the phenomenal world are

> in a state of constant flux.... They may therefore be designated as 'empty' or 'void' because they lack any inherent characteristic by which they can be described ... looked at from the point of view of emptiness, they are seen to have one quality they all share: that of forming a single entity, one that is beyond the power of language to describe because language can deal only with distinctions.[3]

In furthering religious aims, silence-cum-*emptiness* is not a description of a reality, but marks out the aspiration of attaining a personal equilibrium. Nor is it to be equated with a nihilistic nothingness. Indeed, when a Japanese visitor in conversation with Heidegger had observed of the German philosopher's conception of 'being': 'To us, emptiness is the loftiest name for what you mean to say with the word "Being"', Heidegger had concurred.[4] As a commentator noted, 'Heidegger did not object to such associations. He had expressed that Being is but a being-in-the-world that manifests itself in simultaneous movements of concealment and revelation.'[5] In its most pronounced form, however, the emptiness of emptiness aims to discredit ontological questions altogether. It is a form of quietism that rejects all philosophical and meta-philosophical debates and dualisms by maintaining silence on them.[6]

In a twentieth-century setting, a parallelism to such non-dualisms is to be found in Foucault's thoughts on silence. Foucault was exploring not the normality, but the oppressiveness, of binary thought-practices in the following passage, but the lessons he derives appear to have some affinity with Buddhist worldviews:

> Silence itself—the thing one declines to say, or is forbidden to name, the discretion that is required between different speakers—is less the absolute limit of discourse, the other side from which it is separated by a strict boundary, than an element that functions alongside the things said, with them and in relation to them within over-all strategies.[7]

Yet the approach is starkly different. Despite rejecting a binary distinction, Foucault's focus on controlling regimes of discourse prioritizes his desire to control silence itself by exposing the strategies employed in its management, in contrast to the Buddhist acceptance of the natural fluidity between speech and silence.

The non-dualism advocated by many Buddhists adds nuances to some of the central representations of silence. In most occidental cultures, a series of ambiguities is attributed to silence on the absence/presence dichotomy as well as on what can be read into tacit knowledge or taciturnity, whether as a form of affirmation and consent or as a form of abstention or negation. Zen-Buddhism adopted a stronger stance on emptiness, when 'all dualities and all unity are being smashed and ruptured'.[8] One Zen aphorism states: 'Has a dog Buddha-nature?/This is the most serious question of all./If you say yes or no,/You lose your own Buddha nature.'[9] Another instructs: 'If you want to express the truth, throw out your words, throw out your silence, and tell me about your own Zen.'[10] Or as expressed by Zhuangzi: 'Words exist because of meaning; once you've gotten the meaning, you can forget the words.'[11] The non-duality of speech and silence is epitomized as 'not-speaking is the Buddha's speaking' or, put differently, 'the Buddha mind, having no fixed form and characteristic, can neither be separated from nor tied to language.'[12] The Buddhist monk Jizang elaborated, 'as emptiness is emptiness-of-existence, it is existence while being emptiness. As existence is existence-of-emptiness, it is emptiness while being existence.' When one represents the word 'existence' by the word 'speech' and the word 'emptiness' by the word 'nonspeech' or 'silence', the result is 'as speech is speech-of-nonspeech, it is nonspeech while being speech. As nonspeech is nonspeech-of-speech, it is speech while being nonspeech.' They are, as Ho explains, 'mutually complementary modes of expression'. Even as one speaks, ineffability is maintained through the refusal to assign 'any attachment to the words spoken and their referents'.[13]

The main ambiguity turns on two facets of language and meaning. First, what words denote cannot be fixed—a truism generally agreed upon among contemporary linguists, philosophers of language, and discourse analysts, though not always by promoters of ideologies. Second, 'What do words rely on, that we have right and wrong? ... Everything has its "that", everything has its "this". From the point of view of "that" you cannot see it, but through understanding you can know it.'[14] Both 'this' and 'that' have a right and a wrong in them, which do away with opposites and produce a 'hinge' of Dao that can respond unendingly with a new clarity of understanding. Ambiguity here leads to resolution and reality, not to the indeterminacy or uncertainty with which it has usually been associated in other interpretative frameworks. Obscured knowledge is revealed in its fullness. Contrast this also with silence in medieval European mysticism which, as a commentary on the sixteenth-century Italian Carmelite mystic Maria Maddalena de Pazzi observes, 'must spread into the very mind which will free itself more and more from all human language, from all earthly imagination, in order to seize as purely as possible the ineffable Being that no word ever can reveal and no sensible reality represent'.[15] Reality is excluded from that ineffable domain, not comprehended through it.

In the broader context of this study, the main significance of these modes of Buddhism, especially Zen, has been to focus awareness on both conceptualizing and practising silence as central to experiencing life. On the one hand, 'silence becomes silence only in relation to speaking ... to maintain an authentic silence or non-speaking, he may have to speak first'.[16] But ultimately in Zen, as Wright has commented: 'The practice of nondiscursive meditation, at its deepest levels, is independent of language and ... the experience of the accomplished meditator is thoroughly nonlinguistic.' And he continues:

> given the range and the subtlety of their vocabulary of meditative silence, the experience of silence in Zen is the most highly nuanced, linguistically articulate—that is, 'significant'—such experience in the world.... Silence in Zen is not just the absence of sound. It is 'symbolic of awakening', 'highly profound', 'the foundation of any authentic practice', 'the atmosphere most treasured and cultivated in monastic life', 'unnerving', 'capable of evoking insight', and so on.

Above all, as Wright observes, silence is catapulted into the core area of scholarly attention:

> What does a 'vocabulary of silence' have to do with its experience besides supplying the term for its communication? Initially, it makes silence noticeable. Although 'silence' was available for experience long before Zen, only when the 'teaching of silence' was generated and regenerated did it really become interesting. Before its articulation in language, silence wasn't much of anything; no one attended to it (at least not in view of Zen interests).[17]

Indeed, as another scholar of Chinese thought, Tong, has intriguingly mused: 'What is silence? This question has perhaps never been raised before—certainly not as a serious philosophical question and not in the Western tradition. In so far as traditional Western philosophy is concerned, this question cannot have arisen because silence has rarely been practiced, if at all, by Western philosophers.'[18] And a comment by Tang is highly pertinent in its cross-cultural validity:

> Paradoxical as it may seem, the tactic of silence possesses advantages unsurpassed by other tactics. It renders to the text gaps and holes that provide the reader's imagination and encourage him to search for its hidden meanings. It liberates the words from their rigid reference so that they are transformed from physical marks into artistic symbols. Language is no longer the shackles or prison-house of thought but a horizon that opens on more horizons. Since truth or meaning does not lie in language but in the horizons it reveals, silence in the forms of suggestion, evocation, 'quiet observation' and 'direct experience' provides Chinese philosophers and poets with a most effective means for obtaining truth or literary understanding.[19]

That observation applies equally to the imaginative visions elaborated in political thinking or, say, to the silences of Virginia Woolf's protagonists discussed in Chapter 4. Whether or not they do indeed obtain truth, they certainly provide insight about the emancipating spaces cleared by silence.

But in those cultural traditions silence is approached as both a state of mind and a state of truth, an inexpressible and mystical awakening or enlightenment. It accompanies language while transcending it and has claims to a superior ranking in non-worldly life. In a subtle and perceptive essay on the rhetoric of ineffability, Varsano explores the Chinese poetic genre of the 'absent-recluse'—unreachable individuals who elude contact or tracking down, and whose ideal identity lies in the values of silence and invisibility. Instructively, she draws attention to those poems as containing 'an eloquent fusion of the contradictory attitudes of acceptance and abhorrence of the compromise [with purity] inherent in language itself'.[20] Through them silence both becomes a language expressed through poetry and—by means of the recurring theme of intending to visit a sought-after but elusive recluse but finding him absent and his room empty—provides the subsequent insight of Daoist enlightened knowledge. Attaining silence begins as a journey whose consequences are not anticipated and only clarified in a transformative realization that the ostensibly thwarted journey has culminated in a very different but nonetheless instructive ending. It is the knowledge secured through encountering lack, a lack embedded in language that falls short of the ineffability of enlightenment.

Varsano's analysis merits close scrutiny, as it touches on many key features of silence that carry comparative significance: silenced silences, disturbed anticipation, the question of boundaries, and the political lessons that silence can offer. The confounding of expectations is a central disruptive ploy of Cage's 4'33", but that ploy was also the turning point for an audience led to cultivate—in secular rather than religious mode—a fresh sensibility to the interactions between sound and silence and a deeper comprehension of the notion of hiddenness itself. When Varsano observes of an absent-recluse poem by Ch'iu Wei that 'silence slips into the vacuum left by the unuttered words',[21] it is a distinctive kind of silence—not as an acoustic ellipsis or hiatus between sounds or words, but as a newly and unintentionally acquired spiritual understanding. But Varsano then adds another strand to the complexity of poetic silence, detecting a further obscured layer that redistributes its significance from the periphery to the unspoken centre of the poem's lesson. In a 'silent adoption of silence itself', a later poem by Chia Tao assumes knowledge of Ch'iu Wei's antecedent poem simply by omitting reference to its well-known narrative.[22] Language is no longer necessary to press home enlightenment when ineffability is relocated at its heart and understanding is diffused through unspoken cultural and spiritual intimations.

At the same time, some of the poems exude strong political implications. Varsano notes another to-and-fro journey, that of the poet-literati who holds a bureaucratic post that entails 'the duty of service to the state' but who then breaches the politically enshrined barrier, the liminality, between the publicly mundane and the personally otherworldly, 'between the socially obligated purveyor of words [opposed] to the unfettered, unknown and wordless hero' who withdraws from human society. The momentary glimpse of enlightenment is incorporated into political life once the poet is back at his public craft. His insight into silence through his evocative poem now 'bear[s] the fruit of this non-encounter'.[23] While the recluse needs the social legitimacy conferred by officialdom, the scholar-official discharges the role of medium between recluse and society through 'his unique ability to see what was hidden and transmit the untransmittable'. Silence thus becomes a moral and spiritual good and the scholar-official, as its detector and conveyer, places the worthy ideals it contains at the service of the state. That Daoist worldview is maintained 'resolutely beyond the sphere of the social while sturdily anchored in its codes'.[24] The desocialized recluse individual and the group vocation of the literati are held in balance, but that is achieved through the spatial relocation that silence undergoes in its purest spiritual form. It migrates from a secluded rural setting to the urban centre that it might subsequently suffuse.

The political sphere requires such an importation of mystical ineffability to enhance and expand the quality of service it can provide, becoming in the process also a covert bearer of spiritual values, and establishing literati as the formalized agents of that regeneration. Yet that very ineffability also constrains its influence on the political realm, as the quality of ineffability is disseminated through a rarefied medium whose imaginative impact depends on its appeal to the effective wielders of power.

2 Thresholds and Transitions

There is another insight to be reinforced from the above. The establishing of boundaries is an indispensable characteristic of the political, whether in its distribution and allocation roles, or in the imposition of order on the words it seeks to control. An aphorism in the Daodejing is illuminating here in identifying the two sides of power, both wielding it and desisting from it: 'When we start to regulate the world we introduce names. But once names have been assigned, we must know when to stop. Knowing when to stop is how to avoid danger.'[25] The challenging and disruption of boundaries is the political inverse of boundary drawing. It is itself a prime feature of thinking politically, ultimately serving to establish new—and always temporary—boundaries, new forms of order and regulation, and new measures of pacing temporality. But in Zen philosophy a further dimension is in play—the ontological negation of the concept of boundaries. What this does is not to eradicate that crucial property of the political, but to interrogate it. Aspects of the political are thus assimilated and integrated as undifferentiated components of a wider experience of the world, both material and spiritual. The political moments of silence as effacing ideas and practices, or as affirming them, lose their distinctiveness. The ancillary consequences are that the political as the arena of social organization and directives, expressed through speech or performance, is brought back into line by demoting its aspiration to be the purveyor of finality in the affairs of people, by querying its methods of communicating, and by shedding its specificity, which of course throws another cloak of inaudibility over it.

Sites of worship are another salient arena of silence. Manners and conventions of silence—as distinct from communal occasions of ceremonial silences—are typical of the conduct of some, though decidedly not all, Christian congregations. To illustrate, they may be observed intermittently in the hush on entering awe-inspiring cathedrals, more substantially in the unwritten rules of Quakers' meetings. Leaving aside the spiritual dimensions of those experiences, they create an exaggeratedly abrupt juncture between the external and the internal, the deliberate and the customary, parcelling out a protected domain of refuge and retreat, in which silence is a mark of that transition. Retreat is of course itself a movement, a folding away from, and it is often accompanied by a scalar distribution of significance in which the secular and the public are removed, and implicitly demoted, from the spiritual and the private, while the institutional force of established religion is experienced in its formal intensity.

Vainiomäki finds such threshold-crossing moments in several culturally and collectively assimilated practices. They occur when 'as a means of signification, silence can function as a channel for many kinds of transitional phases'. Thus, the momentary hush that settles on an audience before a concert begins serves as a preparatory stage prior to a modification in behaviour.[26] Those silences constitute a boundary for mood change, for awareness of altered surroundings, and for switching to a different set of social rules. Concurrently, they supply the political imprimatur for ranking certain public activities by ushering in a redistributed significance as people migrate through their social roles, each demanding a specific and tight organization of conduct. While superficially voluntary, such silences become ingredients of structured and semi-formal occasions into which one enters routinely and largely unthinkingly through unwritten, but not uncoded, understandings.

Under conditions of worship, group identity is privileged over the sole individual, not least because such devotion is located in designated areas. The difference between the cathedral experience and Quakers' meetings is, however, stark. A silence with a quasi-authoritarian resonance is juxtaposed to a democratic one. Cathedrals impose a time-honoured and ritually expected, top-down, silence on a potentially wayward assembly of individuals, both casual and worshippers—an elite, hierarchical conception of silence is initiated by stepping over the threshold, the boundary. Their cavernous architecture miniaturizes and effaces individuals—architecture itself serves as an enhancer of sanctity, a regulator of conduct, and a silencer, even for non-believers. In the case of Quakers, the silence is at grass-roots level, egalitarian, voluntary, and horizontally spread rather than vertically structured. The meeting room is relatively sparse and of modest proportions, bereft of liturgical signs, and offering withdrawal from the world. Silence, stillness, and calm do not emanate from an engulfing space or an awareness of tradition but from a sense of commonality.[27]

Alternatively, the intensity of silences may be a function of a deep physical quiet and absence of sound, as experienced in wildernesses. Even though the known universe is frequently described in human terms as actively restless, and far from still, the space provided by a wilderness becomes the prototypical setting for either the lyrical harmony, or jarring clash, between human and nature. We have already encountered its stillness as a site of spiritual or mystical communion. By contrast, the phrase 'in space no one can hear you scream'[28] is an evocation of utter isolation, as well as terror. Either way, another threshold is there to be traversed, for the idea of a silent, primordial wilderness feeds the theory that silence is the default position that precedes sound, so that the metaphor of 'breaking the silence' points to an abrupt shattering of a 'thing' possessing both initial solidity and brittleness. The semantic vagueness of the phrase is evident: it may gently introduce a break, a hiatus, in which noise or voice are temporarily enabled to take over. But alternatively breaking requires effort, and results in fracturing. The Israeli non-governmental organization 'Breaking the Silence' is composed of veteran soldiers who offer testimony on the effects of military rule on Palestinian civilians in the occupied territories.[29] Its political aspect as a sudden, and vocally forceful, intervention in a previous public quiescence, with the aim of effecting a change, is undeniable. There is of course an ambiguity here, less in the deliberate rupture or ending of the practising of silence and more in the unclear intentionality of the silence itself: is it a secretive muffling of the known or an unreflective cultural condoning of violence against particular individuals and groups, combined with an internalized ingestion of assumed national interests? In Israeli society the widespread reliance on recruiting citizens for reserve duty past their initial conscription period helps to blur the distinction between military and national-civic norms and to blend private and public patterns of conduct. But breaking that silence emerges precisely from the greater maturity found among some of those slightly older reservist citizens.

Commonly, too, people are 'rendered speechless' for a host of deeply emotional reasons. One of them may be a sense of outrage at a deed or expression that violates their standards of fairness or acceptability, in which case it resets the capacity to counteract. Another may follow from a very moving scene in a film or a TV report that touches or shocks viewers intensely. Here, their silence provides a disruptive, but temporally limited, suspension of an individual's capability, brought on by external triggers that impact on one's emotional equilibrium. A third may reflect surprise and wonder, as in the following newspaper caption: 'Egypt archaeologist rendered speechless by treasure: "Never seen anything like it"', although one suspects that may be metaphorical.[30] In all three instances, people are subject to a powerful exterior encounter or occurrence that requires personal recovery and recalibration and the restoring of order and balance.

3 The Modalities of Silence and Their Social Roots

The modalities of silence elaborated in Chapter 7 are all subject to social processing, though some more than others. Acting them out and reacting to them are assimilated both into the everyday lives, languages, routines, imaginations, and grievances of societies and individuals at large, and into the various bodies of professional knowledge that the civilizations of the globe craft and develop. The distribution of their effect, however, is uneven within a specified society, let alone across nations and cultures. The unthinkable is the product of a host of different factors, any of which can dampen or eliminate the capacity for reflection. One is the spread of forms of education that not just limit the quantity of available information but discourage the spirit of inquiry and curiosity, the testing of assumptions, the imagining of alternatives, and what can colloquially be called a healthy scepticism. Hofstede, for example, has explored uncertainty avoidance in learning contexts in which security seeking and intolerance are cultural characteristics of sectors within a society and that consequently diminish question posing.[31] Another is the speed with which knowledge paradigms alter—a function at least in part of the autonomy of knowledge centres and the general receptivity to outside influence. A third concerns the political control deliberately or unwittingly exercised by leaders of opinion and defenders of public morality. The unthinkable can never be a constant through either space or time. The silences it causes affect groups differentially and their capacity to remain undetected may vacillate between the robust and the fragile.

The unspeakable is a combination of durable and ephemeral factors. There are nigh-universal subjects whose details induce repugnance among most people: mass murder, sexual violence towards children, and extreme forms of torture, alluded to above. Other acts—especially those that violate a 'code of honour'—are met by a silence of shame, or occasionally of complicit guilt. Yet in the same society, outspokenness may be inculcated within some groups or individuals, whose immunity from shock and abhorrence may be culturally acquired; or it may reflect cultural practices of speaking one's mind, untrammelled by what are termed 'social niceties'. The ephemerality of the unspeakable, like the unthinkable, can fluctuate. In segments of many societies—though far from all—attitudes towards homosexuality and children born out of wedlock are undergoing change and no longer erased from both public and private spheres. Different categories of what is deemed unmentionable abound in the same social context, for instance in care communities and religious groups. In the former, the linguistic move away from 'handicapped', 'special needs', and 'disabled' illustrates the search for new terminology, as in turn existing terms fall foul of negative connotations. In the latter, those shifts occur in reverse by the sacralization of words such as the name(s) of the deity. Silences concerning 'unspeakable' taboos are socially common, but the topics concerning such taboos and the areas in which those prohibitions prevent expression vary tellingly: from superstitions, through religious injunctions, to national ordeals, to discussing death or sexual conduct, and to 'politically correct' language—the latter tending to be the province of culturally and ethnically sensitive or militant groups and their supporters.

A very different account of the unspeakable emanates from critical theory. Although critical theorists do not necessarily espouse the agentic view of so-called Anglo-American analytical philosophy, they see human beings as endowed with a voice, with the attribute of being vocal, if not simplistically rational, and—as do the flatter—they too superimpose on that understanding the normative enabling of ethical involvement in social and political life. For them, however, silence is suspicious and disturbing, occasioned not by the failure of certain individuals to realize fully their intellectual and performative capabilities, but by the failure of the societies of which they are part to discharge their elemental duties towards their members. It suggests that voices have been suppressed or deliberately obliterated and that the unspeakable is determined by systemic and invasive social and political intrusions into autonomy. One scholar in that camp has remarked that 'silence by a victim of injustice is a kind of political neurosis',[32] while another has referred to the 'demise of identity'.[33]

Euphemisms are a widespread variant of the unspeakable as the unsayable. Referring to death as passing or slipping away, passing on, losing the battle, or indeed losing a specified human being, is a common practice that combines delicacy, superstition, fear (of the event and of causing offence), and self-protection.[34] It is not only that silencing the signifier is an indirect attempt to erase the signified, when all it actually does is to divert attention from an ultimately unavoidable event. 'Passing' refers to a relocation, a move, to another world, rather than to the more appropriate stillness or extinction, two states that are themselves silenced in ordinary language. Loss has two different prongs: the one insists on a lust for life that is defeated under circumstances beyond individual control, weaving a narrative that may well mute a less heroic reality. The other focuses on the survivors, not the deceased, who become diminished and lapse into a condition of lack that overshadows the graver total absence of the now lifeless person.

At the level of social conduct, the unnoticeable is a particularly common modality. It is not linked to specific social characteristics and can be experienced within any section of society—unlike the unconceptualizable that would be more typical of groups with a relatively low degree of curiosity about existential social issues or a cultural propensity to forgo abstraction and self-questioning. A familiar pattern of unnoticeability relates to the perception of minorities within a dominant culture. Ethnicity and skin colour may be obvious to some casual observers on a case-by-case basis. But even if not minority-hostile, they may nonetheless be minority-insensitive, unmindful that those features are perfectly consonant with the presence of a group that is a full constituent of a plural nation, with its own history, customs, and needs. In his famous prologue to *Invisible Man* (where invisible includes inaudible), Ralph Ellison wrote: 'I am an invisible man. . . . I am invisible, understand, simply because people refuse to see me. . . . When they approach me they see only my surroundings, themselves, or figments of their imagination—indeed, everything and anything except me.'[35]

The unnoticeable is anchored in concrete ways of life. As Zerubavel observes, 'when we notice or ignore something, we . . . often do so as members of particular social communities'—involving 'highly impersonal social traditions of paying attention'.[36] For Zerubavel, that is about learning to ignore, but it also is about the inevitable and non-flagged selectivity of perception and memory. Ignoring possesses two shades of meaning: the one central to the verb 'ignore', which involves a refusal to take notice or an intentional disregard, and the other embedded in the adjective 'ignorant', which can signify being unconscious, unschooled, or innocent of something. That duality stitches together two social happenings: a conspiratorial collusion or an eclipsing caused by cultural proclivities. The latter attribute of unnoticeability may involve an inclination to register only those aspects of an environment that hold particular significance to the observer, whereas what is overlooked or unscanned takes on the status of a default antithetical silence, a deficit of salience.

To illustrate: a cultural-geographical propensity to be silent is often associated with the Finns, described 'as a natural way to be'. It is a practice that 'serves a protective function, giving a social territory for each that is to be honoured socially, or not to be intruded'. It is often a matter 'of being guarded and observant before approaching another to speak to them'. While such silences are deliberate, they are concurrently customary and internalized and do not require spelling out or accounting for. They are an 'unspoken understanding, providing a taken-for-granted feature of unspoken social life'. Importantly, speaking is considered not 'as filling a silence, a presence within an absence, but potentially as a breach, cracking the valuable quietude among those present'.[37] Another study, by Lehtonen and Sajavaara, notes that 'the duration of silences tolerated by Finns in conversation is much longer' than in other cultures. Delayed or silent participation can lead to unintended breakdowns in communication. The rate of speech may also reflect variations internal to a culture, such as 'the relatively conservative morphophonology which lacks the consonant and vowel elision typical of other dialects'. A type of conduct that would be salient in many other societies, as well as to visitors to Finland, goes unnoticed and literally unremarkable on a macro-level, though minute differences will unsurprisingly be detected by the linguistic community alert to local speech patterns. But on a larger stage conversational silences are also understood as marking a cultural-political divide between Finland and its not infrequently verbally 'intrusive' neighbours.[38]

In a follow-up chapter, the authors investigate the stereotype of the silent Finn, a nation wittily, if antiquatedly, referred to by Bertolt Brecht 'as a people who are silent in two languages', Finnish and Swedish. That may be attributed to an alleged collective lack of self-esteem—silence relating here to the low ranking of one's national characteristics. Impressions of national silence—real, exaggerated, or imaginary—can contribute to the diminished status and power attributed to a particular society. Linguistic speed is associated with vitality and capability; perceptions of cultural silence vitiate the impact of those properties. Moreover, the absence of cultural affinity between groups is not always a sign of linguistic barriers, it may occur 'when people speaking the same language do not realise that their respective codes are shared only partially'. Lehtonen and Sajavaara are particularly instructive in addressing some of the implicit political features of the silences they explore. Argumentation may be seen as disrespect for the opinion of another—hence a violation of privacy and of equal regard. Noteworthy is the insistence not on the right to speak, or on the right to be silent—important feature of rights-oriented societies—but on the right of the listener to listen without being disturbed or interrupted.[39] As ever with equivalent cultural manifestations, the conceptual frameworks employed to interpret 'Finnish silence' single out different facets, variably focusing on its intensity, on the communicative range in which it is especially noticeable, on its proportional relation with speech, on its role in socio-political interaction, and on the significance and incommensurability of diverse kinds of absence.

There are other varieties of social silences with salient political content—each differentiated from the others—that share the feature of unnoticeable cultural 'naturalization'. They are all hybrid combinations of conscious but unremarkable silences that are imposed by unquestioned custom: going without saying because they come without saying, to reiterate Bourdieu's inspired formulation.[40] One would be the regular conversation silences of Japanese people described not as pauses for the right words but as their 'gaining mastery over silence for the sake of silence'—a form of self-control.[41] Another may endow silence with protective psychic powers as a barrier intended to ward off harm from conversing with certain classes of individuals.[42] A third is the *constrained*, personalized, initial silence that etiquette might prescribe with respect to encountering people with an ambiguous social or professional standing, or who are strangers, as registered for example in Apache culture—a matter of ordering and ranking culturally discrete groups.[43] That said, such hesitation may indicate internal reticence as well as hallowed external custom. Likewise, Aboriginal people maintain hierarchies of those who can talk and decide and those who have no right to speak—indeed, a duty not to speak—on certain issues,[44] though numerous remnants—even thriving instances—of such conventions are detectable in contemporary Western societies: in the workplace, educational facilities, places of worship, the military, gender-mediated relationships, and others. Goffman has discussed deference in the form of avoidance rituals that—following Georg Simmel—delineate an area of non-penetrability around others, incorporating stand-off arrangements. Central to those is the 'avoidance of other's personal name'[45]—a widely prevalent distancer or, conversely, expression of awe and respect. Gurevitch, too, has suggested that silence can function as spatial distancing when a face-to-face conversation fails to hold.[46] Silence then becomes a marker and mapper of separation between individuals in a physically proximate discursive relationship. Max Picard has described the encounter with an object that cannot be encapsulated by the word signifying it and needs to be introduced in a measured way in order to access and come to terms with it: 'The first time he sees an object, man is silent of his own accord. With his silence, man comes into relationship with the reality in the object which is there before even language gives it a name. Silence is his tribute of honour to the object.'[47]

The social normalizing of silence is thus infused with strong rationales that associate it with the distribution of significance to certain groups or segments above others. It contributes to, or endorses, the ranking and prioritizing processes that constitute one of the most fundamental of political practices. And it operates in two opposite ways: either signalling deference to a vocal group by falling silent in its presence, or discounting the voices of groups attempting to be heard by silently overlooking them. At any event, even plural societies eventually turn a deaf ear to multiple voices if—as an organizational necessity—those voices have to be funnelled into the political delivery of a single outcome, rather than left to an anarchic babble. Selection may involve suppressing or disregarding, but no less centrally it involves commitment, free choice, and the pursuit of desirable as well as desired ends. In a very elementary sense, the normal plurality of voices is transformed into the monolithic finality of decision that political life invariably requires, whether that society has adopted a democratic or autocratic ethos. That too goes without saying, for deprived of such 'end to debate' practices—however ephemeral—societies cannot function.

The political dimension of this is palpable. Language—and its complementary avoidance—appear here as a means of controlling the uncontrollable, imposing organization on the destructive potential of nature, or cosmos, or even more modestly of ignorance, and doing that through human activity—whether individual or collective. Politics is a prime anthropocentric practice, notwithstanding the fact that its features may possess parallel echoes in divinity and in nature. And the introduction of both time and space permits the imposition of measurability and finiteness on the unmeasurability and infinity of silence and on the absence of the unattainable. Man once again professes to be the measure of all things, a pursuit either doomed to defeat or pathetic in its posturing.

4 Dramatic Silences

In artistic and literary imaginations, silence as textual absence can be fashioned to furnish opportunities. Silences are sculpted and elongated in order to clear space that can immediately be filled with activity and movement and grafted on to subsequent text and speech. As the curtain rises, recent theatre directors have indulged in carving contrived pre-textual silences out of that eminently political and personal play, *King Lear*, extending the span of time and the reach of meaning. They have injected the opening scene with dramaturgical performativity that evokes the power and status of the king as his entourage accompanies him in a procession, voicelessly miming pomp and regality.[48] All this is a departure from former practice, as Oliver Taplin notes: 'In the theatre today silences are usually total: there is a hiatus, during which nobody speaks. Most previous theatres, including the Greek theatre, have generally avoided empty pauses, and have tended to a continuity of sound.'[49] If dramatic sound traditionally entailed a succession of voices, the silences extracted at the creative whim of theatre directors permit turning time back on itself, adding a new beginning.

Some of the great theatrical productions in the genre of the 'theatre of the absurd' employ silence as their central, defining idiom. The normalization of silence as a means of theatrical expression can achieve impact as a spectacle in ways that Cage's silent pianist could never do. Cage could confound audience expectations once, and then only as a novelty whose duration would necessarily be short. It bears some resemblance to the famous Milgram experiment when students were asked to inflict what they believed were electric shocks on complicit subjects, who had to pretend that they were enduring increasingly excruciating pain although no current flowed.[50] People eventually become in the know, nullifying the value of future experiments. In contrast, both Pinter and Beckett are in their different ways masters of silence as an art and a vocation. In Part I the significance of Pinter and Beckett was related to diverse realms of studying silence: as spasmodic communicative disconnections, as nihilistic rhythms of unsayability, and as semantic paralysis. But above all, as dramatists and literary innovators, they intertwined a powerful imaginative dexterity with an undertow of philosophical unease. Pinter's plays display a mastery of silences as human miscommunication and abrupt caesuras, as menace and, of course, as humour, employing dialogues of misplaced, non-sequitur, and distracted silences. They simultaneously stem the flow of dialogue and narrative and invest them with an arrhythmic momentum, while concurrently hinting at new possibilities both for the characters and for the spectators-cum-audience, drawn in as they are, intrigued, magnetized, perplexed, startled, and amused. His conversational yet monological blockages erratically unsettle and disarticulate speech, even as they are bound together by the centrality of silence. Indeed, Pinter's silences share a fundamental similarity, as with a well-honed routine of contrapuntal exchanges that meld together and confer a dramatic unity on the halting and muted irregularities of discourse. Below the surface, a plurality of silences operates to accentuate the prominence of silence in human conduct and interaction, as the unexpected in human conduct becomes the norm.

If Pinter's silences are intimidating, ominous, mostly communicative, and laden with semantic import, Beckett's are just as often ostensibly vapid, vacuous, and profoundly bereft of meaning, which injects them, of course, with ulterior significance. Both are craftsmen who make silences work for them, putting them to dramatic usage in their reconstruction of everyday speech, albeit exaggeratedly and often comically. Both playwrights tip the speech–silence balance in favour of silence, not quantitively but qualitatively.[51] But Beckett is often engrossed in direct metaphysical and philosophical cogitations on the meaning of silence and the futility of language, identity, and existence, while Pinter's artistry conveys more elliptical ruminations combined with targeted political critique. And there is also another stark political message in Beckett's work as well as in his life, which saw him severing professional contacts in a nomadic embracing of loneliness. Writing about Proust in a vein redolent of Beckett's own predilections, he commented: '... Art is the apotheosis of solitude. There is no communication because there are no vehicles of communication.'[52] An extreme atomistic withdrawal from social institutions became a signature tune of much of Beckett's opus. Communal discourse is relegated to silence in that dissolution of human ties, not so much a silence of speech as one of structural isolation. Pinter's silences, to the contrary, tease out the overcharged and disconcerting atmosphere of human contact.

Pinter embraces a further insight about language that expresses not one, but two, dual layers. First, two discourses that educe the simultaneity of speech *and* silence. 'So often,' he reflects, 'below the spoken word, is the thing known and unspoken ... a language ... where under what is said, another thing is being said.' Second, two silences. 'One when no word is spoken. The other when perhaps a torrent of language is being employed.'[53] That torrent is central to Stein's discussion of Ionescu's conversations and their 'repetition of banalities', or Beckett's 'speaking characters [who] talk with desperate fervor ... obsessed with talk'. 'It is in the dialogue—disjunctive, circular, contradictory, irrelevant', she writes, 'that the new attitude of metaphorical silence is best manifested.'[54] Ambiguity, indeterminacy, misrepresentations, recrafting realities, are standard weapons in many political armouries. Built into these literary genres is a recognition of contingency and bewilderment as underlying aspects of social life alongside the conditions of disarray that incapacitate purposive action. In parallel, the unpredictability of individual behaviour serves as a reminder of the political challenges to which organization and control must continually adjust and confront. Not least, failure, emotional fragility, and the decontextualization of time, space, and memory permeate human existence and usher in an ironic mirror-image that could be termed a constancy of disorientation. They signal not so much the collapse of political ends as their futility, when sapped of purpose and abandoned to a caricature of neutering, rote, and stagnant exchanges in which random words overwhelm language itself. It is an attitude that 'puts to question the peculiar power, the ancient excellence, of literary discourse—and challenges the assumptions of our civilisation'.[55]

Inasmuch as those given assumptions were shaped—at least in part—by theological narratives of order carved out of chaos or void, they were dismissed by artistic counter-narratives of a silencing chaos nihilistically released—often in anger or frustration—from a straitjacketing order. Literary practice appears torn between its conventional authoritative mainstays and their decomposition by rebellious sceptics and cynics. It conjures up an image not of an uplifting wilderness but of a dysfunctional desert drained of individual cooperation as well as creativity. Or perhaps it simply is a warning that the political fantasies of order and progress need to cede way. Human contact can then be reconciled with the really political—a scattering of permanently unsettled human transactions whose impact repeatedly misfires. The metaphorical silence is lodged in an anti-language unreceptive to decoding that, like the colour white, contains everything while seemingly containing nothing. The spectre of a political dystopia, of course, is never far away—itself unspoken but plainly 'below the spoken word'. Much of Pinter's explicit political *oeuvre* is nourished—if that is the *mot juste*—by exactly those conditions.

Silent 'music', as noted in the Prelude, attains celebrity status in Cage's *4'33"*, controlling, manipulating, and compelling an audience to alter its conventional expectations by eliminating anticipated sound and clearing the way to 'replace' it with ambient, disorganized background noise. But Cage's composition elicits another dimension, one relating to the dual disruption and upholding of socially acceptable conventions. The sustained suppression of coughs and rustling is relaxed, triggering a counterpoint to the normally required—indeed, culturally de rigueur—silence of the audience during a classical music concert. That behavioural pattern entails a strict culture of material and vocal (though not emotional or aesthetic) non-participation and non-involvement, inducing either a contemplative or a conforming silence. As Ramel notes, ducal power in Renaissance Italy was reflected in the concert halls they constructed and that imposed secularized silences on audiences.[56] And as Jacques Attali records, 'the most perfect silence reigned in the concerts of the bourgeoisie, who affirmed thereby their submission to the artificialized spectacle of harmony—master and slave, the rule governing the symbolic game of their domination'.[57] Yet in *4'33"* the confusion is obvious: the constraining norms of concert etiquette somehow still hold even under those topsy-turvy conditions. Ambient noise there is indeed, but unaccompanied by idle audience chatter, such is the power of the conventions of silence dictated by audience behaviour.

Among the social practices related to silence, that of ostracism is an oddity that merits a few observations. 'Sending people to Coventry', ignoring them, cutting them off informally from human contact, is a special case of distributing silence—not imposing silence *on* another, but practising silence *against* another. It is commonly an act of aggressive yet half-hidden harm, verging on abuse, directed against an individual or a (presumably small) group—a deliberate act of wielding power as retribution that is not always or immediately evident or transparent to the recipient. Ostracism supplies three features highly pertinent to a consideration of silence. The first reveals a potential and unusual reversal of the flow of silence. The ostracizing group silences *itself* in the process of eschewing a prohibited interaction—a political practice of considerable self-control, consistency, and finality. It involves mobilizing support and coordination among the self-silencing community and the enforced demotion of the social status of the target to the point of exclusion. Notably, that deliberate self-silencing directed outwards does not involve the imposition of quiet on the ostracized. They may speak, but it is as if they had not spoken and were reduced to inaudibility and invisibility; in other words, the communication line between speech and listening, or performing and reacting, is disconnected. Instead of the oft-sought solitude experienced in non-human nature, theirs is a contrived solitude in the midst of society, a marginalization that instead of stifling sound among those at the receiving end of punitive action, envelops them in a one-way bubble of disregard, even denial, of personhood and an effacement of social identity. As a form of banishment, it conspicuously involves the drawing not of spatial, but discursive, boundaries.

The second feature of ostracism underscores that specific instances of silence possess varying levels of power. A silence in a human context isn't just a silence; it radiates vastly diverse amounts of emotional energy and it too contains considerable dramatic force. As Kipling Williams notes, it covers the defensive, the oblivious, and the punitive.[58] Indeed, it may entail more than one of those simultaneously.

The third aspect of ostracism re-emphasizes the ambiguous character of silence as a feature of human behaviour. Avoiding human contact may have different impacts on receivers and givers of the 'silent treatment'.[59] The silence may be unnoticed by its targets; it may be regarded as insignificant, accidental, or unintentional and consequently not interpreted as an act or occurrence of silence at all. The obverse may also happen: the receiver may identify an interpersonal silence as ostracism, while the assumed perpetrator may simply not regard the receiver as important enough 'to bother acknowledging'.[60] The receiver could register it as a mere act of disengagement lacking strong intent or motivation, or as a consequence of the perpetrator's embarrassment following a previous encounter. One might assume that the ambiguous nature of silence is self-evident; that many meanings can be imposed on or extracted from any practice of silence. But ostracism offers a more specific case of ambiguity—it is not the analysts, the theorists, the observers, who bring with them their doubts, hesitations, or competing criteria. Rather, the experience of silence is often rendered ambiguous by the actors and participants themselves, an ambiguity that can have a profound impact on their behaviour and perceptions.

Notes

1. See the reference to McGilchrist on the left hemisphere in Chapter 3.
2. *The Middle Length Discourse of the Buddha: A Translation of the Majjhima Nikāya*, trans. Bhikkhu Nanamoli and Bhikkhu Bodi (Oxford: Pali Text Society, 2001), pp. 533–536.
3. *The Vilmalakirti Sutra*, trans. Burton Watson (New York: Columbia University Press, 1997), pp. 10, 110–111.
4. M. Heidegger, *On the Way to Language*, trans. P. D. Hertz (New York: Harper & Row, 1971), p. 19.
5. Zhang Wei, 'On the Way to a "Common" Language? Heidegger's Dialogue with a Japanese Visitor', *Dao: A Journal of Comparative Philosophy* 4 (2005), pp. 283–297 at p. 293.
6. In Stefano Gandolfo, 'The Positionless Middle Way: Weak Philosophical Deflationism in Madhyamaka', *Journal of Indian Philosophy* 44 (2016), pp. 207–228, the author explores a weaker version of such quietism through the writings of Nāgārjuna, the Buddhist philosopher.
7. Foucault, *A History of Sexuality*, p. 27.
8. Ueda, 'Silence and Words in Zen Buddhism', p. 13.
9. *Writings from the Zen Masters*, compiled by Paul Reps (London: Penguin, 2009), pp. 5–6.
10. Ibid., p. 34.
11. Zhuangzi, *Basic Writings*, trans. Burton Watson (New York: Columbia University Press, 2003). E-book.
12. Wang, *Linguistic Strategies*, pp. 116–117, 119.
13. Chien-hsing Ho, 'The Nonduality of Speech and Silence: A Comparative Analysis of Jizang's Thought on Language and Beyond', *Dao* 11 (2012), pp. 1–19. The citation of Jizang is from his *Dasheng Xuanlun* (*A Treatise on the Profound Teaching of the Mahayana*).
14. Zhuangzi, *Basic Writings*.
15. J. Souilhé, 'Le silence mystique', *Revue d'Ascétique et de mystique* 4 (1923), pp. 128–9. Cited and translated in Montiglio, *Silence in the Land of Logos*, p. 24.
16. Wang, *Linguistic Strategies*, p. 105.
17. Dale S. Wright, 'Rethinking Transcendence: The Role of Language in Zen Experience', *Philosophy East and West* 42/1 (1992), p. 130.

18 Lik Kuen Tong, 'The Meaning of Philosophical Silence: Some Reflections on the Use of Language in Chinese Thought', *Journal of Chinese Philosophy* 3 (1976), p. 169.
19 Yanfang Tang, 'Language, Truth, and Literary Interpretation: A Cross-Cultural Examination', *Journal of the History of Ideas* 60/1 (1999), p. 20.
20 Paula M. Varsano, 'Looking for the Recluse and Not Finding Him In: The Rhetoric of Silence in Early Chinese Poetry', *Asia Major*, 3rd ser., 12/2 (1999), p. 43.
21 Ibid., p. 48.
22 Ibid., p. 55
23 Ibid., pp. 48–49.
24 Ibid., pp. 69–70.
25 Laozi, *Daodejing: 'Making this Life Significant,' A Philosophical Translation*, trans. Roger Ames and David Hall (New York: Ballantine, 2002). E-book.
26 Vainiomäki, 'Silence as a Cultural Sign', p. 355.
27 J. Norris-Green, 'The Anthropology of Silence: Quaker Silence', http://anthropologyofsilence.com/2018/11/16/quaker-silence/
28 The tagline for the film *Alien* (1979), directed by Ridley Scott.
29 See, e.g., https://www.breakingthesilence.org.il/
30 *Daily Express*, 6 July 2021.
31 G. Hofstede, 'Cultural Differences in Teaching and Learning', *International Journal of Intercultural Relations* 10 (1986), pp. 301–320.
32 P. Lyman, 'The Domestication of Anger: The Use and Abuse of Anger in Politics', *European Journal of Social Theory* 7/2 (2004), p. 138.
33 Ferguson, 'Silence: A Politics', p. 51.
34 D. Jamet, 'Euphemisms for Death: Reinventing Reality through Words?', in S. Sorlin (ed.), *Inventive Linguistics* (Montpellier: Presses Universitaires du Languedoc et de la Méditerranée, 2010), pp. 173–188.
35 R. Ellison, *Invisible Man* (New York: Random House, 1995), p. 3.
36 Zerubavel, *Elephant in the Room*, p. 20.
37 D. Carbaugh, M. Berry, and M. Nurmikari-Berry, 'Coding Personhood through Cultural Terms and Practices: Silence and Quietude as a Finnish "Natural Way of Being"', *Journal of Language and Social Psychology* 25 (2006), pp. 1–18.
38 J. Lehtonen and K. Sajavaara, 'The Silent Finn', in Tannen and Saville-Troike, *Perspectives on Silence*, pp. 189–201.
39 Sajavaara and Lehtonen, 'The Silent Finn Revisited', in Jaworski, *Silence: Interdisciplinary Perspectives*, esp. pp. 264, 268, 274–275.
40 See Chapter 7.
41 Kagge, *Silence in the Age of Noise*, pp. 118–119.
42 Nwoye, 'Eloquent Silence among the Igbo of Nigeria', p. 191.
43 Basso, '"To Give up on Words"'.
44 Billias and Vemuri, *The Ethics of Silence*, pp. 100–101.
45 Goffman, *Interaction Ritual*, p. 63.
46 S. D. Gurevitch, 'Distance and Conversation', *Symbolic Interaction* 12 (1989), pp. 251–263.
47 Quoted in Corbin, *A History of Silence*, p. 12.
48 E.g., in performances by Ian McKellen (RSC, directed by Trevor Nunn, 2007) and Antony Sher (RSC, directed by Gregory Doran, 2016).

49 O. Taplin, 'Aeschylean Silences and Silences in Aeschylus', *Harvard Studies in Classical Philology* 76 (1972), p. 57.
50 S. Milgram, 'Behavioral Study of Obedience', *Journal of Abnormal and Social Psychology* 67 (1963), pp. 371–378.
51 For a detailed textual analysis see L. Kane, *The Language of Silence: On the Unspoken and the Unspeakable in Modern Drama* (London and Toronto: Associated University Presses, 1984).
52 Quoted from Beckett's *Proust* in Esslin, *The Theatre of the Absurd*, p. 4.
53 Pinter, 'Writing for the Theatre', pp. 23–24.
54 K. F. Stein, 'Metaphysical Silence in Absurd Drama', *Modern Drama* 13/4 (1970), pp. 423–431.
55 Hassan, 'The Literature of Silence', p. 78.
56 Ramel, 'Silence as Relation in Music', p. 151.
57 J. Attali, *Noise: The Political Economy of Music* (Minneapolis, MN, and London: University of Minnesota Press, 1985), p. 47.
58 K. D. Williams, *Ostracism: The Power of Silence* (New York and London: Guilford Press, 2001), pp. 53–54.
59 Ibid., esp. pp. 70–98.
60 Ibid., pp. 47–48.

13
State and Government Silences

1 The Quietism of States, Governments, and Constitutions

No assessment of the political implications of silence can sidestep that most prominent of institutions, the state. There are many forms of state silence, or what is assumed to be state silence. At first blush, states are not famed for their silences: they arrogate to themselves major channels of communication through which their voices are strident, overbearing, and frequent. But does it make sense to refer to the silence of states rather than to that of their concrete organs such as governments? Because governments are in the main the vocal, noisy, and assertive agents whose voices are equated in common perception and parlance with those of their state, those questions must be addressed obliquely. The attributes of a state are exercised through those who, legitimately or otherwise, speak and act in its name. And yet, there are silences of the state irreducible to those of governments.

Is there then something particularly significant about a silent state? The sovereign supremacy of the state installs it as the regulator and allocator of social silences, despite that role rarely being acknowledged in political studies and in state-centred analysis. Sometimes that role is overt, although unformalized. A state's silence can be self-assumed when a decision is taken—in its basic constitutional arrangements, or through its agents—to abstain from expressing and publicizing a view, or from entering into a performative act, that could be listened to, read, or understood by a relevant grouping: that is, a grouping actually or potentially subject to a state's influence. Typical areas of those silences may concern issues of abortion, the subscription to religious beliefs, sexual practices, or juridical procedures. A state's silence can also be the result of governmental ignorance or the opacity of certain individual and social practices. The latter may involve the emergence of new technologies when the state is playing catch-up, or when highly private practices are publicly invisible. And a state may be aware of certain classes of conduct but regard them as trivial, or socially inconsequential, as would be the case with hobbies such as philately or trainspotting—though even then the former

Concealed Silences and Inaudible Voices in Political Thinking. Michael Freeden, Oxford University Press.
© Michael Freeden (2022). DOI: 10.1093/oso/9780198833512.003.0015

could be a potential source of state propaganda and income, and the latter a tool for espionage. Not least, a government may profess its commitment to silence on a given matter for reasons of expediency or ideological commitment. Such an unnoticed silence is of particular interest to this study, but none should be confused with the deliberate and often conspiratorial silence in which states tend to shroud some of their activities. Several, but not all, of these categories may be reassessed when boundaries of criminality are redrawn, inasmuch as designating a practice to be criminal is *ipso facto* the formal, though not always operative, ending of state and juridical silences concerning it.

The relationship between a constitution (whether written or not) and the state identifies a basic form of political silence. In older, but still prevalent, understandings of constitutions, a constitution undergirds the fundamental workings of the state—just as the state transcends any specific government. Constitutions provide the anatomy of the state, supporting and sustaining the staple and indispensable arrangements of a society, and they do so in two diverse ways: by securing the rhythmic calm essential to a state's operation, and by enabling silences in the form of absences, gaps, omissions, and indifferences, without which political life would run into even greater difficulties than might otherwise be the case. One might liken a constitution to a lattice that, while holding up the structure of a climbing plant, also provides the spaces through which the vegetation may escape or grow in an unregulated manner. Like lattices, constitutions supply permanent absences through which the potential build-up of political pressure can be avoided or averted.

Crucially, as Michael Foley argues in his pioneering book, 'gaps in a constitution should not be seen as simply empty space'. They are real, because constitutions 'remain dependent upon an instinctive, indefinable, and thoroughly unwritten code of practised obscurity'. Here is the task of the curious legal scholar, for 'by concentrating on the gaps and fissures in a constitution, it is possible to sense the silent strength of a collective and instinctive impulse to condone glaring anomalies'.[1] Constitutional quietude and constitutional absences can occur at two levels of silence: through a process of normalization and routinization akin to the working of Bourdieu's habitus, albeit in a more defined legal sense; and through the deeper silences we have encountered in other contexts—namely, the creation of formal vacuums around which the law skirts and that do not draw attention to themselves as silences. Both kinds of silence act as dissolving threads suturing the state's anatomy—vital to keeping the body intact but kept well out of view, often beyond everyday awareness.

Foley's study focuses on the idea of state silence as the specific absence recognized as constitutional non-involvement or abstention. Legal phraseology employs the term 'abeyance' for a temporary halt or suspension of activities, but Foley employs the term in a far more expansive sense. He draws attention to 'concealed perspectives' among constitutional scholars—an 'obscure and compulsively unwritten' component within written constitutions whose significance lies in its need 'to remain unexpressed and unfathomable, in order for it to maintain its essential character'.[2] Unlike the central idea of superimposition, discussed in Chapter 10, which identifies the silences buried under palimpsests formed by assertive groups or changing historical narratives, the concealed silences of constitutional framing result from abandoning voice, or nullifying the possibility of articulating it in the precise language demanded by legal practice.

Foley elucidates: 'much of a constitution's unwritten element is a function of its being unknowable'. And he continues in a remarkably perceptive vein, worth quoting in full:

> What is being proposed in this context is the existence of an intermediate layer of obscurity sequestered between the micro-dimensional world of uncodified rules and customs and the macro-dimensional world of constitutions as abstract manifestations of cultural and historical conditions. This layer represents not just a difference in scale to the other two layers, but a difference in kind. The layer in question accommodates those implicit understandings and tacit agreements that could never survive the journey into print without compromising their capacious meanings and ruining their effect as a functional form of genuine and valued ambiguity. It is not just that such understandings are incapable of exact definition; rather their utility depends upon them not being subjected to definition, or even to the prospect of being definable.[3]

Foley regards such abeyances as 'barely sensed disjunctions lodged so deeply within constitutions that ... they can only be assimilated by an intuitive social acquiescence in the incompleteness of a constitution ... and by an instinctive inhibition to objecting to what is persistently omitted from the constitutional agenda'. They are, he notes, the core of a constitutional culture.[4] Exploring the constitution of seventeenth-century Stuart England, he sees its ambiguity and imprecision as 'the hallmarks of its strength'. It rested upon 'positions not being pressed beyond the bounds of what was tacitly and intuitively accepted'.[5] Likewise, Sedley draws attention to silences in the unwritten British constitution between the nominal unity of state power in the Crown and the factual and necessary division of that power between discrete and sometimes conflicting bodies of the state. Those unfilled gaps and hiatuses merely confirm that no organization or institutional utterance or practice can fill in all the lacunae or anticipate all eventualities in an open-ended society,[6] and it would be folly for the constitution to step in.

Among contemporary ideologies, liberalism is thought to incorporate— at least in some of its versions—the requirement for state silence. In the early, pre-liberal stages of that notion, Hobbes famously asserted that liberties other than self-defence 'depend on the silence of the law'. Tellingly, silence is attributed to an institution—the wielders of sovereignty—or, put differently, it points to the unavailability of a particular regulatory set of practices for a political society. It is not quite an absence when, one assumes, the sovereign could have prescribed a rule but did not.[7] Rather, it adumbrates a legal *terra incognita* whose political exploration is simply not countenanced.

The idea of silence as quietude has been well captured by Maistre, but in reverse, as extra-constitutional. He saw the French constitutions of the 1790s as the structural mechanisms of an artificial, written idea produced by a priori science and reasoning, but far from silent. Maistre effectively credits the French post-Revolution constitutions with a failure to furnish an economy of means. 'Open your eyes', he writes, 'and you will see that it [the French Republic] does not *live*. What an enormous machine! What a multiplicity of springs and clockwork! What a fracas of pieces clanging away!' By contrast, in nature and in a living, organic society, 'everything being in its place, there are no jerks or bumps, friction is low, and there is no noise, only majestic silence. So it is that in the mechanism of nature, perfect balance, equilibrium, and exact symmetry of parts give even rapid movement the satisfying appearance of repose.' Furthermore, 'all true legislative action has its *Sabbath*, and intermittence is its distinctive characteristic'.[8] While Carlyle extols the earthy noise emitted by the hum of machinery and exalts the extra-governmental entrepreneurship of captains of industry, inspiring workers who speak not but grunt and growl in physical effort, Maistre accuses the state of producing a clanging din. In that context one may note Scollon's observation that silence does not have to be 'heard as the *malfunctioning* of a machine' to remain significant. Changing the way the metaphor works, he reflects, changes the meaning of silence.[9] Rhetoric and metonymy serve as filters through which political practices and processes can be indicated, focused, and directed.

The idea of state silence as quietude is frequently extended in late eighteenth- and nineteenth-century debate to a government. In Jeremy Bentham's much-cited passage, he decreed silence to be not just legal inaction but the active self-restraint of government in certain circumstances:

With the view of causing an increase to take place in the mass of national wealth, or with a view to increase of the means either of subsistence or enjoyment, without some special reason, the general rule is, that nothing ought to be done or attempted by government. The motto, or watchword of government, on these occasions, ought to be—Be quiet.[10]

The success of such an injunction is of course in its eventual invisibility, so that the silence entailed by non-intervention becomes a habitual and thus unnoticed cultural and political norm turned fact. Those processes of naturalization are the optimal indications of a successful ideological precept.

Invisibility is also the key feature of Adam Smith's famed theory of individual wealth creation. 'He generally, indeed, neither intends to promote the public interest, nor knows how much he is promoting it ... he intends only his own gain, and he is in this, as in many other cases, led by an invisible hand to promote an end which was no part of his intention.'[11] Smith often describes that invisibility as silence. It is patently an attribute of an impersonal and universal psychological mechanism with fundamental economic consequences. Referring to the annual produce of England's land and labour, he writes: 'in the midst of all the exactions of government, this capital has been silently and gradually accumulated by the private frugality and good conduct of individuals'.[12] John Stuart Mill echoed a similar sentiment in pointing out that landlords 'grow richer, as it were, in their sleep, without working, risking, or economizing'.[13] These silences are doubly concealed: not only by those who exhibit them while unaware of their public effect, but by the political system that indirectly condones the industrial practices underlying them, for good or bad. A socially shared silence, breached only by a small number of discerning critics such as Smith, masks the actual functioning of both the polity and, under its oblivious aegis, the economy.

Several themes explored in previous chapters resurface in this section: the concreteness of silences as lived practices; silence as displaying not one level but tiered strata of hiddenness; tacit consent—not with regard to a Lockean consent and submission to the government but pertaining to juridical practice; the political value of ambiguity alongside the inevitability of indeterminacy; and the open invitation to flood such silences with meaning, just as van der Rohe's glass walls permitted a proliferation of light to enter an 'enclosed' space. No wonder that the sphere of jurisprudence countenances thick and permanent abeyances and steps back, whether deliberately, intuitively, or ever-thwarted, from the elusive goal of decontestation that ordinary political discourse—especially in its ideological mode—pursues. That ever-present need to bestow definitive sense on language meant that 'the threat of innovative clarity posed the greatest danger'.[14] The inarticulate and the unknowable join forces in the workings of a constitution. The silences they call up serve both to protect and to promote the major political objective of bolstering political solidarity, by diminishing the likelihood of conflict and contradiction that the over-detailed stipulation of mandatory guidelines in a nation's affairs might occasion[15]—even were such stipulation possible in the first place. They do so chiefly by recognizing the importance of 'negative factors such as negligence, ambiguity, fear of dissensus, and a resolve to exclude fundamental constitutional issues from the political agenda'[16]—itself a political choice usually hidden from public view.

2 Neutrality and Abstention

It is only at a much later stage of political thinking that the silence of the state shifts from a simple absence of, or indifference to, given aspects of people's lives to a principle of non-intervention among competing viewpoints and policies. That occurs when it appears in the shape of neutrality: the reluctance to voice or support a view in some areas of belief or policy-preference. The demand to refrain from doing so becomes enshrined as a political practice. To be clear, that practice does not entail the deliberate silencing either *of* the state or *by* it, nor is it normally one of smoothing the path for self-sustaining harmonious activity. It indicates a more complex absence: the ethical requirement not to participate, or to remove oneself from, certain classes of debate and contestation. That has notably been true in the domain of expressing religious faith and exercising religious practices. On some liberal views, religious conviction carries particular weight with regard to determining which social and political silences must be practised, though in rarer instances liberals may baulk at any challenge to a deeply held belief short of those deemed harmful and dangerous. Yet heralding neutrality as an active guiding principle conceals the plain fact that its core simply consists of silence.

For Barthes, however, there is a further element: neutrality as 'the right to be silent—a possibility of keeping silent'. For him, that arises in the double context of 'the right to nature's peacefulness', the refraining from pollution by speech on the one hand, and as a 'tactic to outplay oppressions, intimidations, the dangers of speaking, of the *locutio*'[17] on the other. The latter suggests deliberate ways of defusing potential danger by attempting to ignore it, but the former may well be an unmediated response to an overwhelming ontological sense of personal insignificance, sometimes conveyed in a religious idiom as awe. Of course, as Montiglio shrewdly notes of another cultural context, 'silence is never neutral in the land of logos'.[18] We may add that the modern neutrality espoused by constitutionalists and analytical political philosophers is itself far from a neutral concept. It is firmly anchored in a specific liberal *Weltanschauung* oriented towards treating alike some unlike categories of human activity. From that perspective, neutrality does not consist in an arsenal of strategies permitting a 'time-out from meaning'[19] and a retreat from the world's designs. Neutrality, rather, is a stance well within the universe of meanings, though it may carry its own unintended surplus of meaning. Its effect is to obscure silence—under the aegis of advocating fairness or equality—to the point where it is no longer identified as silence but as a purposive and ethical clearing of the way to enable the free run of certain valued social and cultural practices, or at least to enshrine the merit of having non-harmful ones.

Significantly, however, silence is not just a mark of respect for the privacy of individual and group faith, or a refusal to contaminate the world with speech, or the avoidance of being provoked by certain words, or opting-out of the requirement for verbal assent.[20] It can operate on a completely separate dimension, as a way of dealing with intractable contestations. Here neutrality is the result of the political wisdom—if that is the appropriate term—of steering clear of disruptive policy quandaries. Such spheres include zero-sum clashes of values such as abortion versus anti-abortion, or animal rights versus scientific experimentation, or the right of women to wear what they will as against women's protection from (often unrecognized) masculinist sartorial diktat. They all often entail the silent abandoning by the state and its government—enabled by the constitution—of decision-making responsibility and the consequent vacating of the field to the unregulated mêlée of social voices that takes over. Rather than advocating *neutrality* as a liberal value and as a principle of social conduct, the danger here is that central political authorities may be *neutered* by the prospect of irresolvable conflict. The issue is left to the specific rhythms of power and counter-power among views and interests that may create temporary balances: a way of navigating through an area where the collective ranking of priorities would be socially and ideologically too costly. Such spheres of neutrality are uneasily suspended between a cultural and ethical predilection for a specific kind of political silence displayed in liberal ideologies, and the instrumental and tactical recourse to silence as a general aid to continuous political functioning.

But what about some of the silences evident in political give and take, or relating to the formal requirement for accountability, at least in democratic polities? Although these kinds of silence will be deliberate, if not the outcome of ignorance or incompetence, they also serve to remove issues from the national arena, often without a broader awareness on the part of the democratic electorate. Parliaments, and governmental offices and agencies, habitually manage silences as a method of obfuscation or evasion. Parliamentary question time has honed the art of ignoring, overriding, deflecting, or selectively responding to questions put by MPs to ministers, as is the case with senior politicians' interviews on the media. The Speaker of the House of Commons rations the number of issues MPs can raise through the practice of 'catching the Speaker's eye', which effectively blocks the voices of those passed over. It sets up a ranking order of participants in a debate, although the rationale for selection remains opaque, once the main party leaders have been invited to speak.

These conventions occupy an undefined space between direct silencing and compliance with rules that are customarily applied to political practices. They become at the very least inconspicuous, bordering on the routine and avoiding any suspicion of discrimination. The Speaker, her- or himself, is considered to be impartial and 'completely non-partisan'[21]—a position difficult to maintain when rulings bound to favour one side or the other have to be delivered. However, although the terms can overlap, there are subtle but significant differences between neutrality and impartiality. The *OED* defines neutrality as 'the state or condition of not being on any side; absence of decided views, feeling, or expression; indifference'; and impartiality as 'freedom from prejudice or bias; fairness'.[22] The first is *hors de combat*, above the fray, which implies a non-participatory silence. The second involves participating, by directing the debate without favouring any viewpoint. The silence involved in not making one's views known can be undermined by the preference for allowing certain votes to go forward and others to be disallowed, demonstrating once again that silence as non-intervention is impossible to sustain in the formal political arena, charged as it is with making decisions.

The rules governing electoral systems offer illuminating insights into the silencing side-effects they carry. Political representation involves the distribution of voice in collective decision making, but it invariably also entails the allocation of silence to those excluded from whatever electoral method is adopted. In a broader sense that silencing is unintentional, as all templates for representation privilege some members of a group at the expense of shutting others out. Hence some silencing is structurally inevitable, which distinguishes it from the plainly deliberate and reversible disenfranchisements of women, ethnic minorities, non-citizens, or prisoners, now or over the course of history. But the choice of any specific system within the options open to liberal democracies imposes varieties of silence on particular groups.

Majoritarian constituency-based elections are committed to territorial units, but in striving for geographical equalization they demote ideational and programmatic voice, and in the special case of first-past-the-post voting they silence all but the one ideological viewpoint that forges ahead of its rivals, however marginally. In contrast, pure proportional representation cuts geographical ties and silences interests and opinions pertaining to space and site. Even the practice of direct democracy—as an attempt to eliminate majority-decision based on counting—must then logically veer towards unanimity which, as Rousseau's famous essay demonstrates, imposes a monolithic voice on a potentially plural base, condemning some to political oblivion or to a 'forced freedom' in the name of a putative shared rationality.[23]

Legal and ethical considerations can also be applied to justifying and normalizing the absence of communication. Assertions of confidentiality and privacy frequently obliterate the paths to understanding and knowledge, ensuring their invisibility. The hackneyed and overused phrase 'we do not comment on individual cases' may be either genuine or a smokescreen for a refusal to divulge information, to protect interests, or to avoid embarrassment. In either instance it uses language that confers an aura of legitimacy on silence—as a bureaucratic given that needs no justification, debarring its questioning. Deferring the consideration of an issue, as in 'kicking the can down the road', indicates the securing of silence through temporal displacement. Redacting is a particularly tantalizing method of indicating the existence of a voice while eliminating it through thick black lines. It is a visually bold, emphatic, and impenetrable silence, whose message is: 'We're suppressing information, we're telling you *that* we are doing it and we're indicating *where* we are suppressing it, but not *what* it is that we're keeping a lid on.' Rather than silencing the silence, the reasons for suppressing the message are ostentatiously silenced. During Nixon's 1968 presidential campaign, one of his speechwriters formulated Rule One: 'What the candidate fails to say can be more important than what he does say. Audiences should be stimulated to supply their own interpretations of gaps left by what is unsaid.' And he added: 'It's not the words, but the silence, where votes lie.'[24] Encouraging reading between the lines opens up the field to the voter's (assumedly supportive) imagination.

Disparate silences can be disruptive of various micro-features of the political. Some are obviously intentional, although their repercussions will be unpredictable and their motivation disputed: abstaining from casting a vote on a matter of constitutional importance has an impact on the claim that shaping public life is a key expectation of citizens' responsibility. Others may be hidden from public view: the failure to endorse a change of government through vocal backing affects the mobilization of support. The selective lack of protest about the conditions of certain social groups, say migrants or children, but not others, say the elderly or the poor, mutely creates a hierarchy of valued or devalued categories. The unconscious or ignorant disregard for future eventualities may result in unpreparedness when an unanticipated pandemic bursts on the scene. Conversely, those same fortuitous silences could facilitate continuity, reduce strife over insoluble pecking orders, prop up legitimacy and authority, or bury damaging collective memories. Indeed, any combination of the social combustibility of silence is possible. The surprising contingency of its effects must perpetually be borne in mind. The study of silences requires that all such cases be tracked as they occur and evaluated from multi-perspectival stances, which are liable to undergo continuous change. Yet even as silences introduce uncertainty, they can be classified in loose and permeable categories that enable tentative and adjustable mapping. The categories are not random, even if they are pliant. Cultural ephemerality is conjoined with patterned replicability of sorts, and silences may contain a reservoir of energetic impact.

There is also a burgeoning interest in the silence of states in international law. One instance concerns recommendations emanating from the International Law Commission (ILC) of the United Nations. The question then is how to construe the absence of a response by a state. Taciturnity in the sphere of state relationships is distinct from taciturnity in the domestic setting of a government and its residents or citizens. The former concerns central governmental policy, or its absence, in the international arena and in the name of a sovereign state as an 'actor' among sovereign states. The latter is a down–up silence in lieu of a possible endorsement of a government by its subjects. Although the question of tacit consent in the undetermined areas of state silence is fluid, Azaria contends that, generally speaking, 'the silence of states *vis-à-vis* the ILC's pronouncements and *vis-à-vis* the responses of some states to the ILC's pronouncements within the UN system may not be construed outright as acquiescence', though it may be a step in that direction.[25] Similarly, on the issue of whether state silences have legal effect, Starski argues that with respect to the use of force in the context of Article 51 of the UN Charter such silence is not to be interpreted as acquiescence. Unlike many other disciplinary viewpoints, the author asserts that 'Silence, therefore, is devoid of content', and its communicative substance is 'contingent on conventional patterns of conduct and communication'.[26]

That comment—while not in itself anomalous—drifts some way from most interpretations of silence we have encountered in this study. It sidesteps those for whom silence is not just acoustic, and those who are ready to read notably unconventional messages into human silences. Starski notes the difficulties in the emergence of a 'legally eloquent', that is to say meaningful, state silence but contends that 'law-generating effects of silence do not depend on the intentions of the silent state, but on the legitimate expectations of other states, and the international community as a whole, that a state should speak'. That is an important observation for two reasons. It posits that in the realm of jurisprudence, a state is not supposed to be voiceless; as well as that there is a legitimate presumption on the part of other states that they may insert that voice on the basis of a reciprocal silent consensus amongst them. Moreover, military or economic power discrepancies between states will have a bearing on the 'acquiescence' of weaker states, casting further doubt on what is concealed beneath silent acquiescence.[27]

3 Commemoration

Alongside silences *of* the state are silences promoted or endorsed *by* the state in its domestic affairs, in particular those honouring momentous events of sacrifice and death. The state undertakes the organization of silences that carry heavy symbolic weight, both in signalling highly ranked socio-political values and in offering solace to their grieving or indebted populations. The ritual public silences imposed on communal remembrance are fuelled by national pride and glory, or by attributing higher significance to the deaths of some individuals over those of others, not least to the manner in which they died, a manner generalized as a group attribute, to which each individual is made to conform. These are socially shared silences that prompt a reaching out to, and with, others in an act of solidarity. But that practice will include concealed reinforcements of loyalty and support for specific causes that may not accrue universal support. As a rule, ceremonial commemorative silences exhibit a high emotive intensity, difficult to resist or dissociate from, but made more manageable by their relatively short duration. As Vinitsky-Seroussi and Teeger observe of such memorial events in Israel, 'The annual reenactment of the moment of silence is so powerful that individuals often find that when the siren sounds, they stand still, keep silent and contemplate the day even if the demarcated moment finds them alone in their homes or offices.'[28] In collective acts of mourning, such high-intensity silences are also to be found among those attending funeral services for victims of atrocities or accidents, an intensity understandably augmented when the casualties are young and when the tragedy was in the immediate past, albeit later abating with the passage of time.

Here the social practice is manifest and observable—it has even been redescribed as a 'performative speech-act', with a strong sense of silence as a conveyer of emotionality,[29] but the silence it triggers may well not be a matter of considered choice. States can manipulate their members through quasi-mandatory conformity to values entrenched in national narratives that transform private into public, choreographed silences. Those silences indicate a common memory and fate, as well as the indisputable determining and ranking of 'defining events' in a society's life. Enlisting support for behaviours embedded in national identity may involve obscured instances of political control and marshalling. In such instances 'the ritualized moment of silence becomes the ultimate manifestation of social control in that it comes to be internalized without external surveillance, creating "docile bodies" disciplined in the act of memory'.[30]

Exercises in collective silence on the performative, ceremonial level are also not uncommon on the local stage. One remarkable instance took place for several years in the small English town of Wootton Bassett located near an air force base into which the coffins of UK soldiers killed in the Afghanistan war were flown between 2007 and 2011, often week after week. The route passed through the town, which became the pivotal space in which the fallen soldiers were accorded public acknowledgement and where collective private grief could be vented, as thousands of its denizens and visitors mutely lined the main street. 'The silence of it all is very important', observed Chris Wannell, the leader of Wootton Bassett town council. Silence became a powerful political language of solidarity and national pride. As with much ritual, there was no interaction between the masses and the performers, not even the mechanical responses of religious ritual. Silences were layered over, and enclosed within, other silences. The spectacle was silent on both sides, punctuated only by the sound of the church bell with its latent religious significance. The ceremonial structure was characterized by the monotonous repetitiveness of the death cortèges—the silence of the one group of the dead mirrored in the silence of the living, while the horizontal stillness of the spectators was contrasted with the vertical motion of the dead, concealed in their coffins. Wannell went on to bemoan that 'with so many journalists there it was no longer a silent affair'. It had become a silence now habitually broken by the detailed accounts of the nature of the ritual given by leading members of the community to the press descending on the town. Underpinning that was a second, roaring political silence, submerged in a sea of patriotism and of local self-satisfaction: the bypassing of any mention of the rights or wrongs of the war in Afghanistan.[31]

There is another idiomatically masked silence in commemorating the war dead, for they are named 'the fallen' (*la caída, i caduti, die Gefallenen*), a term associated with toppling in silent dignity as does a felled tree—usually in marked distinction from their actual horrific deaths—as well as with descriptors such as nobly, bravely, heroically, self-sacrificingly, or martyr fashion. The silence of forgetfulness can, of course, be induced by a collective lapse of memory, when a voice of past social import is lost, or simply through the covering over and displacing of ideas and occurrences,[32] which should be distinguished from the mundane case of individuals forgetting what they were going to say. The desire to draw a veil over a past event or concept may initially be deliberate among survivors who experience pain, humiliation, or embarrassment in their bid to consign their recollections to the realm of the unsayable. Winter observes of those who refuse to talk about their war memories, whether generally or selectively: 'Silence is neither forgetting nor oblivion. Silence is a language of memory.'[33] But it also is a language of what is emotionally inarticulable, and as time passes the social pool of those memories can be drained into a depleted unawareness.

The rationale of ceremonies and the enshrining of memories such as these stand in utter contrast to the chilling erasure of memory remarked on by Lyotard, when words or phrases that initially signify acts and events of deliberate obliteration become themselves a shell that houses an irretrievable silence. On the mass extermination during the Holocaust, he writes: 'The individual name must be killed (whence the use of serial numbers), and the collective name (Jew) must also be killed in such a way that no we bearing this name might remain. ... This death must therefore be killed.' Following that willed and wilful extinction, a completely hidden silence covers both act and memory, permanently banished from human consciousness. 'Auschwitz ... cannot engender anything. ... The name would remain empty ... put into mecanographical or electronic memory. But it would be nobody's memory, about nothing and for no one.'[34] That dual silence envelopes the silences brought about by the murder of Nazi victims with a more profound silence that eradicates the evidence about the very existence of those individual and collective annihilations. Indeed, contends Lyotard, the Nazi atrocities have been terminated through the destruction of Nazism, but Nazism has not been—and due to the absence of appropriate language, cannot be—refuted.[35] In another instance, he sees Marxism as identifying a generalized wrong perpetrated against the proletariat, 'expressed through the silence of feeling, of suffering.'[36] In that version, silence is counter-political as well as extra-legal: its indeterminate generality ensures the absence of the concrete finality and resolution—whether real or illusory—that is insisted on by the political.

4 Univocality

Voice and vocalization naturally emerge from an empirically undeniable plurality, and the test of a legitimate government, especially a democratic one, hinges on how it handles such plurality fairly and sensitively. Nonetheless, silence occasionally makes an appearance as distinctly monolithic, or indivisible, against the current of recent interpretations. That is one of many reasons why silence cannot comfortably serve democratic, pluralistic, or heterogeneous ends, unless a plethora of voices is inventively or deceptively teased out of it. With that in mind, some scholars persevere in regarding silence as the absence of a specific practice. Zumbrunnen's analysis of silence in ancient Greece juxtaposes silence to the practice of deliberation, a collective enterprise. Instead, 'noisy plurality has been subsumed by silent unity'.[37] In an act of manifest superimposition, 'the silence of contending voices amounts to a recognition of the merit of the single remaining voice'.[38]

Montiglio also highlights 'the negative disposition of an Athenian audience towards the use of silence in political deliberation', when silence entailed marginalization from the democratic polis.[39] In the *Iliad*, the ancient Greek term *akên*—being quiet—applies among others when an audience listens to an authoritative speaker in wonder or amazement.[40] It is the quiet silence of the subordinate or the subaltern that is necessary to secure the authority of the dominant. Often that process is understood as the silencing of a range of competing voices, as a muting capacity, in order to demarcate the one remaining voice as meaningful and unchallenged.[41] Instead of the superimposition of voice as an attempt of private or civic groups to hog the limelight at the expense of competitors vying for the control of a national podium, in this instance silence is imposed as a central hierarchical convention serving political univocality. One recurring lesson is that, although many of the silences explored in these pages are susceptible to an imaginative and tentative deciphering through cross-cultural comparison or through psychoanalysis, others could best be unpacked against the backdrop of the thought-practices that take place in cultural and political proximity to them.

Building silences into state-regulated transactions extends the right to silence beyond the issues of neutrality. Contrary to those silences that enhance the solidarity of those who take part in them and reduce difference by letting through shared emotions, the legal right of an accused to remain silent enshrines the importance of space between state and individual. As in contemporary architectural practice, space between structures serves the dual role of extolling the value of shared and open areas to the benefit of all who may use them, and creating a buffer between edifices that diminishes intrusiveness. Although the right to remain silent is intentional and openly known, it indicates a conceptual bundle of protection that extends the idea of harm to one's own self, and that safeguards personal space, including privacy, protection, and the prioritization of the individual over an inquisitive system of public accountability and answerability. In legal and political frameworks, what is presented as the right of individuals not to incriminate themselves—most famously in the Fifth Amendment of the Constitution of the United States—incorporates the latent endowing of individuals with control over certain freedoms and the removal of the state and its legal instruments from enforced pressure on its members. More specifically, that has been extended to the Miranda rights that the police have to read out to an arrested suspect and that include that person's right to remain silent.[42] Those Miranda rights are, however, silent on the risks of remaining silent once a case proceeds to a trial, pitting the concerned party against the force of the law in a potentially shifting balance of power relationships and raising suspicions about the reasons for that silence. They are conceived within a legal culture that carries with it a rhetorical routine of reading out rights, in which the letter of the law often masks the threat of violence hanging over police-individual confrontations. Under such conditions the right to remain silent may be transformed into a de facto stifling of voice—voice now recast as a costly and hazardous medium, a danger best to be avoided. The pluralism and openness of voice is suspended, and a person's presumed innocence is converted into the univocal silence of one who cannot even protest it.

Finally, some states have introduced a right to oblivion, or to be forgotten. Under general data protection regulations, certain information on individuals—particularly on the internet—can be permanently removed when it is no longer relevant. This has a bearing on corresponding rights to privacy, but it is more instructive to see it as the erasure and public silencing of segments of one's past.[43] Individuals may need to be protected against their own digital history

Notes

1 M. Foley, *The Silence of Constitutions: Gaps, 'Abeyances' and Political Temperament in the Maintenance of Government* (London: Routledge, 1989), pp. 81–82.
2 Ibid., pp. 7–8.
3 Ibid., pp. 8–9.
4 Ibid., p. 10.
5 Ibid., pp. 22, 32.

6. S. Sedley, 'The Sound of Silence: Constitutional Law without a Constitution', *Law Quarterly Review* 110 (1994), p. 272.
7. Hobbes, *Leviathan*, ch. 21, p. 271.
8. J. de Maistre, *Considerations on France*, ed. R. A. Lebrun (Cambridge: Cambridge University Press, 1994), pp. 54–57.
9. R. Scollon, 'The Machine Stops: Silence in the Metaphor of Malfunction', in Tannen and Saville-Troike, *Perspectives on Silence*, pp. 21–30 at p. 28.
10. J. Bentham, *A Manual of Political Economy*, 'Introduction', p. 33, http://oll.libertyfund.org/titles/bentham-the-works-of-jeremy-bentham-vol-3 (accessed 17 October 2017). In most older UK writings the distinction between state and government is elided.
11. A. Smith, *An Inquiry into the Nature and Causes of the Wealth of Nations* (Oxford: Oxford University Press, 1979), book 4, ch. 2, p. 456.
12. Ibid., book 2, ch. 3, p. 345.
13. J. S. Mill, *Principles of Political Economy* (London: D. Appleton & Co., 1885), p. 630.
14. Foley, *The Silence of Constitutions*, p. 32.
15. See also M. Loughlin, 'The Silences of Constitutions', *International Journal of Constitutional Law* 16 (2018), pp. 922–935 at p. 927.
16. Foley, *The Silence of Constitutions*, p. 129.
17. Barthes, *The Neutral*, p. 23.
18. Montiglio, *Silence in the Land of Logos*, p. 289.
19. R. Teeuwen, 'Roland Barthes's "Neutral" and the Utopia of Weariness', *Cultural Critique*, no. 80 (Winter 2012), pp. 1–26 at p. 7.
20. For a case study exploring some avoidance and omission manoeuvres see C. Halbrock, 'Nicht-Handeln und Nicht-Mitmachen: Nicht erfüllte Erwartungen und politisch abweichendes Verhalten in der DDR', in T. Jung (ed.), *Zwischen Handeln und Nichthandeln* (Frankfurt: Campus Verlag, 2019), pp. 101–126.
21. UK Parliament, 'The Speaker, Impartiality and Procedural Reform', https://www.parliament.uk/about/living-heritage/evolutionofparliament/parliamentwork/offices-and-ceremonies/overview/the-speaker/procedures-and-impartiality/ (accessed 17 December 2021).
22. *OED* online.
23. Rousseau, *Social Contract*, pp. 151–154.
24. William F. Gavin, quoted in R. L. Johannesen, 'The Functions of Silence', pp. 32–33.
25. D. Azaria, '"Codification by Interpretation:" The International Law Commission as an Interpreter of International Law', *European Journal of International Law* 31/1 (2020), pp. 171–200 at p. 200.
26. P. Starski, 'Silence within the Process of Normative Change and Evolution of the Prohibition on the Use of Force: Normative Volatility and Legislative Responsibility', *Journal on the Use of Force and International Law* 4/1 (2017), pp. 14–65 at p. 22.
27. Ibid., pp. 26, 37.
28. V. Vinitsky-Seroussi and C. Teeger, 'Unpacking the Unspoken: Silence in Collective Memory and Forgetting', *Social Forces* 88/3 (2010), p. 1109.
29. F. Donnelly, 'Silence is Golden: Commemorating the Past in Two Minutes', in Dingli and Cooke, *Political Silence*, p. 78.
30. Vinitsky-Serouossi and Teeger, 'Unpacking the Unspoken', *passim*.

31 M. Freeden, 'Editorial: The Politics of Ceremony: The Wootton Bassett Phenomenon', *Journal of Political Ideologies* 16 (2011), pp. 1–10.
32 Vinitsky-Serouossi and Teeger, 'Unpacking the Unspoken', passim
33 J. Winter, 'Between Sound and Silence: The Inaudible and the Unsayable in the History of the First World War', in A. J. Murray and K. Durrheim (eds.), *Qualitative Studies of Silence: The Unsaid as Social Action* (Cambridge: Cambridge University Press, 2019), p. 227.
34 Lyotard, *The Differend*, p. 101.
35 Ibid., p. 106.
36 Ibid., p. 171.
37 Zumbrunnen, *Silence and Democracy*, p. 56.
38 Ibid., p. 6.
39 Montiglio, *Silence in the Land of Logos*, pp. 282, 292.
40 Ibid., p. 65.
41 Achino-Loeb, *Silence: The Currency of Power*, p. 6.
42 http://www.mirandarights.org/
43 See, e.g., D. Erdos, 'The "Right to be Forgotten" beyond the EU: An Analysis of Wider G20 Regulatory Action and Potential Next Steps', *Journal of Media Law* 13/1 (2021), pp. 1–35; Biguenet, *Silence*, pp. 106–108.

14
Ideological Assimilations of Silence

1 Ideological Networks and Ideological Spaces

Ideologies are codifications of what their proponents claim is 'correct', 'meaningful', or 'appropriate' political discourse. All ideologies specialize in typical silencing procedures, such as exclusion, naturalizing, and simplifying, but within each ideological family further codes apply regarding the overt or covert handling of silence. The issue of inclusion and exclusion derives from three defining features of ideologies. The first and main feature is that no ideology can logically hold all the political meanings available to the concepts it employs—after all, many of those meanings cancel each other out *ab initio*, making it impossible to subscribe to them *in toto*. Thus, concerning the method of distributing valued social goods, equality of need is incompatible with mathematical equality or equality of merit. That follows from the inbuilt morphology of ideologies: the conceptual clusters that ideologies contain adopt a profusion of highly pliant permutations at the disposal of a political community or communities. Those fluid patterns are subject to constant recalibration over time and across space, adding or jettisoning the interpretations, arguments, and purportedly factual statements that ideologies employ in making sense of the socio-political world. Because each political concept within an ideological frame is itself a container of micro-conceptions pulling in many directions—think of liberty as licence, as emancipation, or as autonomy—ideologies function as complex significance-distributing devices that allocate and reallocate variable weightings to their components.

Ideologies are not understood here as sets of hegemonic biases, distortions, or dogmas—a relic of the Marxist approach. Their features are more intricate and subtle, calling up patterns of commission and omission that different ideological families adopt of necessity. Ultimately, all ideologies are eliminators as well as promoters, advocates, and endorsers. Nor are they merely occasional silencers: the practice of silencing, even when unacknowledged, is wired into the rationale of any ideological position. At their most fundamental, ideologies are discursive competitions over the control of public political language necessary to formulating shared policy objectives. They do so mainly through a process of decontestation that opts for specific meanings of each essentially contested concept, choosing, alighting on, or replicating their favoured ones and, by default, silencing or abandoning others. And because ideologies are first and foremost mechanisms of ideational and interpretative preference, the flipside is that large areas of political thinking and configuration will be structurally omitted from any ideological family. In other words, because selectivity is at play in the articulation of ideologies—albeit always subject to modification—its inevitable corollary is the parallel presence of equally selective, fluid, and shifting silences under the surface. Alongside its promotion of specific ideas and policy prescriptions, any ideology can be conspicuously identified for the deliberate absence of several conceptual clusters, and for the inadvertent concealing and suppression of other components. The resulting semantic patterns are patchworks of knowledge or imagination knitted together in ways that cover up major gaps and absences, employing a mixture of forceful intentionality and casual ignorance.[1]

Additional defining features of an ideology are important adjuncts to the first. There are conflicting cultural reasons that determine why any ideology contains several arguments and positions that are unacceptable, or even meaningless, to competing ideologies and their social frames of reference. Cultures that cultivate a strong collective ethos on matters of public health and welfare will clash with those with an inbuilt libertarian suspicion of the state and an insistence on the supremacy of individual choice making. A further feature is that ideologies labour under the crucial operational constraint that they can only be effective when they streamline and gloss over ideational complexity as a prerequisite to recruiting large-scale political support. Trevor Pateman has commented on the disparity between an increased volume of information and the declining capacity to process it, a capacity deficient in two respects, conceptual and verbal: 'In the first place, people lack theory, that is, interpretive and organising schemes which would allow the appropriation of information in a coherent form. . . . In the second case, there is ignorance of substantive or verbal organisation and classification.' One consequence is that 'people are socialized *out of* certain linguistic and organisational skills, and in this way socialised into a necessary acceptance of particular substantive ideologies and social systems'.[2] Even as ideologies assert and promote schemes of political order and reordering—which is their main function—they simultaneously possess a concealing logic built into every dimension of their modus operandi.

The focus of this chapter is not on what discourse analysts refer to as a 'language ideology', by which they mean 'the relationships between discourse on the one hand and social conflict, struggle and inequality on the other hand' that entails addressing the manner in which language acts as an instrument transmitting 'conflict, inequality, injustice, oppression'.[3] That is indisputably a topic of considerable importance to political theorists—including those who focus on ideologies—but it is a separate research agenda flagging a particular set of *substantive ethical* concerns. It deflects from the fuller attention devoted to the political implications of language and its attendant silences pursued in these pages. That broader purview is distinguished by another antecedent framework: namely, an overarching *methodological* concern with political practices that suffuse the entire category of silences across the field of absence and lack in human expression, whether harmful or beneficial. Ideologies are no exception to the politically indispensable practice of concealed silences. Indeed, concealed silences are crucially sustained and reproduced by the pervasiveness of ideologies as a mode of thinking politically. Silence has only rarely been discussed as a significant feature of ideologies, but it nevertheless is. In line with the criteria adopted in this study, ideological silences will chiefly attract our full attention only when they have become assimilated into modes of belief and articulation beyond the awareness of the community harbouring them.

In conveying their ideas, ideologies may do so in distinctive rhythms and with a wide-ranging assortment of communicative devices at their service, but they may also display bouts of randomness and unpredictability. Ideology studies benefit from incorporating several manifestations of silence already explored in previous chapters: repetitions and disruptions, ponderous prose and staccato soundbites, simplifications and elaborations, vagueness and precision, caesuras and counterpoints. Their randomness includes kneejerk reactions to unanticipated urgency, or ad hoc emotionally uncontrolled outbursts of fantasy, anger, or fear. Ideologies also embrace a major part of the performativity that is practised in producing, uttering, writing, acting out, conveying, resisting, altering, and consuming political discourse. They choreograph the political, badly as well as elegantly. All that takes place at different levels of unnoticeability for those involved.

There is another structural reason why ideologies are silencing devices. That follows from the distinction between the two categories of full (or comprehensive) versus thin ideologies. Full ideologies such as liberalism and socialism offer positions on as broad a range as feasible affecting the central political concepts in general circulation. They are ambitious and, on the whole, well thought out, irrespective of their ethical qualities. Thin ideologies focus on a narrower selection of issues and concepts that relate to specific political and ethical concerns and tend to remain uninterested in, hence silent on, more extensive issues. Thus nationalism, for instance, does not have its own distinctive views on internal social justice but adopts them from a broad palette of other ideologies; populism—often emaciatedly thin as an ideology[4]—is muted on many major social problems, such as distributive justice and the environment. It is not that such issues and problems are marginalized; they simply are irrelevant to the basic thrust of nationalist or populist arguments, even when not inimical to them. Alternatively, when thin ideologies—for instance, feminisms—do have a voice on such topics, each of their sub-variants will assimilate disparate and competing positions of other ideologies, whether liberal, social-democratic, Marxist, or anarchist. Just as likely, other ideologies will 'muscle in' and occupy the vacant spaces the thin ideologies leave uninhabited.[5]

Inclusion and exclusion thus give us only a limited taste of the multifaceted interplay of silence with the socio-cultural world of ideologies. Laclau identified a further obfuscating characteristic present in ideologically discursive mode, which he called the logic of equivalence. It occurs when different words are employed in a contiguous chain of partially substitute signifiers that creates slippage to the point of eliminating distinctions in meaning, locking together disparate and plural views. The nuances of difference collapse and linguistic indeterminacy is concealed when one word or phrase is so arranged that it substitutes for another or others, leaving no gaps. As Laclau explained: 'The specificity of equivalence is the destruction of meaning through its very proliferation.'[6] Thus 'law and order', when uttered in the same breath, suggests a fused linkage of meaning amenable to conservative argumentation, despite the very different connotations each term carries on its own. By remaining silent on the non-overlapping ranges of meanings such pairings contain, the successful dissemination of ideologies can be enhanced through the impoverishment of background discourse. Reform, reason, hierarchy, discipline, and harmony are just some of the alternative, competing meanings that can be drawn into the orbit of 'law and order', but not necessarily simultaneously.

In the analysis of ideologies, however, the 'shading' of silence offers special heuristic benefits—more for the discerning analyst than the participant—because ideologies are flexible, mutating configurations, far from the dogmatic or dichotomous freeze-frames some assume them to be. The absolute distinction between silence and sound/voice is appropriate for several of the contexts this study has considered, but ill-suited for the malleability of ideological morphology and content, tempering contrasts to establish varying nuances in a semantic field. A move from conceiving the borders between voice and silence as hard and abrupt or fuzzy and pliable parallels the growing tendency to regard ideological boundaries not as rigid but as permeable and, indeed, artificial.

Naturalizing a belief or a specific political procedure is a common means of obscuring their contestable, and often tenuous, underpinnings. They conceal the very opposite: natural political beliefs do not exist and—although societies possess inevitable generic political features—they will adopt numerous and vastly diverse configurations. Ideologies operate by making something appear to be obvious, as Bourdieu contended from a socio-cultural perspective. That 'normality' becomes invisible and inaudible and, as a rule, is secured from questioning and protected from change. Radical, conservative, and liberal worldviews are all equipped with their immutable 'naturalities' which they seek either to protect or—if previously removed by apparently misguided or malicious human design—to reinstall.

Simplifying a set of arguments or an ideational map is essential for the mass, or large-scale, dissemination of an ideology in order to make it attractively consumable and to carry an effective political punch. Ideological silence removes clutter. Broad-brush portrayal elides vital distinctions and hides the minutiae that inevitably come into view in the nitty-gritty concrete course of political implementation. Their absence conceals the multiple paths that ideologies can actually tread, once the cloak of simplicity is ripped off, while providing bolder, and thus inevitably less accurate, maps of political choice. Silences not only disrupt order; they disrupt disorder by shoehorning it into an impression of harmony and symmetry.

The socio-political silences contained in, and circling around, ideologies are selective, moveable, and porous. Each ideological family is typified by templates that let voice through under certain circumstances, while rationing, regulating, or thwarting its access in other areas, as well as being occasionally closed to and dismissive of voices knocking at its gates. The silences ideologies harbour always paint a particular, if transient, picture of a discursive scene and can be differentiated on a number of dimensions. How is silence dispersed across an ideological terrain: at the centre, the periphery, or scattered over certain areas? What determines how silences travel—quickly or laboriously—across ideological space and time? One distinction that can shed light on those issues is that between high- and low-impact silences. High-impact silences can reflect and even change a society's basic social relationships, or its power structures. In conservative or religious ideologies they remove articles of faith and conventional beliefs from contention, while progressive ideologies—notwithstanding tendencies to increasing transparency—are more likely to tolerate silence in areas demarcated as private. Low-impact silences may relate, say, to social embarrassment or respect, and have a decreasing or ephemeral effect on the political practices of a society.

On all these counts, silence contributes tone, structure, detail, and resolution. It lends texture, tinting, and further meaning to the verbal components transmitted by ideologies as they circulate. Just as importantly, the silencing roles of ideologies may be due to quite distinct causes: the replacement role of narratives, as seen above in historical accounts; the epistemological overlooking of subjects irrelevant to, or unregistered by, the decontestations they adopt; or the introduction of specific themes in which silences are built into their ideational arsenal and play a substantive role, though not always in a form recognized by their creators and adherents.

In sum, ideologies integrate silence, and specific silences, into their patterned thinking and they may even lend themselves to classification on that basis. Totalitarian ideologies are, of course, deliberate silencers, and their dampening and stifling silences are located at the epicentre of their political practices; but all ideologies command, and insist on, certain silences. Actively, ideologies may denounce other ideologies for their unconscionable silences on certain subjects, such as conditions of equitable living or refusal to condemn human rights abuses. They may conceptually transform an absence in a rival ideology into an ascertainable silence, whether in accusatory or in commendatory fashion: 'why did no one speak out in the name of the victims?' Or—as has been shown in Chapter 10—they may burrow through silence to rejig or invent pieces of information and of imagination that are modelled and imposed to satisfy the urge for a communal vade mecum and to screen a society from its own ignorance and cluelessness, from the residual silence that still rules on matters such as environmental health.

The conceptual meanings and discursive possibilities that are 'surplus to requirement' in any ideology are cloaked in inevitable silences that demote or marginalize them from the available pool of concepts in a political language. The excluded meanings are not necessarily unconceptualizable or unknowable, nor even unthinkable or unspeakable, but within a specific ideological framework something has to give, as there simply is no space available for all. Those inevitable structural exclusions are partly magnified by the presence of topics intellectually and emotionally unacceptable to some articulate sections of a society. Their mention is at the very least heavily muted, at most proscribed—informally as well as formally. Proscribed silences travel as a matter of routine across ideologies, infecting each in turn for a disparate range of reasons. Traditional and conservative ideologies underpinned by unassailable religious beliefs have stringent no-go areas. Emerging ideologies orbiting around social and ethical critique employ woke and cancel-culture proscriptions with equal passion, fervour, and arsenals of justification, but also with increasing automaticity fuelled by a revulsion triggered off by specific words. What is omitted is left unworthy of consideration, or a target for intellectual or rhetorical demolition. The silences they incur point to an epistemological refusal to give credence to all manner of policies, programmes, visions, and maps other than the ones deliberately or latently endorsed through permitted conceptual arrays.

But silence is also a precious ideological resource. It offers a seductive tabula rasa on which to chart a preferred and optional route to securing the political prerequisites of order, harmony, progress, and collective purpose. Because the contents of silence are not predetermined, it yields its apparent secrets in an arbitrary and malleable form that ideologies will work to their advantage. After all, the order and harmony most ideologies seek in their separate idiosyncratic ways are just as frequently attained by removing knowledge or fantasy from the political agenda as by harnessing them to forge coherence. Forging—in the sense of crafting—is indeed the operative word, for strands of interpretation or stark storytelling are imperative even when adhering strictly to scientific methods of evidence, let alone when the foolishness of reckless fact-free invention rushes in to occupy the spaces that silence releases. Remembering and forgetting is the name of the ideological game as ideologies covertly and often without self-conscious intent move to harness time-parameters to their benefit.

The study of ideological silences has been given a boost by questioning the old assumption, carried over from Marx and Engels, that ideologies were above all masking devices—a mixture of deliberate and socially constructed practices that served to obscure and suppress truths. Consequently, the declared task of both participants and scholars was chiefly to unmask—that is to say, un-silence—those concealments and liberate social knowledge. That mode of concealment is procedurally ingrained in the concept of ideology that Marxists entertain, and one adopted by the *Ideologiekritik* School. There, the issue of dogma introduces itself not merely as the attribute of a particular, closed ideology, unwilling or unable to deviate from doctrinaire assertions and beliefs. Instead, the dogmatic element was inserted into the *methodology* of early Marxist scholars of ideology and emanated from their assumptions about the general nature of political thinking under conditions of human alienation. Their scientific certainty in the withering away of ideologies as distorting, class-dominated perspectives regrettably discourages the cultivation of any interest in what those distortions actually look like. It ignores any analytical conclusions the scholarly study of ideology might extrapolate from a microscopic examination of its minutiae, culturally, rhetorically, and ideationally, as they present themselves in the public arena, leaving aside questions of 'authenticity', dissembling, or ethical value. The Marxist disregard for all manifestations of ideology stems from an abhorrence of that allegedly derivative and inferior mode of thinking. In short, Marxists identified ideologies as the silencers of truth and concurrently imposed an epistemological silence on those who sought to pursue alternative interpretations of ideology.[7]

However, the growing appreciation of the unintentional and the unconscious instigated a significant shift among students of ideology. It changed the balance of interpretation, through requiring analysts to perform an act of deciphering rather than unmasking. It accepted that the warping of truth—though in itself far from uncommon—was largely immaterial to the functional rationale of ideologies, while concurrently recognizing that many criteria of truth were dependent on interpretation rather than set in stone.[8] The silencing in which ideologies may or may not have engaged as a form of social warfare and manipulation paled against the very disparate silences that were built into the nature of language and discourse and were at the service of those elemental attributes. Anglo-American political theory was coupled with Marxist epistemology in being too unbending—the former, on its own terms, also too rigorous in its abstract universalism and normative certainties—to permit such intellectual flexibility, the sidestepping of cognitive thought, and the relocation of silences. Although, as we have seen, under the influence of Lacan and Laclau post-Marxism welded psychoanalysis to notions of semantic social control and distortion in an endeavour to revitalize thinking about ideology, even that development could not easily extricate ideology from Marx's shadow.

There has been a more radical alternative, of which Slavoj Žižek has been one of the chief advocates, linking ideology to the issue of lack aired in Chapter 5. On that account, ideology reflects a fantasmatic symbolic projection in Lacanian mode of what cannot be symbolized, precisely because it deals with an unfathomable 'reality'. Ideology then becomes the product of a psychological necessity arising from the need to escape the emptiness of the subject.[9] In that sense ideology does have an empirical purpose, both for the population at large and, indirectly, for the scholar. For the former, its semblance of certainty crafted through decontestation is a requisite for preserving social order and constructing individual identity when such certainty is patently unavailable. For the latter, it assists in pinpointing crucial lacks that delineate areas where knowledge is unavailable, or profound absences where the object pursued is unconceptualizable.

As a result, new methodologies arose of detecting silence through, and in, ideology. Ideologies were now interpreted as paramount examples of particular kinds of hiddenness: the hiddenness of lack that enticingly invites detection; the hiddenness of meaning that intriguingly demands decoding; and the hiddenness of postulations that painstakingly requires unpacking. In that latter respect especially, ideologies share a feature with political and philosophical theory: the words, ideas, and arguments used to construct their claims host far greater underlying variability than those who employ them—practitioners and ideologues—are either willing or able to embrace, impose, or comprehend. In such instances, and given that silence challenges certainty, harnessing the constraining logic of decontestation is inevitable in order for sense—not truth—to be extracted from a semantic tower of Babel.

The crucial adjustment lay in departing from the Marxist conviction that hidden assumptions could be not only detected, but overcome once and for all in the battle against alienation and suppression and in the campaign to remove distorting binaries. Marxist theory, it transpired, was not geared to accepting that some form of concealment was a necessary consequence of developing *any* course of reasoning and explanation pertinent to social life. Neither tacit consent nor tacit dissent was in play here, either. The new aim of ideology studies became to reveal the widespread narrowing of focus typical of any *Weltanschauung*, a narrowing serving to exclude and obscure whatever appeared to be irrelevant to that *Weltanschauung*'s purposes. In contradistinction to Marxist theories of ideology, that filtering-out practice was emphasized by scholars not because it could be eliminated, nor because it was oppressive, but to announce its normal membership of the family of silences.

One consequence is that all ideologies, with differing measures of assurance, stifle the typical uncertainty surrounding the languages they employ and their styles of argumentation, overriding both their indeterminacy and their inaccessibility. They do so by advertising their pretentions to ideological precision, by shrinking ideational pluralism—in different degrees for each ideological family or grouping—and by removing semantic competitors from the ideological arena, viewing them through a glass darkly and muffling the sounds they emit. But that is only one side of the coin. Ideologies may conversely resort to vagueness rather than precision. In such cases, through muting and glossing over the availability of contending meanings they seek advantage in the political objective of recruiting support, by permitting their consumers to read their own positive understandings into the messages they pick up. The silence of semantic singlemindedness—by disregarding other voices—is matched with the silence of surreptitiously exploiting the semantic range of the selected concepts within each ideology so as to optimize its dissemination.

In international relations theory, Hom approaches that vagueness from a slightly different perspective. He has argued that some trends of critical theory that engage with the problems of time and timelessness 'offer little practical traction because all the heavy lifting is done by assumptions, abstractions or productive silences'. Thus, in analyses of rupture, an exaggerated commitment to indeterminacy and unlimited political possibilities—rather than weeding out some options while endorsing others—'reinforces silent doxas, which . . . reduce temporal analysis to loose theorising and rhetorical provocation'.[10] In other words, excessive fluidity of meaning and method, or the assigning of equal weight to all possibilities, decreases the visibility and audibility of worthy perspectives that merit a closer look. Blurring the political validity of differences and obliterating the qualitative distinctions among them is one forceful form of silencing. However, what Hom regards as a defect of some critical theories can—on the expansive understanding of politics on which this study builds—be turned by ideologies to their political advantage in their quest for support.

In light of such nuances, one needs to bear in mind the distinction between an ideology's overt self-portrayal and the actual ideational arrangements and clusters that it contains. That elementary distinction is central to the role of silence in each and every ideological family: it is no surprise that the formulators and conveyors of ideologies rarely construct their case with open eyes and critical self-awareness. This leads to another kind of ideological silence: the denial by the adherents of ideologies of different stripes that they possess an ideology in the first instance. That standpoint is common to many conservatives, neoliberals, populists, Marxists, and critical left-radicals, though not for the same reasons. Claims to shake off the label of ideology can of course be anchored in older premises. If liberalism wasn't an ideology, it was due to the definitional fiat of ideology as closed and doctrinaire. If conservatism wasn't an ideology, it was due to the definitional fiat of ideology as abstract and non-empirical. But there was no overt acknowledgement that those definitional reasons precluded subscribers to ideologies from admitting their nature.

Specific denials such as those were gathered under a more categorical refutation of ideology *in toto*: the 'end of ideology' thesis that flowered twice and faded twice, once in the mid-twentieth century and then towards its end. The age of ideology was over, declared its proponents, because the passion and vehemence that had typified the clash between the grand democratic and totalitarian ideologies had petered out, replaced by a convergence between different worldviews now seeking economic stability, material comforts, and similar welfare systems.[11] As a result, three forms of silencing were generated, the consequence not so much of deliberate obfuscation but of analytical error. First, it was held that if all ideologies shed their differences there would be no ideology, rather than one common one. If—the argument dubiously went—ideology necessarily entailed polarized disagreement, not consensus, then shared or overlapping views of the world could not constitute an ideology. Second, ideological convergences on major issues—assuming that was possible—could not eliminate 'technical' differences on policy implementation that would themselves reveal ideological micro-nuances. A third variant retained the construct of ideology but declared liberalism—famously by Francis Fukuyama in the 1990s—to be the winning one, putting all others in the shade of insignificance, if not chasing them off the world stage completely.[12] That simply disregarded both the proliferation of all other collective, action-oriented political ideas still found in current societies, and the inevitably open-ended nature of history qua time. The 'end of ideology' school of political theory categorically condemned a rich range of voices to unnoticeability and came close to succeeding. The underlying question then became: which ideology is itself unknowingly secreted in the notions of the political that do not recognize 'ideology' as a legitimate phenomenon and object of study? To what is the thought-practice of ideology reduced if its notable manifestations can be eliminated both from the historical stage and from the cut and thrust of political debate and confrontation?

2 The Proliferation of Ideological Silences

Turning to specific unacknowledged or veiled silences within various ideologies, the scholarly challenge includes the following. First, and very significantly, to establish how different ideational maps and groupings confer the status of the unspeakable, the unthinkable, and even the unknowable on the subject-matter of their discourses. Second, to distinguish between 'open' and 'silencing' ideologies on many dimensions, not least by interrogating 'open' ideologies for their nonetheless characteristic 'trademark' silences; and questioning dogmatic, 'closed' ideologies for voices that steal through the absences forced on them. That requires identifying how open ideologies switch between using silence to further their ends or to obscure them, and exploring the effective limits on the capacity of 'closed' ideologies to control the latent ideological decontestation that bubbles under the surface of even the most rigid polities. Third, to ascertain whether a specific population is subject to particular or selective silences and how such silences are distributed ideologically across it. Fourth, to establish whether silence is perceived by its adherents as a valued social good that enables an ideology to flourish, or whether they consider it to be a hindrance in attaining that flourishing. Overlaying these is a parallel perspective: the six defining axes of the political discussed in Chapter 2 are traceable in each ideological family, while, unavoidably, some *variants* of each feature are destined to be muted, forgotten, or eliminated.

The unthinkable and the unspeakable occupy very different slots in ideological practices. On the whole, radical-right ideologies are more prone to contemplate and enunciate the ethically 'unthinkable': namely, topics that for many other 'progressive' ideological families are ruled out of court. Negative eugenics, involving the disabling or forbidding of procreation for certain groups, depriving people of citizenship or residence rights, and in extreme cases mass incarceration and extermination can be part of a political and cultural imagination-cum-reality with 'no holds barred'. Many such modes of racial abuse, economic discrimination, and cultural prejudice were until recently—and still often are—accepted silently by some sectors of any population as permissible or, even more emphatically, as unquestionable. Liberals and progressives, however, are more likely to curtail the unthinkable among their own ranks. They will not, of course, practise silence about its manifestations but convey vocal views chiefly as vehement opposition to expressed 'unthinkable' measures voiced by others.

By contrast, in societies that privilege unfettered open discourse over the emotional damage such openness may spark, there will be fewer inhibitions on what can be said and a tendency to voice the unspeakable in the name of free speech or the public airing and deliberation of issues, however distasteful or painful. It is thus a matter of considerable disagreement—within those ideological families themselves—whether practices that have become partially internalized and that garner cultural support, such as political correctness, no-platforming, and enforcing taboos on certain words, are liberal features. Schröter plausibly regards the political correctness aimed at protecting the sensibilities of those in the discursive firing line as an ideological instrument that can point both ways, benefiting the political right by portraying left-liberals as engaged in silencing procedures that undermine their professed advocacy of 'openness and discourse accessibility for all'.[13]

In general, ideological silences are most prevalent when epistemological constraints incur their unnoticeability or conceptual opacity. A compact selection of these silences will now be sketched out as illustrative of distinctive ideological discourses, focusing on the most significant and intriguing instances in each ideological family.

2.1 Liberal Silences

Turning specifically to liberalism, preventing harm still is a central first pillar that has understandingly undergone expansion and adaptation since its prominent exposition by Mill. A silence concerning the very identification of harm is uneasily built into liberal thinking, although physical harm is the easiest to identify, epitomized by the questionable nineteenth-century adage: 'sticks and stones may break my bones, but words will never hurt me'. Liberals were seemingly inured to offensive speech by the detached rationality they used to swear by. Since then, many liberals have accepted the extension of harm to the domains of emotional and psychological damage and distress. Social liberal variants promote strong welfare agendas on basic incomes, and access to basic goods such as education and health in order to counter damaging hindrances to human autonomy and development. Nonetheless, harm remains a culturally and temporally flexible criterion, and the standards it meets are fluid both subjectively and objectively.[14]

A second, connected pillar relates to the communal extension of rights holders. Early liberal thinking, with its initial focus solely on individuals, was silent about collective groups that bear rights. A gradual enlargement of such units to embrace local communities, nations, and peoples has removed vital social elements from disregard and obscurity. Peoples, in particular, a term usually referring to indigenous populations, are a recent addition to the liberal insistence on self-determination, including the right to their cultural, national, linguistic, and ethnic identity.[15] That conceptual legitimation is rejected by ideological opponents who dismissively refer to it as invoking a non-existing group-mind.

Neutrality—discussed in the previous chapter in conjunction with the state—is a strong contender for a third pillar of the liberal ideological imaginary, particularly in some academic philosophical constructions of optimal, abstract liberalism that practises variable degrees of value-agnosticism in major personal and social areas, and even more so in popular understandings of liberalism.[16] Contemporary philosophical liberalism exudes a potential for fairness and equality, but neutrality functions also as a harmonizing sheen that deflects attention from its de facto, inbuilt, inability or even failure to mitigate dissatisfaction and conflict as normal, concrete political outcomes. Those endemic tensions and imperfections may result from the usual discord and disagreement engendered by all social interaction, but also from the ambivalence of the role of the pluralism often seen to typify liberalisms—either as a praiseworthy protector of diversity, or as a series of parallel internal ideological routes, stretching from social liberalism to neoliberalism to libertarianism—that cannot agree on central minutiae of public conduct. Each path obscures the costs incurred by the other.

For those unschooled in the fine arts of politics, the constitutional anchoring of the alleged accolade of depoliticized neutrality in the legal practices of court institutions is emphasized by images of blind justice and balanced scales. Perceptions of the US Supreme Court draw a veil of silence over the latter's dual political nature. To begin with, that eminently political body is appointed through clear political procedures, and it then goes on to deliver certain classes of decisions that directly reflect the ideological balance, or imbalance, of its composition. But even disregarding its activist ideological affiliations, and the obvious partisanship of such institutions, the very act of distributing significance to events, processes, and arguments, and of delivering judgments—an activity shared by all courts—is a core political practice, all too often cloaked under the dignified guise of a purely legal and constitutional one. For the politically streetwise that should be evident, yet for those taken in by a cementing and insulating myth-making narrative that insight is hushed up by the promotion of an allegedly supra-political and socially prominent vantage point, in which the professionally 'objective' legal prevails over the political.[17]

Depoliticization and neutrality are central weapons in the arsenal of political concealment, if often unintentionally so, and they are sped on under the guise of dispensing justice and exercising reflectiveness. Construing the law, and applying it to collective social procedures in such a formally regimented manner, fosters a silence that gnaws away at the reality of a set of practices. That silence is achieved simply by ensuring that the insights of one discipline—politics—are not permitted to spill over onto the domain of another—jurisprudence. Maintaining the boundary between the two is paramount when protecting the legitimacy and integrity of some of the most fundamental order-preserving institutions and rules of a society, particularly when legitimacy and integrity rest on shaky and contested ground. The silent mythology surrounding Supreme Court opinions and decisions is a highly apposite illustration of the fundamental political feature of shoring up support for a collective entity.

The notion of 'holding the ring' with reference to keeping order and setting out the boundaries of a boxing match is a good exemplification of a neutrality/silence treble move. The arbitrator is *neutral* (i.e., silent) about preferring one side or the other; the actual monitoring of the practice is *impartial* and unbiased; but that monitoring also simultaneously conceals the strong, *non-neutral*, value-laden preference for observing rules by means of an external regulation of the combatants. That latter interventionist practice is silently taken for granted.

A fourth pillar is the harnessing of change to liberal discourse. Although liberals do not embrace disruptive change, they subscribe to a strong belief in the natural rhythm of social progress and civilizational improvement. Gradual and rational advance airbrushes away upheavals and revolutions as glitches in human development, unless such major disturbances are designed to smooth the path of progress itself, as with liberation movements. Many ideologies invent their own historical continuities, as we will presently note. But the liberal faith in social and cultural evolution is ingrained as a fundamental value and it is preserved in the face of bumps and twists in the road.[18]

There is a further dimension to liberal change as flexibility. Liberals—if not neoliberals—may be open to listening to messages from a hitherto 'acoustically' blocked sphere. Their flexibility is facilitated through occasionally porous boundaries, transferring ideas from the previously culturally unthinkable, or undesirable—as in attitudes towards homosexuality—to a reconfigured domain of ideological possibilities, thus allowing novel voices to become audible and take their place in the family of liberalisms. Liberals may permit silences to be lifted to enable reflective and self-critical adjustments, while cultural silences are relocated and recalibrated in order to dampen previous distaste and disapproval.

A fifth pillar of liberalism is the conventional distinction between the public and the private spheres, with the corollary that not only is the private sphere deemed apolitical—a conclusion now heavily challenged—but its occupants have no pressing claim to be heard in the larger social arena. What happens in the private domain is squirreled away for reasons of both irrelevance and discretion, equally underserving of a public platform and legally shielded. Those silences have accorded carte blanche to those who take advantage of that dichotomy and they camouflage harms and discrimination. As Carole Pateman has contended, 'the profound ambiguity of the liberal conception of the private and public obscures and mystifies the social reality it helps constitute'.[19] The highly valued family sanctuary carved out by liberals may shroud an unanticipated dark side that is a site of oppression and abuse but it raises significant questions concerning the adverse effects of liberal silences.

2.2 Feminist Silences

So-called first-wave liberal feminists placed their faith in an impartial state that—through legal and constitutional means—would secure the full rights of women.[20] The laudable intent of liberals and egalitarians to universalize human rights originally referred to the 'rights of man'. But it concealed differential gender-based claims to rights, as well as sidelining the need for the largest gender category—women—to catch up with men, given their serious disadvantages in the actual social and cultural assignment of rights. The 'rights of man' buried such rights terminologically and did almost nothing to redress concrete discriminatory practices that predominantly not only concerned women but also affected LGBT people. Even the later replacement of the 'rights of man' with 'human rights' offered an abstract syllogism: 'human beings have rights; women are human beings; therefore, women have rights'. By formulating the issue in the shape of a universal truth claim, or fact, it rendered any debate on the subject superfluous and immune to human practices that contravened it.

Hence later feminists towards the end of the twentieth century contended that, through subsuming women within the category of men, liberals had made them invisible. To cite Pateman again, the strong patriarchal understanding of full citizenship meant that 'at best, citizenship can be extended to women only as lesser men'.[21] Liberal universalism extended gender identity only in areas where it was believed women could match men in a narrow constitutional sense, or by pursuing separate paths of individual development. The legitimation of women's political roles as a lack in relation to men saw that lack gravitating towards an enduring deficiency—an absence—rather than a potential to be realized at a future point.

The ongoing cultural subjection of women to the public–private dichotomy, moreover, confined them to a political silence on the 'passive' side of that divide, before theory caught up with reality and acknowledged that 'the personal (too!) is the political'—and not only in relation to gender segregation and devaluation. Rhetorically speaking, however, a dilemma emerges. The singularity of the claim to human rights attracts powerful slogans, while skipping over vital disparities. But enumerating the increasingly gender-fluid distinctions of language that can give voice to those differences and subtle overlaps may also dilute the universal rallying force of rights demands. It furthermore flags up the issue of naming. Previous sections of this book drew attention to the naming of the phenomenon of silence itself as part of a reification process. But renaming events, processes, and narratives frequently operates as an act of eradication. Past histories of women and of racial and cultural minorities, as demonstrated by Trouillot, have been silenced in their historical contexts. Ideologies operate by simplifying concepts in a search for the demotic and catchy, without which their aspirations to broad social appeal would suffer. That entails passing a veil over, or sidestepping, distinctions that are still contentious, or that have not yet bedded down. Those generalizations conceal the deeper silences about gender status that have maintained their grip over centuries.

Renaming can also be a reclaiming process, rearranging the morphological patterns of ideologies, often replacing not merely words but concepts—not just by extending conceptual combinations, or debarring certain conceptual patterns that have become unsayable, but by infusing ideological families with new discursive power ostensibly under the same umbrella.[22] A well-known instance is Carol Gilligan's advocacy of a hitherto marginalized ethic of care alongside, and occasionally instead of, an ethic of justice in order to reflect women's experience of social responsibility.[23] In the words of Dale Spender: 'The silence of women has been a cumulative process. Conceptually and materially excluded from the production of knowledge, their meanings and explanations have been systematically blocked. . . . Women's meanings cannot just be added on . . . new *cerebration*, a new way of knowing is required.'[24]

The complexity of women's silences through the critical lens of feminists is well articulated by Holub, not only as a change over time but as a recognition of the duality of silence itself. 'As a master category', she writes,

> 'silence', conceived of as presence and absence, permeates and informs the architectural designs of feminist discourse at first as a synonym of powerlessness, of the places, rights, symbolic orders and privileges which had been denied to many women, and with the inflexibility of some of the symbolic systems to express that which had hitherto remained inexpressible. In a subsequent move, feminist discourses recognize that silence was not always to be seen in a negative key, that the cultural silences which appear to have been imposed on women perhaps reveal, as much as they conceal, presences which fuelled the various historical phallocratic ascents to power.

Identifying oppression and exploitation becomes then only one kind of change for the analyst. The other—no less demanding—is to 'archaeologize the silent sites of power present in those silences'.[25] The movement from critical advocacy to excavating and decoding practices emerges as an instrument of comprehending silence within the framework of the political.

The ideologies of feminism have censured the grand narratives that construct social identity as 'tacitly reproducing a masculinist view of the world'. But, as McNay has argued, that contention underplays women's participation in social practices: 'If women's narratives are always placed at the margins of sociality, an analysis of the socio-historical dynamics through which feminine gender is both included and excluded from mainstream social experience is foreclosed.' That 'obscures the extent to which narratives of female identity are caught up in a complex fashion with more general categories of self, personhood and history'.[26] Edifyingly, that does not imply deliberate silencing. But silencing creeps in on a massive scale nonetheless, not only hiding the specific practices that women pursue but, further, emphatically reducing the social capacity to place women's experiences and histories in public view.

2.3 Anarchist Silences

The silences that anarchists display are most prominent on issues of power and harmony, occasionally on the very nature of the political. Many of their thinkers and texts regard anarchism as a promising transcendence of conflict and struggle, as well as hierarchy and inequality. While these remain conscious ends, they obscure the embedded but often unacknowledged politicization, organization, and leadership required both to attain and to maintain them. The wielding of power occurs at two anarchist nodes. Performatively, it is evident in the campaigning occupations of urban spaces that operate as attacks on establishment domination. Ideationally, it is built into the theorizing of an anarchist society in which government is ostensibly replaced by spontaneously coordinated and self-sustaining social arrangements, but that entails the optimistic assumption that self-regulation (which itself is the self-exercise of power) can actually do away with control as socialization, influence, and the marshalling of human conduct. The silence that covers the inescapable and perennial indications of power is necessary to safeguard the tenets of anarchism from an ideologically suppressed reality that would otherwise invalidate many of its core beliefs. As several theorists of anarchist ideology recognize, anarchism may exclude tiered and centrist forms of power—particularly the power of the state—but is committed to continuous reformist or revolutionary activism that bears all the hallmarks of an intense engagement with power.[27] Nor can that just be written off as the temporary means to a power-free society.

2.4 Conservative Silences

Conservatism subscribes to extensive ideological silences. In parallel to several religious belief systems, it curtails the self-questioning of many human practices, sanctioning them through a principled and ingrained refusal to contemplate anything other than their foundational and unchallengeable character. By appealing either to God, nature, science, history, or biology as extra-human sources of the social order,[28] conservatives place a raft of preferred ideas and practices beyond dispute and thus accord them tacit consent. Indeed, the anxiety attached to uncontrolled or 'unnatural' change raises a host of 'unthinkable' possibilities in conservative minds that require them to be dismissed out of hand. The indisputability conservatives assign to the sources of the social order, and their conviction in the validity of those propelling lodestars, rules out any possibility of working outside them and shuts down the cultural and epistemological horizons in which they are located. Hierarchy and leadership are subsumed under the rubric of 'what you see (and hear) is what you get', dismissing the plausibility of alternatives. As with some other ideologies, conservatives can display an aggressive dismissal of counterarguments or counterfactuals. 'Science' and 'history' in this case do not embrace methods to be endorsed in a professional disciplinary sense but a mode of naming ideas and events, asserting their finality and removing their precepts and findings from debate and contestation.

As an example, consider the economist and philosopher Friedrich von Hayek. His self-declared contribution to liberal theory has been rendered questionable because of the manner in which he implicitly foregrounded certain silences. Hayek replicated the conservative insistence on the natural balance of a society through his theory of a spontaneous order—the catallaxy. When individuals pursue their own ends the result is a harmonious market that eliminates the role of collective human design. Hayek remained conspicuously silent on the role of power in shaping that order, obscuring its workings through the well-aired ideological tactic of neutralizing and depoliticizing it. By likening the rules of a market to a game dependent on unforeseen and uncontrollable circumstances, Hayek ignored the social and cultural forces that enabled and sustained that market.[29] This is a case not of lack, superimposition, or unconceptualizability, but of a prior ontological stance that precludes the relevance of such forces in accounting for socio-economic order.

2.5 Reformist and Radical Silences

Silences are markedly woven into socialist argumentation, one instance of which emanates from the interfaces between its Marxist and utopian tendencies. Karl Marx's disinclination to spell out the details of his view of future socialist society and his unease with the blueprints of utopian socialist writers is significant. David Leopold observes three possible—and broadly incompatible—explanations for that reluctance, though he casts doubt on Marx's unalloyed commitment to any one of them. The first is that such blueprints would foreclose the future in an undemocratic way because 'they inappropriately restrict the freedom of individuals to determine for themselves the kind of society that they want to live in'. The second is that the historical process makes any blueprint design redundant and unnecessary. The third relates to the epistemological impossibility of available knowledge about future society.[30] However patchy the accounts given by various scholars may be, and however unmindful of the complexity of Marx's thinking on those issues, they permit us to illuminate different interpretations of future absence. This case accentuates the unwillingness to superimpose a voice on such absence; specifically, by letting future silences be. Marx's qualms and democratic decision making aside, however, the very imagining of a utopia necessarily superimposes a blue-printed path held hostage to present imaginations.

Taking each account in turn, the first explanation elicits an ethico-political insistence on enabling human beings to engage in the immediacy of their own voices. Silence here assumes and condones non-intervention in the autonomy of others. That is not, however, the liberal abstention from intervention in value-contested preferences under the umbrella of neutrality, but the deeper respect for the right of groups to choose the course of their social and political identity. The second ascribes to history and social evolution a relentless logic, ensuring that socio-economic mechanisms will leave no space for silences. It holds that the forward-marching trajectory of social forces and relations allows us at the very least to infer the macro-contents of such voices, if not their specifics. The third is particularly interesting as a concealed silence. It signals a form of conceptual silence emanating not from unawareness on the part of an existing population, or from obstacles that hinder the role of detection in scholarship, but from the unfathomability of impending epistemologies. Whereas past and present blockages to conceptualization may sometimes dangle indirect but existing clues that invite decoding, that does not apply to patterns of thought and conduct that may never materialize. Underpinning these is a broader sociological consideration, curtailing the possibility and appropriateness of legislating for a future generation, or for a present one that knows where it might be going but currently lacks the full conditions for thinking clearly.

Needless to say, holding back is not typical of most utopian (or for that matter dystopian) writers, who are inventively tempted to spell out the particulars of their private visions in eloquent and often loquacious terms. Unlike the operational practices adopted by ideologies, utopias are not as a rule widely shared programmes or blueprints. The political silence-cum-indifference they display reflects unconcern with the recruitment of broad social support for their proposals—not least because so many of them are individual literary ventures, not actively campaigning political movements. By contrast, the anticipation of the future in varieties of mainstream socialism follows an extrapolation from the present in often sanguine terms.[31] Socialisms trace a cycle of lack, initiated through human and social misorganization and alienation but harbouring a restorative potential. That said, for an ideology strongly fixated on future temporal dimensions, the obvious silence that the future offers serves as a politically secure 'haven' for attractive political plans, especially long-term ones. Their political vision holds out an escape route from the immediate criticism of their applicability or success. The silence of the future provides a vitally important tabula rasa for the appeal and survival of current socialist templates through which to inscribe policies and to solicit support, while not staying around long enough to be held accountable.

The radical left nurtures its own silences. Many of them follow the logic of critical ideologies focused on drawing sharp distinctions between them and their opponents—or enemies, to recall Schmitt's dichotomy. That dialectical logic feeds off the Hegelian–Marxist heritage that still holds considerable sway within left-radicalism and its commitment to the notion of antagonism. Dichotomies and opposites exist, of course, but rarely in regular political thinking and practice. Those contrasts tend, as contended above, to blur the continua that run between polarities. Indeed, polarities are hardly the most methodologically astute heuristic devices for analysing ideologies to begin with. In crusading or censorious mode, however, that tendency—no stranger to other ideologies as well—is built into the conceptual worldview of the radical left, producing conspicuous discursive silences when the main current enemy, neoliberalism, is excoriated. As Phelan observes in a recent analysis, 'Critics of neoliberalism do not want to talk much about markets in anything other than a critical mode because of the (at least unconscious) fear that they will sound like Tony Blair if they do so'[32]—i.e., adopting an accommodatory stance typical of a Third Way blending of markets with mild social-democratic adjustments. Behind that lies the reasoning, emotional as much as intellectual and not always grasped by those who subscribe to it, that 'the ideological authority of what we might call a sedimented antagonism to neoliberalism potentially inhibits our ability to construct other more potent kinds of political and ideological antagonism ... that typically go unarticulated in critiques of neoliberalism'.[33]

The advocacy of animal rights presents a case study contending with a very different problematic: standing up for 'the weakest, the voiceless in our society: people, animals and environment'.[34] With regard to animals, human voice is superimposed on a silent group who—on the whole—are both vocal and highly performative, though far from noiseless or lacking in expression. The superimposition of voice travels across species (though predictably in one direction only!). The Australian Animal Justice Party has appealed to citizens to 'lend animals your political voice' and pledged 'to provide a voice for policies and practices that promote respect, kindness, compassion and understanding toward other animals'.[35]

But there is a preliminary issue firmly connected to historically mutating reconceptualizations of rights. Obliviousness to the rights of animals is hardly surprising if they do not pass the test of rights-bearing entities. If the prerequisites for claiming rights are held to emanate from being able to make and communicate conscious claims over the conduct of others, or being capable of constituting part of a moral community, or possessing human qualities that merit protection as an enshrinement of worth, including complex linguistic ability—all well-known arguments in human rights theories[36]—then variably shaded silences about animal rights will follow. For those silences to dissipate, not only must human rights-bearers cease to maintain exclusive status, but it has to become politically legitimate for others to claim rights on behalf of non-verbal sentient creatures, human as well as non-human. Specifically, that requires two silences to be disregarded: the concrete absence of animals' verbal voice and conceptual flexibility,[37] and the ontological silence within several areas of rights scholarship concerning the interspecies validity of rights-claims.

2.6 Populist Silences

Populists possess their own noticeable sets of shrouds and shields that nurture significant silences. One prominent instance is the ubiquitous phrase 'the will of the people', found in—or should one say appropriated by—right-wing populist discourse, already discussed in Chapter 10. A slogan that appears at first impression to epitomize the incorporation of the entire population under a profusion of historically valued banners such as communitarianism, egalitarianism, and popular sovereignty is revealed on closer analysis to be an ideological power grab that deprives sizeable segments of a people from uttering their views and fosters the very division that it proclaims to eliminate. Concurrently, it promotes significant silences concerning the persistence of power hierarchies that are supposed to have been eradicated through such ostensible displays of togetherness. The anti-pluralist—and on some interpretations anti-democratic—spirit of any will encompassing all members of a society permits a 'spokesperson' of that will to articulate it by superimposing a private hypothetical voice on a postulated 'unanimous' consensus that resists disaggregation. The part—often the small part—masquerades as the totality.[38]

In populist parlance, democracy can be effectively divested of emancipatory or egalitarian values or of constitutional practices fostering reflection and accountability, which are instead spirited out of view. It becomes an abstract and conceptually vacuous reference to an assertion *en masse* of crude power, eschewing dialogue and diversity and shunning liberal majoritarianism. When populists refer to a dualist confrontation between the elites and the people, they overlook, ignore, or hide the fact that challenges to existing elites in the name of populism emanate without exception from other articulate and *parti-pris* political elites, or aspirants to elite status, who bedeck themselves in the trappings of direct democracy without the mechanisms for securing its voices. Such challenges are harboured by rival groups who nourish resentment towards those they perceive to inhabit positions of influence, and who accordingly arrogate to themselves the rhetorical force with which to override other perspectives.[39]

Right-wing populism is seen by its proponents as an ideology of the dispossessed, yet it is characterized by the absence of an agenda designed to benefit the socio-economic groups that constitute a large part of the people. The populist notion of deprivation is reserved for the 'authentic' primacy of natality: namely, the cultural precedence of 'natives'—a specific and imagined dominant ethnicity—over immigrants, foreigners, and alternative ethnicities. It is justified by the unique and proudly heralded distinguishing features of a fantasized original occupancy of a geographical space, and the insistence on monopolizing a temporal trajectory of national origins and 'natural', unsullied, evolution.[40] And it is reinforced by a profound silence over the claims of multiple other contenders to such occupancy and to their role in shaping cultural, national, and sub-national identities.[41]

2.7 Nationalist Silences

Finally, the silences of right-wing populism stand out in comparison to the far more complex family of nationalist ideologies. Right-wing populism is rarely focused on a multifold movement of parallel yet distinct populisms across different countries, preferring instead to homogenize the phenomenon as undifferentiated. Liberal nationalisms, however, exhibit a subtle interweaving of nationalism with other core concepts, such as the national and personal values of liberty, emancipation, rights, and self-development. They are also tuned into the formative creation of a nation, while populism tends to locate that birth in the extra-historical mists of time, muting the possibility that nations can emerge *de novo* as a political act out of human will and energy. The intensity of right-wing populists' engrossment with the failings of their own society blanks out a comparative vista. Nationalisms, by contrast, are far more content to accept that each country may develop its own version of nationalism precisely due to fundamental and respected cultural dissimilarities—dissimilarities glossed over by populist discourse.[42] In an international context, nationalists are acutely aware of their competitive role among other nation-states. There is no institutional equivalent of competing, cooperating, or conflictual populist states on the basis of alternative populist ideologies, as populism fails to attain a clear-cut organizational incarnation. The nationalist appeal to universal values of self-determination and equality is also notably absent among right-wing populisms. Here again, the political silence and elusiveness of populism are conspicuous.

That said, conservative and fascist nationalisms may display overlap with right-wing populisms on issues of unity. Major trends within conservatism subscribe to an organic idea of community, but it is community in a concrete sense rather than postulating the abstract and depersonalized populist version of an invented people—or, for that matter, the idealized universalist notion of a global, or ethically inspired, humanity. Fascists have valorized their own nation, much as populists valorize their own people ('America first' in Donald Trump's staccato slogan), and they both do that in an aggressive, exclusive, and uncompromising manner.[43] As for nationalists, Perry Anderson's term 'imagined communities' is a seminal device utilized by those anxious to maintain a story of historical continuity. Anderson specifically shines a light on cases where 'official nationalism concealed a discrepancy between nation and dynastic realm. . . . Slovaks were to be Magyarized, Indians Anglicized, and Koreans Japanified.'[44] Nationalists fill in the inevitable disruptions to accounts of national continuity either by invented detail or, to the contrary, by erasing them with an obscuring silence. The latter was made famous by Renan: 'Forgetting, I would even say historical error, is an essential factor in the creation of a nation.'[45] If anything, populists treat history as a distraction and are content to replace it with the ahistoricity of conjectural and nebulous myth.

Another approach to nationalism attaches it to a Bourdieu-like naturalization of social experience. The term 'banal nationalism' has been suggested by Billig. It refers to the commonplace assimilation of a territorial and psychological sense of individual and social belonging in and of a nation, reflected in everyday deeds and thoughts such as specific usages of the pronoun 'we'. This association becomes so routine as to be undetected; consequently "our" daily nationalism slips from attention' as befits 'the powers of an ideology which is so familiar that it hardly seems noticeable'.[46] Nationalist identity and its narrowing is another potent example of a hybrid case of concealed silencing, when the imposition of silences may have been deliberate but its broader awareness as an instance of silencing has since faded, eliminating any traces of such intentionality or consciousness. Regional languages may be marginalized, dialects become unintelligible, and symbols and memorized history are wiped out when a national identity becomes standardized. These silences hover between the unknowable and the inarticulable, between lost and buried knowledge and the faint remnants of a vanished folk culture, abetted by the dying away of cultural actors. The political practices involving the superior ranking and promotion of a specific expressive identity operate here relatively smoothly up to the point where previously silenced, or new, groups find their voice as well as rediscovering the voices of some of their predecessors. The entire cycle may then resume, or fragment and reassemble into different units of social identity. Noteworthy are quasi-silences, as in Svetogorska Street in Belgrade, where a sign on a corner registers seven successive name changes, one over the other, not as a palimpsest but as a visible, sequential list. The visual layering bears witness to a simultaneous replacing and recording of the past and of the places and people who played a role in it. A transparent silencing and redemption of that national and municipal history—both as past shadow and as a current living site—go hand in hand.

2.8 Illiberal Silences

Authoritarianism, totalitarianism, and fascism have their own forms of silence. Much of it is deliberate, directly employed to instil terror and obedience—artistically phrased as 'the natural demonic power of silence'.[47] But it also adopts the guise of a systemically internalized averseness to divulging information or the habitual submerging of truth in lies. At that point, intentionality fades away to be replaced by a gradually ingrained bureaucratic routine—a customary acquiescence or muteness—becoming an almost imperceptible disengagement that has long ceased to be practised purposively. Totalitarianism adopts a manufactured comprehensiveness that seals innumerable holes in the fabric through which values such as individuality and diversity might pass, and which are removed from public view unless challenged by opposing ideologies. Seamlessness in a world of social pluralism is a form of silencing, eliminating 'subversive' knowledge and even taboos themselves from sight. By rejecting political participation and popular voices that are not manipulated, faked, or superimposed, non-democratic ideologies utilize the widespread occurrence of silence as a vital fuel, a resource through which to obviate legitimacy and (tacit) consent issues and to protect rulers. Its most horrific form—obliteration—is poignantly recreated on the banks of the Danube below the Hungarian Parliament building, where dozens of empty pairs of bronze shoes are affixed to the promenade to symbolize the annihilation of denizens of Budapest, many of whom were Jewish, who were shot and dumped in the river by members of the Hungarian Arrow Cross in 1944–5. The double silence—of absent people and of a proper debate on the circumstances of their murder—draws out the many layers of Hungarian national memory.

A crucial but elusive difference repeatedly identified in the course of this book continues to dominate the silences of political theorizing as well as ordinary ideological expression. It is that between not listening or not discerning, when the evidence is capable of being grasped but is hidden to the eye and ear; and not knowing due to the unavailability of a serviceable intellectual apparatus, persistently resisting detection by the participants in a discourse. The problem, of course, is that the advance of knowledge lies in those very interstices where that distinction blurs, when an Archimedes can jump out of their bath and transform the forgotten, discarded, or unnoticed into the permanently and transformatively knowable. Defensive and preserving silences are then undermined by the creation of tools that reveal silences as gaps in understanding: their durability difficult to crack but, once the missing pieces of the jigsaw are supplied, bereft of their previous order-sustaining functions, and transferred to more precarious ground. Silence, as with Sherlock Holmes, then becomes a mystery—a challenge to puzzle out and ultimately to clarify. But we need to heed different senses of mystery here. In the world of sleuths, mystery is a rational and intellectual conundrum to be solved and the silence surrounding it eliminated. That is a far cry from the wondrous, ethereal, and sacred idea of mystery as represented, *inter alia*, by the Greek and Roman child god Harpocrates—the god of silence, mystery, and secrecy, the combination of which was a fixture in the imaginations of the ancients. Here silence is a preserve to be revered and guarded, rather than an invitation to unlock and explore. Either way, the question of barriers, screens, and interventions dictates patterns of abstinence or activism, and in ideologies—those political constructs par excellence—they find their apotheosis.

Notes

1. Freeden, 'The Morphological Analysis of Ideology', pp. 116–118.
2. T. Pateman, *Language, Truth and Politics*, pp. 19, 68.
3. J. Blommaert, 'The Debate is Open' in J. Blommaert (ed.), *Language Ideological Debates* (Berlin and New York: Mouton de Gruyter, 1999), pp. 2, 8.
4. Freeden, 'Editorial: After the Brexit Referendum'.
5. Ibid.; M. Freeden, *Ideologies and Political Theory: A Conceptual Approach* (Oxford: Clarendon Press, 1996), pp. 485–487.
6. Laclau, 'The Death and Resurrection', p. 207.
7. See A. Vincent, *Modern Political Ideologies*, 3rd edn (Chichester: John Wiley & Sons, 2010), pp. 1–22.
8. Freeden, *Ideologies and Political Theory*, pp. 33–36; Freeden, *Ideology Studies*, pp. 183–186.
9. S. Žižek, 'The Spectre of Ideology', in S. Žižek (ed.), *Mapping Ideology* (London: Verso, 1994), pp. 1–33.
10. Cf. A. R. Hom, 'Silent Order: The Temporal Turn in Critical International Relations', *Millennium* 46 (2018), pp. 325, 327–329.
11. D. Bell, *The End of Ideology: On the Exhaustion of Political Ideas in the Fifties* (London: Collier-Macmillan 1961).
12. F. Fukuyama, 'The End of History?', *National Interest*, no. 16 (summer 1989), pp. 3–18. The three misconceptions of the 'end of ideology' thesis are discussed in Freeden, *Ideologies and Political Theory*, pp. 17–19.
13. M. Schröter, 'The Language Ideology of Silence and Silencing in Public Discourse: Claims to Silencing as Metadiscursive Moves in German Anti-political Correctness Discourse', in Murray and Durrheim, *Qualitative Studies of Silence*, pp. 165–185.
14. M. Freeden, *Liberalism: A Very Short Introduction* (Oxford: Oxford University Press, 2015).
15. 'Universal Declaration of the Rights of Peoples', 2001. https://unpo.org/article.php?id=105
16. Most liberal philosophers shy away from strong notions of neutrality, but several are prepared to entertain circumscribed neutrality claims. See R. E. Goodin and A. Reeve, *Liberal Neutrality* (London and New York: Routledge, 1989), and J. Rawls, *Political Liberalism* (New York: Columbia University Press, 1996), pp. 191–194.
17. See, e.g., J. Iuliano, 'The Supreme Court's Noble Lie', *UC Davis Law Review* 51 (2018), pp. 911–977.
18. See my 'Twentieth-Century Liberal Thought: Development or Transformation', in M. Freeden, *Liberal Languages: Ideological Imaginations and Twentieth-Century Progressive Thought* (Princeton, NJ: Princeton University Press, 2005), pp. 19–37.
19. C. Pateman, *The Disorder of Women* (Cambridge: Polity Press, 1989), p. 120.
20. A. M. Jaggar, *Feminist Politics and Human Nature* (Totowa, NJ: Rowman & Littlefield, 1983).

21 Ibid., p. 197.
22 See Freeden, *Ideologies and Political Theory*, pp. 497–501.
23 C. Gilligan, *In a Different Voice* (Cambridge, MA: Harvard University Press, 1993), pp. 97–98, 174.
24 D. Spender, *Man Made Language* (London: Routledge & Kegan Paul, 1980), p. 59.
25 R. Holub, 'This Silence Which Is Not One: Towards a Microphysics of Rhetoric', *Differentia: Review of Italian Thought* 2 (1988), art. 21, pp. 251–259, at p. 257.
26 McNay, *Gender and Agency*, pp. 82–84.
27 U. Gordon, 'Anarchism Reloaded', *Journal of Political Ideologies* 12 (2007), pp. 29–48.
28 Freeden, *Ideologies and Political Theory*, pp. 317–347.
29 See, e.g., the chapter 'Liberalism' in F. A. Hayek, *New Studies in Philosophy, Politics, Economics and the History of Ideas* (London: Routledge & Kegan Paul, 1978), esp. pp. 135–137.
30 D. Leopold, 'On Marxian Utopophobia', *Journal of the History of Philosophy* 54 (2016), pp. 111–134, at pp. 118, 122–123, 129. I have altered the sequence in which Leopold discusses these three points.
31 D. Sassoon, *One Hundred Years of Socialism* (London: HarperCollins, 1997).
32 S. Phelan, 'What's in a Name? Political Antagonism and Critiquing "Neoliberalism"', *Journal of Political Ideologies* 27 (2022), pp. 147–167 at p. 157.
33 Ibid., p. 158.
34 'Manifesto of The Dutch Party for Animals (Partij voor de Dieren, PvdD)' ('Verkiezingsprogramma Partij voor de Dieren'), in Joop van Holsteyn et al. (eds.), *Verkiezingsprogramma's 2002 & 2003* (Amsterdam: Rozenberg, 2003), p. 502 [quoted in P. Lucardie, 'Animalism: A Nascent Ideology? Exploring the Ideas of Animal Advocacy Parties', *Journal of Political Ideologies* 25 (2020), pp. 212–227].
35 https://animaljusticeparty.org/about/manifesto/ (accessed 6 May 2020).
36 M. Freeden, *Rights* (Milton Keynes: Open University Press, 1991).
37 See, e.g., W. T. Fitch, 'Animal Cognition and the Evolution of Human Language: Why We Cannot Focus Solely on Communication', *Philosophical Transactions of the Royal Society B* (2019), https://royalsocietypublishing.org/doi/10.1098/rstb.2019.0046
38 See J.-W. Müller, *What Is Populism?* (Philadelphia, PA: University of Pennsylvania Press, 2016), p. 22.
39 For an elaboration of the above arguments, see Freeden, 'Editorial: After the Brexit Referendum'.
40 P. Taggart, 'Populism and Representative Politics in Contemporary Europe', *Journal of Political Ideologies* 9 (2004), pp. 269–288.
41 Freeden, 'Editorial: After the Brexit Referendum'.
42 See M. Viroli, *For Love of Country* (Oxford: Clarendon Press, 1995).
43 M. Freeden, 'Is Nationalism a Distinct Ideology?', *Political Studies* 46 (1998), pp. 748–765.
44 P. Anderson, *Imagined Communities* (London: Verso, 1983), p. 110 and *passim*.
45 Ernest Renan, 'What is a Nation?', text of a conference delivered at the Sorbonne, 11 March 1882, in Ernest Renan, *Qu'est-ce qu'une nation?*, trans. Ethan Rundell (Paris: Presses-Pocket, 1992), http://ucparis.fr/files/9313/6549/9943/What_is_a_Nation.pdf (accessed 7 April 2020).
46 M. Billig, *Banal Nationalism* (London: Sage Publications, 1995), pp. 8, 12.
47 Picard, *The World of Silence*, p. 37.

Coda

Drawing this study to its conclusion, it behoves us to pause and ask: What does the renewed interest in silence tell us about contemporary research into the field? How has recent scholarship, through its mutating ontological paradigms and its unfolding epistemologies, extracted, elaborated, and stumbled upon the politically rich features of silence? How are diverse theories, interpretations, and usages of silence reflected in academic and public discourses, recalibrating the standing of silence within knowledge communities? And, conversely, how does the detection of concealed silences illuminate our awareness of the expansive understanding of the political addressed in these pages? As we extend our view well beyond the conventional confines of politics as a self-contained field of enquiry and trace its filtering into literature, art, theology, and other domains, can we get a better handle on the manner in which it functions and malfunctions?

The partial and tentative answers that can be offered to these questions relate to some of the following. There is a collective appreciation that 'face-value' enquiry, and what used to be referred to as positivism, have to allow much more space to the existence and value of palimpsests and layers as central to the processes of writing, thinking, and speaking. In a culture where philosophers of ethics, and guardians of public standards, increasingly demand transparency and excoriate dissembling, scholarship is taking on the tasks of excavation and deciphering in order to remove the coatings and decrypt the codings that overshadow current reference points. Not that everything deserves to be brushed aside in the bright light of forensic logic. Quite the contrary: esotericism and enigma are situated at the heart of the human condition and need to be respected as indispensable modes of engaging with the world, not least in their artistic and religious manifestations. Often that engagement is accompanied by disillusionment with, or at least a focus away from, the spoken or written word as the apex of creativity and articulateness, and by an intensified embrace of feelings and performativity. That remains a difficult predicament for many political theorists, myself included, principally educated to analyse texts, utterances, and arguments. If it might seem odd that a study of silence requires the use of words, we must recall that words are separated by spaces-cum-silences in any intelligible language. Be that as it may, words remain the most subtle instrument at the disposal of scholarship.

Lifting up enigmatic veils should be seen as a service to knowledge, although potentially at a cost. Nothing ventured, nothing gained, even if something may be lost in the process. One consequence has been the secularization of mysticism as a process of human creativity. The unsaid and the alluded to are conundrums that hint at something else—transcendental, secretive, or forbidding, circling around the impenetrability of experience—or possibly emotional and intellectual ploys that human beings devise, appeal to, or enjoy. They all drive home the paradoxes of being, of which silence is a notable element. From a different angle that challenge may be approached as wrestling with indeterminacy—that rising staple of linguistics, post-structuralism, science, or ideology studies—as the 'new normal', essential to social knowledge, underpinning ordinary language, as well as macro-ontologies.

In a very 'non-mystical' way, students of the social sciences and the humanities have come to terms with parallel worlds, and with transiting between them, as they forage, test, and borrow insights and tools from across several explanatory systems and domains, each of which nonetheless asserts and protects its own rationale for autonomous recognition. These tentative forays are reinforced by the growing—but separate—trend to emphasize the connectivity, interdependence, and complexity of abutting spheres of study whose findings and frames of reference frequently overlap, even as diverse professional languages are marshalled to interpret them. Although different disciplines are keen to demarcate their distinct areas in method and in substance, they share far more than they are willing to concede across the humanities and the social sciences, and way beyond them as well. The indispensability of silence in every corner of organized knowledge and of ordinary language is a testimony to that reach. That ubiquity is matched with plasticity. Both boundary crossing and interdependence serve to acknowledge the many variants tucked into apparently similar social phenomena. That has particular significance for silence, in the past often conceived to be a deathlike absolute, but now—especially in its political guises—the subject of multifarious and prolific vistas and inspirations. Silence could have become crushingly static but has turned out to be excitingly dynamic, though not so much shape-shifter as ceaselessly re-experienced and reimagined.

We may now be able to appreciate the unbreakable and profound relationship of silence to the manifold dimensions of the political. Let us summon up again the six central political axes enumerated in Chapter 2. Silence-cum-stillness extends the *finality* attribute of the political: the ontological *fons et origo* of being and doing, vying with sound and movement as the default position of existence and conferring a conclusiveness on beginnings and endings. It can be interpreted as the antidote to existence, operating as a photographic negative that highlights and emphasizes the presence of features of social interaction whose absence is consequently striking and resounding. But it can also indicate the limits of human sovereignty and understanding—drawing an authoritative line under the knowable and reinforcing human fallibility. In so doing, silence signals the ultimate feature of the human condition—combining finality with counter-finality.

Silence (re)distributes social and ethical significance by *ranking* whatever it engenders, responds to, or opposes, through honouring individuals and events or by giving them the cold shoulder and marginalizing them. It can *mobilize or withhold support* for social practices by tacitly endorsing prevalent patterns of social thinking or tacitly rejecting them when support is sought. It can be a powerful and instant remover of evidence as well as dissent, a sinkhole into which knowledge and awareness are flushed, or a mirror without reflection: intervening through concealing and deflecting. It can isolate individuals and groups from, or link them to, their communities of choice or necessity. It can reduce the diversity of action and language to an indistinguishable state of nothingness: unifying and *integrating* through hiding plurality. It can iron out the bumps that obstruct and roughen up shared space or *dislocate* the continuity of political institutions and ideas, repressing or releasing bundles of creative, intellectual, and imaginative energy: fostering or unsettling social stability. It can eradicate, store up, or juggle with collective memory, rechannelling communal *visions of the future*, not least by filtering the present and by erasing or allowing the reinscribing of both private and public pasts. It can introduce dynamism through the idea of lack, and openness by challenging closure. It can concurrently play its own part in inserting itself directly into the substantive desirable or dreaded accounts of the passing or anticipation of time, controlling and managing their reception and impact, setting calming or contrapuntal rhythms. It can also fashion and interpret the prime tool of social life—language—not only by rationing it but through the prominence of silence as a crucial *constituent of language*, introducing tone, intensity, or coolant to human discourse, both collaborative and discordant. And it can indicate the limitations of language, skirting around or evading the unfathomable reaches of communication that engulf our interactions with the world.

Ultimately, the power of silence combines its role as the repository of potential and the extinguisher of capacity, not in dichotomous mode but as a series of scattered and disjointed occurrences and weightings. Its function in political life, as in other spheres, remains permanently ambiguous and indeterminate, as does the political thinking with which it intersects and that it sporadically obscures. Silence's frequent double-bind of concealing itself might be its greatest political master-stroke.

Bibliography

Abû Zayd, N., *Rethinking the Qur'an: Towards a Humanistic Hermeneutics* (Amsterdam: Humanistics University Press, 2004).
Achino-Loeb, M.-L., *Silence: The Currency of Power* (New York and Oxford: Berghahn, 2006).
Achterberg, W., 'Sustainability, Community and Democracy', in B. Doherty and M. de Geus (eds.), *Democracy and Green Political Thought: Sustainability, Rights and Citizenship* (London: Routledge, 1996), pp. 170–187.
Aminzade, R. and D. McAdam, 'Emotions and Contentious Politics', in R. R. Aminzade, J. A. Goldstone, D. McAdam, E. J. Perry, W. H. Sewell, S. Tarrow, and C. Tilley, *Silence and Voice in the Study of Contentious Politics* (Cambridge: Cambridge University Press, 2001), pp. 14–50.
Amir-Moezzi, M. A., *The Silent Qur'an and the Speaking Qur'an* (New York: Columbia University Press, 2016).
Anderson, P., *Imagined Communities* (London: Verso, 1983).
Aristotle, *Metaphysics*.
Arkoun, M., *The Unthought in Contemporary Islamic Thought* (London: Saqi, 2002).
Attali, J., *Noise: The Political Economy of Music* (Minneapolis, MN, and London: University of Minnesota Press, 1985).
Atwood, M., *The Blind Assassin* (London: Bloomsbury, 2000).
Azaria, D., '"Codification by Interpretation:" The International Law Commission as an Interpreter of International Law', *European Journal of International Law* 31/1 (2020), pp. 171–200.
Bachrach, P. and M. S. Baratz, 'Two Faces of Power', *American Political Science Review* 56 (1962), pp. 947–952.
Baker, S. J., 'The Theory of Silences', *Journal of General Psychology* 53 (1955), pp. 145–167.
Barthes, R., *The Neutral* (New York: Columbia University Press, 2005).
Basevic, J., 'There's No Such Thing as Just "Following the Science"—Coronavirus Advice is Political', *The Guardian,* 28 April 2020.
Basso, K. H., '"To Give up on Words": Silence in Western Apache Culture', *Southwestern Journal of Anthropology* 26/3 (1970), pp. 213–230.
Beasley-Murray, T., 'Reticence and the Fuzziness of Thresholds: A Bakhtinian Apology for Quietism', *Common Knowledge* 19 (2013), pp. 424–445.
Beckett, S., *Waiting for Godot* (London: Faber & Faber, 1956).
Beckett, S., *Proust, and Three Dialogues with Georges Duthuit* (London: John Calder, 1965).
Beckett, S., *The Unnamable* (London: Faber & Faber, 2010).
Bell, D., *The End of Ideology: On the Exhaustion of Political Ideas in the Fifties* (London: Collier-Macmillan, 1961).
Bentham, J., *A Manual of Political Economy*, http://oll.libertyfund.org/titles/bentham-the-works-of-jeremy-bentham-vol-3.
Biguenet, J., *Silence* (New York and London: Bloomsbury Academic, 2015).
Billias, N. and S. Vemuri, *The Ethics of Silence* (Cham, Switzerland: Palgrave Macmillan/Springer, 2017).
Billig, M., *Banal Nationalism* (London: Sage Publications, 1995).

Bibliography

Billig, M., *Freudian Repression: Conversation Creating the Unconscious* (Cambridge: Cambridge University Press, 2004).
Bion, W. R., *Second Thoughts: Selected Papers on Psycho-Analysis* (London: Maresfield Reprints, 1984).
Bion, W., *The Complete Works of W. R. Bion*, ed. Chris Mawson (London: Routledge, 2014), vol. VII, Brazilian Lectures.
Blommaert, J., 'The Debate is Open', in J. Blommaert (ed.), *Language Ideological Debates* (Berlin and New York: Mouton de Gruyter, 1999), pp. 1–38.
Blommaert, J., *Discourse: A Critical Introduction* (Cambridge: Cambridge University Press, 2005).
Book of Common Prayer.
Bourdieu, P., *Outline of a Theory of Practice* (Cambridge: Cambridge University Press, 1977).
Bourdieu, P., *In Other Words: Essays Towards Reflexive Sociology* (Stanford, CA: Stanford University Press, 1990).
Bourdieu, P., *The Logic of Practice* (Cambridge: Polity Press, 1990).
Bourdieu, P., *Language and Symbolic Power* (Cambridge: Polity Press, 1991).
Braine, D., 'Negative Theology', in *The Routledge Encyclopedia of Philosophy*, https://www.rep.routledge.com/articles/thematic/negative-theology/v-1.
Brito Vieira, M., 'Representing Silence in Politics', *American Political Science Review* 114 (2020), pp. 976–988.
Brito Vieira, M., 'Silence in Political Theory and Practice', *Critical Review of International Social and Political Philosophy* 24/3 (2021), pp. 289–295.
Brox, J., *Silence: A Social History of One of the Least Understood Elements of Our Lives* (Boston, MA, and New York: Houghton Mifflin Harcourt, 2019).
Brubaker, R., M. Loveman, and P. Stamatov, 'Ethnicity as Cognition', *Theory and Society* 33/1 (2004), pp. 31–64.
Bruneau, T. J., 'Communicative Silences: Forms and Functions', *Journal of Communication* 23 (1973), pp. 17–46.
Budick, S. and W. Iser, *Languages of the Unsayable: The Play of Negativity in Literature and Literary Theory* (Stanford, CA: Stanford University Press, 1987).
Burke, E., *Reflections on the Revolution in France* (Harmondsworth: Penguin, 1968).
Burke, E., 'Privation', in *A Philosophical Enquiry into the Origin of our Ideas of the Sublime and Beautiful* (Cambridge: Cambridge University Press, 2014). doi:10.1017/CBO9781107360495.028.
Buswell, R. E. Jr. and D. S. Lopez Jr., *The Princeton Dictionary of Buddhism* (Princeton, NJ: Princeton University Press, 2014).
Byrd, R. E., *Alone* (Washington, DC, Covelo, CA, and London: Island Press/Shearwater Books, 1938).
Cage, J., *A Silence* (Middletown, CT: Wesleyan University Press, 1961).
Carbaugh, D., M. Berry, and M. Nurmikari-Berry, 'Coding Personhood through Cultural Terms and Practices: Silence and Quietude as a Finnish "Natural Way of Being"', *Journal of Language and Social Psychology* 25 (2006), pp. 1–18.
Carlyle, T., *Past and Present*, Collected Works, https://www.gutenberg.org/ebooks/26159.
Chafe, W., 'Some Reasons for Hesitating', in D. Tannen and M. Saville-Troike (eds.), *Perspectives on Silence* (Norwood, NJ: Ablex, 1985), pp. 77–89.
Chasseguet-Smirgel, J., 'Foreword', in I. Kogan, *The Cry of Mute Children* (London: Free Association, 1995), pp. xii–xiv.
Christoff, P., 'Ecological Citizens and Ecologically Guided Democracy', in B. Doherty and M. de Geus (eds.), *Democracy and Green Political Thought: Sustainability, Rights and Citizenship* (London: Routledge, 1996), pp. 159–169.

Cobb, J., 'The Death of Floyd George in Context', *New Yorker*, 27 May 2020.
Conan Doyle, A., 'The Adventure of Silver Blaze', in *The Memoirs of Sherlock Holmes* (London: George Newnes, 1894).
Cook, A. and G. Kirk, *Greenham Women Everywhere: Dreams, Ideas and Actions from the Women's Peace Movement* (London: Pluto Press, 1983).
Corbin, A., *A History of Silence* (Cambridge: Polity Press, 2018).
Coupland, N. and J. Coupland, 'Discourses of the Unsayable: Death-Implicative Talk in Geriatric Medical Consultations', in A. Jaworski (ed.), *Silence: Interdisciplinary Perspectives* (Berlin and New York: Mouton de Gruyter, 1997), pp. 117–152.
Crawford, M., *The World beyond Your Head* (London: Penguin, 2016).
Dahl, R. A., 'The Concept of Power', *Behavioral Science* 2 (1957), pp. 201–215.
Dahrendorf, R., 'Out of Utopia: Toward a Reorientation of Sociological Analysis', *American Journal of Sociology* 64/2 (1958), pp. 115–127.
Danze, E. A., 'An Architect's View of Introspective Space: The Analytic Vessel', *Annual of Psychoanalysis* 33 (2005), pp. 109–124.
Dauenhauer, B. P., *Silence: The Phenomenon and its Ontological Significance* (Bloomington, IN: Indiana University Press, 1980).
Day, L., 'The Greenham Common Contest: A Participant Observer's Account', *Rain*, no. 62 (1984), pp. 3–4.
de Saussure, F., *Course in General Linguistics* (London: Duckworth, 1983).
Dean, T., 'Cumulus Head' and 'Artist's Book', in A. Harris, A. Hollinghurst, and A. Smith (eds.), *Tacita Dean* (London: Royal Academy of Arts, National Portrait Gallery, The National Gallery, 2018), pp. 8–9, 86–106.
Dean, T., 'Merce Cunningham performs STILLNESS', 6 x 16 mm colour films (2008). Exhibited at the National Portrait Gallery, London, 2018.
Deleuze, G., *Negotiations 1972–1990*, trans. M. Joughin (New York: Columbia University Press, 1995).
Derrida, J., *Writing and Difference* (Chicago, IL: University of Chicago Press, 1978).
Derrida, J, *Margins of Philosophy*, trans. Alan Bass (Brighton: Harvester Press, 1982).
Derrida, J., 'How to Avoid Speaking: Denials', in H. Coward and T. Foshay (eds.), *Derrida and Negative Theology* (Albany, NY: SUNY Press, 1992), pp. 73–136.
Dingli, S. and T. N. Cooke, *Political Silence: Meanings, Functions, and Ambiguity* (London and New York: Routledge, 2019).
Donnelly, F., 'Silence is Golden: Commemorating the Past in Two Minutes', in S. Dingli and T. N. Cooke (eds.), *Political Silence: Meanings, Functions, and Ambiguity* (London and New York: Routledge, 2019), pp. 78–95.
Douglass, R., 'Tuck, Rousseau and the Sovereignty of the People', *History of European Ideas* 42/8 (2016), pp. 1111–1114.
Dunn, J., *The Political Thought of John Locke* (Cambridge: Cambridge University Press, 1969).
Durkheim, É, *Suicide: A Study in Sociology* (London: Routledge & Kegan Paul, 1952).
Durkheim, É., *The Division of Labor in Society* (New York: The Free Press, 1964).
Edsall, T. B., 'Conservatives Are from Mars, Liberals Are from Venus', *The Atlantic*, 7 February 2012.
Eliot, T. S., *Four Quartets*, 'Burnt Norton' (London: Faber & Faber, 2001).
Ellison, R., *Invisible Man* (New York: Random House, 1995).
Ephratt, M., 'The Functions of Silence', *Journal of Pragmatics* 40 (2008), pp. 1909–1938.
Erdos, D., 'The "Right to be Forgotten" beyond the EU: An Analysis of Wider G20 Regulatory Action and Potential Next Steps', *Journal of Media Law* 13/1 (2021), pp. 1–35.
Esslin, M., *The Theatre of the Absurd* (New York: Doubleday & Co., 1961).
Faimberg, H., *The Telescoping of Generations* (London and New York: Routledge, 2005).

Fawcett, E., *Conservatism: The Fight for a Tradition* (Princeton, NJ, and Oxford: Princeton University Press, 2020).
Fellmeth, A. X. and M. Horwitz, *Guide to Latin in International* Law (Oxford: Oxford University Press, 2009).
Ferenczi, S., 'Silence is Golden', in *Further Contributions to the Theory and Technique of Psychoanalysis* (London: Hogarth Press, 1926), pp. 250–251.
Ferguson, K., 'Silence: A Politics', *Contemporary Political Theory* 2 (2003), pp. 49–65.
Fernando, M. L., 'Ethnography and the Politics of Silence', *Cultural Dynamics* 26 (2014), pp. 235–244.
Fink, B., *The Lacanian Subject* (Princeton, NJ: Princeton University Press, 1995).
Fink, B., *Lacan to the Letter* (Minneapolis, MN: University of Minnesota Press, 2004).
Fitch, W. T., 'Animal Cognition and the Evolution of Human Language: Why We Cannot Focus Solely on Communication', *Philosophical Transactions of the Royal Society B*, 2019. https://royalsocietypublishing.org/doi/10.1098/rstb.2019.0046.
Fivush, R., 'Speaking Silence: The Social Construction of Silence in Autobiographical and Cultural Narratives', *Memory* 18/2 (2010), pp. 88–98.
Foley, M., *The Silence of Constitutions: Gaps, 'Abeyances' and Political Temperament in the Maintenance of Government* (London: Routledge, 1989).
Foucault, M., *The Archaeology of Knowledge and the Discourse on Language* (New York: Pantheon, 1972).
Foucault, M., *A History of Sexuality*, vol. 1 (New York: Pantheon, 1978).
Freeden, M., *Rights* (Milton Keynes: Open University Press, 1991).
Freeden, M., *Ideologies and Political Theory: A Conceptual Approach* (Oxford: Clarendon Press, 1996).
Freeden, M., 'Is Nationalism a Distinct Ideology?', *Political Studies* 46 (1998), pp. 748–765.
Freeden, M., 'Twentieth-Century Liberal Thought: Development or Transformation', in *Liberal Languages: Ideological Imaginations and Twentieth-Century Progressive Thought* (Princeton, NJ: Princeton University Press, 2005), pp. 19–37.
Freeden, M., 'Editorial: The Politics of Ceremony: The Wootton Bassett Phenomenon', *Journal of Political Ideologies* 16 (2011), pp. 1–10.
Freeden, M., 'The Professional Responsibilities of the Political Theorist', in B. Jackson and M. Stears (eds.), *Liberalism as Ideology: Essays in Honour of Michael Freeden* (Oxford: Oxford University Press, 2012), pp. 259–277.
Freeden, M., 'The Morphological Analysis of Ideology', in M. Freeden, L. T. Sargent, and M. Stears (eds.), *The Oxford Handbook of Political Ideologies* (Oxford: Oxford University Press, 2013), pp. 115–137.
Freeden, M., *The Political Theory of Political Thinking: The Anatomy of a Practice* (Oxford: Oxford University Press, 2013).
Freeden, M., *Liberalism: A Very Short Introduction* (Oxford: Oxford University Press, 2015).
Freeden, M., 'Editorial: After the Brexit Referendum: Revisiting Populism as an Ideology', *Journal of Political Ideologies* 22 (2017), pp. 1–11.
Freeden, M., 'The "Beginning of Ideology" Thesis', in *Ideology Studies: New Advances and Interpretations* (Abingdon and New York: Routledge, 2022), pp. 99–105.
Freeden, M., *Ideology Studies: New Advances and Interpretations* (Abingdon and New York: Routledge, 2022).
Fukuyama, F., 'The End of History?', *National Interest*, no. 16 (summer 1989), pp. 3–18.
Gandolfo, S., 'The Positionless Middle Way: Weak Philosophical Deflationism in Madhyamaka', *Journal of Indian Philosophy* 44 (2016), pp. 207–228.
Gere, C., *Knossos and the Prophets of Modernism* (Chicago, IL: University of Chicago Press, 2009).

Gertrude Bell Archive, Newcastle University, Letters.
Gilligan, C., *In a Different Voice* (Cambridge, MA: Harvard University Press, 1993).
Glenn, C., *Unspoken: A Rhetoric of Silence* (Carbondale, IL: Southern Illinois University Press, 2004).
Goffman, E., *Interaction Ritual* (New York: Pantheon, 1967).
Goodin, R. E. and A. Reeve, *Liberal Neutrality* (London and New York: Routledge, 1989).
Gordon, U., 'Anarchism Reloaded', *Journal of Political Ideologies* 12 (2007), pp. 29–48.
Gray, C., *A Cautious Silence: The Politics of Australian Anthropology* (Canberra: Aboriginal Studies Press, 2007).
Gray, S. W. D., 'Mapping Silent Citizenship: How Democratic Theory Hears Citizens' Silence and Why It Matters', *Citizenship Studies* 19/5 (2015), pp. 474–491.
Guillaume, X., 'How to Do Things with Silence: Rethinking the Centrality of Speech to the Securitization Framework', *Security Dialogue* 49/6 (2018), pp. 476–92.
Gurevitch, S. D., 'Distance and Conversation', *Symbolic Interaction* 12 (1989), pp. 251–263.
Halbrock, C., 'Nicht-Handeln und Nicht-Mitmachen: Nicht erfüllte Erwartungen und politisch abweichendes Verhalten in der DDR', in T. Jung (ed.), *Zwischen Handeln und Nichthandeln* (Frankfurt: Campus Verlag, 2019), pp. 101–126.
Hartley, L. P., *The Go-Between* (London: Penguin, 1997).
Hassan, I., 'The Literature of Silence', *Encounter* (January 1967), pp. 74–80.
Hawkins, P. R., 'The Syntactic Location of Hesitation Pauses', *Language and Speech* 14 (1971), pp. 277–288.
Hayek, F. A., *New Studies in Philosophy, Politics, Economics and the History of Ideas* (London: Routledge & Kegan Paul, 1978).
Hayes, P., 'Hobbes's Silent Fool: A Response to Hoekstra', *Political Theory* 27 (1999), pp. 225–229.
Heidegger, M., *On the Way to Language*, trans. P. D. Hertz (New York: Harper & Row, 1971).
Hindman, M., *The Myth of Digital Democracy* (Princeton, NJ, and Oxford: Princeton University Press, 2009).
Hirschman, A. O., *Exit, Voice, and Loyalty: Responses to Decline in Firms, Organizations, and States* (Cambridge, MA: Harvard University Press, 1970).
Ho, Chien-hsing, 'Saying the Unsayable', *Philosophy East and West* 56 (2006), pp. 409–427.
Ho, Chien-hsing, 'The Nonduality of Speech and Silence: A Comparative Analysis of Jizang's Thought on Language and Beyond', *Dao* 11 (2012), pp. 1–19.
Hobbes, T., *Leviathan* (Harmondsworth: Penguin, 1961).
Hofstede, G., 'Cultural Differences in Teaching and Learning', *International Journal of Intercultural Relations* 10 (1986), pp. 301–320.
Hogan, C., 'The Sounds of Spacetime', *American Scientist* 94/6 (2006).
Holbraad, M., B. Kapferer, and J. F. Sauma (eds.), *Ruptures: Anthropologies of Discontinuity in Times of Turmoil* (London: UCL Press, 2019).
Holiday, A., 'Wittgenstein's Silence: Philosophy, Ritual and the Limits of Language', *Language and Communication* 5/2 (1985), pp. 133–142.
Holub, R., 'This Silence Which Is Not One: Towards a Microphysics of Rhetoric', *Differentia: Review of Italian Thought* 2 (1988), art. 21, pp. 251–59.
Hom, A. R., 'Silent Order: The Temporal Turn in Critical International Relations', *Millennium* 46 (2018), pp. 303–330.
Huspek, M. and K. E. Kendall, 'On Withholding Political Voice: An Analysis of the Political Vocabulary of a "Nonpolitical" Speech Community', *Quarterly Journal of Speech* 77/1 (1991), pp. 1–19.
Imam Muslim, *The Book of Marriage (Kitab Al-Nikah) of Sahih Muslim*.

Iser, W., 'The Play of the Text', in S. Budick and W. Iser, *Languages of the Unsayable: The Play of Negativity in Literature and Literary Theory* (Stanford, CA: Stanford University Press, 1987), pp. 325–339.

Ishiguro, K., interview, *Imagine*, BBC 1 TV, 29 March 2021.

Iuliano, J., 'The Supreme Court's Noble Lie', *UC Davis Law Review* 51 (2018), pp. 911–977.

Jaggar, A. M., *Feminist Politics and Human Nature* (Totowa, NJ: Rowman & Littlefield, 1983).

Jamet, D., 'Euphemisms for Death: Reinventing Reality through Words?', in S. Sorlin (ed.), *Inventive Linguistics* (Montpellier: Presses Universitaires du Languedoc et de la Méditerranée, 2010), pp. 173–188.

Jaworski, A. (ed.), *Silence: Interdisciplinary Perspectives* (Berlin and New York: Mouton de Gruyter, 1997).

Jensen, J. V., 'Communicative Functions of Silence', *ETC: A Review of General Semantics* 30 (1973), pp. 249–257.

Johannesen, R. L., 'The Functions of Silence: A Plea for Communication Research', *Western Journal of Communication* 38 (1974), pp. 25–35.

Joseph, Branden W., 'John Cage and the Architecture of Silence', *October* 81 (1997), pp. 80–104.

Jung, T. (ed.), *Zwischen Handeln und Nichthandeln* (Frankfurt: Campus Verlag, 2019).

Jung, T., 'Mind the Gaps: Silences, Political Communication, and the Role of Expectations', *Critical Review of International Social and Political Philosophy* 24/3 (2021), pp. 296–315.

Kagge, E., *Silence in the Age of Noise* (London: Viking, 2017).

Kahn, E., 'Functions of Silence in Life and Literature', *Contemporary Review* 194 (1958), pp. 204–206.

Kane, L., *The Language of Silence: On the Unspoken and the Unspeakable in Modern Drama* (London and Toronto: Associated University Presses, 1984).

Kant, I., 'On the Common Saying: "This May be True in Theory, but It Does Not Apply in Practice"', in *Kant: Political Writings*, ed. H. Reiss (Cambridge: Cambridge University Press, 1991), pp. 61–92.

Katy, J. H., 'Contract Law and the Social Contract: What Legal History Can Teach Us about the Political Theory of Hobbes and Locke', *Ottawa Law Review* 31/1 (1999), pp. 73–91.

Kawabata, M. and D. Gastaldo, 'The Less Said, the Better: Interpreting Silence in Qualitative Research', *International Journal of Qualitative Methods* 14/4 (2015), pp. 1–9.

Keane, J., 'Silence and Catastrophe: New Reasons Why Politics Matters in the Early Years of the Twenty-First Century', *Political Quarterly* 83 (2012), pp. 660–668.

Keller, R., 'Michel Foucault: Discourse, Power/Knowledge and the Modern Subject', in R. Wodak and B. Forchtner (eds.), *The Routledge Handbook of Language and Politics* (Abingdon: Routledge, 2018), pp. 67–81.

Kidron, C., 'Toward an Ethnography of Silence: The Lived Presence of the Past in the Everyday Life of Holocaust Trauma Survivors and Their Descendants in Israel', *Current Anthropology* 50 (2009), pp. 5–27.

Klein, M., 'On the Development of Mental Functioning (1958)', in M. Klein, *Envy and Gratitude and Other Works 1946–1963* (London: Hogarth Press, 1984), pp. 236–246.

Kølvraa, C., 'The Discourse Theory of Ernesto Laclau', in R. Wodak and B. Forchtner (eds.), *The Routledge Handbook of Language and Politics* (Abingdon: Routledge, 2018), pp. 96–108.

Kurzon, D., *Discourse of Silence* (Amsterdam/Philadelphia, PA: John Benjamins, 1998).

Kurzon, D., 'Towards a Typology of Silence', *Journal of Pragmatics* 39 (2007), pp. 1673–1688.

Laclau, E., 'The Death and Resurrection of the Theory of Ideology', *Journal of Political Ideologies* 1 (1996), 201–220.

Laclau, E. and C. Mouffe, *Hegemony and Socialist Strategy* (London: Verso, 1985).

Langton, R., 'Speech Acts and Unspeakable Acts', *Philosophy and Public Affairs* 22 (1993), pp. 293–330.

Laozi, *Daodejing: 'Making this Life Significant,' A Philosophical Translation*, trans. Roger Ames and David Hall (New York: Ballantine, 2002).
Laplanche, J. and J.-B. Pontalis, 'Repression', in *The Language of Psycho-Analysis* (London: Hogarth Press, 1985), pp. 390–394.
Laurence, P. O., *The Reading of Silence: Virginia Woolf in the English Tradition* (Stanford, CA: Stanford University Press, 1991).
Lehtonen, J. and K. Sajavaara, 'The Silent Finn', in D. Tannen and M. Saville-Troike (eds.), *Perspectives on Silence* (Norwood, NJ: Ablex, 1985), pp. 189–201.
Leopold, D., 'On Marxian Utopophobia', *Journal of the History of Philosophy* 54 (2016), pp. 111–134.
Linehan, J. and P. Lawrence, *Giving Future Generations a Voice: Normative Frameworks, Institutions and Practice* (Cheltenham: Edward Elgar, 2021).
Little, A., *Temporal Politics: Contested Pasts, Uncertain Futures* (Edinburgh: Edinburgh University Press, 2022).
Locke, J., *Two Treatises of Government, Second Treatise* (New York: Mentor, 1965).
Locke, J., *Essay Concerning Human Understanding* (Oxford: Oxford University Press, 1979).
Loughlin, M., 'The Silences of Constitutions', *International Journal of Constitutional Law* 16 (2018), pp. 922–935.
Lyman, P., 'The Domestication of Anger: The Use and Abuse of Anger in Politics', *European Journal of Social Theory* 7/2 (2004), pp. 133–147.
Lyotard, J.-F., *The Differend* (Minneapolis, MN: University of Minnesota Press, 1988).
MacCulloch, D., *Silence: A Christian History* (London: Penguin, 2014).
Maistre, J. de, *Considerations on France*, ed. R. A. Lebrun (Cambridge: Cambridge University Press, 1994).
Maitland, S., *A Book of Silence* (London: Granta, 2009).
'Manifesto of The Dutch Party for Animals (Partij voor de Dieren, PvdD)' ('Verkiezingsprogramma Partij voor de Dieren'), in Joop van Holsteyn et al. (eds.), *Verkiezingsprogramma's 2002 & 2003* (Amsterdam: Rozenberg, 2003).
Marais, M., '"A Step Towards Silence": Samuel Beckett's *The Unnamable* and the Problem of Following the Stranger', *Journal of Literary Studies* 32/4 (2016), pp. 89–106.
Marx, K., 'Theses on Feuerbach', in *Early Writings*, ed. Quintin Hoare (Harmondsworth: Penguin, 1975), pp. 421–423.
Matt, D. C., 'Ayin: The Concept of Nothingness in Jewish Mysticism', in Robert K. C. Forman (ed.), *The Problem of Pure Consciousness: Mysticism and Philosophy* (New York and Oxford: Oxford University Press, 1990), pp. 121–159.
Mauriac, C., *The New Literature* (New York: G. Braziller, 1959).
Mazour-Matusevich, Y., 'Historical Roots of Russian Silence', *CrossCurrents* 64 (2014), pp. 295–311.
McGilchrist, I., *The Master and his Emissary: The Divided Brain and the Making of the Western World* (New Haven, CT: Yale University Press, 2009).
McNay, L., *Gender and Agency* (Cambridge: Polity Press, 2000).
McNay, L., 'Suffering, Silence and Social Weightlessness: Honneth and Bourdieu on Embodiment and Power', in S. Gonzalez-Arnal, G. Jagger, and K. Leon (eds.), *Embodied Selves* (London: Palgrave Macmillan, 2012), pp. 230–248.
Merleau-Ponty, M., 'Indirect Voices and the Language of Silence', in G. A. Johnson (ed.), *The Merleau-Ponty Aesthetics Reader: Philosophy and Painting* (Evanston, IL: Northwestern University Press, 1993), pp. 76–120.
Merleau-Ponty, M., *Phenomenology of Perception* (London and New York: Routledge, 2002).
Merton, R. K., *Social Theory and Social Structures* (Glencoe, IL: The Free Press, 1957).
Merton, T., *The Silent Life* (Dublin: Clonmore & Reynolds, 1957).

Merton, T., *Thoughts in Solitude* (New York: Farrar, Straus & Cudahy, 1958).
The Middle Length Discourse of the Buddha: A Translation of the Majjhima Nikāya, trans. Bhikkhu Nanamoli and Bhikkhu Bodi (Oxford: Pali Text Society, 2001).
Milgram, S., 'Behavioral Study of Obedience', *Journal of Abnormal and Social Psychology* 67 (1963), pp. 371–378.
Mill, J. S., *Principles of Political Economy* (London: D. Appleton & Co., 1885).
Montiglio, S., *Silence in the Land of Logos* (Princeton, NJ: Princeton University Press, 2010).
Moraitis, G., 'Prologue', *Pychoanalytic Inquiry* 15/3 (1995), pp. 275–279.
Mori, H., 'An Analysis of Switching Pause Duration as a Paralinguistic Feature in Expressive Dialogues', *Acoustical Science and Technology* 30/5 (2009), pp. 376–378.
Morton, P., *Fire across the Desert: Woomera and the Anglo-Australian Joint Project 1946–1980* (Canberra: Australian Government Publishing Service, 1989).
Mouffe, C., *On the Political* (London: Routledge, 2005).
Müller, J.-W., *What is Populism?* (Philadelphia, PA: University of Pennsylvania Press, 2016).
Murray, A. J. and K. Durrheim, *Qualitative Studies of Silence: The Unsaid as Social Action* (Cambridge: Cambridge University Press, 2019).
Nagar-Ron, S. and P. Motzafi-Haller, '"My Life? There Is Not Much to Tell": On Voice, Silence and Agency in Interviews with First-Generation Mizrahi Jewish Women Immigrants to Israel', *Qualitative Inquiry* 17/7 (2011), pp. 653–663.
Nancy, J.-L., *Listening* (New York: Fordham University Press, 2007).
Neuwirth, K., E. Frederick, and C. Mayo, 'The Spiral of Silence and Fear of Isolation', *Journal of Communication* 57 (2007), pp. 450–468.
Nietzsche, F., *Thus Spake Zarathustra* (New York: Boni & Liveright, 1917).
Nixon, R., *President Nixon's Address to the Nation on the War in Vietnam*, 3 November 1969, http://watergate.info/1969/11/03/nixons-silent-majority-speech.html.
Noble, A., 'Apophatic Elements in Derrida's Deconstruction', in P. Pokorný and J. Roskovec (eds.), *Philosophical Hermeneutics and Biblical Exegesis* (Tübingen: Mohr Siebeck, 2002), pp. 83–93.
Noelle-Neumann, E., 'Turbulences in the Climate of Opinion: Methodological Applications of the Spiral of Silence Theory', *Public Opinion Quarterly* 41/2 (1977), pp. 143–158.
Norris-Green, J., 'The Anthropology of Silence: Quaker Silence' (2018) http://anthropologyofsilence.com/2018/11/16/quaker-silence/.
Norum, R., 'Trading Silence for a Voice: Ethnography of Lack for the Contemporary Classroom', *Teaching Anthropology* 9 (2020), pp. 93–97.
Nwoye, G. O., 'Eloquent Silence among the Igbo of Nigeria', in D. Tannen and M. Saville-Troike (eds.), *Perspectives on Silence* (Norwood, NJ: Ablex, 1985), pp. 185–191.
Panagia, D. and J. Rancière, 'Dissenting Words: A Conversation with Jacques Ranciere', *Diacritics* 30/2 (2000), pp. 113–126.
Pateman, C., *The Disorder of Women* (Cambridge: Polity Press, 1989).
Pateman, T., *Language, Truth and Politics: Towards a Radical Theory for Communication* (Lewes, East Sussex: Stroud, 1975).
Patton, P., *Deleuzian Concepts: Philosophy, Colonization, Politics* (Stanford, CA: Stanford University Press, 2010).
Pérez, J., 'Functions of the Rhetoric of Silence in Contemporary Spanish Literature', *South Central Review* 1/1–2 (1984), pp. 108–130.
Persak, C., 'Rhetoric in Praise of Silence: The Ideology of Carlyle's Paradox', *Rhetoric Society Quarterly* 21 (1991), pp. 38–52.
Phelan, S., 'What's in a Name? Political Antagonism and Critiquing "Neoliberalism"', *Journal of Political Ideologies* 27 (2022), pp. 148–167.
Picard, M., *The World of Silence* (Chicago, IL: Henry Regnery, 1964 [1948]).

Pieters, J., *Speaking with the Dead: Explorations in Literature and History* (Edinburgh: Edinburgh University Press, 2005).
Pinter, H., 'Writing for the Theatre', in *Various Voices: Prose, Poetry, Politics 1948-2005* (London: Faber & Faber, 2005), pp. 20-26.
Plato, *The Sophist*.
Polanyi, M., *The Tacit Dimension* (New York: Doubleday & Co., 1966).
Polsby, N. W., *Community Power and Political Theory* (New Haven, CT: Yale University Press, 1963).
Pope, A., 'Ode on Solitude' (1700), poetryfoundation.org/poems/46561/ode-on-solitude.
Rai, S. M., M. Gluhovic, S. Jestrovic, and M. Saward (eds.), *The Oxford Handbook of Politics and Performance* (Oxford: Oxford University Press, 2021).
Rawls, J., *Political Liberalism* (New York: Columbia University Press, 1996).
Rawnsley, A., 'A No-Deal Brexit may be Unthinkable but that Doesn't Mean it Can't Happen', *The Observer*, 26 August 2018.
Renan, E., "What is a Nation?", text of a conference delivered at the Sorbonne, 11 March 1882, in *Qu'est-ce qu'une nation?* (Paris: Presses-Pocket, 1992).
Ricoeur, P., *Interpretation Theory: Discourse and the Surplus of Meaning* (Fort Worth, TX: Texas Christian University Press, 1976).
Ricoeur, P., *Lectures on Ideology and Utopia* (New York: Columbia University Press, 1986).
Ritter, M., 'Silence as the Voice of Trauma', *American Journal of Psychoanalysis* 74 (2014), pp. 176-194.
Robinson, A., 'The Political Theory of Constitutive Lack: A Critique', *Theory and Event* 8/1 (2005).
Robinson, C. J. Bradbury, 'A Way with Words: Paradox, Silence, and Samuel Beckett', *Cambridge Quarterly* 5/3 (1971), pp. 249-264.
Rogers, R. A., 'From Cultural Exchange to Transculturation: A Review and Reconceptualization of Cultural Appropriation', *Communication Theory* 16 (2006), pp. 474-503.
Rollo, T., 'Everyday Deeds: Enactive Protest, Exit, and Silence in Deliberative Systems', *Political Theory* 45 (2017), pp. 587-609.
Rollo, T., 'Democratic Silence: Two Forms of Domination in the Social Contract Tradition', *Critical Review of International Social and Political Philosophy* 24 (2021), pp. 316-329.
Rousseau, J. J., *The Social Contract* (Harmondsworth: Penguin, 1968).
Ruggles, D. Fairfield, 'The Stratigraphy of Forgetting: The Great Mosque of Cordoba and its Contested Legacy', in H. Silverman (ed.), *Contested Cultural Heritage* (Urbana, IL: Springer, 2010), pp. 51-68.
Sajavaara, K. and J. Lehtonen, 'The Silent Finn Revisited', in A. Jaworski (ed.), *Silence: Interdisciplinary Perspectives* (Berlin and New York: Mouton de Gruyter, 1997), pp. 263-283.
Sanders, S., 'Trump Champions the "Silent Majority," But What Does That Mean in 2016?', NPR.org, 22 January 2016.
Sassoon, D., *One Hundred Years of Socialism* (London: HarperCollins, 1997).
Saunders, G. R., 'Silence and Noise as Emotion Management Styles: An Italian Case', in D. Tannen and M. Saville-Troike (eds.), *Perspectives on Silence* (Norwood, NJ: Ablex, 1985), pp. 165-183.
Schröter, M., *Silence and Concealment in Political Discourse* (Amsterdam: John Benjamins, 2013).
Schröter, M., 'The Language Ideology of Silence and Silencing in Public Discourse: Claims to Silencing as Metadiscursive Moves in German Anti-political Correctness Discourse', in A. J. Murray and K. Durrheim (eds.), *Qualitative Studies of Silence: The Unsaid as Social Action* (Cambridge: Cambridge University Press, 2019), pp. 165-185.

Schröter, M., and C. Taylor (eds.), *Exploring Silence and Absence in Discourse: Empirical Approaches* (Cham, Switzerland: Palgrave Macmillan, 2018).

Scollon, R., 'The Machine Stops: Silence in the Metaphor of Malfunction', in D. Tannen and M. Saville-Troike (eds.), *Perspectives on Silence* (Norwood, NJ: Ablex, 1985), pp. 21–30.

Sedley, S., 'The Sound of Silence: Constitutional Law without a Constitution', *Law Quarterly Review* 110 (1994), pp. 270–291.

Sells, M. A., *Mystical Languages of Unsaying* (Chicago, IL: University of Chicago Press, 1994).

Shakespeare, W., *Julius Caesar*.

Sider, G., 'Between Silences and Culture: A Partisan Anthropology', in M.-L. Achino-Loeb (ed.), *Silence: The Currency of Power* (New York and Oxford: Berghahn, 2006), pp. 141–157.

Sifianou, M., 'Silence and Politeness', in A. Jaworski (ed.), *Silence: Interdisciplinary Perspectives* (Berlin and New York: Mouton de Gruyter, 1997), pp. 63–84.

Silverman, H. (ed.), *Contested Cultural Heritage* (Urbana, IL: Springer, 2010).

Silverstein, J., 'The Global Impact of George Floyd: How Black Lives Matter Protests Shaped Movements around the World', *CBS News*, 4 June 2021.

Simmons, A. J., *On the Edge of Anarchy: Locke, Consent, and the Limits of Society* (Princeton, NJ: Princeton University Press, 1993).

Simon, P., 'The Sound of Silence', https://www.paulsimon.com/track/the-sound-of-silence/.

Skinner, Q., *Forensic Shakespeare* (Oxford: Oxford University Press, 2014).

Smith, A., *An Inquiry into the Nature and Causes of the Wealth of Nations* (Oxford: Oxford University Press, 1979).

Smith, J. D., M. Wilson, and D. Reisberg, 'The Role of Subvocalization in Auditory Imagery', *Neuropsychologia* 33 (1995), pp. 1433–1454.

Sobkowiak, W., 'Silence and Markedness Theory', in A. Jaworski (ed.), *Silence: Interdisciplinary Perspectives* (Berlin and New York: Mouton de Gruyter, 1997), pp. 39–61.

Sontag, S., 'The Aesthetics of Silence', p. 14. http://www.ubu.com/aspen/aspen5and6/index.html.

Spender, D., *Man Made Language* (London: Routledge & Kegan Paul, 1980).

Spivak, G. C., 'Can the Subaltern Speak?', in P. Williams and L. Chrisman (eds.), *Colonial Discourse and Post-colonial Theory: A Reader* (New York: Columbia University Press, 1994), pp. 66–111.

Starski, P., 'Silence within the Process of Normative Change and Evolution of the Prohibition on the Use of Force: Normative Volatility and Legislative Responsibility', *Journal on the Use of Force and International Law* 4/1 (2017), pp. 14–65.

Stavrakakis, Y., 'Jacques Lacan: Negotiating the Psychosocial in and beyond Language', in R. Wodak and B. Forchtner (eds.), *The Routledge Handbook of Language and Politics* (Abingdon: Routledge, 2018), pp. 82–95.

Stein, K. F., 'Metaphysical Silence in Absurd Drama', *Modern Drama* 13/4 (1970), pp. 423–431.

Steiner, G., *Language and Silence* (Harmondsworth: Penguin, 1969).

Steiner, J., *Psychic Retreats* (London and New York: Routledge, 1993).

Steinmetz, W., *Das Sagbare und das Machbare* (Stuttgart: Klett-Cotta, 1993).

Sterling, J., J. T. Jost, and C. D. Hardin, 'Liberal and Conservative Representations of the Good Society: A (Social) Structural Topic Modeling Approach', *Sage Open*, April–June 2019, pp. 1–13.

Taggart, P., 'Populism and Representative Politics in Contemporary Europe', *Journal of Political Ideologies* 9 (2004), pp. 269–288.

Talmud, *Kiddushin*.

Tang, Y., 'Language, Truth, and Literary Interpretation: A Cross-Cultural Examination', *Journal of the History of Ideas* 60/1 (1999), pp. 1–20.

Tannen, D., 'Silence: Anything But', in D. Tannen and M. Saville-Troike (eds.), *Perspectives on Silence* (Norwood, NJ: Ablex, 1985), pp. 93–111.
Taplin, O., 'Aeschylean Silences and Silences in Aeschylus', *Harvard Studies in Classical Philology* 76 (1972), pp. 57–97.
Teahan, J. F., 'The Place of Silence in Thomas Merton's Life and Thought', *Journal of Religion* 61 (1981), pp. 364–383.
Teeuwen, R., 'Roland Barthes's "Neutral" and the Utopia of Weariness', *Cultural Critique*, no. 80 (winter 2012), pp. 1–26.
Tie, W., 'Radical Politics, Utopia, and Political Policing', *Journal of Political Ideologies* 14 (2009), pp. 253–277.
Toadvine, T., 'The Reconversion of Silence and Speech', *Tijdschrift voor Filosofie* 70/3 (2008), pp. 457–477.
Tong, L. K., 'The Meaning of Philosophical Silence: Some Reflections on the Use of Language in Chinese Thought', *Journal of Chinese Philosophy* 3 (1976), pp. 169–183.
Torresan, P., 'Silence in the Bible', *Jewish Bible Quarterly* 31/3 (2003), pp. 153–60.
Trimboli, C. and M. B. Walker, 'Switching Pauses in Cooperative and Competitive Conversations', *Journal of Experimental Social Psychology* 20 (1984), pp. 297–311.
Trouillot, M.-R., *Global Transformations: Anthropology and the Modern World* (New York and Houndmills, Basingstoke: Palgrave Macmillan, 2003).
Trouillot, M.-R., *Silencing the Past: Power and the Production of History* (Boston, MA: Beacon Press, 2015 [1995]).
Tuck, R., *The Sleeping Sovereign: The Invention of Modern Democracy* (Cambridge: Cambridge University Press, 2016).
Ueda, S., 'Silence and Words in Zen Buddhism', *Diogenes* 43/170 (1995), pp. 1–21.
UK Parliament, 'The Speaker, Impartiality and Procedural Reform', https://www.parliament.uk/.
Umbach, M. and M. Humphrey, *Authenticity: The Cultural History of a Political Concept* (Cham, Switzerland: Springer, 2017).
'Universal Declaration of the Rights of Peoples', 2001. https://unpo.org/article.php?id=105.
Vainiomäki, T., 'Silence as a Cultural Sign', *Semiotica* 150/1–4 (2004), pp. 347–361.
Varsano, P. M., 'Looking for the Recluse and Not Finding Him In: The Rhetoric of Silence in Early Chinese Poetry', *Asia Major*, 3rd ser., 12/2 (1999), pp. 39–70.
Vincent, A., *Modern Political Ideologies*, 3rd edn (Chichester: John Wiley & Sons, 2010).
Vincent, D., *A History of Solitude* (Cambridge: Polity Press, 2020).
Vinitsky-Seroussi, V. and C. Teeger, 'Unpacking the Unspoken: Silence in Collective Memory and Forgetting', *Social Forces* 88/3 (2010), p. 1103–1122.
Viroli, M., *For Love of Country* (Oxford: Clarendon Press, 1995).
Voegelin, S., *Listening to Noise and Silence: Towards a Philosophy of Sound Art* (London: Continuum, 2010).
Vogel, S., 'The Silence of Nature', *Environmental Values* 15 (2006), pp. 145–171.
von Hassell, M., '"Issei" Women: Silences and Fields of Power', *Feminist Studies* 19/3 (1993), pp. 549–569.
Walker, A. G., 'The Two Faces of Silence: The Effect of Witness Hesitancy on Lawyers' Impressions', in D. Tannen and M. Saville-Troike (eds.), *Perspectives on Silence* (Norwood, NJ: Ablex, 1985), pp. 55–75.
Wang, Y., *Linguistic Strategies in Daoist Zhuangzi and Chan Buddhism: The Other Way of Speaking* (London: Routledge Curzon, 2003).
Wardle, B., 'You Complete Me: The Lacanian Subject and Three Forms of Ideological Fantasy', *Journal of Political Ideologies* 21 (2016), pp. 302–319.

Wei, Z., 'On the Way to a "Common" Language? Heidegger's Dialogue with a Japanese Visitor', *Dao: A Journal of Comparative Philosophy* 4 (2005), pp. 283–297.

Weller, R. P., 'Salvaging Silence: Exile, Death and the Anthropology of the Unknowable', *Anthropology of This Century*, no. 19 (2017), pp. 1–14.

Willet, A., *Hexapla in Exodum: The Second Booke Of Moses Called Exodus* (London: Thomas Man, Paul Man, and Jonah Man, 1633).

Williams, K. D., *Ostracism: The Power of Silence* (New York and London: Guilford Press, 2001).

Williams, Z., 'What Used to Define Us was Irony. Now It's Self-Importance', *The Guardian*, 30 October 2017.

Winter, J., 'Thinking about Silence', in E. Ben-Ze'ev, R. Ginio, and J. Winter (eds.), *Shadows of War: A Social History of Silence in the Twentieth Century* (Cambridge: Cambridge University Press, 2010), pp. 3–31.

Winter, J., 'Between Sound and Silence: The Inaudible and the Unsayable in the History of the First World War', in A. J. Murray and K. Durrheim (eds.), *Qualitative Studies of Silence: The Unsaid as Social Action* (Cambridge: Cambridge University Press: 2019), pp. 223–235.

Wiseman, M. E., 'Still', in A. Harris, A. Hollinghurst, and A. Smith (eds.), *Tacita Dean* (London: Royal Academy of Arts, National Portrait Gallery, The National Gallery, 2018).

Wittgenstein, L., *Tractatus Logico-Philosophicus*, Ogden and Ramsey translation (London: Routledge & Kegan Paul, 1922).

Wodak, R., *The Politics of Fear* (London: Sage, 2015).

Wolosky, S., 'Samuel Beckett's Figural Evasions', in S. Budick and W. Iser (eds.), *Languages of the Unsayable: The Play of Negativity in Literature and Literary Theory* (Stanford, CA: Stanford University Press, 1987), pp. 165–186.

Wordsworth, W., *The Prelude*, ed. Jonathan Wordsworth (London: Penguin, 1995).

Wright, D. S., 'Rethinking Transcendence: The Role of Language in Zen Experience', *Philosophy East and West* 42/1 (1992), pp. 113–138.

Writings from the Zen Masters, comp. Paul Reps (London: Penguin, 2009).

Yandell, K. E., 'Some Varieties of Ineffability', *International Journal for Philosophy of Religion* 6/3 (1975), pp. 167–179.

Zajda, J. and R. Zajda, 'The Politics of Rewriting History: New History Textbooks and Curriculum Materials in Russia', *International Review of Education* 49 (2003), pp. 363–384.

Zerubavel, E., *The Elephant in the Room: Silence and Denial in Everyday Life* (New York: Oxford University Press, 2006).

Zerubavel, E., 'Listening to the Sound of Silence: Methodological Reflections on Studying the Unsaid', in A. J. Murray and K. Durrheim (eds.), *Qualitative Studies of Silence: The Unsaid as Social Action* (Cambridge: Cambridge University Press, 2019), pp. 59–70.

Zhuangzi, *Basic Writings*, trans. Burton Watson (New York: Columbia University Press, 2003).

Žižek, S., 'The Spectre of Ideology', in S. Žižek (ed.), *Mapping Ideology* (London: Verso, 1994), pp. 1–33.

Zumbrunnen, J. G., *Silence and Democracy: Athenian Politics in Thucydides' History* (University Park, PA: Pennsylvania State University Press, 2008).

Index

A
abeyance 225, 227
Aboriginal societies 163–4, 165, 166, 173, 214
absence 1–2, 3, 5, 29, 151, 160, 271
   analysing silence 38, 41, 44, 52, 54
   historical silences and forgetfulness 83–4, 84–5
   ideological assimilations of silence 245, 246, 248, 260, 256, 262
   indeterminacy of 73–7, 82
   layers of silence 15, 16, 20
   listening 91, 96
   modalities of silence 111, 115, 117, 128
   state and government silences 224, 225, 228, 231, 232, 235
   stillness/solitude 58, 60–1, 63, 65–6
   taciturnity and tacit consent/dissent 182, 183, 197
'absent-recluse' 205–6
abstention 225, 228–33, 260
Abû Zayd, Nasr 173
academic circles and scholarship 269–70
   disciplinary circumspection/erasure 165–8
   methodological predispositions 99–101
access rights 30
Achino-Loeb, M.-L. 95, 96, 97
acoustic purism 41–6, 58, 63
acquiescence 20, 232, 233, 265
Afghanistan 234
agency/non-agency 17, 19–23, 32, 59, 61, 76, 94, 95, 98, 103, 176, 184, 201
aglôssos (being tongueless) 59–60
agreement: tacit consent 181
'alternative facts' 173
ambiguity 255, 271
   socio-cultural filters of silence 203–4, 209, 217, 219–20
   state and government silences 225, 227, 228
   taciturnity and tacit consent/dissent 195, 196–7
Aminzade, R. 165
Amir-Moezzi, M. A. 173–4
anarchism 244, 258
Ancient Greece 45, 59, 113, 216, 236
Andersen, Hans Christian 97
Anderson, Perry 264
animal rights 262
annotation techniques 147
anomie 117–18

Antarctica 66, 67
anthropology 18, 31, 46, 49–50, 61, 123, 173, 215
   disciplinary circumspection/erasure 165–8
   linearity 161–5
anthropomorphization 175–6
anti-political thinking 27
Apache people 214
apolitical thinking 27
apophatic thought 112, 115
archaeology 21, 160, 161, 210
architecture 3, 4, 5, 208–9, 236
Aristotle 126
Arkoun, Mohammed 129, 130
Article 51 (UN Charter) 232
artistic/poetic phenomena 37, 40, 46, 62, 75, 85, 116, 131-2, 144, 205–7, 215
aspirational silences 35, 36
Attali, Jacques 218
attitudinal research 99
Atwood, Margaret 41
audibility of silence 30
Auschwitz 117, 235
Australian Animal Justice Party 262
authenticity 96
authoritarianianism 172, 208, 265
authority: acceptance of 30
authors: fiction 50
autonomous agency 22
avant-garde literature: emptiness 43
avoidance rituals 214
awareness 103, 119, 126, 184, 201
ayin (nothingness) 112
Azaria, D. 232

B
Bachrach, Peter 82
Baker, S. J. 144
Bakhtin, Mikhail 188
'banal nationalism' 265
Baratz, Morton S. 82
barriers 38, 44
Barthes, Roland 61–2, 63, 66, 155, 228
Basilides 42
Bataille, Georges 115
Beckett, Samuel 35, 68, 110–11, 131, 146–7, 216–17

286 Index

'Being' 202
Bell, Gertrude 66
Bentham, Jeremy 226–7
Bergman, Ingmar 143, 193
Big Bang theory 128, 156
Billig, M. 85–6, 265
Bion, Wilfred 86, 121
Birthday Party, The (Pinter) 147
Black history 106, 158
'Black Lives Matter' 126
blocking and blockages 36, 85, 86, 109, 127, 172, 173, 260
Blommaert, J. 92
Book of Common Prayer 192, 193
boundaries, political 25, 26, 48, 143, 207, 219, 245, 270
Bourdieu, Pierre 140, 158, 214, 224, 245, 265
    modalities of silence 119, 124–5, 130, 131
    removal 86, 87
    superimposed/invented voice 171, 178
    taciturnity and tacit consent/dissent 183, 184, 191–2
brain functions 50–1
'Breaking the Silence' 209
Brecht, Bertolt 213
Brexit 173, 194
Brito Vieira, M. 195
Brubaker, R. M. 125
Bruneau, T. J. 141, 142, 143
Budapest 266
Buddhism *see* Zen-Buddhism
buried silence 43, 225
Burke, Edmund 67–8, 177
Byrd, Admiral 66

C

Cage, John 1–6, 54, 58, 138, 206, 216, 218–19
'Can the Subaltern Speak?' (Spivak) 107, 108
Caretaker, The (Pinter) 147
Carlyle, Thomas 44, 64–5, 183, 226
catachresis 108–9
catallaxy 259
cathedrals 208–9
Cat on a Hot Tin Roof (Williams) 109–10
'cautious silences' 165
censorship 87, 106, 130, 196
ceremonial silence 192–3, 208
Chafe, W. 138–9
Chia Tao (poet) 206
Ch'iu Wei (poet) 206
Christianity 40, 154, 157, 160, 192
climate change 176
codes 35–7, 117
collective memories 26, 36, 83, 84, 234, 271

collectives and groups 25, 26, 67, 120, 156
colonialization 107–8, 161, 163, 165, 166
Columbus, Christopher 159, 175
commemorative silences 11, 23, 45, 46, 57, 233–5
communicative silences 43, 141–4, 146–7, 166, 183
communitarianism 262
comparative silences 152
compliance 10, 23, 25–6, 30, 190, 191, 230
Conan Doyle, Sir Arthur 92
concealed silences 39, 48, 83, 91, 112, 127, 176, 225, 243, 260
    layers of silence 17, 18, 20, 21, 22, 23
concreteness 75, 87, 151, 159, 171, 212, 227, 253
    analysing silence 37, 39, 40
    listening 97, 98
    modalities of silence 110, 118, 130
    stillness/solitude 57, 65, 68
    taciturnity and tacit consent/dissent 186, 189, 195
confidentiality agreements 47
conforming silence 218
consciousness 66, 86, 95, 104, 126, 129, 186, 235, 265
consensualism 79, 99
consent *see* taciturnity and tacit consent/dissent
conservatism 245, 246, 250, 258–9, 264
conspiratorial silence 22, 31, 109, 127, 212, 224
constitutions 224–6, 228–9, 254, 263
Constitution (United States) 237
contemplation 156, 218
contention 99, 144, 177
contestation/decontestation 81, 82, 142, 145, 195, 196
    ideological assimilations of silence 242, 246, 248, 249, 251, 259
    state and government silences 227, 228, 229
    temporality 164–5, 167
contextualized silence 36, 93
continuity 141, 158–9, 264, 271
controversy 82
conversation 38, 139, 141, 145, 146, 149, 175–6, 213, 214, 216
conversation preventers 106
conveyed meaning 61
Corbin, A. 118
coronavirus pandemic (2020) 11
counter-power 31, 229
cover-ups 25, 113, 121
Covid-19 pandemic (2020-22) 179
Cratylus 126
creative writing 113
criminality 224
critical discourse analysis 38, 47, 75, 76, 81
critical theory 79, 211, 250

crowding out 171–4
cultural appropriation 107
cultural practices 21, 25, 28, 39, 50, 125, 152, 158, 163, 212–13
Cunningham, Merce 1, 2–3, 4, 6, 146, 149

D
Dahrendorf, Ralf 164
Daodejing 207
Daoism 206-7
Darstellung 171, 172
data protection 237
Dauenhauer, Bernard 155
dead silences 172, 174–9
Dean, Tacita 1, 2, 3, 4, 6, 42, 57, 58, 63, 146, 149
death 64, 113, 211–12, 233–5
decision making 25, 27, 30, 82, 139, 146, 154, 177, 188–9, 197, 223, 229, 230
decontestation *see* contestation/decontestation
deferential silence 10, 16, 36, 45, 110, 157, 214, 215
Defoe, Daniel 68
degrees of silence 45
deistic creationism 91, 100, 128, 129, 153, 154
delayed action/reaction 146, 213
delegitimization 11, 81, 85
Deleuze, Gilles 157
deliberate silencing 9, 20, 23, 31-2, 174, 183, 201, 213, 219, 242, 246, 258, 265
  state and government silences 224, 228, 229–30
democracy 32, 173, 178, 184, 196, 231, 244, 250, 263
denial: history 85
De Pazzi, Maria Maddalena 204
depoliticization 29, 129, 254
Derrida, Jacques 60, 83, 108, 114–16, 123, 128–9, 131, 132
De Saussure, Ferdinand 137
detectable silences 16–19, 57, 95
dichotomies 76, 99, 100, 101
différance 115–16, 128–9, 132
differend 116–17, 120
'diffused' perspective of silence 49
digitalization 196
discontinuity 26, 100, 110, 147
discriminatory language 95, 106
disguising 98, 158
disjunctive silences 139, 158, 166
disorientation 117–18, 217
disparate silences 231–2, 248
displacement 21, 85, 144, 153, 173, 175, 191, 231, 235
dispossession 31, 263
dissensus 79, 99
'dog that did not bark' 92

dominant ideologies 118–19
domineering silencing 22
dramatic silences 215–20
dramatizations 146–8, 149, 236
duality of silence 257
Duchamp, Marcel 5
dumb: double meaning 19
Dunn, J. 186
Durkheim, Émile 100, 117–18
duty not to speak 214

E
earthly silence 156
Easton, Susan 118
Eckhart, Meister 113
eclipsed silences 21
Edgar, A. 4
education and learning 210
egalitarianism 262, 263
ego: splitting of 86
electoral systems 230–1
'elephant in the room' study (Zerubavel) 109
Eliot, T. S. 131–2
ellipses 140, 141
Ellison, Ralph 212
elusiveness 92–8
emotional reaction 38, 233–4
emphasis: rhetorical strategy 138
emptiness 43, 64, 74, 154, 160, 162, 190, 202, 203
'end of ideology' thesis 250–1
enforced silence 31, 156
Engels, Friedrich 247
enigma 269, 270
enlightenment 205, 206
Ephratt, M. 118
esotericism 269
Essay Concerning Human Understanding (Locke) 190, 191
Esslin, Martin 146
ethics 243
ethnicity 17, 31, 47, 125, 162, 212, 230, 253, 263
ethnography 123, 166
etiquette 145, 218
euphemisms 211–12
Evans, Arthur 161
exclusion/inclusion 25, 87, 119, 157, 241, 244
existence-of-emptiness 203
existential silences 35, 36, 66
expressiveness 103, 141, 146

F
face-value enquiry 269
facts 85, 127, 178–9
'fallen' (war dead) 235
fascism 264, 265

fast-time silences 142
fear-inducing silences 35, 36
feminism 244, 256–8
Ferguson, K. 19
Feuerbach, Ludwig 28
Fifth Amendment (Constitution of the United States) 237
finality 25, 80-81, 82, 142, 144, 154, 173, 235, 270, 271
 socio-cultural filters of silence 207, 215
 taciturnity and tacit consent/dissent 188, 190
Fink, B. 80, 117
Finns 39, 69, 120, 213, 214
first-past-the-post voting 231
Fivush, R. 140, 148, 162, 173
Floyd, George 126
Foley, Michael 224, 225
fore-and-after silence 154, 155–6
Foucault, Michel 45, 87, 94, 106, 110, 115, 203
4′33 (music composition) (Cage) 1–6, 206, 218–19
Four Quartets (Eliot) 131
France 167, 226
Freeden, M. 29
freedom of expression 107, 140
Freud, Sigmund 86, 129
friend–enemy dichotomy 99
Fukuyama, Francis 251
future generations 176–7

G
Garfunkel, Art 62
gender and gender-fluidity 18, 31, 48, 87, 118, 158, 162, 172, 244, 256–8
Genesis, Book of 59
Gere, Cathy 161
German language 137–8
Gilligan, Carol 257
Glenn, C. 75
Gnosticism 112
Go-Between, The (Hartley) 164
God 66, 97, 112, 113, 114–15, 128, 129, 146, 154, 156, 191
Goffman, Erving 139, 214
government silences *see* state and government silences
Greenham Common (US nuclear missile base) 120–1
Grenell, Richard 195
groups *see* collectives and groups
Gurevitch, S. D. 214

H
habitus 86, 124, 130, 158, 186, 224
Haiti 83–4, 85, 160–1

Hamlet 97
harm 109, 176, 237, 253
Harpocrates 266
Hartley, L. P. 164
Hasidism 112
hearing 92–3
Hegel, Georg Wilhelm Friedrich 261
Heidegger, Martin 202
Heraclitus 126
'heroic' status 174–5
hesitancy 139–40, 141, 194
hiatuses 21, 26, 38, 100, 154, 193, 226
 language and communication 139, 141, 145
 socio-cultural filters of silence 206, 209, 216
hiddenness 16–19, 249
high-impact silences 245–6
Hirschman, A. O. 188
historical silences and forgetfulness 18, 39, 46, 145, 235, 271
 absence 83–5
 ideological assimilations of silence 247, 264
 temporality 157–61
Hobbes, Thomas 181, 185, 188, 191, 192, 226
Ho, Chien-hsing 114, 203–4
Hofstede, G. 210
'holding the ring' 254–5
Holocaust, The 105–6, 122, 123, 235
Holub, R. 257
Hom, A. R. 250
Horniman Museum (London) 41
hostile silencing 22
Huangbo Xiyun 62
humanities 270
Hungarian Arrow Cross 266
Huspek, M. 28, 118
Huygens, Constantijn 175
hyperessentiality 114–15

I
identity and identitarian politics 86–7, 96, 105, 162, 172
ideological silences
 anarchism 258
 conservatism 258–9
 feminism 256–8
 illiberalism 265–7
 liberalism 226, 229, 253–5
 nation and nationalism 263–5
 networks and spaces 241–51
 populism 262–3
 proliferation of silences 251–3
 reformist/radicalist silences 259–62
ideological morphology 80–1, 84, 99, 100, 152, 241, 244, 257
Ideologiekritik School 247

Igbo people (Nigeria) 182
ignoring 212, 219, 232
ILC *see* International Law Commission (United Nations)
Iliad 236
illiberalism 265-7
'imagined communities' 264
immigrants 17, 162, 172
impartiality 230, 255
inaccessible silence 93-4, 130, 249
inarticulable silence 21, 28, 39, 94, 171, 265
  modality of silence 103, 105, 116-24
  state and government silences 228, 235
inaudibility 21, 80, 93, 127, 128, 208, 219, 245
inclusion *see* exclusion/inclusion
incomprehensible speech 43-4, 45, 118
inconceivability 128
incontrovertible verification 178
indeterminacy 73-7, 126, 129, 227, 244, 249, 250, 270, 271
indigenous cultures 163-4, 165-6, 214, 253
individuality 5, 66, 149, 266
industrialism 64-5, 226
ineffability 38, 39, 76, 103, 112-16, 129, 155, 161, 202-7
inequality 76, 117, 242, 243, 258
information and communication 38, 172, 196, 242
inhibition 31, 36, 116, 225, 252
insensitivity: depictions of people 95, 105
institutional politics 28
intentionality 23, 61, 87, 184, 209, 242, 265
interactive silences 61, 143
intergenerational justice 178
international law 232-3
International Law Commission (ILC) (United Nations) 232
international relations theory 250
interpretations of silence 28-9, 77, 99, 158, 184, 248, 269
  listening 91, 92, 93, 94, 96-7
interruption 115, 139, 145
interviews (ethnological) 166
invalidation 85
invented voice *see* superimposed and invented voice
invisibility 219, 227, 231, 245
Invisible Man (Ellison) 212
irrelevance 46, 85, 125, 126, 157, 161, 182, 217
  ideological silences 244, 246, 249, 255
Iser, Wolfgang 28, 111
Ishiguro, Kazuo 75
Islam 129, 130, 160, 167, 173, 192
Israel 119, 162, 209, 233
Italy 218

J
Japan 166, 174-5, 214
Jizang 203
jouissance 78, 79, 117
Judaism 112, 113, 157, 191-2
justice/injustice 178, 192, 211, 244, 254, 257

K
kabbalists 112
Kafka, Franz 146
Kagge, Erling 61, 66-7, 144, 145, 175, 189
Kary, J. H. 185
Keane, John 47, 49
keening 43, 52, 120
Keller, R. 87
Kendall, K. E. 28, 118
Kidron, Carol 123-4
King Lear (Shakespeare) 215-16
Klein, Melanie 86
Knossos 161
knowingly restrictive silence 31
knowledge centres 210
known and unknown unknowns 127
Kølvraa, C. 109
Kurzon, D. 22, 59, 116

L
Lacan, Jacques 77, 78, 79, 80, 81, 83, 114, 117, 248
lack 58, 91, 129, 162, 206, 212, 248, 271
  absence/removal and 73, 74-5, 77-81, 83
  Lacanian 77-81
  modalities of silence 114, 117
Laclau, Ernesto 78, 244, 248
Langton, R. 52, 116
language and communication 161, 183, 205, 217, 218, 242-3, 271
  ambiguity of 196-7
  discursive distribution of silence 137-41
  micro-structures of silence 141-5
  uncommunicative silences 146-9
  see also linguistics and speech
Large Glass, The (Duchamp) 5
latent functions 74
Laurence, P. O. 60, 118, 141
law codes 118, 119
Lawrence, Peter 177
leadership 48, 91, 258, 259
legal practices 225, 231, 233, 237, 254, 256
legitimacy 119, 125-6, 183, 184, 190, 231, 236, 254, 266
Lehtonen, J. 213
Leopold, David 260
liberalism 130, 178, 183, 264
  ideological assimilations of silence 243, 244, 245, 251, 252, 253-5, 256, 260

liberalism (*Continued*)
  neoliberalism 250, 254, 255, 261–2
  state and government silences 226, 228, 229, 230
limitlessness 62
linearity 159, 161–5, 177
linguistic deauthorisation 119
linguistics and speech 81, 116, 140, 145, 188
  analysing silence 37, 38, 41, 43, 52–3
  hearing/listening 92, 93, 97
  layers of silence 16, 21, 22
  silence/stillness/solitude 59–60, 62–3
  socio-cultural filters of silence 204, 211, 213, 215, 217
  unspeakable/unsayable 39, 61, 64, 76, 103, 104–12, 114, 119, 211
  see also language and communication
listening: for/to silence 75–6, 91, 93-7, 121, 142, 266
literature 29, 35, 46–7, 60, 75, 85, 141, 147, 215–18, 260–1
Little, A. 85
lived world 151–2, 227
Locke, John 20, 27, 181–91, 194, 227
logos 58–63, 76, 116, 156
low-impact silences 245, 246
Lyotard, Jean-François 94, 116–17, 120, 235

M
McAdam, D. 165
McGilchrist, Iain 50, 51
McNay, L. 86, 119, 162, 257–8
macro-temporalities 153–4, 157, 158
madness 115
Maistre, J. de 226
Maitland, S. 59, 74, 128, 161–2
majoritarianism 173, 179, 231, 263
maldistribution 158, 196
manifest functions 74
manipulative silencing 22
Marais, M. 111
marginalization 86–7, 162, 172, 219, 246, 265, 271
markedness theory 148
marriage ceremonies 191–3
Marxism 235, 241, 244, 247–8, 249, 250, 260–1
masculinity 11, 229, 257
Matt, D. C. 112
Mauriac, Claude 113
Mazour-Matusevich, Y. 119, 120
meaningful pauses 16
meditation 64, 204–5
memory 83-4, 142–3, 145, 173, 212, 235, 247, 271
Merleau-Ponty, Maurice 53–4, 60, 74, 116
Merton, Robert 74
Merton, Thomas 144, 145, 157
metonymy 226

Mezquito (Cordoba) 160
micro-temporalities 153–4, 157
Milgram, S. 216
military silence 156
Mill, John Stuart 227, 253
minors: identity 47–8
Mirabeau, Honoré Gabriel Riqueti, Count of 87
Miranda rights 237
Mizrahi people 162
moku (silence, Japan) 63
monastic silence 36, 69, 144–5, 156–7, 194
Montiglio, S. 113, 228–9, 236
Monty Python (comedy series) 139
motionlessness 1, 3, 6, 59, 63
Mouffe, Chantal 78, 99
mourning *see* commemorative silences
movement 2, 3, 5, 6, 10, 63, 65, 66, 154
multiple silences 44, 46, 84, 155, 195, 215, 216
music 44, 50, 51, 218
muting/muteness 9, 19, 84, 143, 175, 236
  ideological assimilations of silences 249, 265
  modalities of silence 109, 119-20, 130
  non-silences 51, 53
mystery 266–7
mysticism 112, 119, 151, 204, 205, 207, 209, 270
myths 166

N
naming/unnaming 29, 79, 80, 161, 175
  analysing silence 41–6
  ideological assimilations of silence 256–7, 259
  modalities of silence 110, 111, 113, 132
Nancy, Jean-Luc 93
narrative voices 175
nation and nationalism 31, 69, 164–5, 175, 194, 213, 234, 243, 244, 263–5
naturalization 241, 245, 265
nature 61, 66–7, 68
Nazism 10, 235
negative theology 112, 114–15, 128
negativity 76, 77, 95, 111
neoliberalism 250, 254, 255, 261–2
networks 241–51
neutrality 228–33, 236, 253–4, 255, 260
neutralizing 140
Nietzsche, Friedrich 65
Nigeria 182
Nixon, Richard 194, 231
Noelle-Neumann, Elizabeth 195–6
noise 3–4, 36, 51–4, 63, 64–5, 92
non-agentic silences *see* agency/non-agency
non-consent 186–7
non-conspiratorial silence 22
non-disclosure 17, 46, 122
non-dualism 38, 51, 62, 202, 203
non-existing voices 171, 172, 174–9

non-identifiable political silences 21
non-meaningful sound/speech 42
non-participatory silence 230
non-silence 51–4, 154
non-sound 42
non-speech 42, 154, 183, 188, 203, 209–10
non-transmittable silence 131
no-platforming 252
Nordic silence 69
nothingness 73, 79, 82, 112, 115, 128, 202, 271

O

obscured silences 21, 107-8
Ode on Solitude (Pope) 68
Oedipus the King/Oedipus at Colonus (Sophocles) 122–3
Old Testament 66
Omertà (Mafia) 92
oneness of silence 44-5
open/closed ideologies 251–2
openness 46, 48, 121, 177, 252, 271
opposed silences 46
oppression 31, 32, 76, 79, 86, 243
ostensibly meaningless sound/noise 21
ostracism 10, 219–20
outspokenness 114, 211

P

parallel silences 84, 86
Parmenides 155
participatory citizenship 32, 86, 184, 196, 230, 256
Pateman, Carole 255, 256
Pateman, Trevor 118–19, 242
patterns of silence 37
Patton, Paul 163
pauses 139, 140, 141–2, 143, 148
Pérez, J. 148
performativity 28, 215–16, 233–4, 243, 258, 262, 269
  taciturnity and tacit consent/dissent 183, 184, 186, 191, 192
perlocutionary frustration 116
Persona (film) (Bergman) 143, 193
personal narratives 29
Petrarch 175
Petschke, K. 59, 60
Phelan, S. 261
philosophical silences 50, 151, 153–7
  see also religious beliefs/practices; spirituality; theological silences
phonetic analysis 140
physiological silence 201
Picard, Max 41, 64, 105, 138, 214
Pieters, J. 175
Pinter, Harold 38, 146–8, 149, 193, 216, 217, 218

Pius XII, Pope 10
Plato 113
pluralism 179, 196, 237, 249, 254, 263, 266, 271
Poe, Edgar Allan 160
Polanyi, Michael 131
policy making 27
political awareness 118–19
political influence 25
political leaders 111
politically central silences 45
politically correctness 46, 211, 252
Political Theory of Political Thinking, The (Freeden) 29
political theory and theorists 18, 19, 26, 27, 29, 47–9, 151-2
Pope, Alexander 68
popular culture 29, 105
populism 244, 250, 262–3
positioning silences 35, 36
positive theology 114-5
positivism 269
possession 182–3, 187-8
potentiality 74, 81
power relations 5, 19, 47, 67, 79, 82, 258, 263
  controlling silence 171, 176, 179, 219
  language and communication 141, 143–4
  listening 96, 98
  maldistributions 158–9
  silence and 25, 26, 27, 31
  state and government silences 225, 229, 233, 237
  taciturnity and tacit consent/dissent 192, 193
pre-conceptualizable 131
'pre-history' 161
printed spaces 148–9
prisons 156, 230
privacy 46, 47, 237
private/public sphere 255
'professionals' 171
profoundly inexpressible 114
property ownership 68, 185–6
proscribed silences 246–7
prospective voices 172
protective shields 31, 47–8, 114, 122
Proust, Marcel 217
psychoanalysis 46, 121–2
psychological role of silence 35–6, 123, 201, 214
psychosomatic behaviour 46
public accountability 47, 237
public conveyance: as a political act 30–1, 124
public voices: articulation and expression 18–19
punctuation 140–1, 147, 148–9
purposive agency 20
Pushkin, Alexander 119, 120

Q

Quakers 208, 209
qualified absence 91
quasi-silences 265
questioning and unquestioning 125, 131, 191, 194, 212, 245
question time (parliamentary) 230
quietism 202, 223–8
quietude 58–9, 68, 213, 224, 226

R

race and racism 31, 87, 106, 162, 167
radical depoliticization 129
radicalism 245, 250, 252, 259–62
Ramel, F. 218
Rancière, Jacques 79, 125
reactions (unintended/intended) 77
'Real' 77–8, 79, 80, 81, 114
redacting 231
reflective silence 138
reflexivity 53–4
reformists 259–62
religious beliefs/practices 10, 22, 31, 97, 156, 173, 191–2, 246
   analysing silence 36, 46, 47, 50
   Buddhist philosophy 38, 40, 51, 62, 76, 157, 194, 202–7
   Christianity 40, 154
   Islam 130, 192
   language and communication 144–5, 151
   modalities of silence 112–3, 128
   silence/stillness/solitude 63–4, 65
   sites of worship 208–9
   state and government silences 228, 229, 234
   see also philosophical silences; spirituality; theological silences
removal 81–8, 91
renaming 161, 256, 257
Renan, E. 264
repressive and imposed silencing 16, 21, 22, 86, 107, 122
resistant 26, 30, 31, 84, 107, 123, 178, 233, 243
'response' silences 139, 145, 151
retreat 43, 52, 69, 145, 157, 208, 229
reverence 113, 156
rhetoric 38, 97, 140, 226
Ricoeur, Paul 98, 117, 142, 190
'rights of man' 256
rights and rights holders 177–8, 186, 197, 213–14, 237, 246, 253, 262
   feminism 244, 256–8
right to oblivion/be forgotten 237
right to remain silent 118, 197, 236–7
right-wing populism 172, 262, 263–4
ritual silences 39

Robinson Crusoe (Defoe) 68
Rollo, T. 183, 184
Romans 182
Rousseau, Jean-Jacques 192, 193, 231
routinizing 140
Rumsfeld, Donald 127
rupture 23, 26, 42, 100, 101, 115, 250
Russia 83, 119–20

S

Sacks, Oliver 50
Sajavaara, K. 213
Saunders, G. R. 53
scarcity: exclusion 87
Schmitt, Carl 99, 261
Schröter, M. 75, 252
seclusion 3, 68, 122, 207
'second nature': mechanical practices 125
Second Treatise of Government (Locke) 181–91, 194
secrecy 31, 83
secularism 39, 47, 66, 74, 97, 270
   modalities of silence 112, 129
   socio-cultural filters of silence 206, 208, 218
   temporality 154, 167
Sedley, S. 225–6
selectivity 92, 212, 242
self-comprehension 30–1, 37, 121
self-imposed silence 9, 17, 98, 219
Sells, M. A. 42, 113
semantic latitude 41–6
semantic singlemindedness 249–50
'sending people to Coventry' 219–20
sensory receptibility 54
sexuality and sexual orientation 22, 106, 158, 255, 256
shading 100, 101, 130, 244, 262
shared silences 140, 144, 227, 233
shielding 48, 53, 66, 167, 175, 255, 262
   modalities of silence 105, 107, 114, 122, 131
shocked silence 43
Sider, G. 45
Sifianou, M. 77
signifiers 80–1
silence
   alternative epistemologies 37–41
   concept of 15–16, 47
   discursive distribution of 137–41
   failure to act 20
   language of unplanned 9–11
   magnifier 109
   micro-structures of 141–5
   pathways of 35–41
   reach of 46–51
   resource/commodity 11

'spaces in between' 41
   stimulating/retarding energy 47
'silence-act' 20
silence-cum-nihilism 146–7
'silence is golden' 10
silence modalities: social roots of 210–15
silence–speech relationship 60–1, 62–3
silences within silences 107–8
Silencing the Past (Trouillot) 83–4
silent communion 144–5, 157
silent futures 178
'silent majority' 9, 21, 194–7
'silent thoughts' 20
'silent treatment' 219–20
'siloed' perspective of silence 48, 138
Simmel, Georg 214
Simon, Paul 62
simplifying 241
Skinner, Quentin 97
slavery 116, 160
'slipperiness' 95
slow-time silences 142–3
Smith, Adam 227
Sobkowiak, W. 42, 43
social conservatism 48
social interaction 25, 28, 38, 77, 141, 213, 214, 271
socialism 243, 260–1
sociality 67, 68
socially deferential positions 10
socially practised silence 45, 46
social media 196
social normalizing 210–15, 216
social potential 26
social practices 18, 25, 156, 218, 219
social resources and stimulants 26
social sciences: role of silence 35–6, 270
socio-cultural filters 5, 201
   Buddhist ineffability 202–7
   dramatic silences 215–20
   social roots of silence modalities 210–15
   thresholds/transitions 207–10
socio-political order/equilibrium 5, 22 3, 26, 18, 106, 107, 154, 218, 247, 259
socio-political thought-practices 13, 25–7, 57, 82, 87, 95, 151
   analysing silence 48, 50
   lived world 182, 203, 236, 245
   ubiquity of 27–32, 57, 270
solidaric silences 35, 36
solitude 38–9, 57, 58, 66–9, 144, 161–2, 189, 217, 219
Sontag, Susan 53, 143, 144, 146, 148, 193
Sophist (Plato) 113
Sophocles 122–3
sotto voce (under the voice) 59

sound 1–4, 42–3, 44, 51–4, 67, 140
'Sound of Silence, The' (song) 62
sovereignty 115, 154, 173, 192, 193, 223, 226, 262, 271
Spain 197
spatiality 189, 214, 215, 241–51
Speaker of the House of Commons 230
speech *see* linguistics and speech
Spender, Dale 257
'spiral of silence' 195–6
spirituality 38–9, 40, 112, 144–5, 147, 209
   see also philosophical silences; religious beliefs/practices; theological silences
Spivak, G. C. 107, 108, 171
Starski, P. 232, 233
state and government silences 151
   commemorative silences 233–5
   neutrality/abstention 225, 228–33
   quietism 223–8
   univocality 236–7
Stein, K. F. 217
Steiner, George 161
Steiner, John 122
Steinmetz, W. 111
stillness 2, 3, 6, 37, 38, 155, 156, 189, 209, 270
   silence/solitude 57, 58, 61, 63–6
subjugation 31, 81, 87
substitution 83, 108, 127
subvocalization ('silent speech') 60
superimposed and invented voice 171–9, 185, 225, 236, 260, 262, 263
suppression 25, 31, 32, 122, 171, 215
   ideological assimilations of silence 242, 249
   layers of silence 20, 22, 23
Supreme Court (United States) 254
Svetogorska Street (Belgrade) 265
switching pauses 139
symbols 80–1

T
taboos 16, 48, 106, 109, 211, 252
taciturnity and tacit consent/dissent 10, 20, 27, 59, 94, 151, 203, 271
   absence 182, 183, 197
   concreteness 186, 189, 195
   finality 188, 190
   ideological assimilations of silences 249, 266
   modalities of silence 103, 109, 116, 121, 123, 126, 131
   performativity 183, 184, 186, 191, 192
   power relations 192, 193
   'silent majority' 194–7
   state and government silences 227, 232
   unwritten implications of 181–94
Tang, Y. 205

Taplin, Oliver 216
Taylor, C. 75
Teeger, C. 233
temporality 25, 85, 128, 142, 151, 172, 190, 215, 250, 261
  anthropology 161–8
  historical silences and forgetfulness 157–61
  theological/philosophical silences 153–7
textbooks: Russian 83
theatre of the absurd 110–11, 146–8, 216
theological silences 153–7
  see also philosophical silences; religious beliefs/practices; spirituality
thought-practices *see* socio-political thought-practices
Thus Spake Zarathustra (Nietzsche) 65
Tie, W. 82
time *see* temporality
Toadvine, T. 54
tohu va bohu (emptiness) (Hebrew) 154
Tong, L. K. 205
totalitarianism 172, 246, 250, 265, 266
traces 16, 174, 265
  absence 76, 81, 84, 86
  modalities of silence 107, 115, 123, 126, 129, 132
tradition 4, 45, 48, 50, 59, 125, 154, 158, 209
tranquillity 3, 5, 58, 66, 147
transcendence 42, 62, 81, 112, 114, 144
transformative silences 151, 154, 160
transparency 46, 47, 114, 177, 245
traumatic events 105–6, 122–4
Trouillot, Michel-Rolph 83–4, 84–5, 145, 159, 160–1, 166–7, 173, 175, 256
Trump, Donald 194–5, 264
'turning a blind eye/deaf ear' 10, 122, 215

U

unacknowledged silences 19–23, 251–2
unborn silences 172, 174–9
uncertainty 139, 204, 232, 249
uncommunicative silences 146–9
unconceptualizability 39, 97, 103, 104, 116, 127–31, 191, 212, 246, 248
unconscious silences 22, 248
uncontested continuity 26
undecipherable messages 118
undermining 85, 147
undetectability: concealed silences 21, 93, 99
undiscussable 109
unexpressed voices 81
unhearability 46
unintelligible speech 43
unintentionality 22, 23, 183, 184, 248
United Nations 176, 232
United States 237

universalism 48, 177, 178, 191, 192, 248, 256, 264
univocality 236–7
unknowability 39, 174, 191, 202
  ideological assimilations of silence 246, 265, 266
  modalities of silence 103, 104, 126–7, 128, 129
  state and government silences 225, 228
unmasking 247, 248
unmentionable 109, 211
Unnamable, The (Beckett) 110–11, 146–7
unnoticeability 17, 18, 21, 39, 42, 158, 163, 184
  ideological assimilations of silence 243, 251, 252, 266
  listening 92, 97
  modalities of silence 103, 124–6, 129, 130, 131, 140
  socio-cultural filters of silence 212–13, 214, 219
  state and government silences 224, 227
unrecognizability 20–1, 23, 126, 131
unspeakable/unsayable 39, 61, 64, 76, 119, 235
  ideological assimilations of silence 246, 251, 252, 257
  modalities of silence 103, 104–12, 113-4, 116, 126
  socio-cultural filters of silence 210–12, 216
unspoken 60, 75, 118, 158, 189, 206, 213, 217, 218
unthinkable 39, 103, 104, 106, 124, 210, 246, 251, 252, 259
unthought 84, 110, 129, 130, 131
untranslatability 43
unutterability 112, 113, 116
utopias 164, 260-1

V

Vainiomäki, T. 44, 208
values 65, 104, 130, 178, 191
  ideological assimilations of silence 263, 264, 266
  socio-cultural filters of silence 205, 207
  state and government silences 229, 233, 234
van der Rohe, Mies 5, 227
Varsano, P. M. 205, 206
verbalization 42, 47, 59, 74
vernacular: expression and speech 99–100
Verstehen 40
Vertretung 171–2
Vietnam War 194
Vilmalakirti Sutra 202
Vincent, D. 69
Vinitsky-Seroussi, V. 233
Voegelin, Salomé 67
Vogel, S. 67, 175–6
voice 9, 20, 28, 59–60, 78, 92, 94, 98, 103, 171-3, 175, 178, 185, 196, 236–7, 262

'Voice for Future Generations at the United Nations? Turning Words into Action, A' (United Nations) 176
'voices-in-waiting' 177–9
Von Hayek, Friedrich 259
Von Holst, Theodor 41

W

Waiting for Godot (Beckett) 146
'wall of silence' 1, 92
Wang, Youru 62
Wanling Lu (Huangbo Xiyun) 62
Wannell, Chris 234
war dead 174, 175, 234–5
Wardle, B. 78
Watson, Burton 202
'weapons of the weak': angry silences 31
welfare agendas 242, 251, 253
Weller, R. P. 137
Weltanschauung 130, 229, 249
'Western' intellectual epistemology 108
'Westminster bubble' 27
Wieseman, Marjorie E. 2
wilderness 66–7, 147, 156, 209, 218
wilful silencing 22
Williams, Kipling 219
Williams, Tennessee 109–10
Williams, Zoe 194
'will of the people' 173, 262
Winter, J. 160, 235
withholding 61, 97
Wittgenstein, Ludwig 105, 126
Wolosky, S. 111
women 17, 48, 91, 95, 118, 158, 162, 230, 244, 256–8
'women in black' (anti-war/violence vigils) 120
wonder 156, 210, 236
Woolf, Virginia 38, 60, 118, 148, 205
Wootton Bassett 234
Wordsworth, William 68
Wright, D. S. 204–5

Y

Yandell, K. E. 114

Z

Zen-Buddhism 38, 40, 51, 76, 101, 132, 157, 194
  ineffability 202–7
  stillness/solitude 62, 63
Zerubavel, E. 109, 125, 212
Zhuangzi 203
Žižek, Slavoj 77, 248
Zumbrunnen, J. G. 236